EUROPEAN SOCIETY OF INTERNATIONAL LAW SERIES

The Judicialization of International Law

EUROPEAN SOCIETY OF INTERNATIONAL LAW SERIES

The ESIL Book Series publishes high quality volumes on the themes of ESIL Annual Conferences and ESIL joint events primarily. The volumes include chapters that are based on selected papers presented at ESIL events, revised to fit the theme and focus of the volume, and complemented by additional chapters that address topics that were not fully explored at the events, but that are essential for a full coverage of the theme.

The Judicialization of International Law

A Mixed Blessing?

Edited by
ANDREAS FOLLESDAL
and
GEIR ULFSTEIN

OXFORD
UNIVERSITY PRESS

OXFORD
UNIVERSITY PRESS

Great Clarendon Street, Oxford, OX2 6DP,
United Kingdom

Oxford University Press is a department of the University of Oxford.
It furthers the University's objective of excellence in research, scholarship,
and education by publishing worldwide. Oxford is a registered trade mark of
Oxford University Press in the UK and in certain other countries

First Edition published in 2018

Impression: 1

Published in the United States of America by Oxford University Press
198 Madison Avenue, New York, NY 10016, United States of America

British Library Cataloguing in Publication Data
Data available

Library of Congress Control Number
Data available

ISBN 978–0–19–881642–3

Printed and bound by
CPI Group (UK) Ltd, Croydon, CR0 4YY

Table of Contents

Table of Cases

INTERNATIONAL COURT OF JUSTICE AND PERMANENT COURT OF INTERNATIONAL JUSTICE

WTO

Appellate Body reports

Panel reports

INTERNATIONAL CRIMINAL COURT

INTERNATIONAL TRIBUNAL FOR THE LAW OF THE SEA

INTERNATIONAL ARBITRATION

ICSID

EUROPEAN COURT OF JUSTICE

EUROPEAN COURT OF HUMAN RIGHTS

INTER-AMERCIAN COURT OF HUMAN RIGHTS

INTERNATIONAL CRIMINAL TRIBUNAL FOR THE FORMER YUGOSLAVIA

INTERNATIONAL CRIMINAL TRIBUNAL FOR RWANDA

SPECIAL COURT FOR SIERRA LEONE

UNITED STATES SUPREME COURT

List of Contributors

Daniel Behn, Senior Research Fellow, PluriCourts Centre of Excellence, Faculty of Law, University of Oslo and Lecturer in Law, The Liverpool Law School, University of Liverpool

Marco Benatar, Research Fellow, Max Planck Institute Luxembourg for Procedural Law

Niels Blokker, Professor of International Institutional Law (Schermers Chair), Leiden University

David Caron, Member, The Iran—United States Claims Tribunal, The Hague, and Professor of International Law, King's College London

Jeffrey L Dunoff, Laura H. Carnell Professor of Law, School of Law, Temple University

Erik Franckx, Professor of Law, Vrije Universiteit Brussel

Christiane Gerstetter, Senior Fellow, Ecologic Institute, Berlin

Malcolm Langford, Professor, Faculty of Law, University of Oslo and Co-Director, Centre on Law and Social Transformation, University of Bergen and CMI

Runar Lie, Researcher, PluriCourts Centre of Excellence and Forum for Law and Social Science, Faculty of Law, University of Oslo

Kjersti Lohne, Postdoctoral Fellow, PluriCourts Centre of Excellence, University of Oslo

Alain Pellet, Researcher, University Paris Nanterre

Jerneja Penca, Research Fellow, Euro-Mediterranean University

Dominika Švarc Pipan, Legal Consultant, Drolec Sladojevic Law Firm and Adjunct Assistant Professor, American University in Bosnia and Herzegovina

Mark A Pollack, Professor of Political Science and Law, Department of Political Science, Temple University

Philippe Sands, Professor of Law, University College London

Esmé Shirlow, PhD Candidate, King's College London

Jochen von Bernstorff, Professor, Eberhard Karls University of Tübingen

International Courts and Tribunals

Rise and Reactions

Andreas Follesdal and Geir Ulfstein

International courts and tribunals (ICs) are increasing in number and importance. They address an expanding variety of issues, ranging from the law of the sea to international criminal law. The ICs are typically of a compulsory character, be it de jure or de facto: states may in practice have little choice whether to accept their jurisdiction if they want to benefit from the relevant regime. They no longer only address disputes among states; several of them are open to non-state actors. And they have functions beyond dispute settlement: they develop or make law, make specialized regimes work through their interpretations, and contribute to compliance with international obligations. In short: international relations are increasingly *judicialized.* The present book maps and assesses this development—and reactions thereto, because the trends have met with mixed responses.

This judicialization of international law has been hailed as a glimmer of more effective and legitimate world governance promoting human rights, justice, and peace. New ICs are called for as offering better governance for ever more problems, be it climate change or corporate wrongdoing. Some envision these ICs as contributions towards a world based on the rule of law rather than politics, where the dignity of human beings rather than the interests of states matter.

But critics abound. The sovereign freedom of well-functioning states is constrained by decisions wrought by ICs, be it the World Trade Organization (WTO) dispute settlement system or foreign investment tribunals. Some critics lament the circumvention of national democratic legislators and the neglect of cultural differences. The independence and professionalism of the judges are questioned, as are the accessibility, accountability, and transparency of IC procedures.

Others question the effectiveness of the ICs, asking whether there are better alternatives to such judicialization. Some fear the systemic impact of turf wars among the existing ICs, and the effects on sectors not covered by ICs, such as the environment. Yet others worry that some ICs will fall victim to their own success, pointing to the overburdened European Court of Human Rights.

These topics were addressed at the 11th Annual Conference of the European Society of International Law, held in Oslo on 10–12 September 2015. The local organizer was the PluriCourts Centre for the Study of the Legitimate Roles of the Judiciary in the Global Order. Four hundred international law scholars and practitioners gathered to discuss the judicialization of international law. The volume contains a selection of contributions presented first at the Conference, then subject to substantial editing.

The volume is composed to give a representative picture of the achievements of ICs, as well as the challenges they face. While only a few of the current international courts and tribunals are covered, those included are among those that have received most critical scrutiny.

The book shows that several of the ICs are living up to the aspirations, and that the fear of institutional fragmentation has only to a limited degree materialized. However, there is a diversity of opinions by different stakeholders of what is to be desired from the ICs. Such diversity applies first of all to their general function. Should they be limited to dispute settlement, or should we expect them to develop international law, especially where there is an impasse among international negotiators? They should mainly promote effective implementation of international legal obligations, but to what extent and how should that objective be tempered by respect for national sovereignty and democratic self-determination? Should interests beyond those expressed in their founding treaty be given emphasis? And is the criticism against ICs really directed to the international judiciary or should it be addressed to the other actors and institutions in the global community? Are there good alternatives to ICs?

Other important questions concern how the ICs work. Are they strategic actors—and if so, in pursuit of which objectives, and how should they perform such a role consistent with their mandate and legal method? How do they respond to criticism, both in their legal and extra-legal approaches? And how do and should other international actors, be they states, international organizations, or non-governmental organizations, try to influence the functions of the ICs?

These questions lead to the issues of independence and accountability of the international judiciary. The basis of their legitimacy is their function as independent interpreters and appliers of international law in concrete cases. But with increasing empowerment more focus is placed on controlling the ICs: Who guards these guardians? How can they be held accountable without compromising the kinds of independence that matter for their functioning and legitimacy? Are there ways to provide control through an international institutional framework which ensures the voice of relevant stakeholders?

This volume gives food for thought on these important issues. But several of the authors underline that more—and interdisciplinary—research is needed.

The contributions to this volume address these critical questions both from general perspectives and as they pertain to particular ICs and concerning specific concerns. Part I provides a general frame for these legitimacy concerns. It discusses the historical expectations of ICs, including their law-making function and how they are governed. Part II considers how the ICs appear to present their judgments in ways that legitimize them vis-à-vis states and other stakeholders; their inner workings; as well as possible alternatives to ICs. Part III then considers the various forms of backlash several of the ICs experience, and how the ICs, states, and civil society seek to respond to these challenges. Part IV deals with the fragmentary character of the international judiciary. An epilogue (Part V) looks to the future of international judicialization.

The first substantive chapters provide general frames for the following discussions. Jochen von Bernstorff identifies the several roles and functions of ICs from the perspective of Hans Kelsen's and Carl Schmitt's accounts of international law. Kelsen saw the international judiciary with compulsory adjudication and de facto law-making authority as the key to a future peaceful world order. This would not require a world legislator. He also held that judges had considerable freedom in their interpretation and application of international law. Schmitt agreed that courts have a central law-making function, and also that judges are subject to few interpretative constraints. While the rise of the international judiciary has been remarkable, it might not have had the wide-reaching importance suggested by these two authors. Furthermore, we can query the desirability of such a prominent role of ICs. But Kelsen and Schmitt were not writing with today's sector-specific international courts in mind. Many current concerns about the legitimacy of ICs can be traced back to tensions with what could be claimed to represent a global judicial imperialism. Von Bernstorff warns against sectorial colonization in the sense that the specialized ICs take control of non-judicialized sectors.

Niels Blokker addresses a central, common legitimacy challenge to the governance of ICs themselves. How can various international organs—such as the General Assembly or the Assembly of States Parties—serve to secure the ICs' requisite independence whilst ensuring their accountability? The governing institutions must ensure this balance in each case, but do so in different ways. Blokker demonstrates some of the dilemmas of 'balancing' the independence and the accountability of ICs. An important question is what would be the best organizational choice(s)—possibly with different answers for different ICs. International accountability is supplemented by domestic checks of IC accountability in terms of states' implementation or non-implementation of international judgments, withholding of funding, and even threats of exit. Further research is needed to assess the factual and desirable relationship between the independence of ICs and international and domestic accountability mechanisms.

The legitimacy of ICs also depends on what are the alternatives. We can think of political deliberations, conciliation, non-compliance procedures, and different forms of hybrids. All of these alternatives are to a great extent state-centred. This raises issues about the role of civil society in resolving international disputes. In Part II concerning the working of ICs, Jerneja Penca contributes to the discussion about the value added by 'The International Rights of Nature Tribunal' in light of the actual needs of potential users who enjoy multiple alternative venues for norm development and dispute settlement. This civil society tribunal borrows some of the language, structure, and procedures from international tribunals. But this tribunal is aiming at giving Earth a voice and to influence the law and the outcome of defined disputes. Thereby, it demonstrates weaknesses of existing courts and tribunals.

The perceptions of legitimacy of ICs also depend on the substantive outcome of their judgments, as well as on their judicial reasoning. Special challenges arise when specialized ICs deal with issues beyond their specialization, such as when the WTO dispute settlement system as a trade mechanism addresses environmental questions. Christiane Gerstetter shows how WTO adjudicators seek to ensure that their decisions are accepted as legitimate where non-trade issues ('trade and . . .') are at stake, both by how the substantive outcome is presented and how this decision is supported by arguments. She concludes that the WTO dispute settlement bodies act strategically in order to win the acceptance of the member states, and ultimately legitimize this dispute settlement system as a judicial entity. This illustrates that ICs as legal organs can also be strategic actors in determining their judicial policy in relation to relevant actors.

Jeffrey L Dunoff and Mark A Pollack discuss the inner working of ICs, such as the drafting of judicial opinions; practices concerning separate opinions; the role of language and translation; and the roles of third parties. They claim that 'social practice' theory can offer insights in how ICs work, and argue that such studies would benefit from inter-disciplinary approaches between international lawyers and international relations scholars. These international judicial practices vary among courts in interesting ways, and are not reducible to the structural features such as the statutes and procedural law of each court. The different practices raise questions about their historical origin as well as their suitability for addressing legal disputes in a fair and effective manner. But it is also pertinent to ask whether the different practices may colour the outcomes of the respective ICs.

Part III addresses several criticisms raised against various ICs. Some may perceive a pattern of backlash against these new, increasingly empowered independent bodies. Kjersti Lohne describes the impact of NGOs for the International Criminal Court (ICC), in particular the relative lack of regard for defendants' rights, especially the difficulties encountered by those acquitted. After the Coalition for the International Criminal Court contributed to the establishment of the ICC itself in the fight against impunity for international crimes, that Coalition has continued a victim-oriented approach, arguably at the expense of defendants' rights. The ICC's focus on victims, 'truth', and 'memory' may challenge the legitimacy of the Court in the longer run. This contribution also demonstrates the particularities with international criminal tribunals compared to other ICs, in that the court's prosecutor has powers to bring cases, whereas other ICs are dependent on the willingness of the relevant rights-holders, be they states, individuals, or companies, to initiate proceedings.

Malcolm Langford, Daniel Behn and Runar Lie begin by identifying various legitimacy critiques of investor-state dispute settlement (ISDS) and the scholarly debate on their empirical validity. The chapter focuses on one concern, the so-called revolving door in international adjudication. Individuals act sequentially and even simultaneously in different roles—adjudicator, legal counsel, expert witness, or secretary. Drawing on the extensive PITAD database, the authors analyze 3910 known individuals in their roles across more than one thousand investment treaty arbitrations. The social network analysis reveals that a group of roughly 25 'powerbrokers'—almost exclusively Western and male—dominate arbitral practice. Besides raising this general legitimacy concern about the system's representativity, the authors also focus on a specific concern generated by the revolving door—conflicts of interests. Taking a point of departure in the long-standing ethical concerns raised by Philippe Sands (reflected in the concluding chapter in this volume), the authors analyse the extent to which individuals act simultaneously as arbitrator and legal counsel (so-called double hatting). Their measurements indicate that there is some justification for the legitimacy concern. A select but significant group of individuals engage substantially and continually in such double hatting, suggesting that international adjudicators may be partly responsible for generating legitimacy concerns about international adjudication. Such legitimacy concerns may in the end prove less worrisome than some critics think, but the issues clearly merit further attention.

David Caron and Esmé Shirlow discuss the widespread criticism against investor-state dispute settlement (ISDS). They argue that these critiques must be disentangled in terms of the actors and substantive concerns. A main conclusion is that the misgivings may not be directed towards the dispute settlement mechanism itself, but rather concern broader worries about globalization. And several changes to the ISDS regime should have dampened such criticisms, raising questions about the protestors' knowledge and motives. Thus the critique will not necessarily provide useful guidance as regards the ISDS system. Similar experiences may be relevant for analysing challenges raised against other ICs: it may be difficult to determine whether the critique really should be seen as addressed to for example the organization of which the IC forms part, such as the WTO, or a more general protest against usurpation of national sovereignty.

Erik Franckx and Marco Benatar consider the peculiar backlash in the form of states rejecting the jurisdiction of ICs. They discuss how the People's Republic of China (PRC) rejected jurisdiction in the *Philippines v PRC* arbitration. The authors draw comparisons with how the Russian Federation rejected the jurisdiction of an arbitration panel in the *Arctic Sunrise* case. But both states participated in the peculiar form of forwarding 'position papers'. This allows states new modes of influencing the bench without formally participating in the proceedings, Franckx and Benatar argue. This may tempt other states to apply a similar approach. For example, Croatia has presented its views to an arbitration panel in a dispute with Slovenia, despite its non-participation after irregularities by one of the arbitrators. The PRC and the Russian Federation have also issued a joint declaration encouraging non-participation in international legal proceedings. These examples, again, show the flexibility of the ICs—within certain bounds. Also, while states may object to ICs through their practice, the examples seem to indicate that they prefer not to leave ICs entirely.

Part IV considers how the ICs respond to the various fears of fragmentation across issue areas and courts. Dominika Švarc Pipan explores the way in which the interstate International Court of Justice (ICJ) deals with individual human rights and international humanitarian law. She argues that ever since the *Interpretation of Peace Treaties* case in 1950, the ICJ has taken an increasingly strong role in recognizing, interpreting, and developing these two disciplines. The Court relies on the cooperation with regional human rights courts and global human rights treaty bodies.

Alain Pellet argues that we should not worry about fragmentation, given the multiplicity of international courts. To the contrary, he defends the dialogue among the many courts as contributing to the responsible development of international law. He responds to several criticisms concerning possible interpretative fragmentation; competing jurisdiction and forum shopping; as well as regional courts as a potential challenge to the global rule of law, holding that whilst fragmentation might be a problem in theory, it hardly ever occurs in practice. Pellet concludes that the several international courts are not a threat, but an enrichment of international jurisprudence.

As an epilogue to the volume, Philippe Sands lays out several of the challenges to international courts. He recalls conversations with the late Professor Vladimir Ibler from Croatia, who recommended that one should not draw conclusions about the legitimacy of ICs too quickly. Sands reminds us that international courts and tribunals are young, compared to national courts. Several of the ICs have encountered challenges, from accusations that the ICC is a neo-colonial instrument, to revelations about leakages and unacceptable communication in the boundary arbitration between Croatia and Slovenia. Sands encourages the relatively small community of practitioners and scholars engaged in the workings of ICs to speak out about the deficiencies of the system. However, he ends on a positive note with a sense of optimism for the future of the international courts and tribunals.

The contributions in this book show that after a period of considerable expansion and increasing importance of ICs, several of them are faced with criticism about their legitimacy, and even backlashes. The criticism is diverse and may relate to the composition of the courts and tribunals, to their procedures, or to their legal interpretations and the acceptability of their outcome. Some of the ICs are more susceptible to critique than others. The investment arbitral tribunals are currently under especially strong attack. They are accused of being composed of a small circle of lawyers, lacking in transparency, and favouring investors.

The authors demonstrate that the ICs have an ability to adapt to changing circumstances. For example, the respective courts and tribunals take into account practice from other ICs in an effort to overcome the increasing institutional fragmentation. Investment tribunals seem also to adjust their outcomes as a result of criticism. But such adaptations matter little if the concern is more general in its character, and in reality is a resistance against what is seen as a development towards undermining national sovereignty.

The ICs enjoy considerable discretion in their interpretation and application of international obligations. Their independence is a cornerstone in their legitimacy. But it does not seem that the institutional frameworks of the different ICs sufficiently reflect the need to secure both the independence and the accountability of the courts and tribunals. More focus should be on the design and functioning of such accountability mechanisms while preserving the independence essential for their credibility.

States may of course become so frustrated with the ICs that they choose to leave. But this is the rare exception. Instead, we have seen that states choose to participate in proceedings in an informal way, rather than how it is envisaged by the relevant treaty. We have so far only a couple of instances where this has happened. But while showing reluctance towards the relevant ICs, these examples seem to confirm that the threshold for a complete withdrawal is high.

Finally, the accountability of ICs should not only be a matter for the states parties. The courts and tribunals operate in an environment of public debate and academic works. There is a need for more information and engagement in the workings, successes, and failures of the ICs—and of what we should reasonably expect from them. This requires further research on the 'mixed blessing' of international courts and tribunals.

PART I

GENERAL PERSPECTIVES

1

Specialized Courts and Tribunals as the Guardians of International Law? The Nature and Function of Judicial Interpretation in Kelsen and Schmitt

Jochen von Bernstorff

Unwavering trust of international lawyers in the beneficial and civilizing power of international courts and tribunals in a world of otherwise untamed sovereigns is one of the strongest twentieth-century scholarly legacies. Many international lawyers continue to identify at least subconsciously with the traditional fight for compulsory jurisdiction in international law by the Hague movement and the cosmopolitan interwar struggle to reform and bolster the Permanent Court of International Justice (PCIJ) and the vision of a judicially controlled rule of law in international relations. Those authors who advocated the introduction of compulsory jurisdiction in the Interwar period faced criticism by more sceptical voices, which held that international law at the time was much too rudimentary or too fragile as a normative structure to allow for compulsory jurisdiction of international courts[1] in vital matters of international concern.[2]

[1] Sir Alfred Zimmern, in his famous monograph *The League of Nations and the Rule of Law 1918–1935* (New York, 1936, reprint of the second, revised edition of 1939, New York: Russel & Russel, 1969), already influenced by the beginning 'realism' within the international legal discourse, revealed a sceptical attitude towards international law: 'There is in fact, whatever the names used in the books, no system of international law—and still less, of course, a code. What is to be found in the treatises is simply a collection of rules which, when looked at closely, appear to have been thrown together, or to have been accumulated, almost at haphazard. Many of them would seem to be more appropriately described as materials for the etiquette book for the conduct of sovereigns and their representatives than as elements of a true legal system', 98.

[2] Hans Joachim Morgenthau, *Die internationale Rechtspflege, ihr Wesen und ihre Grenzen* (1929), Leipzig, Noske; Martti Koskenniemi, *Morgenthau's Books on International Law with Kelsen* (2006); GO Mazur, *Twenty-Five Year Memorial Commemoration to the Life of Hans Morgenthau (1904–2004)* (2004), New York, Semenko Foundation, 152–58; later, in a similar vein, EH Carr, in his famous book *The Twenty Years' Crisis, 1919–1939*, noted, with reference to Lauterpacht, that the view of international law as a legal system that was institutionally completed by compulsory jurisdiction was another 'distinguished international lawyer's dream of an international community whose center of gravity is in the administration of international justice' (Carr 1939: 186).

While the realization of a unified international legal order with compulsory jurisdiction remained an unattained dream up until today, the second half of the twentieth century has brought about the cherished establishment of ever more sophisticated issue-related international regimes that rely on their own mechanisms of adjudication and enforcement.[3] This development took place in the absence of a hierarchical system of courts that judicially guarantees the systemic unity of international law as a legal system. Instead of the aspired structures of a world state regulated by law and controlled by a world court, we face the challenges of issue-related fragmentation in an institutionally decentralized legal order, where individual regimes such as the World Trade Organization (WTO), the international investment protection regime, regional human rights instruments, and the international criminal law regime have their own independent courts and tribunals. International law thus has brought about compulsory adjudication within individual regimes, but these partial regimes are not tied together into a comprehensive legal system institutionalized through centralized courts. These developments have led to heated debates about conflicts between norms from within and outside specific legal regimes and on the role of judges in protecting or endangering the 'unity' of the international legal system.[4]

The issue of judicial interpretation thus is back on the scholarly agenda. In particular, a key area of debate revolves around the question of whether recognized methods of interpretation, such as the ones contained in article 31 of the Vienna Convention on the Law of Treaties, allow sectorial judges to take into account other potentially colliding sectorial regimes in their decisions. Famous examples are the conflicts between Agreement on Trade-Related Aspects of Intellectual Property Rights (TRIPS) rules on patent protection and the human right to health in the context of access to generically produced HIV-AIDS drugs or conflicts between bilateral rules of investment protection and principles of international environmental law. A widely shared scholarly opinion on these matters seems to be that on the basis of recognized methods of interpretation judges can use norms of other sectorial regimes in their judicial reasoning.[5]

A central motive of the discussion seems to be the question to what extent specialized courts and tribunals constitute a danger for other sectorial regimes and how this danger is being mitigated through judicial practice and recognized methods of interpretation in the various regimes. What has been neglected in this debate is the more fundamental question, what general theoretical role judicial decisions have for

[3] See on this development Mario Prost, *The Division of Expert Labour in the International Law Profession: Genealogies of Fragmentation*, ASIL Proceedings (2012). Relatively optimistic as to the role of international courts in the protection of also a general rule of international law despite fragmentation Geir Ulfstein, 'International Courts and Judges, Independence, Interaction and Legitimacy' (2014), 46(3) New York University Journal of International Law and Politics 849–66; Andre Nollkaemper and Ole Kristian Fauchald, 'Conclusion' in *The Practice of International Courts and the (De-) Fragmentation of International Law*, pp. 343, 366.

[4] ILC-Report, *Fragmentation of international law. Difficulties arising from the diversification and expansion of international law*, Report of the Study Group of the International Law Commission finalized by Martti Koskenniemi, 13 April 2006, ILC Doc. A/CN.4/L.682, para 479.

[5] Bruno Simma and Theodore Kill, 'Harmonizing Investment Protection and International Human Rights: First Steps Towards a Methodology' in C Binder, U Kriebaum, A Reinisch et al. (eds), *International Investment Law for the 21st Century. Essays in Honour of Christoph Schreuer* (2009), 678–707.

legal systems and for international law in particular. What do judges actually do when deciding legal cases brought before them? How can from a theoretical perspective internal and external constraints, their degree of discretion, their freedom or even political power in the process of norm-application be conceptualized? To what extent do doctrinal methods of interpretation, such as the methods laid out in article 31 Vienna Convention, limit or control the judicial process of norm-application in the first place? Maybe the doctrinal canon of established methods of interpretation is completely irrelevant for the process of judicial norm-application and the canon is not more than a rather helpless scholarly rationalization of a judicial practice following in essence a completely different logic or routine? In the remainder of this contribution I would like to discuss these issues through the eyes of two particularly salient theoretical positions, namely through the theories of judicial decision-making of Hans Kelsen (1.) and Carl Schmitt (2.). Both as scholars inter alia have in common that they were famous twentieth-century legal philosophers *and* international legal scholars.

1 The Judicial Decision Within Kelsen's Pure Theory of Law

Kelsen's desire to foster the establishment of compulsory jurisdiction in international law must be analysed more closely against the backdrop of the theoretical function of courts in his main theoretical oeuvre, the Pure Theory of Law. The outstanding significance that Kelsen accorded the courts was based not only on his evolutionary theory of the law, but also on his concept of the dynamic legal system that was derived from the theory of the hierarchical structure of the legal system.[6]

1.1 Interpretation as dynamic and contingent concretization of legal 'frames'

For Kelsen, the decision of the court served to concretize abstract general norms.[7] It thus had by no means only a declaratory character, in the sense of merely pronouncing already existing law. Rather, it had a constitutive, law-creating function: 'That there is held to be a concrete material fact at all, which is to be linked with a specific legal consequence, and that this concrete material fact is indeed linked with concrete legal consequences—this entire connection is created by the judicial decision.'[8] As Kelsen saw it, the decision by the court created an individual legal norm by concretizing a norm of customary law or an international legal treaty. According to the previously described hierarchical structure of the law [*Stufenbau*], the application of a higher-ranking norm within the hierarchy of norms was simultaneously the creation of a lower-ranking norm by the authorized legal organ. In this way, following Kelsen, the application could be seen as the dynamic process of concretizing norms.

[6] See the discussion of Kelsen's hierarchical structure of the law in Jochen von Bernstorff, *The Public International Law Theory of Hans Kelsen, Believing in Universal Law* (2014), Chap. 5 B.

[7] Hans Kelsen, *Reine Rechtslehre* (1934), 79; *Introduction to the Problems of Legal Theory* (1992), 68.

[8] ibid.

Law-making was always an empirical act, the performance of which created a norm by having the act satisfy the conditions for the creation of a norm as laid down in a higher norm.[9] For Kelsen there was, however, no guarantee that the concrete decision by a court was still in accord with the general norm that was being applied.[10] Yet in such a case this individual norm still had the force of law.[11] This was the institution of the *res iudicata*, which was central to every legal system.[12] The theory of the hierarchical structure adopted from Merkl allowed Kelsen to see the application of the law by the courts simultaneously as law-making. Moreover, because this was law-making at the last level of concretization, the court decided in the final analysis what was law.[13] Only the application of the law to the individual case, which laid claim to being valid even if it departed from the abstract rule, formed the concrete corpus of law: 'One should not overlook the important fact that in the last analysis the law is not what the legislator more or less clearly sets forth or what the rule of custom more or less comprehensibly implies. The law is what the court finally decides.'[14]

By emphasizing the crucial function of the judiciary within the legal system, Kelsen sought to demonstrate that the importance of a centralized legislature—in the sense of a world parliament—was secondary to that of the courts. Not only was the concretization of the law by the courts the first step—in his theory of legal evolution—towards a modern, centralized legal system, even within the more highly evolved legal systems it remained functionally the most important organ of the legal order. For Kelsen, the still decentralized law-making by treaties and customary law created a sufficient material basis for the introduction of compulsory jurisdiction. A stronger centralization of general law-making could then follow in a later step.[15] By contrast, Kelsen believed that the efforts to create a comprehensive codification of international law by a kind of world parliament before establishing compulsory jurisdiction was potentially dysfunctional. One must in his view not overestimate the function of the legislative. But if one considered the eminent importance of the courts, it becomes clear 'why there can be no legislator without a judge, even though there can very well be a judge without a legislator'.[16]

If one sees the courts as the central organ of the legal system, as Kelsen did, the question about the nature and method of the judge's act of decision takes on special relevance. I shall therefore take a closer look at Kelsen's theory of interpretation

[9] ibid, 82 et seq; 70; cf Carsten Heidemann, *Die Norm als Tatsache. Zur Normentheorie Hans Kelsens* (1997), 78–79.

[10] Hans Kelsen, *Peace through Law* (1944), 162–63.

[11] On the problem of judge-made law as a source of law in the Continental European and the common law tradition see Niklas Luhmann, *Das Recht der Gesellschaft* (1993), 304–10; Josef Esser, 'Richterrecht, Gerichtsgebrauch und Gewohnheitsrecht' in Josef Esser (ed), *Festschrift für Fritz von Hippel* (1967), 95 et seq.

[12] Kelsen (n 10), 163.

[13] Hans Kelsen, 'International Peace—by Court or by Government?' (1941) XLVI The American Journal of Sociology 575.

[14] ibid.

[15] Kelsen works with an evolutionary theory of law, Jochen von Bernstorff, *The Public International Law Theory of Hans Kelsen, Believing in Universal Law* (2010), Chap. 6 A. II.

[16] Kelsen (n 13), 575.

for what it has to say about the boundaries or guiding principles of individual law-making by the person who applies the law.

According to Kelsen, the process of law-making as it moves from a higher to a lower norm is guided by the mental procedure of legal interpretation.[17] In addition to this mental process, the higher norm—to a certain extent—also predetermines the content of the lower norm. But this higher norm formed only the frame, within which the lower norm had to be established.[18] Because the content of the lower norm was thus never completely determined, the interpretation of the norm served to choose one possible concretization of the more general framework provided by the higher norm. In addition, for Kelsen there was no 'method according to which only one of the several interpretations of a norm could be distinguished as correct'.[19] As he saw it, all methods of interpretation developed by the traditional doctrine lead to a possible, but never to the only correct result. The possibility of interpretation arose precisely from the semantic openness of any norm to various inferable meanings.[20] It was futile to try to establish legally one correct concretization by excluding the others.[21] For Kelsen, herewith distancing himself from the Free Law movement, objectively 'right' results of interpretation could not be arrived at either from judicial interpretive techniques such as *analogy*, or from the *argumentum e contrario*, or from the so-called weighing of interests.

In his Pure Theory of Law, Kelsen thus demystified the objectivity of these methods of interpretation along with other classic techniques of legal argumentation. From a scholarly perspective, the only remaining purpose of interpretation was to determine an external semantic framework; one could speak here of the '*Wortlautgrenze*' ['semantic frame'] that circumscribed the subjective act of the judge's decision.[22] In the second edition of his Pure Theory, Kelsen spoke with respect to interpretation by legally authorized organs of 'authentic interpretation'.[23] With this, he demarcated this form of interpretation sharply from scholarly interpretation. Neither the judge as the one applying the law, nor the legal scholar, could claim that he alone was able to determine the only correct way of applying the norm. But in the case of the subjective decision of the judge, we are dealing with an act of application authorized by the legal system, whereas for Kelsen the legal scholar was not embedded within such a functional context.[24] He had to limit himself to demonstrating the various decision options of the one applying the law and place them side by side as equals.[25]

In this way, the application of the norm was largely disconnected from the problem of jurisprudential cognition: 'For if there can be an interpretation of a norm,

[17] Kelsen (n 7), 90; 77. On the theory of interpretation see Heidemann *supra* (n 9), 78–79.

[18] Kelsen (n 7), 91, 78. [19] ibid, 96; 81. [20] ibid, 97; 81. [21] ibid, 96; 81.

[22] In this critical view of the traditional methods of interpretation, Kelsen was in agreement with the realistic theory of international law of McDougal and Schwarzenberger; see Myres S McDougal, 'International Law, Power and Policy: A Contemporary Conception' (1953) 82 RCADI 149–57; Georg Schwarzenberger and Edward D Brown, *A Manual of International Law*, 6th edition (1976), 135–37; on this parallelism see Martti Koskenniemi, *From Apology to Utopia* (2006), 298.

[23] Hans Kelsen, *Reine Rechtslehre*, 2nd edition (1960), 350; Heidemann (n 9), 136–37.

[24] Hans Kelsen, ibid, 353.

[25] It was in this way that Kelsen was trying to write his commentary on the Charter of the United Nations. *Supra* (n 15), final chapter.

then the question as to which is the "correct" choice from among the possibilities given within the frame of the norm is hardly a question of cognition directed to the positive law; it is a problem not of legal theory but of legal policy.'[26] The individual creation of a norm thus becomes a subjective act of will on the part of the judge:

> In applying a statute, there may well be room for cognitive activity beyond discovering the frame within which the act of application is to be confined; this is not cognition of the positive law, however, but cognition of other norms, which can now make their way into the law-creating process, the norms, namely, of morality, of justice—social value-judgments customarily characterized with the catch-phrases 'welfare of the people', 'public interest', 'progress', and so on. From the standpoint of the positive law, nothing can be said about their validity and whether or not they can be identified.[27]

The judge, unlike the legal scholar, was thus free to incorporate personal value-judgments, political maxims, and ideas of justice into his decision—according to Kelsen, he could not but do so.

In order to get a better grasp of how far-reaching Kelsen's concept of judicial law-making is, a comparison with HL Hart's theory of adjudication may be helpful. Hart seems to follow Kelsen in accepting that norms can be indeterminate or 'open textured' which leads to a relatively wide judicial discretion when applying such norms. Instead of a 'frame' provided by the higher law Hart speaks of a 'core of certainty' and a 'penumbra of doubt'.[28] In his view, when being confronted with indeterminacy and lacunae, judges must perform an act of 'interstitial' legislation,[29] which, however, compared to parliamentary legislation operates under various (unspecified) institutional constraints. Despite a slightly diverging metaphor Hart seems to follow Kelsen's move to destabilize the boundary between adjudication and law-making without, however, endorsing Kelsen's strong (continental) notions of hierarchical ordering of the legal system. At first sight, both theories seem to uphold the distinction between 'cognition' and 'decisionism' by reducing judicial discretion to deciding within the 'frame' or the 'penumbra' of the applicable law. A closer look at Kelsen's somewhat ambiguous statements on judicial interpretation however reveals that the determination of the frame itself for Kelsen also cannot be objectified and is a wilful und ultimately subjective act of the judge.[30] Determining the frame thus also is not only a 'cognitive' act. In that sense he even seems to go beyond Hart's explanation that reduces *decisionism* or the political dimension to a limited area of indeterminacy within the law.

[26] Kelsen (n 7), 98; 82.

[27] ibid, 98–99; 83; for a current in-depth analysis of the general problem of interpretation in international law, Ingo Venzke, *How Interpretation Makes International Law* (2013).

[28] HLA Hart, *The Concept of Law*, 1st edition (1961), 119–20; 123–28; 131–35; 143.

[29] HLA Hart, *The Concept of Law*, 2nd edition Postscript (1994), 273.

[30] Hans Kelsen, *Reine Rechtslehre*, 2nd edition (1960), 350; cf Volker Neumann, *Carl Schmitt als Jurist* (2015), 20; Dieter Grimm however portrays Kelsen's theory as upholding a clear distinction between the cognitively accessible 'frame' and the wilful act of 'filling' it, D Grimm, 'Zum Verhältnis von Interpretationslehre, Verfassungsgerichtsbarkeit und Demokratieprinzip bei Kelsen' in Krawietz et al (eds), 149–57, 151.

1.2 The return of the political in the Pure Theory—Kelsenian decisionism?

This brings us to a critical point of the Pure Theory, one to which the secondary literature about the now 'classic' 1931 Weimar dispute over the limits of constitutional adjudication[31] has called attention.[32] Critics see in the possibility granted by Kelsen of a largely free constitutional court with the ability to engage in political law-making as a contradiction to the rule-of-law-limitation on politics, which he actually desired.[33]

What Kelsen asked the enlightened jurist to confront through his view of the court decision, however, was not so much a contradiction in the theoretical approach of the Pure Theory, as one of the central paradoxes of the law. The legal sociologist Kelsen was aware of the central role that binding decisions by courts have for the ability of the legal system to function, but he was realistic enough not to resolve the paradox of the 'undecidability of the decision'.[34] Instead, the Pure Theory of Law sought to constructively capture the objectively uncontrollable and in the final analysis irrational character of the court decision through the dynamic view of the creation of law. That was also the reason why Kelsen did not need to restrict the subjectivity of the court decision through a purified theory of interpretation. The intrusion of the judge's subjective value judgements into decisions of the court should *not* be glossed over by the seeming objectivity of the theories of interpretation. Instead, Kelsen construed the scientifically uncontrollable factor as an act of law-making of the judge that was authorized by the legal system.[35] The degree of freedom granted to the judge by the dynamic idea of law-creation allows the court to adjust the law to the current needs of society.[36]

It thus no longer comes as a surprise that Kelsen was more than receptive to the use of general legal principles and decisions *ex aequo et bono* by international courts and arbitrators. In an analysis of article 38 of the statute of the PCIJ, Kelsen noted

[31] Hans Kelsen, *Wer soll Hüter der Verfassung sein?* (1931), Walther Rotschild, Berlin-Grunewald.

[32] See the critical approaches by M Troper and D Dyzenhaus: Michel Troper, 'Kelsen und die Kontrolle der Verfassungsmäßigkeit' in A Carrino and G Winkler (eds), *Rechtserfahrung und Reine Rechtslehre* (1995), 15–39; Michel Troper, 'The Guardian of the Constitution—Hans Kelsen's Evaluation of a Legal Concept' in D Diner and M Stolleis (eds), *Hans Kelsen and Carl Schmitt: A Juxtaposition* (1999), 81 et seq; David Dyzenhaus, *Legality and Legitimacy. Carl Schmitt, Hans Kelsen and Hermann Heller in Weimar* (1997), 102–60.

[33] Michel Troper, *Kelsen und die Kontrolle der Verfassungsmäßigkeit*, 15–39; David Dyzenhaus, *Legality and Legitimacy*, 149, 157; on this criticism see Clemens Jabloner, 'Verrechtlichung und Rechtsdynamik' in (1999) 54 *ZöR* 270–78.

[34] On the paradox of the 'undecidability of the decision' see Niklas Luhmann, *Das Recht der Gesellschaft* (1995), 317: 'Courts must also decide in cases where they cannot decide; or at least, not within tenable standards of rationality. If the law cannot be found, it must simply be invented.' On the 'affliction of the undecidable' see Jacques Derrida, *Gesetzeskraft. Der mystische Grund der Autorität* (1991), 49.

[35] To that extent, the court, like any other legal organ, can be simultaneously seen, according to Kelsen, as a 'political' organ. But it remains a legal organ only if, in the political act of applying the law or making law, it adheres formally and materially to the framework established by the legal system: Hans Kelsen, 'Science and Politics' (1951) XLV The American Political Science Review 660.

[36] Kelsen (n 13), 575.

the outstanding possibilities of the court to account for the demands of justice and equity through the application of general legal principles.[37] Reference to general legal principles always allowed the court in practice to apply also considerations of equity, even though *ex aequo et bono* decisions by statute require the special consent of the contending parties.[38] In fact, for Kelsen, considerations of fairness—in the sense of the adjustment of the abstract norm to the specific circumstances of the case—by a court rendering compulsory decisions were unavoidable:

> A court which really has compulsory jurisdiction, that is to say, which is competent to decide finally all disputes without any exception, inevitably will adapt positive law in its concrete decisions gradually and imperceptively to actual needs; in other words, will decide on the basis of equity, even if it is not expressly empowered to apply principles other than those of law.[39]

The application of general legal maxims, considerations of equity, and notions of justice, which Kelsen sought to prohibit the legal scholar from using, was not only permitted to the judge, but from a functional point of view was necessary. That subjective value judgements and political preferences flowed into the rendering of a decision and in the end were also cast into the form of the court's decision was the precondition for the necessary, continuous reform of the law. Thus, they found their justified function not in the jurisprudential determination and analysis of the law, but on the level of law creation by the organs set up for that purpose by the legal system.

And yet doubts remain. While exposing the dilemma of interpretation, Kelsen stopped short of contributing to its methodological containment. Instead, he completely removed methodological questions regarding the act of interpretation from the Pure Theory's realm of cognition.[40] Despite Kelsen's illuminating theoretical equation of adjudication and legislation, it remains problematic within this context that the Pure Theory of Law, as a theory of law, promotes the civilizational function of a specific judicial rationality without being able to explain it.

[37] Hans Kelsen, 'Compulsory Adjudication of International Disputes' (1943) 37 AJIL 406.

[38] ibid.

[39] ibid. In contrast to Kelsen, Lauterpacht, in his argumentation, had shied away from describing the administration of the law as law-making. For him, the judge was applying existing law in a creative process. There was no need to depict the function of the judge as a purely automatic, formal deduction from the law, nor cause for the assumption that the decision of a court was the highly subjective affair of a judge who was guided by emotion: Hersch Lauterpacht, *The Function of Law in the International Community* (1966), 103. The judge's freedom to decide should not be overestimated especially in the international arena, since the competence of the court was grounded in the voluntary agreement of states (104). For Lauterpacht, the subjective element inherent in the decision encountered its limit in the respect for the rule of law. The judge's freedom to decide remained a freedom within the law (103). Julius Stone criticized Lauterpacht for what he believed was an inconsistent construct. He maintained that in order to justify a prohibition of 'non liquet' or an obligatory jurisdiction, one had to eventually posit a law creation activity on the part of the judge: Julius C Stone, 'Non Liquet and the Function of Law in the International Community' (1959) 25 BYIL 137. Lauterpacht was concealing this when he pointed in his argumentation to the fruitfulness of the general legal maxims in the judge's finding of law (133–37). Because a judge always had a choice between various legal maxims, he did not apply existing law, but in the end created new law (159). On the debate between Lauterpacht and Stone see Iain GM Scobbie, 'The Theorist as a Judge: Hersch Lauterpacht's Conception of the International Judicial Function' (1997) 2 EJIL 274–98.

[40] On this and the critique, *supra* (n 15), Chapter 6.

The practical significance of Kelsen's insights into the political nature of judicial decision-making is further increased by the role he envisages for judicial decisions in his theory of sources of international law. His theory of customary law must be seen as strongly fixated on international adjudication at that time.[41] Instead of relying on the *opinio iuris* of state organs as the second element (besides state practice) of custom, decisions by international organs, and here especially the decisions of international courts, were for Kelsen the most important pillar in determining customary law.[42] In line with postmodern concepts of law as a systemic communicative practice, court decisions in Kelsen's view do not only have a significance for the case at hand, but influence the legal fabric of international law as a whole by developing and modifying rules of both customary law and treaty law by interpretation.[43] Court decisions thus do not only constitute individualized law-making but also contribute to general international law-making.[44] Taking all of this together, it seems striking that Kelsen, as a staunch defender of liberal democracy, did not hesitate to promote compulsory international adjudication, which he conceived to be a specific form of law-making. Not only does this approach seem to privilege the international judiciary over international political institutions. It moreover considerably strengthens the international level vis-à-vis the national (potentially democratic) level of law-making.[45] Kelsen's quest for compulsory adjudication, however, must be contextualized as part of a post-World War one project to civilize territorial disputes between states as a substitute to war. And even though Kelsen concedes the political role and power of the judges of the new World Court, he trusts in the traditional routines and institutional safeguards of judicial practice, which will bring a 'civilizing' rationality to bear in questions of war and peace in international relations.

2 Carl Schmitt's Theory of Judicial Decision-making

Carl Schmitt is commonly known for his theory of *decisionism* (Dezisionismus), which he developed in his book *Politische Theologie* (1922) and for his associated

[41] Henri Thévénaz was the first to point out this link: 'A Propos de la Coutume' in S Engel (ed), *Law, State, and International Legal Order: Essays in Honor of Hans Kelsen* (1964), 317, 325.

[42] Hans Kelsen, 'Théorie du droit international coutumier' (1939) 253 Revue internationale de la théorie du droit 15–16.

[43] For an in-depth critique of the unhelpful classic claim that international law does not know a concept of *stare decisis* see Marc Jacob, 'Precedents: Lawmaking Through International Adjudication' (2011) 12 German Law Journal 1005; 1008–20.

[44] Such a concept of the law-making effect of international court decisions can as of today hardly be squared with Art 38 I d), 59 ICJ-Statute but could nonetheless be an adequate sociological description of the effects of international adjudication on the international legal system; see on the differentiation between voluntas and ratio maintained in the formulation of Art 38 I d), Armin von Bogdandy and Ingo Venzke, *In wessen Namen?* (2014), 156–67.

[45] According to Michael Hardt and Antonio Negri, this cosmopolitan impetus of the 'Pure Theory', Kelsen's quest for world government through law, enforced by international courts, made him the chief theorist of an 'imperial' global legal order, Michael Hardt and Antonio Negri, *Empire* (2001), Chap 1.1, on this claim see Jochen von Bernstorff, 'Hans Kelsen on Judicial Law-Making by International Courts and Tribunals' (2015) 14 The Practice of International Courts and Tribunals 35–50.

concept of the 'state of exception' (Ausnahmezustand). Most of the secondary literature focuses on these interwar publications of Schmitt in which he tried to construct a theoretical explanation for legal decisions of the strongest political power in situations of existential crisis and confrontation. A legal decision in such a moment of existential crisis of a political community famously according to Schmitt is 'from a normative perspective, something which emerges out of nothingness' ('normativ betrachtet, aus dem Nichts geboren').[46] Schmittian 'decisionism' for a long time has on the basis of these interwar publications been portrayed as a deeply apologetic and power centred theory that—in contradistinction to Kelsenian normativism—accords no autonomous role for law as a constraining element in a situation of crisis and political upheavals. Schmitt's strong support of Hitler's dictatorial rule and his personal involvement in early Nazi rule in Germany add a biographical dimension to this interpretation.[47] This in many ways is a helpful critique of Schmitt's *Politische Theologie*, to which I generally would and actually did subscribe. Interestingly Schmitt himself in a conscious paradoxical move always insisted that these allegedly normatively unfounded decisions remained *legal* decisions and as such an issue of *legal* theory.[48] His relatively short, ambivalent and provocative Weimar statements in *Politische Theologie* have for a long time absorbed most of the scholarly attention and coined the reception of Schmittian *decisionism.*

His pre-First World War writings on *judicial* decision-making, however, which include the monograph *Gesetz und Urteil* (1911), have received less attention in the post-Second World War secondary literature, even though this book constitutes a comprehensive and original theory of the role and function of the judiciary, which the late Carl Schmitt five decades later defended as his most important contribution to a legal theory of judicial decision-making. In *Gesetz und Urteil* Schmitt develops a whole theory of judicial decision-making, which reacted to the Free Law movement with an elaborate and idiosyncratic answer. Like Kelsen, Schmitt dismisses not only the nineteenth century old hermeneutic canon of methods of interpretation but also newer theories, which sought to explain judicial decision-making through the weighing of interests or 'logical' reasoning, such as *analogy, argumentum e contrario.* An objective theory of the 'right' judicial decision for him could not be derived from these approaches. All these theories operated on the flawed assumption that the judge in a concrete case could in a methodologically controlled way determine the will of the law ('Wille des Gesetzes') and subsequently bring it to bear in the decision. All these methods may for Schmitt have a legitimate function for legal scholarship for an *abstract* scholarly interpretation of the law, but they cannot control or regulate the *concrete* (judicial) application of the norm to a particular case ('Subsumption').[49] It is important to note that Schmitt aims at developing an immanent theory of the

[46] Carl Schmitt, *Politische Theologie*, 8th edition (2004), 42.

[47] For his legal justification of early mass killings of potential internal opponents instructed by Hitler: Carl Schmitt, 'Der Führer schützt das Recht' (1947) Deutsche Juristen-Zeitung 947 et seq.

[48] Carl Schmitt, *Politische Theologie*, 16; 44.

[49] Carl Schmitt, *Gesetz und Urteil* (1969), 37.

practice of judicial decision-making, explaining law's 'practical validity' and not a theory of scholarly interpretation of the law.

The basis for Schmitt's theory of judicial decision-making is the 'principle of legal determination' ('Prinzip der Rechtsbestimmtheit') which has the following materially purified theoretical content: Legal practice in all its dimensions works on the basis of a compulsion or force to generate a decision.[50] His explanation of this principle of substantively 'indifferent' legal decisions starts with the decisions taken by the legislator. Assumed moral or political purposes of an abstract law or norm for Schmitt can neither theoretically determine its content nor its subsequent application. Schmitt provides examples from domestic legislation where many norms do not follow a specific moral or political purpose but are being enacted for the *sole* reason that a certain question needs to be regulated or decided. The existence of most laws reflects the societal necessity 'that decisions must ultimately be made' ('dass überhaupt eine Entscheidung gegeben werden muss').[51] Thus it is the legislative decision as such ('die Entscheidung an sich'), reflecting the wish to have a binding legal regulation of a societal issue, and not any supposed pre-legal moral, political, or economic motive, which constitutes the primary purpose of legislation. As a consequence, legal decisions from the perspective of the 'principle of legal determination' must be conceptualized as being 'indifferent' towards any pre-legal purposes and in that sense legal decisions on all levels must be seen as inherently free from normative constraints ('normfrei'). It is a purely formal principle, the content of which is reduced to the compulsion to decide and the formalized factual product of the decision, the publicized law, judgment etc; a principle that cannot be equated with a much more demanding substantive principle of 'legal certainty' ('Rechtssicherheit') of the liberal rule of law tradition.

Compared to Kelsen's realistic approach to interpretation, Schmitt even more radically denies the existence of a semantic 'frame' provided by the higher norm that at least prima facie controls and limits the range of defensible results of the process of judicial norm-application. But how can Schmitt on that rather minimalist and unorthodox basis develop the promised theoretical yardstick for the 'right' judicial decision? Schmitt now introduces a theoretical axiom, which is derived and argued from an institutional perspective on judicial practice and which is compatible with his 'principle of legal determination'. For him 'a judicial decision is correct today when it can be assumed that another judge would have decided in the same way' ('eine richterliche Entscheidung ist heute dann richtig, wenn anzunehmen ist, dass ein anderer Richter so entschieden hätte'). Schmitt herewith further shifts the theoretical perspective into institutionalized legal practice. Judges in modern legal systems do not derive their decisions from the applicable legal norms but from judicial practice. To think Schmitt propagated a sophisticated theory of judicial precedents, however, underestimates how unorthodoxly Schmitt approaches his topic. For him judicial precedents are only being used strategically and instrumentally by judges to demonstrate that their decision would have been taken by every other expertly trained judge—they do

[50] ibid, 48. [51] ibid, 48.

not control or predetermine the decision as such. Equally, all recognized methods of interpretation, both the classic canon as well as balancing of interests and references to societal and moral values, are being employed by judges for this particular purpose. Even the act of a 'smooth subsumption' ('glatte Subsumption') is only supposed to give the decision a justification, which increases the likelihood that another normal judge called 'the empirical type of the modern expertly trained jurist' would have come to the same decision; for Schmitt 'subsumption' is, however, a particularly safe option to generate a 'right' decision.[52]

Schmitt has two central arguments as to why the professional acceptability of a decision is the best scholarly explanation for the 'right' judicial decision. Modern legal systems do operate with collegial judicial bodies for the very reason that the presence of three or more judges is supposed to guarantee that a decision will be taken that is in line with the general expectations of judicial practice.[53] These collegial bodies are used to avoid mistakes, which for Schmitt means that they attempt to avoid unorthodox decisions—to avoid idiosyncratic decisions not in line with such professional expectations. The second argument is the institutionalization of appeal structures in 'modern' legal systems. In line with Schmitt's explanation of collegial judicial bodies, he sees appeal structures established by a hierarchical court system as an instrument to produce judicial decisions, which avoid subjectivity and instead increase the likelihood that the final decision conforms to general expectations of a 'normal' professionally trained judge.[54] Very coherently Schmitt also explains the function of judicial reasoning from his initial axiom. The reasoning is an integral part of the decision not because it produces transparency or as an act of methodological self-control of the judge. Instead for Schmitt it has the function to convince other judges, in particular those sitting in the appeal body, that the decision is correct.[55] Using precedents is a particularly effective way of achieving this result.

Carl Schmitt would not be Carl Schmitt if he at this point missed out on the occasion to push his axiom to the extremes. According to his judicial 'categorical imperative' the decision is 'right' if another normal judge in the same situation would have decided likewise.[56] Hence, professional peer expectations take precedence over both moral inclinations of the judge and even the wording of applicable norms. If this requires deciding *contra legem* or outside of accepted moral standards judges according to Schmitt usually will and must do so.[57] With this internally coherent

[52] Page 87; For Scheuermann this axiom cannot 'work' in practice because of usually missing homogeneity among judges, William E Scheuermann, Carl Schmitt, *The End of Law* (1999), 23. However this might be a misunderstanding of the theoretical status of the axiom, which is despite Schmitt's introductory rhetoric eventually not meant to be a concrete yardstick for individual decisions providing one right decision but has the status of an (hypothetical) 'as-if' assumption in line with the then highly influential *Philosophie als Ob* by Vaihinger; Schmitt gives this explanation himself in: 'Selbstanzeige von Gesetz und Urteil' in Kantstudien, Bd. 18, Berlin (1913), 165, cf Mehring, *Pathetisches Denken*, Berlin (1989), 25 et seq and Ulrich Habfast, *Das Normative Nichts der Entscheidung* (2010), 29.

[53] Carl Schmitt, *Gesetz und Urteil* (1969), 72–76. [54] ibid, 74. [55] ibid, 83.

[56] Schmitt compares his axiom with Kant's categorical imperative, ibid 78.

[57] ibid 111–12; insightful and convincing on Schmitt's position on *contra legem* decisions Ulrich Habfast, *Das Normative Nichts der Entscheidung* (2010), 32–33.

theoretical justification of *contra legem* decisions as potentially 'right' judgments Schmitt ends his treatise on a provocative stance dissolving the notion of the judge being bound by the applicable law. It is important to note that Schmitt's judge in contradistinction to Kelsen's approach is less free to inject subjective moral values in his decisions. Schmitt insists that the judge must justify his decision before the entire body of judicial practice. That is why *contra legem* decisions can never be decisions of individual judges only but will be taken and maintained by collective judicial practice.[58] In deciding a case the individual judge executes an institutional practice and not a subjective feeling. This overall institutional practice for Schmitt helps to realize the idea of justice, which from a legal perspective essentially relies on the notion of predictability.[59] And with the judge merely executing the will of an institutionalized practice, controlled by colleagues and appeal judges, judicial decisions become more predictable.[60]

A comparison between these two approaches and the one developed by Duncan Kennedy at the end of the twentieth century can help to clarify their differences and commonalities. Duncan Kennedy criticizes Kelsen and Hart for the idea that the place of subjectivity and ideology in judicial decision-making is reduced to the act of choosing between alternative interpretations within the frame or penumbra provided by the higher applicable norm. While Kelsen and Hart did understand that judicial decisions are individualized 'legislation' or law-making they still contained the ideological dimension of this act through the notions of semantic 'frames' (Kelsen) and 'cores/penumbras' (Hart). Subjectivity is reduced to deciding how to fill or concretize the 'frame' or 'penumbra'. While this is a correct description of Hart's theory of adjudication, Duncan Kennedy overlooks that Kelsen had himself argued that already at the level of the determination of the 'frame' no objective method of 'cognition' was available.[61] Be that as it may, for Duncan Kennedy those approaches working with a boundary between indeterminate and determinate areas of law overlook—and here he is quite close to Schmitt—that even these containments can be undone by what he calls 'legal work'. Judicial interpretation involving the whole set of doctrinal and judicial materials available ('legal work') can realign 'frames' and the boundaries between 'cores' and 'penumbras'. Judges are thus in an even more powerful position to strategically manipulate decisions in order to pursue their own ideological agendas. Like Schmitt (and arguably Kelsen) and unlike Hart, Kennedy sees no insurmountable limitations imposed by the norm itself for subjective and ideological judicial decision-making. But in contradistinction to Schmitt's position and in line with Kelsen's approach this leaves the judge free to inject subjectivity into judicial practice. Kennedy only in a limited way acknowledges the institutional constraints imposed by judicial practice, which are the very basis of Schmitt's perspective on judicial decision-making.

[58] 113, Habfast, ibid. [59] ibid 75. [60] ibid 75. [61] See above under 1.1.

3 Non-legal Motives and Institutional Constraints Matter

What can be inferred from all of this for contemporary judicial decision-making in international courts and tribunals? If taken seriously both Kelsen's and Schmitt's theory of adjudication can provide two principal insights into the function and nature of judicial decision-making. The first one is that courts with compulsory jurisdiction have a central law-making function for any legal system. Secondly, judges in their decision-making are only in a very limited way controlled by internal 'legal' constraints, such as doctrinal methods of interpretation, the content of applicable norms or any other 'objective' principles, values, or norms arguably contained in the legal system. For Kelsen this leaves ample room for the individual judges to incorporate personal value judgements and political maxims into their decisions. For Schmitt this space of discretion is filled by constraints imposed by a collective judicial practice. In short: International courts and tribunals are powerful institutions primarily controlled by non-legal constraints or guidance be they individual beliefs and values of the judge (Kelsen) or a collective professional practice (Schmitt). Hence, asking who the judges are becomes a very important, if not the central, issue surely of much greater importance than the content of article 31 Vienna Convention on the Law of Treaties (VCLT). How have judges been trained, what is their cultural, economic, and political background and how have judges been selected and socialized into practice? Who were the first judges who coined the self-understanding of the court or tribunal? While being an important question for any legal system it is a particularly pertinent question for an increasingly specialized international judicial landscape.

Specialized courts and tribunals recruit their judges and arbitrators from a small circle of highly specialized regime experts. Human rights lawyers do not end up in WTO panels. You need to be a recognized international trade lawyer to be appointed for a judicial position in this regime. The same holds true to a greater or lesser extent for any other specialized international legal regime. It is thus not unlikely that judges and arbitrators who have for many years been socialized as experts in one particular regime will have internalized the biases and values propagated by this particular 'epistemic community'.[62]

A scholarly observer of the field of international investment law describes the evolution of the discipline in the following way:

> An important part of the history of IIL (International Investment Law) is the technical and sociological process of its establishment as its own distinct professional specialization, a new 'field' of study and work. It has emerged in recent years as not merely a particular application

[62] On the notion of 'epistemic communities' coined by Haas and the issue of interpretation in international law, see Michael Waibel, 'Interpretive Communities in International Law' in A Bianchi, D Peat, and M Windsor (eds), *Interpretation in International Law* (OUP 2015); On elite networks from a Bourdieu-perspective MR Madsen, 'Transnational Fields and Power Elites: Reassembling the International with Bourdieu and Practice Theory' in Didier Bigo, Rob Walker, Tugba Basaran, and Emmanuel-Pierre Guittet (eds), *Transversal Lines in International Relations: Perspectives from International Political Sociology* (Routledge 2016).

of general rules of public international law or procedures for commercial dispute settlement, but as a new discipline requiring specialist (and expensive) knowledge and expertise, provided and supported by an 'epistemic community' with its own networks, conferences, and journals. An interest in promoting this sense of progress in professional development may lead an arbitrator not only to seek to make 'balanced' (or 'rebalanced') decisions in individual cases, but to strive for coherence and consistency across different investment disputes.[63]

Usually these specialized international judges and arbitrators also have much less expertise when it comes to questions of relevant domestic rules and with regard to other external international legal regimes. And the higher the degree of specialization of a judicial regime and its judges, arguably the greater the likelihood that these judges identify in a particularly strong manner with the social values purportedly realized by the implementation of the regime rules. These circumstances taken together can lead to a certain individual or collective bias in favour of the rules of that regime, which has erected the judicial mechanism. Such a bias, in the absence of a higher layer of judicial bodies with cross-sectorial legal expertise, usually cannot be corrected. But why could this be a problem? It is problematic because judicial decisions in these regimes may have an enormous influence on various other areas of life, thereby colliding with other values, norms and international legal rules. All these other societal interests protected by international law then tend to be sacrificed on the altar of powerful specialized regimes leading to a process of incremental judicial 'colonization' of legal regimes with weaker enforcement mechanisms.[64]

Moreover, trust in constraining practical and functional routines of judicial decision-making—as expressed by both Schmitt and Kelsen—is much less warranted in a fragmented judicial landscape than in a centralized and hierarchical court system. Most international courts and tribunals operate in the absence of judicial hierarchies, which guarantee that each tribunal decision can be appealed and controlled by at least one subordinated judicial body.[65] In international investment arbitration many decisions are not even publicized let alone controlled by appeal bodies. With Schmitt we must imagine the arbitrator as an expert who has his community of international investment lawyers in mind when drafting an award. He or she by the way depends much more on this community for being reappointed in the future than a professional domestic judge acting as a civil servant. With Kelsen the world view and the personal belief systems of these judges and arbitrators matter; they strongly impact their decisions. In international investment law this community currently consists mainly of experts from the field of private commercial

[63] Alex Mills, 'The Balancing (and Unbalancing?) of Interests in International Investment Law and Arbitration' in Z Douglas, J Pauwelyn, and JE Viñuales (eds), *The Foundations of International Investment Law: Bringing Theory into Practice* (OUP 2014), 437, 454.

[64] Discussing this issue Dirk Pulkowski, *The Law and Politics of International Regime Conflicts* (2014), 36; on the 'asymmetric' rule of law in international relations, von Bernstorff, 'International Law 1989–2010: Reflections on the Asymmetric Rule of Law in International Relations' in J Crawford (ed), *Select Proceedings of the European Society of International Law* (Hart 2012), S. 381–84.

[65] For international investment law Gus van Harten, *Investment Treaty Arbitration and Public Law* (2007).

arbitration working in Western-based international law firms and of highly specialized international lawyers working also mainly in Western academic institutions.

According to Schmitt's theory, the peer expectations of this expert community shape their decisions and not the Vienna Convention on the Law of Treaties. Such peer expectations are often influenced by specific genetic codes fixed in a formative phase of the regime and by subsequent path dependencies creating general conventions among the judges on how to decide the cases brought before them. If applying a norm from international human rights or international environmental law to an investment case is at odds with these professional expectations, it will only very rarely happen; or arbitrators would apply the rules of other legal regimes through exception clauses and hereby through the eyes of their own specific regime rationale.[66] They will thus at best 'reconstruct' external norms in the light of their own regime's rules or practice.[67] For inserting values, norms, and beliefs from other fields of international law into proceedings of tribunals usually comes with the risk of falling outside of peer expectations and of not being reappointed for a prestigious and lucrative arbitration next time.[68] And even if specialized tribunals refer to a method of interpretation explicitly in their reasoning, the decision itself ultimately will have been taken on the basis of prior subjective (Kelsen) or collective (Schmitt) preferences leading to a strategic choice regarding the applicable method of interpretation.

If anything in more general terms can be inferred from the two iconic theories of judicial interpretation for the present-day fragmented international judicial landscape, it would be that the traditional scholarly quest for compulsory adjudication in international law should be thoroughly reassessed. Such an assessment would have to start from the insight that doctrinal solutions and new scholarly methodological remedies will only have a very limited impact on specialized judicial or arbitral decision-making in practice. Training sectorial judges and arbitrators as well as domestic judges in how to use article 31 of the Vienna Convention on the Law of Treaties surely will not do any harm, it will however not turn a specialized court or tribunal, nor domestic judges, into 'other-regarding'[69] reflexive institutions aiming

[66] Jason Beckett, 'Fragmentation, Openness and Hegemony: Adjudication and the WTO' in MK Lewis and S Frankel (eds), *International Economic Law and National Autonomy* (2010), 54–56; somewhat less sceptical Joost Pauwelyn, *Conflict of Norms in Public International Law. How WTO-Law relates to other Rules of International Law* (2003), 242–43 and Andreas L Paulus, *Subsidiarity, Fragmentation and Democracy. Towards the Demise of General International Law?* in T Broude and Y Shany (eds), *The Shifting Allocation of Authority in International Law. Considering Sovereignty, Supremacy and Subsidiarity* (2008), 193–213, 210; also promoting systemic integration but in a slightly more sceptical tone are Bogdandy/Venzke, *In wessen Namen? supra* (n 44), at 258–64; on various and potentially conflicting 'objectives' of international courts in this context Andreas Follesdal, 'Curb, Channel and Coordinate: The Constitutionalisation of International Courts and Tribunals' in Geert De Baere and Jan Wouters (eds), *The Contribution of International and Supranational Courts to the Rule of Law* (Cheltenham: Edward Elgar Publishing 2015), 355–69.

[67] Beckett, ibid.

[68] On the internal dynamics of the current community of arbitrators: Daphna Kapeliuk, 'The Repeat Appointment Factor: Exploring Decision Patterns of Elite Investment Arbitrators' (2010) 96 Cornell L Rev 47; Jason Yackee, 'Controlling the International Investment Law Agency' (2010) 53 HILJ 391, 401–6; Sergio Puig, 'Social Capital in the Arbitration Market' (2014) 25 EJIL 387.

[69] To use a term coined by Eyal Benvenisti, 'Sovereigns as Trustees of Humanity: On the Accountability of States to Foreign Stakeholders' (2013) 107 AJIL 295–333 (296).

to preserve the unity of international law. Prevailing subjective regime-biases in a specialized epistemic community of judges and a largely self-referential collective regime practice will usually prevent this from happening.[70] Sectorial judicial regimes operating outside of a general hierarchical court system will follow their own regime-specific, and to a large extent legally uncontrollable logic, the effects of which will not necessarily be to the benefit of all those human beings ultimately affected by them.

[70] Elsewhere I have proposed a 'sectorial non liquet' to be rendered in cases before specialized tribunals affecting various international legal regimes, Jochen von Bernstorff, 'Hans Kelsen on Judicial Law-Making by International Courts and Tribunals: A Theory of Global Judicial Imperialism?' in (2015) 14 The Law & Practice of International Courts and Tribunals 35–50.

2

The Governance of International Courts and Tribunals

Organizing and Guaranteeing Independence and Accountability

*Niels Blokker**

1 Introduction

International courts and tribunals have by now become well-established institutions. Some were created long ago: examples are the International Court of Justice (ICJ) and the Administrative Tribunal of the International Labour Organization (ILO). Many more were established in more recent years, in areas such as international criminal law, human rights law, and international economic law. There are now thirty international courts and tribunals;[1] fifty if we include international administrative tribunals which deal with complaints of staff of international organizations. Since the late 1990s much attention has been paid to what is generally referred to as 'the proliferation of international courts and tribunals'. Many books and articles have been published on the law and practice of, for example, the International Criminal Court (ICC), various international criminal tribunals (notably those for the former Yugoslavia (ICTY) and for Rwanda (ICTR)), the International Tribunal for the Law of the Sea (ITLOS), the Appellate Body of the World Trade Organization (WTO), international administrative tribunals,

* Professor of International Institutional Law (Schermers Chair), Grotius Centre for International Legal Studies, Leiden University, the Netherlands. I thank Ms Whitny Kapa for her research assistance and the editors for their comments.

[1] See the 'Taxonomic Timeline' in Cesare PR Romano, Karen J Alter, and Yuval Shany (eds), *The Oxford Handbook on International Adjudication* (OUP 2014). This overview demonstrates that, as of 1 July 2013, thirty international courts and tribunals were operational. Six of them were created before 1990, twenty-four after that year. As far as administrative tribunals are concerned: for many years only the ILO and UN tribunals existed. In 1980 the World Bank Administrative Tribunal was created, and since 1990 seventeen more administrative tribunals were established.

regional courts in Europe, Africa, and America (such as the European Court of Justice (ECJ) and the European Court of Human Rights (ECtHR), the Andean Tribunal of Justice, and the East African Court of Justice).

Significantly less research has been done into the law and practice of international organs ('governance institutions') related to the necessary governance functions over all these international courts and tribunals. Examples of such organs are the General Assembly and the Security Council of the United Nations (UN) (the governance institutions for the ICJ and for some ad hoc criminal tribunals), the Assembly of States Parties (the governance institution for the ICC), the Meeting of States Parties to the UN Convention on the Law of the Sea ('SPLOS', for ITLOS), the Dispute Settlement Body of the WTO (for the WTO Appellate Body), and the Committee of Ministers and the Parliamentary Assembly of the Council of Europe (for the ECtHR). These governance institutions elect the judges of international courts and tribunals, adopt their budgets, supervise the implementation of judgments, and take other decisions that are of fundamental importance for the way in which international courts and tribunals can carry out their judicial tasks independently. This contribution is an appeal for more research into the law and practice of what I will call international judicial governance institutions (injugovins).

2 Some Examples

In recent years, these international judicial governance institutions have dealt with a number of issues that directly or indirectly affect the functioning and the independence of international courts and tribunals. This chapter will briefly discuss three examples, concerning the Tribunal of the Southern African Development Community (SADC Tribunal), the ICC, and the ICJ. These three judicial institutions have been selected, because their recent experiences offer a good illustration of the governance dilemmas facing different types of international courts and tribunals.

2.1 The SADC Tribunal, the SADC Summit, and Zimbabwe—'go big or go home'

The rise of regional courts and tribunals outside Europe has not been accompanied by a similar rise in research into the work of these courts and tribunals, and certainly not into the law and practice of their injugovins. The experience of the SADC Tribunal offers an excellent and unfortunate illustration of the importance of a good relationship between a court and its governance institution.

The Southern African Development Community was created in 1992. Its current member states are fifteen states in southern Africa, including South Africa and Zimbabwe. Its Tribunal became operational in 2005. One of the first cases of this Tribunal was a big case, concerning a delicate issue, the land allocation legislation of Zimbabwe. The Tribunal faced the choice 'to go big or to go home', as it was called in a recent study.[2] In its judgment in this case, of November 2008, the Tribunal decided 'to go big'. It ruled that Zimbabwe had discriminated against the applicants on the basis of race (indirect discrimination of white farmers) and had violated its obligations under the SADC Treaty.[3] Although this was a binding judgment, Zimbabwe decided not to comply with it. A few days after the judgment was delivered, the responsible minister for land reform stated that the SADC Tribunal was 'day-dreaming because we are not going to reverse the land reform exercise. There is nothing special about the 75 farmers and we will take more farms. It is not discrimination against farmers, but correcting land imbalances.'[4] President Mugabe referred to it as 'an exercise in futility', and the High Court of Zimbabwe subsequently ruled that the Tribunal's judgment was null and void because it was ultra vires.[5] Zimbabwe did not only refuse to implement the judgment, it also started a campaign against the Tribunal that resulted in a suspension of its functioning.[6] In 2010 the injugovin of the Tribunal, the Summit of Heads of State and Government (the supreme policy-making organ of SADC), decided to review the role of the Tribunal. In 2012 the SADC Summit agreed 'that a new Tribunal should be negotiated and that its mandate should be confined to interpretation of the SADC Treaty and Protocols relating to disputes between Member States'.[7] In August 2014 the Summit adopted a Protocol limiting the Tribunal's jurisdiction to interstate disputes. The Protocol was signed by some member states including Zimbabwe but has not yet entered into force. It is criticized for the 'rule of law step backwards' it embodies.[8] Some twenty Non-Governmental Organizations have organized themselves as a 'Coalition for an Effective SADC Tribunal'.[9] Therefore, in this first example, the SADC Tribunal decided 'to go big', but in the end it was 'sent home' for this, by its injugovin.

2.2 The ICC and the ASP—Kenyan leaders' presence during the trial

The governance institution of the ICC is the Assembly of States Parties (ASP). The ASP elects the judges and the Prosecutor, adopts the Court's budget, provides 'management oversight to the Presidency, the Prosecutor and the Registrar regarding the administration of the Court', and performs a number of other governance

[2] Karen J Alter, James T Gathii, and Laurence R Helfer, 'Backlash Against International Courts in West, East and Southern Africa: Causes and Consequences', iCourts Working Paper Series No 21, published at <http://papers.ssrn.com/sol3/papers.cfm?abstract_id=2591837> (last visited 29 June 2016), in particular at 18–29. At 42, the authors use the expression 'go big or go home'.

[3] SADC(T)Case No 2/2007, reproduced in (2009) 48 ILM 534.

[4] B Chigara, 'Introductory note to Southern African Development Community (SADC) Tribunal—Mike Campbell (PVT) LTD and others v Republic of Zimbabwe' (2009) 48 ILM 530.

[5] ibid.

[6] See for details Alter, Gathii, and Helfer (n 2).

[7] See <http://www.sadc.int/about-sadc/sadc-institutions/tribun/> (last visited 29 June 2016). This episode in the history of the SADC Tribunal is discussed in more detail in Frederick Cowell, 'The Death of the Southern African Development Community Tribunal's Human Rights Jurisdiction' (2013) 13 HRLR 153–65; Laurie Nathan, 'The Disbanding of the SADC Tribunal: A Cautionary Tale' (2013) 35 HRQ 870–92; Alter, Gathii, and Helfer (n 2).

[8] See Alter, Gathii, and Helfer (n 2), at 28, and <http://www.kas.de/wf/doc/kas_38707-1522-2-30.pdf?140922094447> (last visited 29 June 2016).

[9] See the website of this Coalition: <http://sadctribunalcoalition.org/> (last visited 29 June 2016).

functions.[10] There is no hierarchy in the relationship between these two institutions. Different from the example of the ICJ given below, the ICC and the ASP are not embedded in a larger international organization. The ICC is an international legal person.[11] The ICC Statute lacks provisions about the legal status of the ASP.[12]

Following the investigation of the post-election violence in Kenya in 2007, Pre-Trial Chamber II confirmed the charges against, inter alia, Uhuru Kenyatta and William Ruto in January 2012. On 4 March 2013 Kenyatta and Ruto won the elections and subsequently became President and Vice-President of Kenya. The cases against them at the ICC exacerbated African criticism of the Court. In October 2013 an Extraordinary Session of the Assembly of the African Union was convened, in which it was decided that 'to safeguard the constitutional order, stability and, integrity of Member States, no charges shall be commenced or continued before any International Court or Tribunal against any serving AU Head of State or Government or anybody acting or entitled to act in such capacity during their term of office', and more specifically, that 'the trials of President Uhuru Kenyatta and Deputy President William Samoei Ruto, who are the current serving leaders of the Republic of Kenya, should be suspended until they complete their terms of office'.[13]

Article 63(1) of the ICC Statute states that 'The accused shall be present during the trial.' During the year 2013, the Trial Chamber and the Appeals Chamber took various decisions relating to requests by Kenyatta and Ruto to be excused from continuous presence during their trials. In particular, the Appeals Chamber had decided on 25 October 2013 that 'Article 63(1) of the Statute does not operate as an absolute bar in all circumstances to the continuation of trial proceedings in the absence of the accused'.[14] In addition, the Appeals Chamber mentioned six criteria that could lead to an excuse for the accused not being physically present at the trial.[15]

Three weeks later, on 15 November 2013 a draft resolution was presented but not adopted in the UN Security Council, by which the Council would have requested the Court to defer the investigation and prosecution of Kenyatta and Ruto for a period of twelve months, in accordance with article 16 of the ICC Statute.[16] In the Security Council, seven of the fifteen members stated that they preferred the ASP to deal with this issue, rather than the Security Council. A few days later, on 20 November 2013, the 12th session of the ASP opened in The Hague. This session was dominated by 'the Kenya issue'. Several proposals were presented and discussed, which ultimately led to the adoption by the ASP of amendments to the Rules of Procedure and Evidence (RPE) dealing with the use of video technology (new Rule 134*bis*), excusal from presence at trial (new Rule 134*ter*), and excusal from presence

[10] ICC Statute, arts 36, 42, and 112 (quotation from art 112.2(b)).

[11] ICC Statute, art 4.1.

[12] For that reason, rules on privileges and immunities of the ASP are included in the 2007 Headquarters Agreement between the ICC and the host State.

[13] AU Doc Ext/Assembly/AU/Dec.1 (October 2013), adopted 12 October 2013 <https://www.iccnow.org/documents/Ext_Assembly_AU_Dec_Decl_12Oct2013.pdf> (last visited 29 June 2016).

[14] Judgment ICC-01/09-01/11, 25 October 2013, paras 1, 55.

[15] ibid, paras 2, 62.

[16] UN Doc S/2013/660; see also UN Doc S/PV.7060 (seven members voted in favour of the deferral (including China and the Russian Federation), and there were eight abstentions).

at trial due to extraordinary public duties at the highest national level (new Rule 134*quater*).

Amendments to the RPE must be consistent with the ICC Statute;[17] if they were to conflict, the Statute prevails.[18] A key question is whether the amendments to the RPE adopted by the ASP in November 2013 were consistent with the Statute, in particular with the requirement in article 63(1) that the accused is present during the trial.[19] For the purpose of this contribution it is of interest to look at this from the perspective of the relationship between the ASP and the Court. Obviously it is in the common interest of the Court and the ASP that they operate in harmony. It is for the ASP to 'legislate', in this case to adopt amendments to the RPE. It is for the Court to apply the law, and to exercise its functions and powers in accordance with the Statute and the RPE. Disputes concerning the judicial functions of the Court shall be settled by the Court.[20] In this case, both the Court and the ASP had to walk a fine line between harsh criticism and political pressure from the African states and the rules of the Statute. It was instrumental that the Appeals Chamber, shortly before the session of the ASP, gave a flexible interpretation of the requirement of the Statute that the accused must be present during the trial, in its decision in the case against Ruto. This requirement was softened even more, and also 'generalized', by the ASP amendments to the RPE. Therefore, this second example also demonstrates that it is as important to study the operation of the ASP in cases such as this one as it is to study the relevant decisions of the Court.

2.3 The ICJ and the General Assembly—remuneration of the members of the Court and the principle of equality of all judges

Both the General Assembly and the Security Council perform governance functions in relation to the ICJ. The members of the Court are elected by the General Assembly and by the Security Council.[21] The ICJ budget is part of the budget of the UN and is approved by the General Assembly.[22] There is no hierarchy in the relationship between these three institutions. All three are 'principal organs' of the UN.[23]

The General Assembly determines the salaries, allowances, and compensation of the members of the Court.[24] But it is not entirely free in doing so: the Statute of the Court contains certain restrictions for the Assembly when performing this task. A clear and fundamental restriction is that the salaries, allowances, and compensation of the members of the Court 'may not be decreased during the term of office'.[25]

[17] ICC Statute, art 17(4). [18] ICC Statute, art 17(5).

[19] See further Jonathan O'Donohue, 'The ICC and the ASP' in Carsten Stahn (ed), *The Law and Practice of the International Criminal Court* (OUP 2015) 120–22.

[20] ICC Statute, art 119.1. [21] Statute ICJ, art 4.1. [22] UN Charter, art 17.1.

[23] UN Charter, art 7.1. [24] Statute ICJ, art 32.5, first sentence.

[25] ICJ Statute, art 32.5, second sentence. Does 'term of office' in this provision only cover the period after a judge is first elected (normally for nine years), or also one or more subsequent periods after a sitting judge is re-elected? According to the Court, the latter interpretation is correct, in cases when 'a member of the Court is re-elected for a further term immediately after the end of the preceding term. It would be inconceivable for the salaries, allowances and compensation of judges re-elected to continue exercising their functions to be subject to a decrease after re-election'. However, according to the Legal Counsel of the UN, the former interpretation is correct, as the Statute 'does not stipulate that, for a

Therefore, whenever the Assembly would consider decreases in the remunerations of the members of the Court, such decreases can only be applied at the end of the terms of office. In addition, the Assembly must respect the principle of the equality of the judges. This principle is referred to as follows in article 3, paragraph 1, of the Rules of the Court: 'The members of the Court, in the exercise of their functions, are of equal status, irrespective of age, priority of election or length of service'. In addition, according to article 31, paragraph 6, of the Statute of the Court, judges ad hoc 'shall take part in the decision on terms of complete equality with their colleagues'.[26]

In Resolution 61/262, adopted on 4 April 2007, the General Assembly made certain adaptations to the remuneration of the members of the ICJ.[27] In this resolution, the annual net base salary of the members of the ICJ (and the judges of ICTY and ICTR) was set, effective 1 January 2007, at 133,500 US dollars.[28] However, the adoption of this resolution resulted in a significant difference in the remuneration of judges elected or appointed before and after 1 January 2007. This gave rise to a bitter quarrel between the Court and the Assembly.[29] One day before the adoption of Resolution 61/262, the President of the ICJ, Rosalyn Higgins, sent a letter to the President of the General Assembly, in which she expressed the Court's 'extremely serious and deep concern that the proposed action regarding emoluments, if approved by the General Assembly, would not be in conformity with the Statute of the Court'.[30] The reason for this concern was the expected difference in the remuneration of the judges. As President Higgins indicated in her letter:[31]

> It is very likely, if not almost certain, that the remuneration of newly elected judges, including those due to take office on 5 February 2009, will be substantially lower than the current remuneration, which is to be applied as a transitional measure for the current judges until such time as this amount is overtaken by the new system. (At present, a difference of approximately $2,500 per month has been identified.) Under Article 32, paragraph 1, of the Statute, each member of the Court shall receive an annual salary. As a matter of the principle of equality, the salary shall be the same for each member. Article 31, paragraph 6, of the Statute emphasizes that ad hoc judges shall also sit in equality with the permanent bench.
>
> The equality of all judges is a fundamental principle underlying the Statute. That principle can in no way be set aside by provisions that stipulate that all new members shall be on the same salary, and that the present salary of existing members shall be protected. The proposed

renewed term of office of a re-elected member or for future members of the Court, salaries could not be decreased. Therefore, in principle, a decrease in salary for future members of the Court would not be inconsistent with the Statute' (see UN Doc A/62/538, at 38, 22–23).

26 See also art 7.2 of the Rules of the Court.

27 The most important details of these adaptations are summarized in UN Doc A/62/538, at 9. This resolution also made adaptations to the remunerations of the judges of ICTY and ICTR.

28 UNGA Res 61/262, para 7.

29 This quarrel is briefly discussed in Dominik Zimmermann, *The Independence of International Courts—The Adherence of the International Judiciary to a Fundamental Value of the Administration of Justice* (Nomos/Hart 2014) 182–91; see in general about the finance and administration of the Court Shabtai Rosenne, *The Law and Practice of the International Court 1920–2005* (4th edn, Martinus Nijhoff Publishers 2006), Vol I, 437–503.

30 UN Doc A/61/837, at 1.

31 ibid.

system would still result in discrimination between members of the Court, i.e. those who assumed office before 1 January 2007 and those who will assume office after that date.

In spite of this protest, the resolution was adopted.[32] Subsequently, President Higgins sent another letter to the Secretary-General of the UN, concerning implications of this resolution for judges ad hoc sitting in the cases pending before the Court and those called upon to sit in future cases. In a pending case, the level of remuneration of the judges ad hoc would be unequal as a result of this resolution, because one of the judges ad hoc was appointed prior to the adoption of the resolution while the other was appointed afterwards. In that case, the Court decided to give equal treatment to both judges ad hoc, even though that was not authorized by the General Assembly Resolution.[33]

In addition, the ICJ prepared a seventeen-page document related to this issue, which was transmitted by its President to the Secretary-General of the UN.[34] In this document, the Court explained its position and analysed the issue at stake. It concluded that Resolution 61/262:[35]

> is not compatible with the basic principles underlying the Statute of the Court, in particular the principle of equality of all judges, nor with its Article 31, paragraph 6, and Article 32, paragraph 5. […] Those principles and provisions being pivotal principles of the international judiciary, it might prove difficult to apply the resolution adopted by the General Assembly on 4 April 2007 to the members of the International Court of Justice or to judges ad hoc without seriously compromising the proper administration of justice.

These critical observations by the ICJ were subsequently discussed in other UN bodies. At the request of the UN Office of Human Resources Management, the UN legal counsel prepared a memorandum, in which he concluded:[36]

> provided that the revised annual salary system results in a lower annual salary for new members of the Court or lower compensation for newly appointed ad hoc judges than for members of the Court or ad hoc judges elected prior to 1 January 2007, the concerns raised by President Higgins and Registrar Couvreur regarding the principle of equality of members of the Court are justified.

In March 2008 the Advisory Committee on Administrative and Budgetary Questions considered the issue and stated that it 'cannot but note that this interpretation [by the ICJ] could affect the exercise of the General Assembly's mandate under article 32 of the Statute of the Court',[37] apparently referring to paragraph 5 of article 32 (according to which the salaries, allowances, and compensation of the judges 'shall be fixed by the General Assembly').

On 3 April 2008, the General Assembly adopted Decision 62/547, in which it set, effective 1 April 2008, the annual net base salary of the members of the ICJ (and the judges of ICTY and ICTR) at 158,000 US dollars.

[32] UNGA Res 61/262. [33] See UN Doc A/62/538, Annex II, at 26.
[34] Reproduced in UN Doc A/62/538, at 26–43. [35] ibid, at 41.
[36] Memorandum of 6 June 2007, reproduced in UN Doc A/62/538, at 23.
[37] UN Doc A/62/7/Add. 36, 4.

The dilemma in this quarrel was the inherent tension between two rules of the Court: the prohibition to decrease the salaries, allowances, and compensation of the members of the Court during their term of office, and the principle of the equality of all judges. Since the end of the term of the Court's members is never at the same time for all members, it is practically impossible to decrease their emoluments without distinguishing between the judges. The only way to find optimal solutions in cases such as this one is to proceed in good cooperation, and by having early and full consultations between these two 'principals' of the UN. While the Court should fully take into account the budgetary responsibilities of the Assembly, the Assembly should fully take into account the proper characteristics and fundamental rules of the Court.

3 Organizing Governance of International Courts and Tribunals

The three examples above give an impression of the role and functioning of three injugovins: the SADC Summit of Heads of State and Government, the ICC Assembly of States Parties, and the UN General Assembly. There are many more such injugovins, even more than there are international courts and tribunals. While there is a wealth of books and articles not only dealing with specific international courts and tribunals, but also with these courts and tribunals generally,[38] not much research has been carried out into their governance institutions. It is true that sometimes importance is attached to the governance functions that states perform in relation to 'their' international courts and tribunals, but it is largely neglected that such functions are almost always organized within collective institutions created by these states. The law and practice of these institutions deserves more scholarly attention. Obviously, it is far beyond the scope of this chapter to fill this gap and to present an overview of all existing judicial governance institutions, let alone to give a taxonomy or analysis of them. Instead, a few general observations will be made.

First of all, almost all existing injugovins are composed of representatives of states.[39] States perform an essential role in the creation and independent functioning of international courts and tribunals. This role is paradoxical: international courts and tribunals are independent from states but at the same time fully depend on them for their effective functioning (illustrated in Section 2 and further discussed in Section 4).

Secondly, the states participating in the creation of an international court or tribunal organize their judicial governance cooperation in different ways. Essentially,

[38] Of the recent literature see in particular Romano, Alter, and Shany (n 1); Karen J Alter, *The New Terrain of International Law—Courts, Politics, Rights* (Princeton University Press 2014).

[39] One of the rare exceptions is the Parliamentary Assembly of the Council of Europe, which elects the judges of the ECtHR (European Convention for the Protection of Human Rights and Fundamental Freedoms, art 22).

it appears that the existing governance structures within which international courts and tribunals are embedded largely follow one of the three following models.

- The injugovin is an organ of an international organization. Examples are the General Assembly and the Security Council of the UN (ICJ, ICTY, ICTR), the WTO Dispute Settlement Body (Appellate Body), the Committee of Ministers and the Parliamentary Assembly of the Council of Europe (ECtHR) and a number of governance institutions of courts of regional integration/cooperation organizations.
- The injugovin is a treaty organ.[40] As such, it is not part of an international organization and does not have its own international legal personality. Examples are the ASP (ICC) and the Meeting of States Parties to the UN Convention on the Law of the Sea, SPLOS (ITLOS).[41] Injugovins that are treaty organs may have their own secretariat (as is the case for the ASP), or they may rely on a 'host organization' that provides secretariat functions (eg SPLOS, which is supported by the UN Secretariat).[42]
- In other cases the cooperation between the states concerned is organized within a very loose gathering of relevant states, not created as a treaty organ. Examples are the meetings of the states parties of UN human rights treaty bodies.[43] In addition, the judges of some international courts and tribunals are appointed by the states parties to the constituent instruments establishing these court and tribunals (not by a treaty organ or by an organ of an international organization).[44]

[40] On treaty organs see Geir Ulfstein, 'Reflections on Institutional Design—Especially Treaty Bodies' in Jan Klabbers and Åsa Wallendahl (eds), *Research Handbook on the Law of International Organizations* (Edward Elgar Publishing 2011) 431–47; Geir Ulfstein, 'Treaty Bodies and Regimes' in Duncan B Hollis (ed), *The Oxford Guide to Treaties* (OUP 2012) 428–47.

[41] See further Liesbeth Lijnzaad, 'Formal and Informal Processes in the Contemporary Law of the Sea at the United Nations, a Practitioner's View' (2014) 57 GYIL, 111–42.

[42] The Secretariat of the ASP—which is not mentioned in the ICC Statute—is created by Res ICC-ASP/2/Res.3 of the ASP. For the administrative functions of the UN Secretariat for SPLOS, see the UN Convention on the Law of the Sea, art 319.2(e), and UNGA Resolutions 37/66, 49/28, 52/26.

[43] UN human rights treaty bodies cannot be qualified as courts or tribunals, but the governance issues discussed in this chapter apply equally to them. See Robin R. Churchill and Geir Ulfstein, 'Autonomous Institutional Arrangements in Multilateral Environmental Agreements: A Little-noticed Phenomenon in International Law' (2000) 94 AJIL, 655–56. In 2009, the authoritative Dublin Statement on the Process of Strengthening of the United Nations Human Rights Treaty Body System recommended, inter alia, that 'States, acting multilaterally, consider such reform issues as the enhancement of the role and the potential of meetings of States parties to the various treaties, enhancement of the manner in which the reports of treaty bodies are received by the relevant political organs of the United Nations and the creation of an adequate financing basis for the treaty body system. States should also consider means to improve procedures for the nomination and the election of members of the treaty bodies, whereby the independence and expertise of elected members is fully assured'. <http://www2.ohchr.org/english/bodies/HRTD/docs/DublinStatement.pdf> (last visited 29 June 2016).

[44] Eg, the judges of the Inter-American Court of Human Rights 'shall be elected by the states parties to the Convention, at the OAS General Assembly' (Statute of the Inter-American Court, art 6(1)); the judges of the Court of Justice of the European Union are appointed 'by common accord of the governments of the member states' (Treaty on European Union, art 19(2)).

These three models show that international judicial governance is structured in very diverging ways, covering the whole gamut of institutionalized international cooperation: from almost pure ad hoc meetings having hardly any pre-established rules to fully fledged international organs that may either be a self-standing treaty organ or an organ of an international organization (of which in most cases the relevant international court or tribunal is also an organ). International courts and tribunals sometimes have one single injugovin, belonging to one of the three models mentioned above (for instance, the ASP (for the ICC)). In other cases they have two or more, either belonging to one model or to more. For example, while the injugovins of the Court of Justice of the European Union (Council, European Parliament) prima facie seem to belong to the first model mentioned above, the judges of this Court are not appointed by one of the institutions of the Union, but 'by common accord of the governments of the member states' (the third model mentioned above).[45] Another example is provided by the ECtHR. While its injugovins (the Committee of Ministers and the Parliamentary Assembly of the Council of Europe) prima facie seem to fit in model one, a number of key governance declarations concerning the ECtHR were adopted by ad hoc conferences of the states parties (model three) that took place in Interlaken (2010), Izmir (2011), and Brighton (2012), not by the Committee of Ministers.[46]

Thirdly, the question is relevant as to what extent and how international judicial governance institutions are more than the sum of their members. In some cases there may be legal boundaries which restrict the sovereign discretion of the relevant states and within which these institutions must operate. Such legal boundaries are mostly of a procedural nature: the decision-making and other procedural rules of the governance institution concerned must be respected. For example, member states of the UN are not free to nominate candidate-members of the ICJ in any way they want. The ICJ Statute has detailed rules on the nomination of candidate ICJ members. For reasons related to the independence of judges, nominations are made not by governments of the member states, but by national groups of the Permanent Court of Arbitration. Elections are by the General Assembly and the Security Council. UN member states are not free to elect members of the ICJ in any way they want. They have to do so in their capacity as members of the General Assembly and the Security Council and by following specific procedural rules laid down in the ICJ Statute, applicable since 1945 and reflecting the international community's requirements for the judges of the world court. These rules for nominating and electing the members of the ICJ have also inspired the rules for nominating and electing the judges of the ICC. But the legal boundaries within which judicial governance institutions operate may also be of a substantive nature. When the ASP discussed the 'Kenya case' in November 2013, the interpretation of substantive ICC Statute rules was essential, in

[45] Treaty on European Union, art 19(2).

[46] For the text of the Interlaken, Izmir, and Brighton Declarations, see <http://echr.coe.int/Pages/home.aspx?p=basictexts/reform&c=> (last visited 29 June 2016).

particular the requirement that the accused is present during the trial and the irrelevance of official capacity (such as Head of State) of the accused.[47]

Fourthly, some specific observations may be made with respect to the governance of international administrative tribunals. For decades, only two such tribunals existed: those of the ILO and of the UN.[48] However, in particular since the 1990s a number of organizations have created their own administrative tribunal; in total, some twenty administrative tribunals now exist. They are all embedded within international organizations. In most cases other organs of these organizations perform the governance functions for these tribunals. However, a special case is that of the ILO Administrative Tribunal (ILOAT). Some sixty international organizations (including various UN specialized agencies, WTO, and ICC) do not have their own administrative tribunal but have joined ILOAT. But the governance functions over ILOAT are only performed by ILO organs. Its seven judges are appointed by the International Labour Conference, and its expenses are borne by the International Labour Office.[49] The law and practice of international administrative tribunals has become a *niche* itself. But here as well, the research focus is mostly on the tribunals themselves, not so much on their governance institutions.

Fifthly, there is some unity within diversity. All these judicial governance institutions perform similar functions in relation to 'their' international courts and tribunals. They face similar challenges, such as the following. How to fully respect the independence and rules of the courts and tribunals in an era in which governments want to limit their financial contributions to international organizations? How to ensure that capable judges are elected? Should advisory bodies play a role in the procedures for the nomination and election of judges, and how exactly, or should states essentially control these procedures? More generally, all judicial governance institutions need to function as responsible frameworks to which international courts and tribunals can be accountable. Section 4 below will further discuss some of these questions.

4 Guaranteeing Independence and Accountability

At a more general and fundamental level, there is a need for analysis and better understanding of the role of governance institutions vis-à-vis 'their' international courts and tribunals. This is particularly true in the present context of mounting criticism of the functioning of international organizations, and related calls for greater accountability. On the one hand, even though there is occasional criticism at the notion of judicial independence,[50] the constituent instruments of international courts and

[47] ICC Statute, arts 27, 63(1).

[48] In the 1970s and 1980s, plans were even discussed to merge these two administrative tribunals (see eg UNGA Res 33/119).

[49] ILOAT Statute, arts III.2 and IX.2.

[50] Eg Lewis A Kornhauser, 'Is Judicial Independence a Useful Concept?' in Stephen B Burbank and Barry Friedman (eds), *Judicial Independence at the Crossroads—An Interdisciplinary Approach* (SAGE Publications 2002), 45–55; Eric A Posner and John C Yoo, 'Judicial Independence in International Tribunals' (2005) 93 California Law Review 3–74.

tribunals always prescribe that these judicial institutions and their members must be independent. This is not only an inherent characteristic of judicial organs; it is also in the common interest of the founding states. As Crawford and McIntyre conclude: '[a]s customary principles of international law, expressly adopted in the governing statutes, and necessarily and inherently adopted as a consequence of the judicial function, the principles of judicial independence and impartiality must be taken to apply equally to international judges and to international judicial bodies as they do to domestic tribunals'.[51]

At the same time, the performance—in full independence—of their functions may sometimes lead to results that states may find difficult to accept in practice (as is illustrated by the demise of the SADC Tribunal). In addition, at a more mundane level, there may at times be criticism of the management and internal functioning of international courts and tribunals. In both cases it is likely that there will be calls for greater accountability. However, it is clear that the quest for accountability should take place in full respect of the independence of these judicial organs. The institutional framework within which solutions must be found for these dilemmas is usually the governance institution of international courts and tribunals. While sovereign states play an essential role in these governance institutions, they do not act as individual states, but within a collective body that is functioning on the basis of predetermined rules and established practices. This also raises the question how such a body should best be structured, and whether one of the three models mentioned in Section 3 would be most suitable for the performance of international judicial governance functions.

4.1 Independence

At first sight, it may seem that the requirement that international courts and tribunals are independent is generally accepted and does not need any further study. However, the reality is much more complex. A distinction can be made between the independence of international courts and tribunals as organs, and the independence of their judges. As far as the latter is concerned, significant research has been carried out and recommendations have been formulated, on such issues as the nomination and election of judges, their remuneration and their term of office.[52] In this context reference may be made to proposals by a few WTO members (including the United States (US)) in the context of the WTO dispute settlement reform negotiations. These proposals try to give more control to WTO members over WTO dispute

[51] James Crawford and Joe McIntyre, 'The Independence and Impartiality of the "International Judiciary"' in CF Forsyth and S Shetreet (eds), *The Culture of Judicial Independence* (Martinus Nijhoff Publishers 2012) 189–214.

[52] Eg Ruth Mackenzie and Philippe Sands, 'International Courts and Tribunals and the Independence of the International Judge' (2003) 44 Harvard International Law Journal 271–85; Ruth Mackenzie et al, *Selecting International Judges: Principle, Process, and Politics* (OUP 2010); the 2004 Burgh House Principles on the Independence of the International Judiciary (prepared by a study group of the International Law Association); 'The Position of the International Judge', Resolution adopted by the *Institut de Droit International* (Session de Rhodes, 2011).

settlement. More specifically, in May 2016 the US blocked the reappointment of one of the Appellate Body members, Seung Wha Chang (South Korea). The US was of the opinion that 'his service did not reflect the role assigned to the Appellate Body' and mentioned that it was concerned about 'the manner in which Mr Chang conducted oral hearings' and about 'the Appellate Body's adjudicative approach'.[53] In a meeting of the Dispute Settlement Body (the injugovin of the Appellate Body) many members criticized the US and stated that the independence and impartiality of the Appellate Body was at stake.[54] The other six members of the Appellate Body wrote a letter in support of their colleague to all members of the WTO, emphasizing his 'integrity, independence and impartiality'.[55] Not much later, all the former, living members of the Appellate Body also sent a letter in support of Mr Chang to the Chairman of the Dispute Settlement Body. In this letter, they warned that '[u]ndermining the impartial independence of the Appellate Body now would not only call into question for the first time the integrity of the Appellate Body; it would also put the very future of the entire WTO trading system at risk'.[56] They also suggested to abolish the system of reappointments, and instead to have a single, longer term for the members of the Appellate Body.[57] This example demonstrates how issues relating to the independence of members of international courts and tribunals are seen as fundamental and may trigger heated and intense discussions.

As to the independence of international courts and tribunals as organs, research is more limited, although this 'organic independence' is also important: even if all the judges are fully independent, their international court or tribunal would not be able to perform its functions independently were it not to have the proper status, privileges, and immunities, and were it not properly organized. For example, significant problems have occurred because the staff of the Registry of the ECtHR is appointed not by the Court itself but by the Secretary-General of the Council of Europe.[58] In addition, while some international courts and tribunals are international legal persons and as such capable of arranging their own privileges and immunities, others are not and for this purpose depend on the organization of which they are part.

4.2 Accountability

International courts and tribunals have important judicial powers, and there must be an external authority, an institution to which they are answerable, a place where they explain and show responsibility for what they do and how they do it. This place

[53] See the report of the meeting of the Dispute Settlement Body of 23 May 2016, available at <https://www.wto.org/english/news_e/news16_e/dsb_23may16_e.htm> (last visited 29 June 2016), at 2.

[54] ibid. Some members stated that 'the United States' statement of opposition based on previous Appellate Body decisions could create a dangerous precedent for other reappointment proceedings and affect an Appellate Body member's decision-making during their first term' (at 3).

[55] Quoted by B Cooreman, 'Politics vs judicial impartiality: A systemic crisis at the WTO', Leiden Law Blog 13 June 2016, available at <http://leidenlawblog.nl/articles/politics-vs-judicial-impartiality-a-systemic-crisis-at-the-wto> (last visited 29 June 2016).

[56] Available at <http://worldtradelaw.typepad.com/files/abletter.pdf> (last visited 29 June 2016).

[57] ibid. [58] See further Zimmermann (n 29), 450–61.

is their injugovin. Injugovins are the bodies to which international courts and tribunals are accountable.

An obvious, most basic accountability instrument for an international court or tribunal is its annual report. Nevertheless, some constituent instruments do not require the court or tribunal to prepare an annual report. Examples are the Charter of the UN and the Statute of the ICC.[59] The ICJ itself took the initiative to send annual reports to the General Assembly in 1968, following the much-criticized 1966 judgments in the South West Africa cases.[60] The ICC has done so at its own initiative from the beginning. In practice, the General Assembly and the ASP normally 'take note' of these annual reports—a neutral term, recognizing the independence of these courts.[61] There is usually no discussion on substance. In practice an important function of these annual reports is that it creates a reason for the President of the Court to be present in the relevant meeting of the injugovin.[62] It offers a framework for informal consultations.

An important instrument by which judicial governance institutions may influence the functioning of international courts and tribunals is the budget. The third example discussed above illustrates what problems and issues may emerge in this context. Consultations preceding the adoption of the budget are not only of a purely financial nature, but also concern the substantive work of these courts and tribunals.

Apart from annual reports and budgets, there may be other accountability instruments. An example are the 'diplomatic briefings' by the ICC, now usually three times a year. In these briefings, the President of the Court, the Prosecutor, and the Registrar inform representatives of the states parties about recent developments at the Court, and there are exchanges of views.[63]

In most cases, the applicable constituent instruments do not contain detailed rules about the accountability functions of governance institutions. An exception is article 112(2)(b) of the ICC Statute, according to which the ASP shall 'provide management oversight to the Presidency, the Prosecutor and the Registrar regarding the

[59] While the UN Charter does not contain a provision on reports by the ICJ to the General Assembly, there is such a provision for reports by the Security Council to the Assembly (UN Charter, art 24(3)).

[60] See Rosenne (n 29), Vol I, 111–12. Rosenne explains that the Court 'had become "conscious of the need for closer co-operation with the other organs of the United Nations". It was a public relations exercise, not a political or organizational requirement' (at 112). See also Salo Engel, 'Annual Reports of the International Court of Justice to the General Assembly' (1970) 44 BYbIL, 198–99.

[61] See eg UNGA Decision 67/510 (1 November 2012; UN Doc A/67/49 (Vol II), Resolutions and Decision adopted by the General Assembly during its sixty-seventh session, at 15); most recently, decision adopted by the General Assembly on 5 November 2015 (UN Doc GA/11719 (GA meetings coverage)); ASP, 2nd session, Official Records, ICC-ASP/2/10, at 6 (para 22) and ASP, 13th session, Official Records Volume I, ICC-ASP/13/20, at 9 (para 36). In contrast, the UN General Assembly 'welcomes' the report prepared by the ICC in the context of the UN-ICC relationship agreement (see eg GA Res 69/279, para 1 (2015)).

[62] Cf in this context the address by President Ronny Abraham of the ICJ before the UN General Assembly on 5 November 2015, in which he both referred to the modest resources of the ICJ and to the endeavours by the Court to use these resources efficiently: '[. . .] la Cour entend s'efforcer d'utiliser de façon optimale les ressources modestes qui sont mises à sa disposition [. . .]'. For the text of this address, see <http://www.icj-cij.org/presscom/files/4/18824.pdf>, at 10 (last visited 29 June 2016).

[63] See the overview of these briefings on the Court's website: <https://www.icc-cpi.int/en_menus/icc/reports%20on%20activities/Pages/reports%20on%20activities.aspx> (last visited 29 June 2016).

administration of the Court'. Referring to this obligation, the ASP created a Study Group on Governance in 2010, to facilitate 'a structured dialogue between States Parties and the Court with a view to strengthening the institutional framework of the Rome Statute system and enhancing the efficiency and the effectiveness of the Court while fully preserving its judicial independence'.

It is important for these accountability mechanisms to be effective and successful. Future research into injugovins should examine this. Those who participate in such mechanisms know that the general impression of the functioning of these mechanisms is far from promising or reassuring. On the one hand, staff and members of courts and tribunals criticize injugovins for their 'micromanagement'. On the other hand, diplomats (representatives of member states of injugovins) say that courts and tribunals all too often hide behind their independence, to prevent any interference or involvement in their 'organic jurisdiction'. The urgency and delicacy of these issues was reaffirmed when, in November 2015, the President, the Prosecutor, and the Registrar of the ICC wrote an exceptional joint letter to the President of the ASP, in which they expressed 'great concern that a number of issues have been proposed for discussion at the Assembly which relate to matters falling clearly within the judicial and prosecutorial competence of the Court', and urged the ASP 'to ensure that the Court's judicial and prosecutorial independence is not undermined, or perceived to be undermined, by proceedings of the Assembly'.[64]

It is clear that it is not easy to develop mechanisms within which a meaningful dialogue can take place between international courts/tribunals and their injugovins. No doubt this is partly due to the fact that the requirements of independence and accountability are almost by definition at odds with each other. As is more often, individuals may sometimes make the difference in the functioning of these mechanisms. It would seem useful to know more about the existing accountability mechanisms and to research this more professionally and systematically.

In addition, it is interesting to look at the requirements of independence and accountability from another perspective. These are also requirements for national courts. At the national level, in developed and developing countries, these requirements are often mentioned in the context of discussions about the judiciary, for instance reform discussions. They may play a role in matters such as nomination and election of judges, the budget of the judiciary, but also when it comes to more mundane issues such as housing and information technology. Over the years, international organizations have become increasingly involved in such national discussions. For example:

- EU conditions for membership also include conditions concerning the judiciary of countries applying for membership. For example, the judiciary must be independent and efficient; legal guarantees for a fair trial must be in place;[65]

[64] Letter of 13 November 2015. The letter is now publicly available via: <http://coalitionfortheicc.org/documents/Letter_from_the_Courts_Principals_to_President_of_the_ASP_final.pdf> (last visited 29 June 2016).

[65] See for these conditions of membership the so-called chapters of the acquis, in particular Chapter 23 (Judiciary and fundamental rights): <http://ec.europa.eu/enlargement/policy/conditions-membership/

- the European Commission for Democracy through Law of the Council of Europe (Venice Commission) may adopt recommendations related to the position of the national judiciary. For example, in 2015 it gave opinions on the proposed constitutional amendments regarding the judiciary of Ukraine;[66]
- the International Monetary Fund (IMF) may be involved in governance discussions relating to the national judiciary, within the context of its loans to a country and demands for macro-economic reforms. For example, the IMF played a role in the reform of the judiciary in Portugal.[67] More specifically, IMF demands in the context of the fight against corruption may also concern the judiciary.

It would be interesting to see whether and to what extent such requirements by international organizations relating to the national judiciary may or must also be applied to international courts and tribunals. Do international courts and tribunals need to meet the same rule of law standards as national courts? Obviously this has implications for the work of injugovins. To what extent must injugovins apply the same standards as *national* governance institutions have to apply in relation to the national judiciary?

5 Conclusion

The role and functioning of international judicial governance institutions is to some extent a *terra incognita*. 'To some extent' because those who work for or with these institutions are more or less familiar with 'their' institution. But it is not well-known and understood more broadly because most of the attention in scholarship is devoted to the international courts and tribunals themselves. The purpose of this contribution is not at all to criticize such a focus. Rather this is an invitation for more research into international judicial governance institutions. Such research could analyse specific individual institutions. But it would seem useful and necessary as well to carry out comparative research into the law and practice of these institutions, also in view of their increased number.

Such research could be done in particular within the disciplines of political science and law. In recent years, some political scientists have done important research

chapters-of-the-acquis/index_en.htm> (last visited 29 June 2016). On the application of these conditions in practice, see Dimitry Kochenov, *EU Enlargement and the Failure of Conditionality—Pre-accession Conditionality in the Fields of Democracy and the Rule of Law* (Wolters Kluwer 2008), in particular Chapter 6 ('The Commission and the Pre-accession Reform of the Judiciaries').

[66] Opinion No 801/2015, together with the Council of Europe's Directorate of Human Rights of the Directorate General on Human Rights and Rule of Law (20–21 March 2015); see <http://www.venice.coe.int/webforms/documents/?pdf=CDL-AD(2015)007-e> (last visited 29 June 2016); Opinion No 803/2015 (24 July 2015), see <http://www.venice.coe.int/webforms/documents/?pdf=CDL-PI%282015%29016-e> (last visited 29 June 2016).

[67] See IMF Working Paper WP 15/279, 'Reforming the Legal and Institutional Framework for the Enforcement for Civil and Commercial Claims in Portugal' (prepared by Sebastiaan Pompe and Wolfgang Bergthaler), December 2015.

in this area, sometimes noting the relevance of the organizational context within which international courts and tribunals are embedded.[68] Within the discipline of law, research in this field would also be part of international institutional law, which has emerged since the Second World War as a separate branch within public international law. International institutional law is mostly based on comparative research into the law and practice of international organizations. It covers such issues and themes as the relationship between international organizations and their members, the relationship between organs, the financing of international organizations, their independence and accountability, etc, and is therefore a suitable reference frame when carrying out research into the governance institutions of international courts and tribunals.

[68] Eg Tom Ginsburg, 'Political Constraints on International Courts' in Romano (n 1), 492: 'Many international courts are embedded in broader international organizations, such as the UN or WTO. The bundling of international courts with broader regimes insulates the tribunals from certain forms of pressure, but also provides a point of leverage to pressure the courts into greater alignment with state preferences.'

PART II

THE WORKINGS OF ICS

3

Escaping from Law, Appealing to it

The Experience of a Civil Society Tribunal

Jerneja Penca

1 Introduction*

The assessment of whether the increasing international judicialization is a positive development entails also a reflection on the proliferation of the *language* of international judicial institutions. In certain instances, what is taking place is not the actual implementation of the concept of courts and tribunals, but of their alternatives, which borrow from the judicial institutions and critique them at the same time. The appearance of the judicial 'mode of operation' and the emergence of the 'fashion' of courts is an issue deserving of attention both in itself, and in so far as it speaks directly to judiciary.

This chapter examines the International Rights of Nature Tribunal (IRNT). This civil society initiative has met three times since 2014 to hear certain cases of disputes involving environmental, investment, and human rights issues. The initiative functions in a tribunal-like format, drawing on some elements of a judicial process, but failing on the crucial principle of a fair trial. While not an international court proper,[1] I consider the IRNT to be of concern to public international law and revealing of some of the topical issues in the debates about international judiciary. My interest is to explore how and why the language and concept of an international tribunal is being used in its case. The aim of the chapter is to describe the endeavour

* The research for this chapter was done during my postdoctoral position at PluriCourts, University of Oslo. The research was concluded in May 2016. All information about the IRNT was last updated then.

[1] I follow the definition of an international court as a permanent body that meets the following criteria: (1) decides the question(s) brought before it on the basis of international law; (2) follows predetermined rules of procedure; (3) issues legally binding decisions or opinions; (4) is composed of independent members; (5) requires that at least one party to a dispute be a state or an international organization; Cesare Romano, Karen Alter, and Yuval Shany, 'Mapping International Adjudicative Bodies, the Issues, and Players' in Cesare Romano, Karen Alter, and Yuval Shany (eds), *The Oxford Handbook of International Adjudication* (OUP 2014) 6. Philip Allott underscores the *isolation* of the courts as its fundamental characteristics and as key to its function. He calls a court 'a self-contained social phenomenon', physically, symbolically, and systematically distinct from other institutions. It is doubtful that the IRNT would fulfil this condition. Philip Allott, 'The International Court and the

Escaping from Law, Appealing to it: The Experience of a Civil Society Tribunal. Jerneja Penca.

aiming at legal authority, as an empirical fact, and flag some of the issues deserving of wider theoretical and practical study. The claim being made is that the disputes contemplated by the IRNT (which consist of disputes that fail to reach courts as well as those that are dissatisfied with the judicial rulings) constitute a valuable critique of where the existing international judiciary fails. As an institution, the IRNT articulates some expectations that both international judiciary and international law are vested with.

From the beginning, it is crucial to associate this institution with voices of indigenous groups and local communities, whose environment, identity, and lives have been impacted by development projects, and also with opponents of the dominant economic trajectories, technological solutions, and power relations, which are promoted in international agreements and dominant discourses. As such, the IRNT's existence and engagement with cases offer an account of how some core interest groups or categories of stakeholders understand legitimacy of international judiciary, a critique of where the existing institutions fail, and one proposal for how a reformed international judiciary could look. The study contributes to the recent wave of scholarly assessments of whether the existing international judiciary arrangements adequately cater for the needs, particularly in the environmental field[2] and more broadly.[3]

In examining the IRNT, the chapter exposes some biases of the courts, namely their political origin and architectural inadequacies. It underscores that environmental dispute settlement institutions are built through an intrinsically political process, as is the case with the establishment of environmental regimes generally. It also asserts how the architecture of the international environmental dispute settlement machinery in some cases impedes access to justice by non-state actors, but also how these non-state actors are addressing the international community through their struggle. Nevertheless, the same legal concepts which are criticized for being an instrument of oppression, remain tools for resolving the clashes in the plurality of norms.

The chapter is structured as follows. The next, second part describes the emergence and the functioning of the IRNT, including an overview of the cases in its docket, to provide an empirical background. The third part is devoted to specifying—despite all the criticism—the value of the IRNT project. I inquire into the intentions and messages of the IRNT with a view to distilling the legitimacy perceptions about existing institutions and the legal framework. Motivating this central part is the question of location of the IRNT within the international law: Are its claims only political, or

Voice of Justice' in Vaughan Lowe and Malgosia Fitzmaurice (eds), *Fifty Years of the International Court of Justice* (CUP 1996) 23.

[2] Eg Tim Stephens, *International Courts and Environmental Protection* (CUP 2012), Chapter 2 and the accompanying bibliography; Jeffrey L Dunoff, 'Institutional Misfits: The GATT, the ICJ & Trade-Environment Disputes' (1993) 15 Michigan Journal of International Law 1043; Robin L Juni, 'The United Nations Compensation Committee as a Model for an International Environmental Court' (2000) 7(1) The Environmental Lawyer 53; special issue of the International Journal of Court Innovation 3(1) 2010; International Court for the Environment Coalition, <http://icecoalition.com/> (last accessed 20 June 2016).

[3] Richard Lempert, 'More Tales of Two Courts: Exploring Changes in the "Dispute Settlement Function" of Trial Courts' (1978) 14 Law and Society Review 91, 99–100.

do they have any relevance for international law and, consequently, for the body of law, on which international judiciary draws? The conclusion points out, through the case of the IRNT, that adjudication is much closer to law-making than what is commonly maintained in international legal scholarship. The conclusion reflects on, rather than decries, this approximation between law-making and adjudication.

2 About the International Rights of Nature Tribunal

2.1 Background to the IRNT

Historical and comparative study can help us to understand the occurrence and intended impacts of the IRNT. Civil society tribunals have developed in the second part of the twentieth century in the environmental and non-environmental context as part of wider civil society resistance to a set of inadequacies and injustices, associated with globalization.[4] These tribunals primarily targeted world public opinion and sought to act as the moral authority in identifying problems not addressed by international law.[5] But rather than simply informing about gaps, these initiatives almost always sought to demonstrate how law acted as a tool of oppression and how existing institutions are implicated in the relations of dominance. The first among such tribunals was the so-called *Russell Tribunal*, which was conducted over a few months in 1967, with the aim of denouncing and legitimating large-scale public opposition to the Vietnam war. The tribunal involved eminent individuals as judges, such as legal academics, philosophers, writers, journalists, and campaigners, including the French philosopher Jean-Paul Sartre in his role of chair. The tribunal took principles, which were used in the Nuremberg Trials against Nazi war criminals, to judge conduct of American forces in the Vietnam conflict with the intention to 'institutionaliz[e] the extraordinary popular feeling that Nuremberg [sic] was in fact applicable through creating a "court" just as the victorious powers had done in 1946'.[6] The model of the first Russell Tribunal has been replicated in the following decades with the focus on individual conflicts around the world. Thus, subsequent Russell Tribunals were held on human rights violations in dictatorships of Argentina and Brazil (1973), on Chile's military coup (1974–76), on human rights in psychiatry (2001), on Iraq (2004), on Palestine (2009–12), and on human rights issues in the East Ukraine war (2014).[7] Based on the model of, but independently from the Russell Tribunal, other initiatives developed, such as the *Permanent peoples' tribunal*

[4] Mario Pianta, 'Parallel Summits of Global Civil Society' in H Anheier et al (eds), *Global Civil Society* (OUP 2001), 169–94.

[5] ibid, 173.

[6] Robert M Cover, 'The Folktales of Justice: Tales of Jurisdiction' (1985) 14 Capital University Law Review 179, 200.

[7] RT Question more, 'Guilty! "Russell Tribunal" condemns Obama, Poroshenko "war crimes" in E. Ukraine' (13.9.2014), <https://www.rt.com/news/187584-russell-tribunal-obama-ukraine> (accessed 1 February 2016).

in Mexico, which focuses on gross and systematic violations of the rights of peoples, minorities and individuals by States, by other authorities or private organizations.[8]

Similar initiatives have developed within the particular environmental context as part of the efforts to shape a more effective environmental governance architecture. One example is the non-governmental organization (NGO)-led *The International 'Court' of Environmental Arbitration and Conciliation*, established in Mexico in 1994. It was inspired by the need to enhance compliance with international environmental law and open to submissions by natural or legal, private, and public persons.[9] But while the above-mentioned 'court' 'has had virtually no influence on the environmental problems raised in "cases" before it',[10] other attempts seemed to have had more impact on the resolution of environmental disputes, even if these contributions are not immediately obvious. Notable among those are water tribunals, which developed in Rotterdam, the Netherlands (in 1983), and were subsequently held also in Amsterdam, the Netherlands (in 1992) and Florianopolis, Brazil (in 1993),[11] before spreading all across Latin America in subsequent years.[12] In some cases they have managed to resolve the conflicts in the usage of water by helping the parties to find a solution, while in other instances they have enhanced compliance with environmental norms by heightening the visibility.[13]

It is important to highlight the intention of these tribunals to represent alternatives to both protests as political actions and litigation in courts as legal actions. Equally significant is to highlight their reliance on morality rather than enforcement potential.[14] The civil society engagement of this kind sees itself as an ethical or parallel mechanism, devoted to *alternative* justice.[15]

These past efforts are referenced in the explanation of the IRNT's ambition.[16] The IRNT also builds on them in the particular design and function, in particular the fact that, like the water tribunals, it represents an entirely non-governmental,

[8] Tribunal Permanente por los Pueblos <http://www.tppmexico.org/> (accessed 20 June 2016).

[9] See Eckard Rehbinder and Demetrio Loperena, 'Legal Protection of Environmental Rights: The Role and Experience of the International Court of Environmental Arbitration and Conciliation' (2001) 31 Environmental Policy and Law 282.

[10] Tim Stephens, *International Courts and Environmental Protection* (CUP 2009), 58.

[11] Tribunal Latinoamericano del Agua, Fundamentos, <http://tragua.com/quienes-somos/fundamentos-vision-mision-objetivos/> (accessed 1 February 2016).

[12] Tribunal Latinoamericano del Agua, Historia <http://tragua.com/quienes-somos/historia/> (accessed 1 February 2016).

[13] Belén Olmos Giupponi, 'Transnational Environmental Law and Grass-Root Initiatives: The Case of the Latin American Water Tribunal' (2015) Transnational Environmental Law; see also Carmen Maganda, 'The Latin American Water Tribunal and the Need for Public Spaces for Social Participation in Water Governance' in J Feyen, K Shannon, and M Neville (eds), *Water and Urban Development Paradigms: Towards an Integration of Engineering, Design and Management Approaches* (CRC Press 2009), 687–92.

[14] Mikita A Weaver, '"El Agua No Se Vende: Water is Not For Sale!" The Latin American Water Tribunal as a Model for Advancing Access to Water' (2011) 11 Pepperdine Dispute Resolution Law Journal 519, 522–24.

[15] Tribunal Latinoamericano del Agua, Historia, <http://tragua.com/quienes-somos/historia/>.

[16] Cormac Cullinan, 'A Tribunal for Earth: Why it matters', <http://therightsofnature.org/a-tribunal-for-earth-why-it-matters/> (accessed 1 February 2016).

'peoples' tribunal, unrelated to any state structures.[17] The IRNT represents a true transnational *movement*,[18] which organizes itself around the principle, rather than the state authority.

The substantive context of the movement represent the 'rights of nature'. These encompass multiple aspects of 'our relationship with nature, a new legal framework, a set of ethical principles, a strategy with which to question the superpowers of transnational corporations'.[19] Embodying a historically marginalized, but enduring ecocentric philosophy of law,[20] the articulation and promotion of 'rights of nature' gained a momentum in 2009. It was then that the United Nations Framework Convention on Climate Change (UNFCCC) summit in Copenhagen failed to, contrary to the popular and expert expectations, reach a legally binding agreement on arresting climate change.[21] To counterbalance the then stalled process of the climate change regime but also to impact on the direction of environmental governance more broadly, the president of Bolivia convened the *People's Conference on Climate Change and the Rights of Mother Earth* in Cochabamba, Bolivia. Some months later it's outcome was a document titled *Universal Declaration of the Rights of Mother Earth* ('Declaration').[22] The document consisting of a Preamble and four articles, inter alia, notes that 'we are all part of Mother Earth, an indivisible, living community of interrelated and interdependent beings with a common destiny'[23] and proclaims that Mother Earth and all beings have the inherent rights to life and to exist, and to continue its vital cycles and processes free from human disruptions.[24] The document consistently promotes a world-view that sees human relationship with the planet and biosphere not in terms of dominance and subordination, but in a more balanced way that acknowledges interdependency between beings and calls for mutual respect. The 'rights of nature' encompass Earth's (nature's) rights as well as individual and community rights.

The proposal to discuss the 'rights of nature' at the highest political level involved some controversy. It was condemned to represent 'an attempt [by socialist

[17] Article 1(2) of the People's Tribunal Convention for the Establishment of the International Rights of Nature Tribunal (2005), <http://therightsofnature.org/peoples-convention-tribunal/> (accessed 20 June 2016).

[18] I follow the inclusive approach to 'environmental movements', which sees them as 'broad networks of people and organisations engaged in collective action in pursuit of environmental benefits'; Christopher Rootes, 'Environmental Movements: From the Local to the Global' in Christopher Rootes (ed), *Environmental Movements: Local, National and Global* (Routledge 2014), 2.

[19] Global Alliance for the Rights of Nature, The Notes for the Debate The Rights of Mother Earth, <http://therightsofnature.org/notes-debate-rights-of-mother-earth/> (accessed 20 June 2016).

[20] Vito de Lucia, 'Towards an Ecological Philosophy of Law: A Comparative Discussion' (2013) 4(2) Journal of Human Rights and the Environment 167; see also Roderick Frazier Nash, *The Rights of Nature: A History of Environmental Ethics* (History of American Thought and Culture) (University of Wisconsin Press 1989).

[21] Daniel Bodansky, 'The Copenhagen Climate Change Conference: A Post-Mortem' (2010) 104(2) American Journal of International Law 230.

[22] Universal Declaration of Rights of Mother Earth, 22 April 2010, Cochabamba, Bolivia; <http://therightsofnature.org/universal-declaration/> (accessed 1 February 2016).

[23] Preamble of the Declaration.

[24] Article 2, paras 1(a) and 1(c) of the Declaration.

governments] to blame environmental degradation and climate change on capitalism'.[25] Nevertheless, the motion gained political success at the United Nations (UN). In 2009, the General Assembly proclaimed 22 April as the International Mother Earth Day[26] and launched a discussion process on the meaning and impact of 'harmony with nature'.[27] While the goal of adopting a document representing 'a common standard of achievement for all peoples and all nations of the world',[28] comparable to that of the Universal Declaration of Human Rights, was not reached, the movement remains active both at the UN level, where seven resolutions have been adopted so far,[29] and at the grassroots level—precisely through the implementation of the IRNT.

The legal status of the claims by the IRNT is not a straightforward issue. On the one hand, its statements are aspirational: the 'rights of nature' are a concept seeking recognition but with an unsure future in the international legal context. Recognition is sought precisely in order to change the practice of states. As such, the IRNT's statements are thus far removed from one of the key conditions to qualify, hypothetically, for customary law.[30] On the other hand however, the Declaration of the Rights of Mother Earth entails ideas that are laws in certain jurisdictions. For instance, laws recognizing the rights of nature have been adopted by certain municipalities in the US.[31] Rights of nature are recognized in a legal agreement between the government of New Zealand and the Maori Iwi peoples.[32] They have motivated a set of Bolivian laws,[33] and have since 2008 been enshrined in the Ecuadorian constitution.[34] Overall, 'rights of nature' are a mixture of national and subnational laws, and international political values.

As part of the movement's goal to aim at (accelerating) the recognition of the rights of nature by the states and international bodies, the idea emerged about a *tribunal* devoted to the concept. The IRNT convened for the first time in January

[25] Jonathan Wachtel, 'UN Prepares to debate whether "Mother Earth" Deserves Human Rights Status, <http://www.foxnews.com/world/2011/04/18/prepares-debate-rights-mother-earth.html> (accessed 20 June 2016).

[26] UNGA Res 63/278 (22 April 2010) UN Doc A/RES/63/278.

[27] 'An Interactive Dialogue of the General Assembly on Harmony With Nature', see UNGA Res 64/196 (21 December 2009) UN Doc A/RES/64/21 which invited Member States and organizations to submit their views on living in harmony with nature.

[28] See n 22.

[29] The most recent was UNGA Res 70/208 (22 December 2015) UN Doc A/RES/70/208, see also the website of the initiative <http://www.harmonywithnatureun.org/index.html> (accessed 20 June 2016).

[30] Apart from state practice, the other condition for customary law is *opinio juris*.

[31] Allegedly, about twelve municipalities have relevant laws; see Global Alliance for the Rights of Nature, Frequently Asked questions, <http://therightsofnature.org/frequently-asked-questions/> (accessed 20 June 2016).

[32] Linda Sheehan, 'Realizing Nature's Rule of Law through Rights of Waterways' in Christina Voigt (ed), *Rule of Law for Nature* (CUP 2013), 233.

[33] The Law of the Rights of Mother Earth; Law 071 adopted by the Plurinational State of Bolivia; the Bolivian Framework Law for Mother Earth and Integral Development for Living Well.

[34] The Constitution of Ecuador, Articles 71–73 recognize the right to exist, persist, maintain and regenerate its vital cycles, structure, functions, and its processes in evolution; the right to restoration; require caution and the banning of the acquisition of the functions of nature and recognizes that all people, nations, and nationalities have the responsibility to protect nature. Further details on this and other examples of constitutionally entrenched environmental protections James R May and Erin Daly, *Global Environmental Constitutionalism* (CUP 2015).

2014 in Quito, Ecuador. In December of the same year the second Tribunal was held in Lima, Peru, simultaneously with and only a few kilometres away from the official UNFCCC COP (Conference of the Parties) 20 meeting. The third session was held in Paris in 2015, again concurrently with the UNFCCC COP 21.

2.2 The functioning of the IRNT

The IRNT follows the format of a tribunal in some, but overall in very few aspects. From the beginning, justifying the name of a 'tribunal' is the existence of certain roles in the process ('prosecutor', 'judge') and of the institute of a 'verdict'. The consideration of cases follows roughly the same procedural pattern, but the statute[35] and the rules of procedure were put in place only after the second session.[36]

The process at the tribunal unfolds as follows. First, the jurisdiction is asserted based on the Universal Declaration of the Rights of Mother Earth. The Declaration also represents the applicable law in the IRNT's proceedings. The cases are presented by the 'Prosecutor for the Earth' and 'Case experts', which have a great extent of freedom in their task. Finally, 'judges' give rulings. As it has been the case with civil society tribunals in the past (see above), the role of judges is not limited to lawyers. Rather than the profession or legal education, the Tribunal places importance on the individuals' (high) ethical and moral standards or reputation in society, but attention is also placed on the variety of judges' backgrounds. Among the large numbers of individuals who have served as judges in the IRNT are writers, academics, public servants, NGO founders and members. The respect enjoyed by those individuals involved acts as an investment into sociological legitimacy and it is crucial to note that law is distinct from that conception. A rather limited role of the legal can be attributed to the intention of the IRNT to campaign for the concept of the 'rights of nature' as a broad concept that goes beyond existing legal constructs.

A most important feature of the process at the IRNT is that there is no representation of the defendant. The Tribunal makes no serious effort to involve the accused States or companies in the trial: it does not inform them of the beginning of the trial against them, nor does it ensure their participation in the proceedings. There are hardly any steps taken to safeguard reasonable procedural fairness to defendants. The Statute of the IRNT explicitly states that the 'Tribunal may make orders, findings and judgments in spite of the absence of any affected party'.[37] It is in this aspect of not conducting a fair trial that the tribunal decidedly fails to qualify as a quasi-legal entity.

2.3 An overview of the cases

So far the IRNT has heard over fifteen cases involving situations, where the 'rights of nature' have allegedly been violated. A more precise number is difficult to assert

35 Statute of the International Tribunal of Mother Earth Rights, <http://therightsofnature.org/statute-of-the-international-tribunal-of-mother-earth-rights/#_Toc436978245> (accessed 20 June 2016).

36 People's Tribunal Convention, <http://therightsofnature.org/statute-of-the-international-tribunal-of-mother-earth-rights/#_Toc436978245> (accessed 1 February 2016).

37 Article 2(2) of the Statute.

as the docket is not as neatly organized as is the case with international tribunals; there are instances of overlapping cases where the same case has been framed in at least two different ways (eg the Chevron/Texaco case is considered on its own terms and again as an example of an ecocide; the reduced emissions from deforestation and degradation (REDD) mechanism is slated on its own terms and again as part of a problematic 'financialization of nature'). There is also no standard format for the presentation of the background and legal facts. As a result, some cases offer a long file of relevant materials while others hardly a few words of the context and the names of those presenting them. According to the IRNT, the cases have been chosen for having a 'broad international appeal and application' and for involving a variety of environmental topics, including the relevance of cases to the host region of each meeting of the tribunal.[38] The selection has resulted in a diverse set of issues, which are—to give a flavour of substance—briefly summarized in Table 3.1 below.

Table 3.1 The summary of the cases presented at the IRNT in its three sessions

Case name, location	Summary of the conflict
Conga Cajamarca Mine, Peru	The Peruvian government, backed by the World Bank, has made a political agreement with foreign investors allowing mining to take place in an ecologically vulnerable environment and a water source, despite an unfavourable environmental impact assessment (EIA) (whereas the commissioned EIA was technically inadequate and thus misused), and existing domestic legislation that protects vulnerable ecosystems.
Condor Mirador, Ecuador	Despite stringent domestic laws protecting nature, the Ecuadorian government awarded a licence to a mining company, which is now accused of destroying rainforest, one of the ecologically most fragile ecosystems in the world, and home to Shuar people.
British Petroleum, Mexico / USA	An oil company's negligence caused a widespread and damaging oil spill and massive damage to wildlife. Domestic courts have charged the operator to pay penalties, but the fines are believed to be too low to represent meaningful compensation, and do not take into account the long-term effects of the damage.
Belo Horizonte Dam, Brazil	The governmental decision to prioritize clean energy and investment has prevailed over the indigenous opposition to the construction of a large dam. Indigenous peoples claim that their right to free, prior, and informed consent and the recommendations by the Inter-American Commission on Human Rights have not been respected.
4 river basins, Peru	Four decades of oil extraction in Amazon basins has resulted in grave damage to ecosystems and in heavy economic, social, and cultural ramifications for lives of the indigenous. A health and environmental emergency has even been declared in the affected areas and a long-term relationship to nature has been lost. Allegedly, the established operational guidelines are not respected. Besides, the state is weakening environmental legislation with a view of reviving economy and attracting investment. There is a further problem with police contracting private companies in order to repress protests.

[38] Interview with a representative of the International Alliance for the Rights of Nature (January 2016).

Table 3.1 Continued

Case name, location	Summary of the conflict
Chevron-Texaco, Ecuador	Four decades of presence of the oil industry in the Ecuadorian rainforest and its use of inadequate technology, as well as the negligence on the side of the oil company, are blamed for extermination of some indigenous peoples and reduction of others, and for vast environmental damage. Justice was sought at US courts and again at Ecuadorian courts. The latter finally decided in favour of plaintiffs, but the judgment is not respected.
Defenders of the Earth: Bagua, Peru	Peruvian decrees that had been enacted to conform Peruvian law to FTA requirements provide new access to exploit lands of Amazonian indigenous people for oil, gas, and logging, to which indigenous peoples are opposed as lands have been impacted heavily by extractive projects. EIA has demonstrated heavy impacts but has not stopped the project. State security forces are used to repress resistance by civil society.
Hydraulic Fracking, a global issue	The practice of fracking is allowed (and spreading rapidly), despite the fact that it is widely opposed. It uses fresh water in the process, and pollutes underground water by wastewater, results in air pollution (including with greenhouse gases), soil contamination (including radioactive waste), increases likelihood of earthquakes, destroys large areas of land, and causes some social problems.
Climate Change and False Solutions, a global issue	High-risk technologies, such as geo-engineering or climate-smart agriculture, are opposed for they preclude more progressive answers to climate change.
REDD, a global issue	The practice of REDD (Reduced Emissions from Deforestation and Forest Degradation) is fundamentally opposed by some groups because it treats nature as commodity. These opponents refuse to seek legal solutions within the framework that accepts the idea.
Great Barrier Reef, Australia	The expansion of ports, especially for the export of coal, dredging, agricultural sediments, and industrial developments endanger the reef, while further development of the area is planned. Several challenges at Australian domestic courts and World Heritage Convention warnings have been unsuccessful in stopping the proposed development projects.
Yasuní, Ecuador	The Ecuadorian president announced exploration of oil reserves in the Yasuní park, which is home to extreme biodiversity and two indigenous peoples in isolation. A number of rights and freedoms are allegedly violated: the right to call a referendum by popular initiative, the right to association, freedom of movement, and expression; the rights to life and self-determination of the indigenous peoples in voluntary isolation; the right of indigenous peoples to continued access to and use of their ecological environment on which they depend. Electoral fraud and intimidation were instigated to defeat the opponents of the initiative. The rights of nature, as defined in the Constitution, are violated.
Agro-food industry/ GMOs, a global issue	The agro-food industry actions to define and process life through patents of genetically modified seeds violate, on a large scale, the fundamental right of Mother Earth to her vital life cycles. In addition, the agro-food industry operations are increasing the financial dependence of cotton seed farmers in India (leading some to commit suicide), impacting on the health of citizens around the world and contributing to much more than the commonly believed 15% of global greenhouse gas emissions.

The cases vary among themselves on a number of issues, including the central themes of the disputes, parties to the dispute, and their use of courts. This variety makes the IRNT a rich project but also one where evaluating its impact is more difficult. In any event, discerning patterns across cases is not the purpose of this section; rather, it serves as a reference point for the discussion on the IRNT as an institution, which follows.

3 Lessons by a 'Tribunal'

The IRNT represents an attempt of bringing justice to affected communities. But while it could be debated as an activist project, a civil society venture with no relevance to international law, it could also invite deeper theoretical and practical considerations. My claim is that contrary to the exclusion from the study of the international law, the IRNT highlights some fundamental issues surrounding its study.

The first of the analytical challenges that the IRNT poses is the question of its location within international law and international institutions. The Tribunal's intentions can be understood as projections of the struggle to influence both adjudication and legislation. For analytical purposes, I thus suggest framing the initiative in two different ways: within the analysis of adjudicative institutions and within the investigations of law-making and distil important lessons to both bodies of law. The IRNT should be understood as speaking simultaneously to judiciary (as a substitute thereof) and to politics (as an attempt at law-making).

3.1 The IRNT and judiciary

There are a number of reasons to question the adequacy of the IRNT's (self) attribution 'tribunal'. The lack of rigorous rules of procedure, the absence of the defendant, the absence of the jurisdiction over the cases, and the fact that norms which the IRNT uses are not law in all jurisdictions over which the IRNT rules, are the most obvious points on which the project can be criticized. Further, the significant marginalization of lawyers questions the extent to which the initiative seeks to seriously engage with law.

Nevertheless, the IRNT can legitimately be put on the radar of the literature on international judiciary. Not least because, perhaps surprisingly, a venture like the IRNT is captured by some of the definitions of international adjudicative institutions that have been put forward in the recent literature. In coming to terms with the rapid expansion of international judiciary institutions since the 1990s, the literature has sought to provide inclusive definitions. Attempts were thus made to accommodate the variety of bodies, which emerged as 'second-generation tribunals',[39] and

[39] These would include arbitral tribunals constituted pursuant to investment treaties, such as the North American Free Trade Agreement and the International Centre for Settlement of Investment Disputes Convention; international commercial-arbitration tribunals, such as the Iran-US Claims

encompass 'not only entities officially designated "courts", such as the [International Court of Justice], but also less formal or permanent bodies established to resolve specific disputes'.[40] The PluriCourts research project on the role of international judiciary in the global order 'considers [international courts] in a wide sense, encompassing international institutions whose formal function is *dispute settlement*, even if not called a "court" (as in the World Trade Organization) or if only able to make non-legally binding decisions (such as the UN human rights treaty bodies)'[41] as long as they are intended to '*aid* resolution of international needs'.[42] By all means, this definition captures the IRNT in the same vein as, for instance, the International Tribunal on the Law of the Sea or the Permanent Court of Arbitration or any other established adjudicative body.[43] But faced with such a finding, this and other current definitions of courts might turn out to be overly expansive for meaningful comparison or pattern-drawing. They might consider adding additional criteria of legality, including the role for law, lawyers, and rules of procedure. The discomfort of having to delineate between the IRNT and the recognized adjudicative bodies reminds us of the diversity of existing institutions and of the difficulty of distilling the essence of what courts are.

If we—as a theoretic exercise—square the IRNT within these loose definitions of judiciary, the project can be considered an indicator of the weaknesses in the existing judiciary and a means to rectify those. Below I discuss two such aspects.

3.1.1 Towards a true 'transnational' judiciary

One area in which the IRNT broadcasts a message to the existing international adjudication is in the need to integrate, more fully than so far, non-state actors. There is a very real urge to consider a true transnational judiciary in terms of its contribution to settling disputes between *two* non-state actors, pushing State and international organizations to the margins of the equation.

Many disputes considered by the IRNT have occurred in a relation between two non-state actors, for example indigenous peoples or environmental groups and investors. These disputes have a clear transnational dimension, and while a set of principles of international law applies to them, they can hardly be brought in front of existing international judicial fora. Limiting the access of such disputes is the condition that at least one party is a governmental or intergovernmental actor.

Tribunal and the UN Claims Commission; the WTO; and national courts adjudicating claims against foreign states; Gary Born, 'A New Generation of International Adjudication' (2012) 61(4) *Duke Law Journal* 775.

[40] Laurence R Helfer and Anne-Marie Slaughter, 'Toward a Theory of Effective Supranational Adjudication' (1997) 107 Yale Law Journal 273, 285.

[41] PluriCourts research plan, <http://www.jus.uio.no/pluricourts/english/about/pluricourts-plan.pdf> (accessed 1 February 2016), 4.

[42] ibid, 2.

[43] See, eg, the database of the Project of the International Courts and Tribunal, <http://www.pict-pcti.org/> (accessed 20 June 2016).

In certain domains of international law non-state actors have shaped the format of adjudicatory bodies.[44] But in the context of 'environmental disputes' non-state actors have long struggled to access justice through courts.[45] Their inclusion was one of the key features in the experiments of, or considerations about, international environmental courts, that would ostensibly better serve environmental goals.[46] A development in this direction would follow the recognition of growing significance of non-state actors and multi-level governance in legal and regulatory developments.[47] Interestingly enough, while 'law beyond the state', at either domestic or international (inter-state) level, has impacted on the empirical and normative examination of law-making (as captured by 'transnational law'),[48] we seem to be further away from a fully-blown conceptualization of 'transnational judiciary'. The design of international courts and the scholarship on judiciary have been, more than the domain of law-making, reluctant to entirely dismiss the state and inter-governmental relations from their equation.

To be clear, the literature on courts now notes that international courts are no longer equal to inter-state fora.[49] International relations scholars have described the rise of 'transnational judicial bodies', where 'access to courts and tribunals and the subsequent enforcement of their decisions are legally insulated from the will of individual national governments [... and which] are therefore more open to individuals and groups in civil society'.[50] But the conception of international courts has been relaxed only to a limited extent—by extending access to judicial institutions to non-state actors and no longer demanding that both *parties* are states. Both the design of courts as an empirical fact and the normative definitions expect at least one state or inter-governmental organization to be a party to the dispute.[51] Engaging with the IRNT reminds us of the extent to which international judiciary remains rooted in a State conception. It also provides an occasion to consider whether

[44] See eg Francisco Orego Vicuna, 'Individuals and Non-state Entities in International Courts and Tribunals' (2001) 5 Max Planck Yearbook of United Nations Law 53.

[45] Peggy R Kalas, 'International Environmental Dispute Resolution and the Need for Access by Non-State Entities' (2001) 12 Colorado Journal of International Environmental Law and Policy 191.

[46] See eg above the description of *The International 'Court' of Environmental Arbitration and Conciliation* in section 2.1; Ole Pedersen, 'An International Environmental Court and International Legalism' (2010) 22 Journal of Environmental Law 461.

[47] See Gunther Teubner (ed), *Global Law without a State* (Dartmouth 1996); Gralf Peter Calliess and Peer Zumbansen, *Rough Consensus and Running Code: A Theory of Transnational Private Law* (Hart 2010); Patrick H Glenn, 'A Transnational Concept of Law' in Peter Cane and Mark Tushnet (eds), *The Oxford Handbook of Legal Studies* (OUP 2003).

[48] Eg Colin Scott, '"Transnational Law" as Proto-Concept: Three Conceptions' (2009) 10 German Law Journal 859; Peer Zumbansen, 'Transnational Legal Pluralism' (2010) 1(2) Transnational Legal Theory 141.

[49] See Karen J Alter, *The New Terrain of International Law: Courts, Politics, Rights* (Princeton University Press 2014). In fact, only a minority of today's international courts maintain the traditional inter-state model.

[50] Robert O Keohane, Andrew Moravcsik, and Anne-Marie Slaughter, 'Legalized Dispute Resolution: Interstate and Transnational' (2000) 54(3) International Organization 457, 458.

[51] The definition by Romano, Alter, and Shany (n 1) remains authoritative.

the State-centred images of international judiciary are ill-prepared to capture real-world situations that seek judicial redress.

3.1.2 The narrative and visibility function of transnational courts

The second aspect, in which the IRNT contributes to the scholarship on adjudication is in the scholarly listing of the roles attributed to international judiciary.[52] This scholarship—despite some differences in the classification—has uniformly assumed that international courts aim at providing authoritative messages, not inherently contestable claims. The IRNT disturbs that image of courts and tribunals as authorities and instead locates them within multiple notions of justice.

The IRNT has been set up as a way of giving voice to victims, and to break the silence about injustices implicated in the cases. Most of the time and effort involved in the process at the IRNT is spent on presenting the social context to and the implications of the legal disputes by the affected individuals and communities. The IRNT's verdicts on the cases are predictable, routinely affirming the accusations of violations of the 'rights of nature' and local communities.

This activity asserts the IRNT in its role of an 'agent of memory' that constructs a particular collective memory of past events and offers a counter-narrative to the prevailing one.[53] In this instance, documenting injustices and critical perspectives seems to serve two purposes. Most immediately, the IRNT functions as an instrument of reparation for the victims of the ecological disasters, human rights violations, and an ineffective judiciary. But the IRNT provides also a mechanism to warn against the repetition of the abuses in the future.

The significance of judicial narratives has been examined in the context of the role of memory in international law. That scholarship draws attention to the role of trials in establishing the truth of events and constructing a historical

[52] Armin von Bogdandy and Ingo Veznke, 'On the Functions of International Courts: An Appraisal in Light of Their Burgeoning Public Authority' (2013) 26(1) Leiden Journal of International Law 49 state the following functions for the courts: settling disputes, the stabilization of normative expectations, law-making, the control and legitimation of authority exercised by others; Karen J Alter, 'The Multiple Roles of International Courts and Tribunals: Enforcement, Dispute Settlement, Constitutional and Administrative Review' in Jeffrey L Dunoff and Mark A Pollack (eds), *Interdisciplinary Perspectives on International Law and International Relations: The State of the Art* (CUP 2013) divides the functions of the courts into dispute settlement, enforcement, administrative review, and constitutional review; see also Richard Lempert, 'More Tales of Two Courts: Exploring Changes in the "Dispute Settlement Function" of Trial Courts' (1978) 14 Law and Society Review 91–138, at 99–100 states that courts contribute to dispute settlement but differentiates between various ways in which they do so.

[53] This point draws on Mosche Hirsch, 'The Role of International Tribunals in the Construction of Collective Memories' (12 November 2016). Proceedings of the Second Workshop on Sociological Inquiries into International Law (Munk School of Global Affairs, University of Toronto, 9–10 October 2015); Proceedings of the Annual Conference of the European Society of International Law (Oslo, 10–12 September, 2015); Hebrew University of Jerusalem Legal Research Paper No. 16-43; Hebrew University of Jerusalem International Law Forum Working Series 08-16. Available at SSRN: <https://ssrn.com/abstract=2868416> or <http://dx.doi.org/10.2139/ssrn.2868416>.

memory.[54] More recently, judicial organs have begun to determine memory-related initiatives as measures of reparation.[55] The intention of the IRNT and its current impact does not exactly support any of these findings. In its case, *the judicial process itself* represents a measure of reparation, a means of redress and a measure of satisfaction for the victims. The IRNT does not expect to form the predominant historical account in the cases it tackles. Nor does it issue material orders which will repair the past wrongs. It functions to provide an avenue for articulating a moral narrative that goes some way to providing satisfaction to the victims.

Leaving aside the normative question of whether creating historical memory should be the role for courts, there remains the issue of whether the operation of the IRNT has had any ramifications for the settlement of disputes presented to the IRNT. The IRNT litigation is capable of bringing some publicity about the injustices involved in the disputes. Awareness is an important compliance-boosting factor for potential violators, especially in cultural contexts, where environmental norms have traditionally been disregarded.[56] But it is unsure whether the message by and about the IRNT has reached anyone outside those audiences, participating in the disputes.[57] From this point of view, the limited impact gives little in the way of expecting a result on the future disputes.

The IRNT is nevertheless a testament to the eternal hope invested into a judicial process. Many cases examined by the IRNT had disappointing experience in courts, mostly in their domestic settings. They saw courts fail in effective judicial protection for various reasons. They had either failed to admit the victims of the disputes (eg *Conga Cajamarca*), act independently and impartially (*Condor Mirador*), rule on the substance and award remedies (*Belo Horizonte, Great Barrier Reef*), or enforce their sentences (*Chevron Texaco, Yasuni*). Yet, the cases are re-considered in a transnational setting—projecting the hope that chances for legal redress can be improved. That is despite the questionable ability of the IRNT to meet those expectations of greater independence and impartiality, to ensure a better access to citizens and offer a better potential for enforcement.

3.2 The IRNT and law-making

If we separate the IRNT from the language it uses, there is very little of judiciary left in it. The supporting material of the IRNT makes it clear that the concept of a 'tribunal'

[54] Marc Osiel, *Mass Atrocity, Collective Memory, and the Law* (Transaction Publishers 1999); Martti Koskenniemi, 'Between Impunity and Show Trials' (2002) 6 Max Planck Yearbook of United Nations Law, 1–35; Richard Ashby Wilson, *Writing History in International Criminal Trials* (OUP 2011).

[55] Maria Chiara Campisi, 'From a Duty to Remember to an Obligation to Memory? Memory as Reparation in the Jurisprudence of the Inter-American Court of Human Rights' (2014) 8(1) International Journal of Conflict and Violence 61.

[56] Giupponi (n 13).

[57] The IRNT itself does not publish media reports about its activities on its website. A simple research on the media outreach seems to not show a large impact.

and the activities around it are only instrumental to the goal, which is to influence law. The IRNT openly works to put the concept of 'the rights of nature' on the map and alongside the established rights with the final aim of universal acceptance and universal observance of the 'rights of nature'. [58] Before that, the movement is expected to educate civil society, the legal community, and governments about that concept and envisage a world, based on that alternative paradigm. A tribunal format was chosen as a tool to that end, that is as an awareness-raising activity and 'the framework for focused analysis of Rights of Nature and the implications on existing and proposed legal systems through the hearing process'.[59]

It is important to separate the described objective of the movement and the actual activity of the IRNT from so-called alternative dispute resolution (ADR) mechanisms. While both ADR mechanisms and the IRNT are designed as alternatives to litigation in courts, the IRNT is not, contrary to the ADR mechanisms, 'spurred by desire to avoid the cost, delay, and adversarial nature of litigation'.[60] It cannot be compared to arbitration, mediation, or conciliation, which are among the common types of ADR. Considerations of cost and time savings, which are ADR's biggest advantages,[61] are not among the IRNT's priorities, and neither is confidentiality. If anything, decreasing confidentiality and increasing visibility is at the very focus of the IRNT.

If we accept that the IRNT is foremost a law-making endeavour, what lessons for international law-making can be discerned from its operation? First, that the construction of authority of judicial institutions is contested because it is embedded in legal pluralism. Second, that some see ethics as transcending law, but nevertheless seek to redress injustices through law. These aspects are considered in turn.

3.2.1 'Rights of nature' within international legal pluralism

The operation of the IRNT can be located within the context of legal pluralism, which stresses a coexisting diversity or even conflict of sources of legal authority.[62]

[58] People's Tribunal Convention (n 17), Article 2(c). [59] Interview, see n 38 above.

[60] World Bank, *Topic Brief on Alternative Dispute Resolution (ADR)*, <http://web.worldbank.org/WBSITE/EXTERNAL/TOPICS/EXTLAWJUSTINST/0,,contentMDK:20755904~menuPK:2035565~pagePK:210058~piPK:210062~theSitePK:1974062,00.html> (accessed 20 June 2016).

[61] Inessa Love, 'Settling Out of Court: How Effective is Alternative Dispute Resolution' (2011), The World Bank Group *Viewpoint* Note Number 329, <http://siteresources.worldbank.org/FINANCIALSECTOR/Resources/282044-1307652042357/VP329-Setting-out-of-court.pdf> (accessed 20 June 2016).

[62] See William Twining, 'Normative and Legal Pluralism: A Global Perspective' (2010) 20 Duke Journal of Comparative & International Law 473; Brian Z Tamanaha, 'Understanding Legal Pluralism: Past to Present, Local to Global' (2008) 30 Sydney Law Review 375; A Fischer-Lescano and G Teubner, 'Regime-Collisions: The Vain Search for Legal Unity in the Fragmentation of Global Law' (2004) 25(4) Michigan Journal of International Law 999; PS Berman, 'A Pluralist Approach to International Law' (2007) 32(2) Yale Journal of International Law 301; Ralf Michaels, 'Global Legal Pluralism' (2009) 5 Annual Review of Law & Social Science 243.

The clash between the 'rights of nature' is a standard clash between the state legal system and the indigenous system. 'Rights of nature' draw on the indigenous Andean goddess of Pachamama, a web of interconnected organisms, including people.[63] The relationship of Pachamama with human beings exemplifies indigenous values and constitutes the core of the cultural integrity of indigenous people in the Andes. While these principles were not strictly treated as rules or commands, they represented the framework for organizing lives of the indigenous, including how to avoid the disputes between people and nature. 'Rights of nature' thus qualify as an institutionalized non-state normative order, which makes a claim to authority and which is competing with the official legal claim. [64]

This descriptive conception of legal pluralism seeks not to legitimate and justify the 'rights of nature' or the IRNT but to benefit the analysis in a conceptual way. In contrast to considering it as a political initiative, situating the 'rights of nature' within global pluralism highlights the intrusive involvement of inter- and transnational law with indigenous population and its disregard for indigenous laws. This framing bears relevance for the judicial institutions in so far as they exercise dominance over the substantive norms and processes, which stand to protect (competing) indigenous normative orders.

Framing the IRNT within pluralistic normative systems also enables us to consider the ability of the IRNT to participate in transnational law. The UN Dialogue on Harmony with Nature is a discussion generated by the IRNT about the suitability of the existing (official) legal framework to relate to the environment. It is inviting a self-reflection of the mainstream legal framework. The awareness of the inconsistency between the two normative systems may force the official legal system to diminish the clash of norms and temper the official order.[65] It is not unlikely that the activity of the IRNT will cause the approximation of the (official) international law to the 'rights of nature'.

3.2.2 The IRNT's ambiguous relationship to law

A curious feature in the IRNT's law-making strategy is that it oscillates between ethical and legal claims. It chooses to introduce ethics as substantively transcending law but simultaneously resorts to law and legal institutions in order to empower its claims and to influence behaviour of stakeholders. The deliberations of the proponents by the IRNT whether to present the project as *ethical* or as *legal* tribunal touch upon the core of the puzzles in the scholarly debates about the legitimacy of international law and adjudication:[66]

[63] See Frazier Nash (n 20). [64] Tamanaha (n 62), 400–1. [65] ibid, at 405.

[66] See eg Mattias Kumm, 'The Legitimacy of International Law: A Constitutionalist Framework of Analysis' (2004) 15(5) European Journal of International Law 907–31; Allen Buchanan, 'The Legitimacy of International Law' in Samantha Besson and John Tasioulas (eds), *The Philosophy of International Law* (OUP 2010); John Tasioulas, 'The Legitimacy of International Law' in Samantha Besson and John Tasioulas (eds), *The Philosophy of International Law* (OUP 2010).

> At one point early on, we referred to it [the IRNT] as an 'Ethical' tribunal in recognition of our ethical and moral authority but also our current lack of legal authority. We dropped the 'ethical' descriptor because we ultimately don't want to limit the Tribunal to only 'ethical' considerations; we are examining the legal as well as moral and broader societal considerations.[67]

The IRNT's struggle to come to terms with its mission bluntly spells out the role of law as both a legitimizing and limiting tool. The official law is limiting the application of the IRNT's normative claims, but legal concepts and institutions play a central role in the setup of this entire alternative. The movement perpetuates the 'myth of rights', [68] where despite the questionable utility of rights for advancing progressive social goals, the appeal of the language of rights 'is premised on a direct linking of litigation, rights, and remedies with social change'.[69] The proponents of the IRNT believe that the existence of 'the rights of nature' as positive law, by virtue of their place at the top of the hierarchy of norms, would ensure better decisions both at the policy level and in litigation. The courts, attuned to the 'rights of nature', are a key part of the equation.

On this view, the legitimacy of courts in the environmental field is tied to the endorsement of a particular ethical framework. This *part* of the legitimacy community would seem to consider the existing (environmental) judiciary more relevant and responsive to its needs, if it moved closer to the ethics that the IRNT promotes. This proposal quite directly exposes the political bias in the existing adjudicative institutions, where the 'rights of nature' appear exotic and unreal. But the proposal is fundamentally problematic because it considers ethics as a uniform concept. This is a futile strategy in a pluralist international society, in which there are multiple, competing conceptions of righteousness, and especially in the ideologically divided environmental domain.[70] Not equating the verdicts of courts with justice may be the only meaningful explanation left to the IRNT.

4 Conclusion: Careful Broadening of the Examination of International Environmental Judiciary

The purpose of this chapter was to explore the contribution of the IRNT project to the debates about global judiciary. As the IRNT fails to fulfil some basic conditions to qualify as a 'tribunal' or 'court' (namely respect for fair procedure), the discussion of the involvement of the IRNT in the international judicial order is itself irrelevant. But the consideration of where exactly in the global structures to locate the IRNT nevertheless provides a convenient frame for thinking about the critiques

67 Interview, see n 38 above.

68 Stuart A Scheingold, *The Politics of Rights* (2nd edn, University of Michigan Press 1974), at 5.

69 ibid.

70 See for a focused discussion in the field of biodiversity, Jerneja Penca, 'Marketing the Market: The Ideology of Market Mechanisms in the Field of Biodiversity' (2013) 2 Transnational Environmental Law 235.

of the existing judiciary and its scholarship, as well as about parallel law-making endeavours in the transnational context.

The increased judicialization in the past two decades has diffused through every part of the society, including civil society advocacy with primary interests in law-making. Studying these transnational initiatives, such as the IRNT, introduces important conceptual and normative questions not only for those on the margins of international law, but also those more dogmatically oriented, who unexpectedly have to revisit the definition of a court. Surely, 'not everything that calls itself a court, is a court'.[71] But it is significant to examine why some initiatives claim legal authority, present themselves as courts, why some lawyers are involved in them, why legal concepts are used, and what implications that may have for transnational law. Disregarding the legal aspects of the IRNT and similar initiatives means not paying attention to the wider normative order, in which the courts operate and which is an important source of legal messages.

I have suggested viewing the IRNT as one articulation of expectations about international judiciary and international law that remain unfulfilled. The portrait of the IRNT can be considered as a portrait of a judicial institution that is, in the view of some, a missing piece in the structure of global judiciary. On this framing, the institution foremost invites us to rethink rules of access, reflect on moral foundations of international adjudication, and admit a bias in the officially valid (state-centred) law. On another view, the IRNT is an antidote to the judicial process. Instead of thinking seriously about a reform of the judicial process, it is interested in promoting an international debate on 'rights of nature' among the global environmental stakeholders and their implementation as an instrument of better protecting the environment. Both these activities are run on the established (state-centred) legal concept of courts and by mimicking its functioning.

Although the IRNT is not doing what we expect courts and tribunals to do (which could also be termed an abuse of the institution of a judicial process as we recognize it), the IRNT might have a point about the powerful and void concept of *a court*. Mirroring the dilemma concerning rights, there is something of a 'myth of courts' going on. The concept is eternally attractive because of the faith that it leads to justice and social change, but with doubtful evidence and even possibility that it actually does deliver.

The portrait of the IRNT is thus only a portrait of the continuity between dispute settlement and law-making. It unequivocally shows that litigation continues the unfinished legislation process and reflects the political struggles involved in developing environmental regimes. It does away with the view, which operates as a commonsense in a large part of the legal community (and is reflected in the structure of international law textbooks), that legislation and litigation belong to separate and relatively autonomous realms. The blurring of the legislative and judicial functions was demonstrated in the case of advisory jurisdictions,[72] and more explicitly in the

[71] Martti Koskenniemi, Keynote panel, ESIL Annual Conference, Oslo, 10 September 2015.

[72] See, eg, Karin Oellers-Frahm, 'Lawmaking Through Advisory Opinions' (2011) 12 German Law Journal 1033.

conversation on the legitimacy of courts.[73] This chapter suggests to continue challenging the image of courts' independence from the struggles on the law-making ground. One trigger for the study of the courts' location in global governance is the disputes that have not made it to the existing, official, or authoritative courts. Asking about the reasons for their exclusion from the analysis of the adjudication is one way of addressing the contours of adjudicative institutions.

[73] See Armin von Bogdandy and I Venzke, 'In Whose Name? An Investigation of International Courts' Public Authority and Its Democratic Justification' (2012) 23 European Journal of International Law 7, 19–23; Armin von Bogdandy, 'The Democratic Legitimacy of International Courts: A Conceptual Framework' (2013) 14 (2) Theoretical Inquiries in Law 361; Daniel Bodansky, 'Legitimacy in International Law and International Relations' in Jeffrey Dunoff and Mark Pollack (eds), *Interdisciplinary Perspectives on International Law and International Relations: The State of the Art*, 321–42 (CUP 2013); Nienke Grossman, 'The Normative Legitimacy of International Courts' (2013) 86 *Temple Law Review* 61.

4

Substance and Style—How the WTO Adjudicators Legitimize their Decisions

*Christiane Gerstetter**

1 Introduction**

The dispute settlement system (DSS) of the World Trade Organization (WTO) has been described as the 'most powerful dispute settlement system at the international level that we have today or perhaps ever in the history of the world'.[1] Its high level of activity makes the WTO DSS an important element of the multilateral trading system and international law more broadly. There is today consensus that the WTO's Appellate Body (AB) can be described as a court or at least a 'quasi-judicial'[2] entity which is, in relevant respects, similar to other international tribunals.[3] Thus, if one seeks to investigate the judicialization of international law, one cannot do so without looking at the WTO DSS.[4]

* Senior Fellow, Ecologic Institute (www.ecologic.eu).

** This chapter is based on a PhD thesis completed at the University of Bremen but not yet published: Christiane Gerstetter, 'Substance and Style: Judicial Decision-Making at the World Trade Organization (WTO) in "trade and ..." Cases' (unpublished draft version, University of Bremen 2015). The work on this chapter was essentially completed in summer 2015. Of the academic contributions published afterwards, Robert Howse, 'The World Trade Organization 20 Years On: Global Governance by Judiciary' (2016) 27 European Journal of International Law 9, as well as some of the commentaries on his article published in 27 European Journal of International Law (November 2016) were taken into account during revision as they are very closely related to some of the topics and arguments of this chapter. I wish to thank Andreas Føllesdal and Geir Ulfstein for their comments on an earlier version; all errors remain mine.

[1] Statement by Jackson during a panel discussion, see Yasuhei Taniguchi and others, 'Panel Discussion: Examining the Dispute Settlement System: How Has It Performed?' in Merit E Janow, Victoria Donaldson, and Alan Yanovich (eds), *The WTO: Governance, Dispute Settlement & Developing Countries* (Juris Publishing 2008) 388.

[2] See William J Davey, 'WTO Dispute Settlement: Segregating the Useful Political Aspects and Avoiding "Over-Legalization"' in Marco Bronckers and Reinhard Quick (eds), *New Directions in International Economic Law* (Kluwer Law International 2000) 293ff.

[3] Giorgio Sacerdoti, 'The Dispute Settlement System of the WTO in Action: A Perspective on the First Ten Years' in Alan Yanovich, Jan Bohanes, and Giorgio Sacerdoti (eds), *The WTO at Ten: The Contribution of the Dispute Settlement System* (CUP 2006) 42ff.

[4] I will in this chapter not describe in detail the institutional set up, procedural rules etc of the DSS, as many such descriptions exist already, see for example Kati Kulovesi, *The WTO Dispute Settlement System. Challenges of the Environment, Legitimacy and Fragmentation* (Wolters Kluwer 2011) 130ff.

I look in this chapter at how the WTO dispute settlement bodies legitimize their decisions and by implication also the WTO DSS as well as the WTO as an institution more broadly. 'Legitimacy' is neither easily defined nor measured. An established distinction is the one between legitimacy in a normative and an empirical sense. Legitimacy in a normative sense means that 'a claim of authority is well founded' or concerning its 'worthiness of acceptance'. Legitimacy in an empirical sense means actual acceptance of a norm, decision, or policy by relevant constituencies as normatively legitimate.[5] I will make clear in which of these senses 'legitimacy' and related terms will be used in the following where not evident from the context. As the title of this chapter implies, the underlying assumption of the present analysis is that the WTO judicial decision-makers actively legitimize their decisions, that is they (consciously or unconsciously) make and justify their decisions in a way that makes them legitimate, worthy of recognition, in the eyes of relevant actors and leads to their acceptance.

The focus of the analysis is on what I call 'trade and ...' or 'non-trade cases'. These are cases where the national measure under judicial scrutiny was—according to the WTO Member taking the measure—adopted in pursuit of public policy goals other than promoting trade. Typical examples are environmental or health measures. This focus is chosen, because the non-trade cases tend to pose the most serious legitimacy issues for the WTO DSS. This is linked to the fact that the WTO is seen by critics as (inappropriately) promoting trade at the expense of other public interests and preventing WTO Members from adopting regulatory measures in support of such interests. Therefore, WTO judicial cases where non-trade interests are at stake tend to receive more critical public attention than other types of cases. As a consequence, the need for legitimizing the WTO's judicial decisions is most pressing in these cases. Therefore, the approaches used by the WTO adjudicators for legitimizing their decisions should become visible in particular in the decisions made in non-trade cases.

I argue that two dimensions are relevant for understanding how judges legitimize judicial decisions:[6] the substantive outcomes of cases, that is who wins and loses and what interpretations are adopted, and the way a judicial decision is justified. A judicial outcome that is perceived as unjust or inappropriate or not in line with the law is likely not to gain the acceptance of relevant constituencies (ie the parties to a case), the actors using an international dispute settlement mechanism, communities of legal practitioners and academics, or the larger public. At the same time, a judicial decision that is poorly reasoned, refers to arguments that by conventional wisdom should not be relevant for a judicial decision, or is contradictory, is not likely to be

[5] See eg Daniel Bodansky, 'The Legitimacy of International Governance: A Coming Challenge for International Environmental Law?' (1999) 93 American Journal of International Law 596, 601; Markus Krajewski, 'Democratic Legitimacy and Constitutional Perspectives of WTO Law' (2001) 35 Journal of World Trade 167, 168.

[6] Generally, a third dimension that is relevant when looking at whether a court's decisions are accepted and deserve to be accepted is the procedural and institutional one, including such issues as how judges are selected. Yet these factors are beyond the control of the judicial body itself and will hence not be discussed in the following for the WTO DSS.

accepted, either. Therefore a court's judicial style, that is the type of arguments, the reasoning, and the rhetoric that a court uses, are important for legitimizing judicial decisions as well. These assumptions and insights are explained in section 2 of the chapter.

I will then look at each of the two dimensions described, the substantive outcome of WTO judicial proceedings (section 3) and the WTO's judicial style (section 4); in the present context, it is only possible to point to examples supporting my overall conclusions.

Concerning the substantive outcome (section 3), the research question is how the WTO dispute settlement bodies have in practice decided cases where non-trade issues were at stake. In these cases, is there a pattern that the WTO adjudicators favour trade and economic concerns over other regulatory objectives to an extent not required by the law? To assess whether WTO law requires a certain interpretation or whether there are defensible alternative interpretations, I will rely primarily on existing comments by legal observers, and on differences between Panel and AB reports. This approach is based on the assumption that WTO adjudicators could have defensibly interpreted the law in a different way if there are alternative interpretations that a number of renowned legal scholars or practitioners agree on. By implication, their actual interpretation must be considered a deliberate choice.

Section 4 is dedicated to selected aspects of the WTO's judicial style and explains how it contributes to legitimizing the WTO's judicial decisions. Section 5 develops the idea that WTO judicial decisions have indeed had a legitimizing effect so far, as indicated by the absence of far-reaching countermeasures by WTO Members.

2 Judicial Decision-making in Substance and in Style: Insights from Existing Research

In a simplifying statement one could say that more recent theories on judicial decision-making largely agree that law is—sometimes/often/usually—indeterminate and that hence judicial decision-makers have a—limited/certain/large—degree of discretion when deciding a case. In the present context, the law is described as 'indeterminate' to refer to a situation where it is not evident to a qualified legal professional acting in good faith, be it immediately or after some reflection, what the law mandates in a certain factual constellation. Indeterminacy is a matter of degree. For example, the term 'like products', contained for example in Art. III of the General Agreement on Tariffs and Trade (GATT), requires a significant degree of elaboration by the WTO adjudicators for a finding whether two products are actually 'like'. By contrast, a clause such as article II.1 b) GATT prohibiting tariffs in excess of the tariff levels defined in a WTO Member's tariff schedule is relatively determinate. The assumption that there are norms that are 'clear, self-executing, fully specified in advance and not in need of interpretation'[7] and others that are not is widely accepted.[8]

However, if one assumes that the law is indeterminate, at least to a degree, it cannot be the law alone that determines judicial decisions. What other factors motivate judicial decisions then? Scholars have given various answers to this question—not only at a theoretical level, but also empirically. The most important approach in the present context, mainly adopted by political scientists and applied to courts at the national as well as international levels, perceives courts as rational and strategic actors that seek to maintain and enhance their own legitimacy, authority, and power.[9] An international court, it is argued, should not be expected to take decisions that are not liked by those having some form of control over the respective court, in the case of an international court the states that created it. Taking such decisions could lead to a legislative backlash, that is a legislative overturn of certain decisions taken or a permanent clipping of the court's wings by changing its mandate or cutting its funding.[10] In other cases, a court might not be motivated by fear of legislative roll-back, but—in particular in international law—by fear that the parties might not comply with a ruling.[11] Frequent non-compliance would also weaken a court's normative and empirical legitimacy.

With regard to the WTO, Kelemen has undertaken a study on a limited number of cases involving environmental measures. He finds that where legal indeterminacy is relatively pronounced and the political threat posed by a state's or a group of states' potential defiance to a certain outcome is great, both the WTO dispute settlement bodies and the European Court of Justice (ECJ)[12] are likely to yield to

[7] Joel P Trachtman, 'The Domain of WTO Dispute Resolution' (1999) 40 Harvard International Law Journal 333, 338 <http://www.wto.org/english/forums_e/public_forum2007_e/session2_trachtman_e.pdf> who draws on the distinction between rules and standards developed in the law and economics literature.

[8] Herbert LA Hart, *The Concept of Law* (2nd edn, Clarendon 1994) 124–35 describes at some length the 'open texture' of law; Ronald Dworkin, *Taking Rights Seriously* (Duckworth 1981) 83 speaks of 'hard cases', in which 'no settled rule dictates a decision either way'; Jürgen Habermas, *Faktizität und Geltung: Beiträge zur Diskurstheorie des Rechts* (Suhrkamp 1992) 266 writes that all legal norms with the exception of a few highly specified ones, are originally (*von Haus aus*) indeterminate.

[9] See eg Alec Stone Sweet, *The Judicial Construction of Europe* (OUP 2004) 20; Robert D Cooter and Thomas B Ginsburg, 'Comparative Judicial Discretion: An Empirical Test of Economic Models' (1996) 16 International Review of Law and Economics 295 <http://works.bepress.com/robert_cooter/28/>; Fuad Zarbiyev, 'Judicial Activism in International Law—A Conceptual Framework for Analysis' (2012) 3 Journal of International Dispute Settlement 1, 9f, 17ff.

[10] See Jared Wessel, 'Judicial Policy-Making at the International Criminal Court: An Institutional Guide to Analyzing International Adjudication' (2006) 44 Columbia Journal of Transnational Law 377, 382.

[11] Alec Stone Sweet and Thomas L Brunell, 'Trustee Courts and the Judicialization of International Regimes: The Politics of Majoritarian Activism in the European Convention on Human Rights, the European Union, and the World Trade Organization' (2013) 1 Journal of Law and Courts 61, 67.

[12] With the Lisbon Treaty, the name of the Court has changed to 'Court of Justice of the European Union' which is usually abbreviated CJEU. In this work, I still use the old terminology, given that the events and cases I refer to are mostly from the pre-Lisbon era.

the political pressure.[13] Garrett and McCall Smith argue that there is evidence, based on the analysis of a limited number of cases, that at least partially supports the hypothesis that when the defendant in a WTO case is a powerful state, the dispute settlement bodies are more likely to rule in favour of the defendant than in other cases.[14] Stone Sweet and Brunell find that the AB seeks to identify consensus among WTO Members on the legal issues at hand and then orients its decision along these lines. At the same time, the authors also conclude that the AB engages in such a strategy less often than other courts like the ECJ and the European Court of Human Rights (ECtHR); they relate this to the different mandate of the WTO.[15] A similar account is provided by Knox, who argues that the AB's 'incorporation of moderate environmental proposals' into its jurisprudence stems from a desire to win support for its decisions from the WTO Membership.[16] Another scholar, Krüger, states the following:

> [I]n its efforts to strengthen its own position and that of the WTO in general, while similarly avoiding political opposition and noncompliance, the AB will leave its generally conservative stance towards interpretation and activism only in the wake of a certain degree of member state support.[17]

Yet does the fact that courts' decisions are partially motivated by other factors than the wording of the law, when the latter allows several interpretations, also mean that courts would be explicit about these non-legal factors motivating their decisions? The answer depends on the courts and the position of the scholar studying judicial decision-making, and is somewhere between 'not at all' and 'only partially'. A poignant formulation to describe the first position has been coined by Shapiro who states: 'Courts and judges always lie.'[18] The use of the term 'lying' is provocative, because it has connotations of bad faith and someone intentionally not telling the truth. Yet one does not have to go as far: The fact that judges do not make explicit in their judgments how non-legal factors motivate a decision is due to professional norms as well as concepts of the appropriate role of judges (as opposed to law-makers). In some legal orders the latter are also incorporated in explicit legal rules. The arguments that a judge can give in a judicial decision are part of what Bourdieu calls a 'field'. There is an 'internal logic of juridical functioning, which (…) constrains the range of possible actions'.[19]

[13] R Daniel Kelemen, 'The Limits of Judicial Power: Trade-Environment Disputes in the GATT/WTO and the EU' (2001) 34 Comparative Political Studies 622.

[14] Geoffrey Garrett and James McCall Smith, 'The Politics of WTO Dispute Settlement' (UCLA International Institute 2002) 44f <http://escholarship.org/uc/item/4t4952d7#page-1>.

[15] Sweet and Brunell (n 11) 85.

[16] John H Knox, 'The Judicial Resolution of Conflicts between Trade and the Environment' (2004) 28 Harvard Environmental Law Review 1, 3, 47ff.

[17] Tilman Krüger, 'Strategic Litigation in the World Trade Organization' (Doctoral thesis, microfiche version, University of Bremen 2013) 57.

[18] Martin Shapiro, 'Judges As Liars' (1994) 17 Harvard Journal of Law & Public Policy 155, 156.

[19] Pierre Bourdieu, 'The Force of Law: Toward a Sociology of the Juridical Field' (1986) 38 Hastings Law Journal 805, 816.

By implication, judges have been said to 'always aim to generate a particular rhetorical effect (…): that of legal necessity of their solutions without regard to ideology'.[20] Other commentators have offered similar conclusions.[21]

Thus, judges may be motivated by the best of intentions when deciding not to mention for example the politics behind a given judicial decision in the written judgment. Moreover, in cases where the law is relatively determinate the wording of the law (in conjunction with precedents and established rules on legal interpretation) is likely to be indeed the main driver behind a judicial decision. In order to legitimize their decisions, to not be criticized as being 'activist' and win the acceptance of the relevant constituencies courts tend to produce judicial decisions that look as if the law determined the outcome of the case even when it did not.

Yet this statement applies to different courts to varying degrees; courts have different judicial styles. Such styles have been investigated by Lasser who focuses on the French *Cour de Cassation*, the ECJ, and the United States (US) Supreme Court. Although all of these courts have a functionally equivalent position within the respective legal system, their judgments differ fundamentally in style or what Lasser calls 'models of judicial control, debate and legitimacy'.[22] At the one extreme, the French court[23] publishes very short, impersonal judgments in which the decision is presented as resulting immediately and inevitably from the wording of the law by manner of syllogistic deductions. Discussions of more political or normative aspects are confined to the interaction of the different judicial players in the courtroom and do not appear in the judgments. The explanation of the judgments with a view to doctrinal as well as social and political consequences is left to academic observers. The US Supreme Court, as the other extreme, produces long decisions and strives to make the reasons for taking them transparent to the utmost degree. The US judicial style incorporates two kinds of discourse: a formal legal discourse and a more socially-responsive, equity-oriented one. An intermediate position is occupied by the ECJ. Originating in the French tradition the court's judgments are comparatively short and rather formalist, textualist in style. However, one particular feature of the ECJ's jurisprudence is the Court's teleological approach of frequently justifying decisions with reference to the overall objectives of the European legal and political order. The centrality of the overall objectives of the European Union (EU) legal order in the ECJ's reasoning is in part indebted, according to Lasser, to the existence of the

[20] Duncan Kennedy, *A Critique of Adjudication {fin de Siècle}* (Harvard University Press 1997) 2.

[21] Armin von Bogdandy and Ingo Venzke, 'Beyond Dispute: International Judicial Institutions as Lawmakers' in Armin von Bogdandy and Ingo Venzke (eds), *International Judicial Lawmaking: On Public Authority and Democratic Legitimation in Global Governance* (Springer 2012) 10; Gunnar Beck, *The Legal Reasoning of the European Court of Justice* (Hart 2012) 19; Zarbiyev (n 9) 29.

[22] Mitchel Lasser, *Judicial Deliberations—A Comparative Analysis of Judicial Transparency and Legitimacy* (OUP 2004); Mitchel Lasser, 'Anticipating Three Models of Judicial Control, Debate and Legitimacy: The European Court of Justice, the Cour de Cassation and the United States Supreme Court' (2003) Jean Monnet Working Paper 1/03 <http://centers.law.nyu.edu/jeanmonnet/archive/papers/03/030101.html>.

[23] The Cour de Cassation is the highest court in France and unique in that it is the only such court in France, with responsibility for civil, criminal, or other cases, see 'The Role of the Court of Cassation' at the court's website, <http://www.courdecassation.fr/about_the_court_9256.html>.

Advocate General. The tone of the Advocate General's reasoning is much more subjective and policy-oriented than that of the ECJ, and the Advocate General's opinions also take scholarly doctrines into account. Therefore, they draw attention to the fact that the decision of the ECJ represents a choice; it is incumbent upon the Court to justify that choice—and it does so by resorting to *telos*. As this overview shows, the line between the judicial and the political realms, marking what is a permissible legal and judicial argument, varies between different jurisdictions and courts. Moreover, the line between the judicial and the political may change its position over time.[24]

These theoretical and empirical insights have two important implications for WTO judicial decision-making: first, it is indeed plausible to assume that the WTO dispute settlement bodies are actors that, faced with the indeterminacy of WTO law, make deliberate choices between different legally defensible interpretations of WTO law and hence between different substantive outcomes. Second, we cannot necessarily expect to find the real reasons for why a certain decision was taken in the dispute settlement reports; conversely, we can expect to see a distinct WTO judicial style of justifying the decisions taken.

3 WTO Judicial Decision-making in Non-trade Cases: Substance

This section discusses how WTO law has been interpreted in non-trade cases so far and to what extent the AB's interpretations have been more restrictive or less restrictive of WTO Members' regulatory freedom as compared to possible alternative interpretations suggested, among others, in legal scholarship. As it is not possible to give a comprehensive overview of all non-trade cases and interpretations offered therein so far in this chapter, examples relating to the interpretation and application of WTO provisions that have played a key role so far in non-trade cases are provided.

3.1 Interpretations favouring the regulatory autonomy of WTO Members

A few important interpretations that the AB has adopted and that in comparison with alternative possible interpretations broaden the regulatory leeway of WTO Members to regulate in favour of various non-trade goals are the following.[25]

First, the AB has not subscribed to the view that exceptions to the trade discipline should *eo ipso* be construed narrowly. It rejected such an understanding explicitly in *Hormones I*, for example.[26] As the exception provisions allow WTO Members

[24] Claus-Dieter Ehlermann and Nicolas Lockhart, 'Standard of Review in WTO Law' (2004) 7 Journal of International Economic Law 491, 493.

[25] A more extensive overview of examples can be found in Robert Howse, 'The World Trade Organization 20 Years On: Global Governance by Judiciary' (2016) 27 European Journal of International Law 9, 46f.

[26] WTO Appellate Body, *European Communities: Measures Concerning Meat and Meat Products* (16 January 1998) WT/DS26/AB/R and WT/DS48/AB/R [104]; by contrast, the ECJ interprets exceptions narrowly, see Armin von Bogdandy, 'Law and Politics in the WTO: Strategies to Cope with a Deficient Relationship' (2001) 5 Max Planck Yearbook of United Nations Law 609, 665f.

to deviate from the trade-liberalizing disciplines of WTO law, this approach tends to favour the regulatory autonomy of WTO Members seeking to pursue non-trade objectives, but would negatively affect other countries' trade-related interests.

Generally, the regulatory objectives as mentioned in the exception clauses in Art. XX GATT and Art. XIV GATS that allow WTO Members to take measures pursuing certain regulatory goals that are otherwise inconsistent with the GATT/GATS, have been interpreted in a rather expansive manner;[27] in other words, showing that a measure falls within the range of policies permitted by one of the sub-paragraphs is relatively easy.[28] For example, the morals clause contained in Art. XX(a) GATT and Art. XIV GATS has been interpreted in broad terms in at least one respect: These clauses can textually be read to allow measures that give 'force to intrinsic moral institutions or shared values',[29] which may relate to circumstances outside of the territory of the country invoking the public morals exception. In the EU Seals case, the controversial measure was an EU ban on the import of seal products. The issue was not that within the EU a large part of the population was involved in hunting seals; citizens were concerned about what happened elsewhere. In other words, the EU measure was outward-directed, not inward-directed.[30] It has been suggested that WTO law should be interpreted to allow only the latter category of measures under Art. XX(a) GATT.[31] Yet other commentators[32]—and ultimately the AB[33]—have rejected this view. On this aspect, the AB has consequently not embraced the most 'pro-trade' interpretation conceivable.

Another example of an interpretation favouring the regulatory autonomy of WTO Members is the interpretation of 'relating to' in Art. XX(g) GATT. In earlier Panel reports, this phrase had been interpreted to mean 'directly aimed at'[34] and

[27] Panagiotis Delimatsis, 'Protecting Public Morals in a Digital Age: Revisiting the WTO Rulings on US—Gambling and China—Publications and Audiovisual Products' (2011) 14 Journal of International Economic Law 257, 261 who claims that the dispute settlement bodies' interpretation goes 'beyond the ordinary meaning or the negotiators' intent'.

[28] See for example Christopher Doyle, 'Gimme Shelter: The Necessary Element of GATT Article XX in the Context of the China—Audiovisual Products Case' (2011) 29 Boston University International Law Journal 143, 153.

[29] Robert Howse and Joanna Langille, 'Permitting Pluralism: The Seal Products Dispute and Why the WTO Should Accept Trade Restrictions Justified by Noninstrumental Moral Values' (2011) 37 Yale Journal of International Law 367, 412.

[30] For this distinction, see Mark Wu, 'Free Trade and the Protection of Public Morals: An Analysis of the Newly Emerging Public Morals Clause Doctrine' (2008) 33 Yale Journal of International Law 215, 216; the author himself proposes, however, a distinction between three categories of measures: (1) measures safeguarding the morals of inhabitants of the country taking the measures; (2) measures aimed at those producing a product or rendering a service; and (3) restrictions aimed at products or services in an exporting state involving actions morally offensive to the importing state, but where these practices are not directly involved in the production of the products or services banned, see 235.

[31] ibid 243 seems to prefer this narrow interpretation over others.

[32] For a discussion of Wu's position, see Howse and Langille (n 29) 414f.

[33] The AB accepted that the EU's trade restrictions relating to seal products could in principle be justified under Art. XX GATT, see WTO Appellate Body, *European Communities: Measures Prohibiting the Importation and Marketing of Seal Products* (22 May 2014) WT/DS400/AB/R and WT/DS401/AB/R [5.131ff].

[34] WTO Panel, *United States: Standards for Reformulated and Conventional Gasoline* (29 January 1996) WT/DS2/R [6.39f].

hence involved a rather strict standard, which does not result in a compelling manner from the wording of WTO law.[35] However, this standard was explicitly given up in *China—Raw Materials*.[36] As a consequence, Art. XX(g) GATT presents, as things stand, the more lenient standard to pass as compared to Art. XX(b) GATT.[37]

The interpretation offered by the AB on Art. 3 SPS (Sanitary and Phytosanitary Agreement) also makes it easier for Members to adopt SPS measures than, for example, the Panel's approach in *Hormones I* would have done. The AB stated that the terms 'base on' and 'conform to' in Art. 3.1 SPS and 3.2 SPS needed to be interpreted differently.[38] The interpretation of the term 'based on' in Art. 5.1 SPS that the AB has embraced also gives WTO Members broader space for SPS measures than, for example, the Panel's approach in *Hormones I* would have done. The AB has done away with the additional procedural or subjective requirement that the risk assessment actually must have been taken into account by the WTO Member adopting a measure and embraced a more objective reading.[39] Several scholars consider this objective requirement easier to satisfy.[40]

3.2 Interpretations favouring trade liberalization

By contrast, there are also some important interpretative decisions of the AB that narrow the space for regulatory action by WTO Members in pursuit of non-trade objectives.

One example is the jurisprudence on the possibility to rely on the exceptions contained in Art. XX GATT to justify violations of agreements other than the GATT. The AB has only dealt with this question in relation to violations of China's Accession Protocol. In one case it decided that Art. XX GATT could justify a departure from one of the provisions of China's Accession Protocol, as a reference to China's 'right to regulate trade in a manner consistent with the WTO Agreement' was contained in that provision. The AB concluded that this clause was a reference to 'the WTO Agreement as a whole, including its Annexes'.[41] One of the Annexes of the WTO Agreement is the GATT 1994, which according to its Art. 1 'consists of' the GATT

[35] Brandon L Bowen, 'The World Trade Organization and Its Interpretation of the Article XX: Exceptions to the General Agreement on Tariffs and Trade, in the Light of Recent Developments' (2000) 29 Georgia Journal of International and Comparative Law 181, 185.

[36] WTO Appellate Body, *China: Measures Related to the Exportation of Various Raw Materials* (7 August 2014) WT/DS394/AB/R, WT/DS395/AB/R and WT/DS398/AB/R [356].

[37] Bradly J Condon, 'GATT Article XX and Proximity of Interest: Determining the Subject Matter of Paragraphs B and G' (2004) 9 UCLA Journal of International Law and Public Affairs 137, 12; Arthur E Appleton, 'Shrimp/turtle: Untangling the Nets' (1999) 2 Journal of International Economic Law 447, 482.

[38] *European Communities: Measures Concerning Meat and Meat Product* (n 26) [163].

[39] ibid 189.

[40] See for a brief overview of the literature Lukasz Gruszczynski, 'The Role of Science in Risk Regulation under the SPS Agreement' (European University Institute 2006) EUI Law Working Paper 2006/03 19.

[41] WTO Appellate Body: *China—Measures Affecting Trading Rights and Distribution Services for Certain Publications and Audiovisual Entertainment Products* (21 December 2009) WT/DS363/AB/R [222].

1947 with its Art. XX GATT, among others. In consequence, China could invoke Art. XX GATT in defence of a certain measure if 'the measure has a clearly discernible, objective link to the regulation of trade in the goods at issue'.[42] By contrast, in a later case where no such reference was contained in China's Accession Protocol, the AB declined to apply Art. XX GATT to another provision in China's Accession Protocol.[43] Therefore, some commentators read the AB to say that Art. XX GATT defences are generally only available outside of GATT where there is explicit language to this effect.[44] If that was the correct reading of the AB's line of reasoning—which is not clear, given that the relevant appellate cases dealt with a violation of China's Accession Protocol only—this would mean that the AB is more restrictive in its application of Art. XX GATT than at least some commentators suggest. It has also been proposed that the AB could acceptably have been more 'courageous' and adopted, in the Chinese cases, a less limiting interpretation on the applicability of Art. XX GATT.[45] With regard to the applicability of Art. XX GATT to other WTO agreements, a non-governmental organization coalition argued in an *amicus curiae* brief that Art. XX GATT should be applicable to justify breaches of the Agreement on Subsidies and Countervailing Measures (SCM).[46] Others have pointed out that denying a WTO Member the right to rely on Art. XX GATT 'tarnishes' the legitimacy of the WTO.[47]

Moreover, the chapeau of Art. XX GATT has also been applied in a rather strict way. For example, the Panel's approach towards interpreting the chapeau in *Brazil—Tyres* would have given WTO Members greater regulatory freedom than the AB's.[48] The outcome of the relevant cases is an indicator for how restrictive or lenient the chapeau's application is. With *Brazil—Tyres* and *EC—Seal Products*, there are by now two cases where a measure satisfied the conditions of one of the sub-paragraphs, but was thereafter held to violate the chapeau of Art. XX GATT by the AB because of exception provisions in the respective measures. In both cases, a general ban on the importation of certain products contained some exceptions. In other words, if these measures had not contained the exceptions and had been *more* trade-restrictive, they might have been justified under Art. XX GATT on the basis of the reasoning

[42] ibid [230].

[43] See *China: Measures Related to the Exportation of Various Raw Materials* (n 36) [284ff].

[44] Ilaria Espa, 'The AB Approach to the Applicability of Article XX GATT in the Light of China—Raw Materials: A Missed Opportunity?' (2012) 46 Journal of World Trade 1399, 1407.

[45] ibid 1420; Bin Gu, 'Applicability of GATT Article XX in China—Raw Materials: A Clash within the WTO Agreement' (2012) 15 Journal of International Economic Law 1007; Wenwei Guan, 'How General Should the GATT General Exceptions Be?: A Critique of the "Common Intention" Approach of Treaty Interpretation' (2014) 48 Journal of World Trade 219, 225ff.

[46] International Institute for Sustainable Development (IISD), Canadian Environmental Law Association (CELA) and Ecojustice Canada, 'Amicus Curiae Submission before the Panel Canada—Certain Measures Affecting the Renewable Energy Generation Sector (DS412)' 6ff <https://www.iisd.org/pdf/2012/ecojustice_amicus_curiae_brief.pdf>.

[47] Marco Bronckers and Keith E Maskus, 'China—Raw Materials: A Controversial Step towards Evenhanded Exploitation of Natural Resources' (2014) 13 World Trade Review 393, 402 <http://journals.cambridge.org/article_S1474745614000032> accessed 14 November 2014.

[48] Arwel Davies, 'Interpreting the Chapeau of GATT Art. XX in Light of the "New" Approach in Brazil Tyres' (2009) 43 Journal of World Trade 507, 522.

of the AB. In both cases, the exceptions were considered not to be justified, among others, because the rationale behind them was not connected to the regulatory goal as recognized in one of the sub-paragraphs of Art. XX GATT.[49] Yet in real-world policy-making a measure restricting or forbidding certain behaviour will often contain exceptions to avoid negative impacts on certain constituencies. An approach to interpreting and applying WTO law that considers policies illegal that are the outcome of normal political bargaining and serve different policy objectives at the same time, can only be classified as restrictive of WTO Members' regulatory freedom. With regard to *EC—Seal Products*, several eminent commentators had voiced the opinion that the EU's measure was not WTO-inconsistent in analyses published before the AB report. In their view, even if a violation of GATT was to be found (contrary to what they argued should be the result), the controversial EU measure could be justified under Art. XX GATT.[50] This is a good indicator that the AB's approach to interpreting and applying the chapeau of Art. XX GATT is unnecessarily restrictive of WTO Members' regulatory freedom.

3.3 Conclusion

The conclusion is that so far the case law is rather mixed in terms of the substantive interpretations adopted by the AB.[51] Yet it is noteworthy that statistically speaking the defendants lost in more than 80 per cent of the cases, including non-trade cases.[52] This implies that the defendants lose for other reasons than the way WTO law is interpreted in dispute settlement; one reason might be the way that WTO law is applied to the facts of the case.

Can this outcome be considered to constitute a deliberate and strategic choice of the AB Members? Obviously, only statements by the AB itself, either in the dispute settlement decisions or in an extra-curial capacity, would provide conclusive evidence. Indeed, there are some statements in AB reports indicating that the

[49] *European Communities: Measures Prohibiting the Importation and Marketing of Seal Products* (n 33) [5.320]; WTO Appellate Body, *Brazil: Measures Affecting Imports of Retreaded Tyres, WT/DS332/AB/R* (3 December 2007) [227f].

[50] Howse and Langille (n 29) 411ff; Christian Pitschas and Hannes Schloemann, 'WTO Compatibility of the EU Seal Regime: Why Public Morality Is Enough (but May Not Be Necessary)' (Transnational Economic Law Research Center, Martin-Luther-University 2012) Beiträge zum Transnationalen Wirtschaftsrecht 118 18ff <http://telc.jura.uni-halle.de/sites/default/files/BeitraegeTWR/Heft118.pdf>.

[51] By contrast, Howse (n 25) seems to hold the view that the Appellate Body has adopted a more general judicial policy of deference to national regulation, see for example 13. This assumption is criticized, eg, by Petros C Mavroidis, 'The Gang that Couldn't Shoot Straight: The Not So Magnificent Seven of the WTO Appellate Body' (2016) 27 European Journal of International Law 1107, 1108 who argues that the Appellate Body 'has not adopted a consistent standard of review across domestic instruments and has outlawed many of them on shaky evidence'.

[52] Juscelino F Colares, 'A Theory of WTO Adjudication: From Empirical Analysis to Biased Rule Development' (2009) 42 Vanderbilt Journal of Transnational Law 383, 402ff; John Maton and Carolyn Maton, 'Independence under Fire: Extra-Legal Pressures and Coalition Building in WTO Dispute Settlement' (2007) 10 Journal of International Economic Law 317, 326ff; Sweet and Brunell (n 11) 82.

adjudicators reflect upon what would be a prudent decision in a certain case[53] and there are also some out-of-the courtroom statements to this end.[54] However, such statements are infrequent. Yet even in the absence of 'hard' evidence, it is plausible to assume that the observed pattern of outcomes is not merely accidental—it is too pronounced for that to be the case.

Indeed, many commentators share the view that at least some of the WTO's judicial decisions must be understood as astute and politically responsive judicial drafting that does not favour any of the two sides too much and avoids issues that could be too controversial.[55] For example, with regard to the *EC—Biotech Products* case, the Panel's approach of not considering the EU's moratorium on genetically modified organisms an SPS 'measure' and by implication not reviewing it under the SPS Agreement's science-related disciplines has been interpreted as a deliberate move to eschew scientifically and politically controversial issues.[56] A somewhat different account is that the WTO dispute settlement bodies, at least in some cases, have opted for a 'procedural' approach, that is, deciding a case on other grounds than finding a violation of a substantive obligation.[57] Procedural 'solutions' to WTO controversies are likely to generally provoke less controversy than cases revolving around a finding of a substantive violation; procedural flaws of a measure can often be remedied without modifying the essence of a measure.[58]

4 WTO Judicial Decision-making: The Style

Some aspects of the WTO's judicial style are very obvious: notably the length of the reports and the great level of detail with which the arguments of parties are summarized as well as the habit of the adjudicators to clarify, often at the end of the

[53] WTO Panel, *European Communities: Measures Affecting the Approval and Marketing of Biotech Products* (29 September 2006) WT/DS291/R, WT/DS292/R and WT/DS293/R [7.89]; *European Communities—Measures Concerning Meat and Meat Products* (n 26) [123].

[54] For a compilation of some of these quotes, see Howse (n 25) 25f.

[55] For statements coming in this category see Gilbert R Winham, 'International Regime Conflict in Trade and Environment: The Biosafety Protocol and the WTO' (2003) 2 World Trade Review 131, 140 on *Hormones I*; Andrew Thomison, 'New and Controversial Mandate for the SPS Agreement—The WTO Panel's Interim Report in the E.C.-Biotech Dispute' (2007) 32 Columbia Journal of Environmental Law 287, 297 for *EC—Biotech Products*; Sarah Lieberman and Tim Gray, 'The World Trade Organization's Report on the EU's Moratorium on Biotech Products: The Wisdom of the US Challenge to the EU in the WTO' (2008) 8 Global Environmental Politics 33, 48.

[56] Alexia Herwig, 'Whither Science in WTO Dispute Settlement?' (2008) 21 Leiden Journal of International Law 823, 834.

[57] See eg Gregory Shaffer, 'A Structural Theory of WTO Dispute Settlement: Why Institutional Choice Lies at the Heart of the GMO Dispute' (2009) 41 International Law and Politics 1, 35 with regard to the Panel's *EC—Biotech Products* decision; Bernard Hoekman and Joel Trachtman, 'Continued Suspense: EC—Hormones and WTO Disciplines on Discrimination and Domestic Regulation Appellate Body Reports: Canada/United States—Continued Suspension of Obligations in the EC—Hormones Dispute, WT/DS320/AB/R,WT/DS321/AB/R, Adopted 14 November 2008' (2010) 9 World Trade Review 151, 160 for the *Hormones II* case.

[58] This point is made for example by Howse (n 25), 66f.

decisions, what they did not decide or did not mean to say.[59] In the following, I will discuss three more salient aspects of the WTO's judicial style that are important for understanding how the WTO adjudicators legitimize their decisions. Yet, it is important to keep in mind that these are not the only features defining the WTO's judicial style. Other defining aspects I have analysed elsewhere[60] include the use of balancing language to arrive at a decision, the standard of review, and the role of international law in the interpretation of WTO law.

4.1 Methods of interpretation

First, the methods of interpretation are an obvious part of a court's judicial style. Literal or textual interpretation is the most prominent among the methods of interpretation used in WTO dispute settlement. Many passages can be cited in which the adjudicators' first step is to ascertain the literal meaning of a word or phrase.[61] In WTO dispute settlement practice textual interpretation is often performed with the help of a dictionary. The AB often provides definitions of terms that are neither controversial between the parties nor prima facie unclear:

- 'generalized' schemes had the sense that schemes 'apply more generally; [or] become extended in application';[62]
- a 'legitimate objective' is a 'target that is lawful, justifiable or proper';[63]
- a 'restriction' is 'something that restricts someone or something, a limitation on action, a limiting condition or regulation';[64]
- competitive means 'characterized by competition' and 'substitutable' means 'able to be substituted';[65]
- 'trade seems to refer, generally, to commerce between nations';[66]
- 'normally' is defined as 'under normal or ordinary conditions; as a rule'.[67]

[59] See for example *European Communities: Measures Affecting the Approval and Marketing of Biotech Products* (n 53) [8.3]; WTO Appellate Body, *United States: Import Prohibition of Certain Shrimp and Shrimp Products* (12 October 1998) WT/DS58/AB/R [185].

[60] Christiane Gerstetter, 'Substance and Style: Judicial Decision-Making at the World Trade Organization (WTO) in "trade and . . ." Cases' (unpublished draft version, University of Bremen 2015).

[61] See eg WTO Appellate Body, *United States: Standards for Reformulated and Conventional Gasoline* (29 April 1996) WT/DS2/AB/R [III C, at 20 and n 40]; WTO Appellate Body, *Korea: Measures Affecting Imports of Fresh, Chilled and Frozen Beef* (11 December 2000) WT/DS161/AB/R and WT/DS169/AB/R [161].

[62] WTO Appellate Body, *European Communities: Conditions for the Granting of Tariff Preferences to Developing Countries* (7 April 2004), WT/DS246/AB/R [155].

[63] WTO Appellate Body, *United States: Measures Concerning the Importation, Marketing and Sale of Tuna and Tuna Products* (16 May 2012) WT/DS381/AB/R [313].

[64] ibid [319].

[65] WTO Appellate Body, *Korea: Taxes on Alcoholic Beverages* (18 January 1999) WT/DS75AB/R and WT/DS84/AB/R [116].

[66] *China: Measures Affecting Trading Rights and Distribution Services for Certain Publications and Audiovisual Entertainment Products* (n 41) [220].

[67] WTO Appellate Body, *United States: Measures Affecting the Production and Sale of Clove Cigarettes* (4 April 2012) WT/DS406/AB/R [273].

There is nothing wrong with any of these definitions, but they do not yield any insights that could not just as easily have been inferred from the term used in the treaty itself.

Many see the particular way in which the WTO dispute settlement bodies use the established methods of treaty interpretation as an attempt at winning acceptance for their decisions.[68] I see no reason to disagree with this analysis. Literal interpretation is generally the method of interpretation allowing a judicial entity to present itself as an interpreter of the law, rather than the creator of law, at least where the text is relatively determinate.[69] Therefore literal interpretation is the least risky option for the AB.[70] By using it, the adjudicators can appear as adhering to the intention of the WTO negotiators.[71] An aspect of the AB's judicial reasoning that supports such a reading is the frequent reference to dictionary definitions that do not make things any clearer than the original text: If the dictionary definitions are obviously not used to clarify a controversial term, because they do not provide such clarification, there must be a different rationale for using them so frequently. Legitimizing the judicial decisions taken is clearly a promising explanation for the excessive and unnecessary reference to dictionaries.[72]

4.2 Use of precedents

A second important element of an (international) court's judicial style is the way it uses precedents.[73]

The AB has stated repeatedly that interpretations developed in WTO case law are binding only on the parties to a dispute.[74] Yet the practice of the WTO dispute

[68] See eg Caroline Henckels, 'GMOs in the WTO: A Critique of the Panel's Legal Reasoning' (2006) 7 Melbourne Journal of International Law 278, 284; Knox (n 16) 48ff; William Magnuson, 'WTO Jurisprudence & Its Critiques: The Appellate Body's Anti-Constitutional Resistance' (2010) 51 Harvard International Law Journal Online 121, 123f <http://www.harvardilj.org/wp-content/uploads/2010/09/HILJ-Online_51_Magnuson.pdf>; Yuval Shany and Sivan Shlomo-Agon, 'The WTO Dispute Settlement System' in Yuval Shany (ed), *Assessing the Effectiveness of International Courts* (OUP 2014) 206; Joseph HH Weiler, 'The Rule of Lawyers and the Ethos of Diplomats: Reflections on the Internal and External Legitimacy of WTO Dispute Settlement' (2001) 35 Journal of World Trade 191, 206; Isabelle van Damme, 'Treaty Interpretation by the WTO Appellate Body' (2010) 21 European Journal of International Law 605, 641ff.

[69] Beck (n 21) 149f.

[70] Claus-Dieter Ehlermann, 'Reflections on the AB of the WTO' (2003) 6 Journal of International Economic Law 695, 699.

[71] Hélène Ruiz Fabri, 'Drawing a Line of Equilibrium in a Complex World' in Alan Yanovich, Jan Bohanes, and Giorgio Sacerdoti (eds), *The WTO at Ten: The Contribution of the Dispute Settlement System* (CUP 2006) 132.

[72] For a similar point see David Pavot, 'The Use of Dictionary by the WTO Appellate Body: Beyond the Search of Ordinary Meaning' (2013) 4 Journal of International Dispute Settlement 29, 37f.

[73] Obviously, there are differences in the use of precedents in common law and civil law systems. These differences are, however, not relevant when looking at international courts which are called upon to interpret international agreements.

[74] See eg *United States: Measures Affecting the Production and Sale of Clove Cigarettes* (n 67) [258] with references to earlier reports.

settlement bodies has been described as '*de facto stare decisis*'.[75] AB reports have been described as having almost the same 'stature' as precedents in common law.[76] The AB has made clear that Panels have to take into account earlier AB reports in order to guarantee 'consistency and stability' in the interpretation of WTO agreements.[77]

Generally, AB reports are cited more frequently than Panel reports.[78] In some cases, Panels and parties seem to rely on certain formulations coined by the AB almost as if they were legal rules. For example, in *EU—Seal Products* the Panel argued that in the case of trade-restrictive measures the contribution of a measure to the end pursued needed to be at least 'apt' to make a 'material' contribution, in order to be justified under Art. XX(a) GATT.[79] With this, it took up an earlier similar formulation from the AB's *Brazil—Tyres* report. The AB rejected this approach, indicating that its earlier formulation had been a result of the specific circumstances of the case and was not to be taken as a generally applicable standard.[80]

The most puzzling aspect about the use of precedents in WTO case law is not how often earlier cases have been used, but how. In some cases, the very fact that a past WTO dispute settlement decision contains a certain interpretation of WTO law seems to be enough for the WTO judicial decision-makers for justifying a later decision—even if the earlier case does not actually support the finding it is invoked for. For example, in *Korea—Beef*, the AB coined its by now famous formula for interpreting the requirement that a measure needs to be necessary for the regulatory objective pursued which is contained in various sub-paragraphs of Art. XX GATT and Art. XIV GATS:

> It seems to us that a treaty interpreter assessing a measure claimed to be necessary to secure compliance of a WTO-consistent law or regulation may, in appropriate cases, take into account the relative importance of the common interests or values that the law or regulation to be enforced is intended to protect. The more vital or important those common interests or values are, the easier it would be to accept as 'necessary' a measure designed as an enforcement instrument.[81]

Almost the only way that the AB justified its way of interpreting the necessity requirement in Art. XX(d) GATT was by presenting it as being nothing more than

[75] Raj Bhala, 'The Myth about Stare Decisis and International Trade Law (part One of a Trilogy)' (1999) 14 American University International Law Review 845, 849 and *passim*.

[76] Joost Pauwelyn, 'The Limits of Litigation: "Americanization" and Negotiation in the Settlement of WTO Disputes' (2003) 19 Ohio State Journal on Dispute Resolution 121, 125.

[77] WTO Appellate Body, *United States: Final Anti-Dumping Measures on Stainless Steel from Mexico* (30 April 2008) WT/DS344/AB/R [160].

[78] Zhu Lanye, 'The Effects of the WTO Dispute Settlement Panel and AB Reports: Is the Dispute Settlement Body Resolving Specific Disputes Only or Making Precedent at the Same Time?' (2003) 17 Temple International and Comparative Law Journal 221, 231.

[79] WTO Panel, *European Communities—Measures Prohibiting the Importation and Marketing of Seal Products* (25 November 2013) WT/DS400/R and WT/DS401/R [7.635f].

[80] *European Communities: Measures Prohibiting the Importation and Marketing of Seal Products* (n 33) [5.213]. The earlier formulation by the AB was: 'it appears to us that it would be difficult for a panel to find that measure necessary unless it is satisfied that the measure is apt to make a material contribution to the achievement of its objective'.

[81] *Korea: Taxes on Alcoholic Beverages* (n 65) [162].

an explicit formulation of what had already been built into an earlier (GATT) formula from the *Section 337* case.[82] That an earlier precedent almost single-handedly has to bear the burden of justifying what later becomes an entire line of interpretation of one of the central terms of WTO law is quite astonishing. The picture becomes even more puzzling when one considers that the *Section 337* findings were much less refined than what the AB proposes in *Korea—Beef* and did—contrary to what the AB implies—not involve any explicit 'weighing and balancing' of different factors.[83] The AB's reliance on the *Section 337* case to support its weighing and balancing formula in *Korea—Beef* has therefore been—correctly—described as a 'far stretch and valiant claim'.[84] There are other cases where doubts exist (to say the least) on whether a finding that was presented as having been contained in an earlier report actually existed in the way it was quoted.[85]

In what way does this manner of using precedents contribute to legitimizing the WTO's judicial decisions? Generally, using precedents allows a judge to appear as being compelled by existing legal rules to take a certain decision, thereby avoiding the impression of creating new legal rules; conversely, failure to adhere to precedents is identified by some scholars as an indicator of judicial activism.[86] Continuity and consistency and the application of the same rules to the same factual issues, regardless of the parties involved, are an important source of legitimacy for any adjudicator.[87] Relying heavily on precedents and not acknowledging explicitly frictions and turns in the case law—as the AB does—makes sense, if constructing a uniform and consistent body of law is an important part of a strategy of generating acceptance for judicial decisions by adding authority and credibility to the adjudicators' new decisions.[88]

4.3 Avoidance techniques

In the WTO context, the term 'avoidance techniques' has been used by Davey to relate to certain techniques that the judicial decision-makers have developed to 'dispose of cases or issues within cases where a decision seems unnecessary, inappropriate or perhaps simply too controversial'.[89]

[82] *Korea: Measures Affecting Imports of Fresh, Chilled and Frozen Beef* (n 61) [166].

[83] Panel, *United States: Section 337 of the Tariff Act of 1930* (1989) L/6439-36S/345 [5.26ff].

[84] Ingo Venzke, 'Making General Exceptions: The Spell of Precedents in Developing Article XX GATT into Standards for Domestic Regulatory Policy' in Armin von Bogdandy and Ingo Venzke (eds), *International Judicial Lawmaking: On Public Authority and Democratic Legitimation in Global Governance* (Springer 2012) 205; for a critical position on the AB's incorrect use of the earlier GATT case, see also Kulovesi (n 4) 188.

[85] Compare for example the AB's statements on the interpretation of the phrase 'relating to' contained in Art. XX(g) GATT in the following two instances: *China—Measures Related to the Exportation of Various Raw Materials* (n 36) [358]; *United States—Standards for Reformulated and Conventional Gasoline* (n 61) III B, at 18.

[86] See eg Stefanie Lindquist and Frank Cross, *Measuring Judicial Activism* (OUP 2009) 32ff.

[87] David N Palmeter and Petros C Mavroidis, 'The WTO Legal System: Sources of Law' (1998) 92 American Journal of International Law 398, 402.

[88] See Bhala (n 75) 940.

[89] William J Davey, 'Has the WTO Dispute Settlement System Exceeded Its Authority? A Consideration of Deference Shown by the System to Member Government Decisions and Its Use of

In the WTO context, judicial economy is used most frequently among various avoidance techniques.[90] The term refers to the practice of the WTO dispute settlement bodies to 'rule not to rule on certain of the litigants' legal arguments, deeming these unnecessary to solving the dispute at hand'.[91] Judicial economy is not mentioned explicitly in any WTO provision.[92] Yet the AB has condoned the use of judicial economy in principle by stating that Panels are not required to address all arguments of parties, but only those necessary to resolve a claim.[93]

Some examples where Panels relied on judicial economy are the following: In *EC—Asbestos*, certain claims under the TBT (Technical Barriers to Trade) Agreement were not decided by the Panel, because a violation of GATT and lack of justification under Art. XX had already been found.[94] In the *EC—Biotech Products* case the Panel did not decide on a violation of Art. III:4 and XI GATT after it had already found a violation of certain procedural rules of the SPS Agreement.[95] Moreover, the Panel did not decide on a violation of Art. 5.6, 5.5 SPS, and the first requirements of Art. 2.2 and 2.3 SPS, either, after a violation of Art. 5.1 SPS had already been found.[96]

A second avoidance technique occasionally used in WTO dispute settlement is an argumentation '*arguendo*'. The term denotes situations where one side agrees on a hypothetical basis to accept certain factual or legal points made by another party in order to construe, on this basis, an argument, often for the purpose of refuting the opponent's view. In *Shrimp—Turtles*, the AB observed that *if* a territorial nexus between the state taking the measure and the resources protected was required by Art. XX(g) GATT, it was, in any event, present, given the migratory habits of sea turtles; the AB did not elaborate on whether a territorial nexus was indeed required.[97] In another case, the issue was whether Art. XX(d) GATT was available as a justification for breaching a norm of the Anti-Dumping Agreement. The AB here, instead of first answering the primary question of the applicability of Art. XX(d) GATT, first looked '*arguendo*' at whether the measure at issue was 'necessary' in the sense of Art. XX(d) GATT. Having answered this question in the negative, it did not deal with the logically primary question of whether Art. XX(d) GATT could be invoked at all for justifying a violation of the anti-dumping disciplines.[98]

Issue-Avoidance Techniques' in Robert Howse and Petros C Mavroidis (eds), *The Role of the Judge in International Trade Regulation* (University of Michigan Press 2003) 58.

[90] Marc L Busch and Krzysztof J Pelc, 'The Politics of Judicial Economy at the World Trade Organization' (2010) 264 International Organization 257, 260.

[91] ibid 257.

[92] Joost Pauwelyn, *Conflict of Norms in Public International Law: How WTO Law Relates to Other Rules of International Law* (CUP 2003) 208.

[93] See eg WTO Appellate Body, *European Communities: Measures Affecting the Importation of Certain Poultry Products* (13 July 1998) WT/DS69/AB/R [135].

[94] WTO Panel, *European Communities: Measures Affecting Asbestos and Products Containing Asbestos* (18 September 2000) WT/DS135/R [6.43].

[95] *European Communities: Measures Affecting the Approval and Marketing of Biotech Products* (n 53) [7.2505, 7.3422, 7.3429].

[96] See ibid 7.3377, 7.3384, 7.3393f and 7.3405 respectively.

[97] *United States: Import Prohibition of Certain Shrimp and Shrimp Products* (n 59) [133].

[98] WTO Appellate Body, *United States: Measures Relating to Shrimp from Thailand (16 July 2008) WT/DS343/AB/R* [310].

However, the AB has put some limits to the use of the *arguendo* technique and stated that

> reliance upon an assumption arguendo is a legal technique that an adjudicator may use in order to enhance simplicity and efficiency in decision-making. Although panels and the AB may choose to employ this technique in particular circumstances, it may not always provide a solid foundation upon which to rest legal conclusions. Use of the technique may detract from a clear enunciation of the relevant WTO law (. . .).[99] [footnotes omitted]

There are some instances, where, by these standards, the AB found that a Panel should not have proceeded *arguendo.* The AB did not accept, for example, that in *China—Audiovisual Products* a Panel had assumed *arguendo* that a deviation from China's Accession Protocol could be justified, in principle, under Art. XX(a) GATT. The Panel had then found that the conditions of Art. XX(a) GATT were not met, relieving it of the necessity to pronounce itself on the matter whether Art. XX(a) GATT was actually available as a defence to China.[100] The AB did not approve of this approach, because it led to a lack of clarity and legal certainty in its view.[101]

The above presents a picture that may appear puzzling at first sight. On the one hand, the AB is very committed to precedents. On the other hand, the adjudicators also frequently avoid taking a decision on certain issues. In other words, on the one hand there is an approach of generating interpretations that transcend individual cases and relying on them in later cases. On the other hand, there are attempts to avoid precisely such case-transcendent findings. This picture is probably the result of the fact that both the consistent use of precedents and the avoidance of potentially controversial findings can help legitimize a judicial decision.

In certain instances, creating a precedent may not be opportune. This thinking is evident from the following statement of a former AB member:

> *[M]ore* [reasoning] is sometimes *less* in treaty interpretation. The AB is ever mindful that the words of sentences that are included in appellate reasoning in one case can have a way of taking on life of their own in later cases.[102]

This lends plausibility to observations in the literature that techniques such as judicial economy are used in WTO dispute settlement to avoid (potentially) controversial findings.[103] By not deciding certain issues a judicial body preserves scope for future decisions that may be particularly suitable to the concrete case or for

[99] *China: Measures Affecting Trading Rights and Distribution Services for Certain Publications and Audiovisual Entertainment Products* (n 41) [213f].

[100] WTO Panel, *China: Measures Affecting Trading Rights and Distribution Services for Certain Publications and Audiovisual Entertainment Products* (12 August 2009) WT/DS363/R [8.2(a)(ii)].

[101] *China: Measures Affecting Trading Rights and Distribution Services for Certain Publications and Audiovisual Entertainment Products* (n 41) [215].

[102] James Bacchus, 'Appellators: The Quest for the Meaning of And/or' (2005) 4 World Trade Review 499, 514; for a similar statement from another former AB member, see Claus-Dieter Ehlermann, 'Six Years on the Bench of the "World Trade Court": Some Personal Experiences as Member of the Appellate Body of the World Trade Organization' (2002) 36 Journal of World Trade 605, 638.

[103] For such an observation, see Shany and Shlomo-Agon (n 68) 207.

responding to political pressure in a future case, thereby avoiding criticism of its jurisprudence.[104] At the same time, a court that produces more legal findings than necessary to resolve the case at hand is more likely to be considered activist and law-making.[105]

5 A Legitimizing Effect of the WTO's Judicial Decisions?

In the two preceding sections I have described the interpretation of WTO law in non-trade cases as being rather balanced and analysed the rhetoric effects of certain aspects of the WTO's judicial style. I have argued that both of these aspects have the potential to contribute to the legitimacy of the WTO's judicial decisions. However, have they actually done so and how do we know?

Obviously, an empirically grounded answer to this question would need to rely on a survey among the relevant constituencies to inquire about their views on the WTO case law and the reasons for accepting or criticizing WTO dispute settlement. Given that this has not been feasible in the present context, there is another indicator that allows conclusions on the extent to which WTO dispute settlement and the judicial output it produces are accepted: the (relative) absence of countermeasures from WTO Members. In section 2, I have introduced existing research showing that (international) courts can be conceived of as strategic actors that seek—where possible—to avoid outcomes that could lead to political backlash in the form of attempts at weakening the mandate of the respective court, political decisions reversing the judicial decisions, non-compliance with judgments, and/or non-use of the WTO DSS. Conversely, one could assume that if WTO Members were fundamentally dissatisfied with the WTO DSS and the output it produces, they would take such steps.

Yet such steps have not been taken by WTO Members:

- There has been very little activity from WTO Members aimed at overturning interpretations by the WTO dispute settlement bodies. For example, there has been no decision by WTO Members constituting an authoritative interpretation of WTO law under Art. IX.2 of the WTO Agreement and modifying any of the findings of the AB.[106] No important decision by the dispute settlement bodies has been reversed through a treaty revision.[107] Admittedly, the quorum

[104] This point is made in particular by James McCall Smith, 'WTO Dispute Settlement: The Politics of Procedure in AB Rulings' (2003) 2 World Trade Review 65.

[105] Compare Zarbiyev (n 9) 8.

[106] The point is made by Bacchus (n 102) 518; however, Anne Scully-Hill and Hans Mahncke, 'The Emergence of the Doctrine of Stare Decisis in the World Trade Organization Dispute Settlement System' (2009) 36 Legal Issues of Economic Integration 133, 148f note that the Doha Declaration on TRIPS (Agreement on Trade-Related Aspects of Intellectual Property Rights) and Public Health may have a somewhat similar effect as decisions under Art. IX.2; Krüger (n 17) 74 points to requests by the EU for an authoritative interpretation on which there was no agreement, however.

[107] Sweet and Brunell (n 11) 66.

for adopting such an interpretation would be high.[108] However, if there was very serious or widespread concern about certain findings of the WTO adjudicators, such a decision could still be politically achievable. Indeed, WTO Members have managed to agree over the course of the years on some 'trade and ...' issues. The Doha 'Declaration on the TRIPS Agreement and public health'[109] is an important example.

- WTO Members dissatisfied with the performance of the dispute settlement bodies could also try to change the mandate of these bodies or change the rules of the judicial game in other ways. Indeed, a mandate for negotiating a Dispute Settlement Understanding reform was contained in the Doha Ministerial Declaration.[110] According to the mandate, the negotiations should have been concluded in 2003, but consensus remains elusive to date. There are basically two major directions of the reform proposals,[111] with the EU and US each spearheading one of them: The US proposals are generally aimed at giving Members more control over dispute settlement procedures (eg by enabling them to adopt only certain parts of a report or by introducing an interim review stage also at appellate level).[112] By contrast, the EU proposals are mostly aimed at guaranteeing and even enhancing the independence of the judicial branch of the WTO and making it more effective and court-like. Suggestions include creating a permanent roster of panellists (thereby moving away from the ad hoc nature of Panels) or changing the term of office of the AB members from once renewable four years to non-renewable six years, thus enhancing the AB members' independence from the WTO Members.[113] Even the more ambitious US proposals are, however, relatively modest in reach. For example, if WTO Members were given the opportunity to only adopt certain of the findings made by a Panel or the AB, this would have significant consequences for the Member losing the case—the extent to which it would need to bring its measures in compliance with WTO law could be significantly reduced. However, what precedential effect the part of decisions not adopted by the DSB would have, remains very open. They would be very similar in character to the non-adopted Panel reports under the old GATT; these reports still have some guiding effect in WTO dispute settlement.[114] The systemic implications of such a reform would likely be limited. Or, as Flett writes, the

[108] According to Art. IX:2 WTO a three-quarters majority of WTO Members would be needed.

[109] Online at <http://www.wto.org/english/thewto_e/minist_e/min01_e/mindecl_trips_e.htm>.

[110] Ministerial Declaration, Adopted on 14 November 2001, para. 30, <http://www.wto.org/english/thewto_e/minist_e/min01_e/mindecl_e.htm#dispute>.

[111] A good overview of the debates is contained in the Chairman's report of April 2011 to the Trade Negotiations Committee (document TN/DS/25). The debate does not appear to have made much progress since then.

[112] Manfred Elsig and Mark A Pollack, 'Agents, Trustees, and International Courts: The Politics of Judicial Appointment at the World Trade Organization' (2012) Online first version European Journal of International Relations 17; Krüger (n 17) 81f.

[113] See Krüger (n 17) 87ff.

[114] WTO Appellate Body: *Japan—Taxes on Alcoholic Beverages* (4 October 1996) WT/DS8/AB/R, WT/DS10/AB/R, and WT/DS11/AB/R, at 14f.

proposals 'do not appear to directly threaten the principle of binding "hard law" adjudication in itself'.[115] In addition, none of these proposals has been agreed upon—even though the reform discussions had already been going on before the Doha Ministerial conference. In sum, while there are attempts by some WTO Members to better control the AB, these appear to be limited in ambition or nothing that all WTO Members would agree on. This can, probably, be taken to mean that the degree of dissatisfaction with the AB's functioning is at least not pronounced enough to trigger a stronger political backlash or more far-reaching counter-measures.

- Another option for WTO Members that do not like a decision in cases where they were involved as defendants is non-compliance with that decision. While non-compliance may be politically and also economically costly for WTO Members, it is still an option that the states have in principle. However, in practice, compliance levels with WTO dispute settlement decisions have been very high. Obviously, there are certain major cases where a party did not comply, at least initially, mostly due to internal political pressure. Yet in the broader picture, it is estimated that the losing parties in a WTO dispute comply with the decision in 95 per cent of the cases; this rate is considerably higher than for the International Court of Justice (62%) and the Inter-American Court of Human Rights (5%).[116]
- WTO Members dissatisfied with the decisions produced by the DSS, could also stop using the system. Whether or not disputes are initiated is in the hands of the WTO Members, and so is a decision whether a particular Panel report is appealed. Yet there is no apparent tendency of WTO Members using the DSS less over time. According to a relatively recent statistical analysis, the number of complaints per year that have resulted in Panel reports has remained largely stable over the years and the same is true for AB reports, with a slightly higher average for the first decade of the WTO's existence than the later period.[117] Another statistical analysis, covering the period 1995–2012, also indicates that while the number of Panel and AB reports issued annually varies per five-year period, there is no general downward trend.[118]

In conclusion, if one takes the behaviour of WTO Members vis-à-vis the WTO DSS as an indicator, the adjudicators have indeed been successful at positioning them as a judicial body taking legitimate decisions and at winning the acceptance of WTO

[115] James Flett, 'From the Green Room to the Court Room (and Back): Judicial Clarification of Ambiguity in WTO Law and the Effects on Subsequent Negotiations' (Oñati International Institute for the Sociology of Law 2011) Oñati Socio Legal Series 4/1 39.

[116] Figures compiled by Magnuson (n 68) 134 from different publications. However, he does not indicate the time periods for which these rates apply.

[117] Krüger (n 17) 63.

[118] Kara Leitner and Simon Lester, 'WTO Dispute Settlement 1995–2012—A Statistical Analysis' (2013) 16 Journal of International Economic Law 257, 262f.

Members. This is true at least to a degree that has prevented far-reaching countermeasures by WTO Members.[119]

To conclude, the WTO dispute settlement bodies are, like other international courts, actors that think and act strategically and take decisions that—within the boundaries of indeterminate legal provisions—are likely to win the acceptance of relevant constituencies, most notably WTO Members. Through a combination of judgments that are balanced in substance (and sometimes avoid too controversial issues) and a unique judicial style the adjudicators appear to have won the acceptance of WTO Members and succeeded in legitimizing their decisions—and thus ultimately the WTO DSS as a judicial entity.

[119] It should be noted that the assumption that the WTO DSS has managed to win the acceptance of relevant constituencies, ie garner empirical legitimacy, is shared by many, but not all authors. For example, Joost Pauwelyn, 'The WTO 20 Years On: "Global Governance by Judiciary" or, rather, Memberdriven Settlement of (Some) Trade Disputes between (Some) WTO Members?' (2016) 27 European Journal of International Law 1119, 1121f argues that neither the degree to which the WTO DSS is used by Members nor compliance rates are good proxies for empirical legitimacy.

5

A Typology of International Judicial Practices

*Jeffrey L Dunoff and Mark A Pollack**

1 Introduction

Does the 'judicialization of international law' constitute 'a mixed blessing'? Determining precisely how and why the rise of courts has altered international relations constitutes an urgent research question. In recent years, international courts and tribunals have proliferated; by one count, more than two dozen permanent international courts are operational, and over one hundred judicial bodies and mechanisms hear international disputes. And these entities are increasingly busy; over 90 per cent of the more than 37,000 binding judgments rendered by international courts have been issued since the fall of the Berlin Wall.[1] Moreover, the stakes associated with international adjudication have never been higher. International courts increasingly consider contentious issues involving substantial economic stakes, important regulatory policies, and fundamental questions of international order. Taken together, these developments explain *why* we should study international courts.

Less clear, however, is *how* one should study international courts. International law (IL) scholars employ various methods to explore jurisdictional and procedural matters, courts' diverse argumentative strategies, and the content and coherence of judicial opinions. International relations (IR) writings often employ quantitative analysis, coding judicial decisions to identify relationships between inputs (such as the relative power of the parties, or backgrounds of the judges) and outputs (who wins, who loses); measure judicial independence; and analyse institutional design. More recently, research agendas in both disciplines have converged in examining the democratic legitimacy and effectiveness of courts, and the sociological and professional backgrounds of international judges and arbitrators.

* An earlier version of this chapter was presented at the ESIL Annual Meeting in September 2015. We are extremely grateful to Judge Joan Donoghue and Professor Hélène Ruiz Fabri for their insightful comments on our presentation. We also thank Cosette Creamer, Dinah Shelton, Beth Simmons, and the editors for perceptive comments on earlier versions of this chapter. This chapter is part of a larger interdisciplinary research project on international judicial practices.

[1] Karen J Alter, *The New Terrain of International Law: Courts, Politics, Rights* (Princeton UP 2014) 4.

Notwithstanding the wide variety of methods employed and issues addressed, however, both literatures share an important blind spot. Specifically, they demonstrate little interest in exploring the inner workings of courts. Scholars from both disciplines have devoted little attention to studying the internal, day-to-day practices of courts, including decision making and opinion drafting. Put simply, both IL and IR writings have largely neglected *how international courts actually function*.

This oversight flows quite naturally from the dominant methodological approaches in both fields, which conceptualize international courts as unitary actors whose interests, intentions, and strategies are best understood by examining judicial outputs, that is, court decisions. This focus is useful for many purposes, but has the unintended effect of rendering courts' inner workings outside the scope of mainstream scholarly inquiry.

To fill this gap, we urge scholars to open up the 'black box' of international tribunals and study what international judges do and how they do it. To begin this process, this chapter presents a preliminary effort to identify and examine the everyday practices of international judges. In undertaking this task, we draw selectively upon a large literature on 'practice theory' that has only rarely been applied to international law in general or to international courts in particular. Practice approaches provide conceptual frameworks and analytic tools that can enable scholars to identify and understand underlying patterns and actions within international courts that have heretofore escaped scholarly attention.

Our analysis proceeds in three sections. Section 2 provides a brief introduction to practice theory. It reviews the understanding of 'practices' commonly used in the study of international affairs, examines the application of practice theory to international legal phenomena, and argues that a comparative, practice-based approach offers the promise of revealing the very different ways in which international court judges organize their work. Section 3, the heart of the chapter, provides a typology and synoptic overview of these practices. We divide these practices into two broad categories—those not directly related to the litigation process, and those directly related to the litigation process—and describe a number of practices in each category, demonstrating that international judicial practices are both highly variable across courts, and not reducible to the structural features (the statutes and procedural law) of each court. Finally, in an effort to motivate a new sub-field of research, section 4 briefly sketches a research agenda for the study of international judicial practices. A short conclusion follows.

2 Practice Theory and International Courts

Practice-oriented approaches 'put social practice—as an actual, contingent, evolving and productive set of activities—centre stage'.[2] In the early 2000s, Emanuel

[2] Nikolas M Rajkovic, Tanja E Aalberts, and Thomas Gammeltoft-Hansen, 'Introduction: Legality, Interdisciplinarity and the Study of Practices' in Nikolas M Rajkovic et al (eds), *The Power of Legality: Practices of International Law and Their Politics* (CUP 2016).

Adler and Vincent Pouliot's work helped to popularize practice theory in IR scholarship.[3] As they explain, '[p]ractices are competent performances. More precisely, practices are socially meaningful patterns of action which, in being performed more or less competently, simultaneously embody, act out, and possibly reify background knowledge and discourse in and on the material world.'[4]

From this basic point of departure, Adler and Pouliot highlight five common dimensions of practice. First, and most basically, 'a practice is a *performance*, that is, a process of doing'.[5] Second, practices are *patterned*; they exhibit regularities across space and time. These patterns are found within socially organized contexts, which both provide meaning and structure interactions. Third, practices can be more or less 'competent', as judged by an audience or public against some set of shared standards.[6] Fourth, 'practice rests on *background knowledge*', which is intersubjective and practice-oriented, as opposed to abstract and theoretical. Fifth and finally, 'practices weave together the *discursive* and *material* worlds', featuring a linguistic element that gives practices their meaning, as well as a material element acting in and upon the world.[7] Drawing on Adler and Pouliot, IR scholars have analysed international diplomacy, European security, the early Cold War, the emergence of private military contractors, international organizations, and humanitarian intervention, among other issue areas, through the lens of practice theory.

Jutta Brunnée and Stephen Toope introduced this approach to international legal scholarship in work that sets forth an 'interactional theory of international law' that centres upon the 'practice of legality'.[8] Specifically, Brunnée and Toope argue that legal norms are built, maintained, and evolve through a 'robust practice of legality' undertaken by 'communities of practice'. These communities of practice consist of individuals who, through engagement in a shared domain, develop a shared repertoire of resources, including cases, stories, tools, vocabularies, and ways of addressing recurring problems—in short, practices. Thus, for Brunnée and Toope, '[p]ractice resides in a community of people and the relations of mutual engagement by which they can do whatever they do'.[9] They argue that it is the day-to-day practice of legality in communities of practice, rather than simply the formal sources of law, that determines whether a given norm generates a sense of legal obligation, on the one hand, or falls into desuetude on the other.[10]

[3] See, eg, Emanuel Adler and Vincent Pouliot, 'International Practices' (2011) 3 International Theory 1; Emanuel Adler and Vincent Pouliot (eds), *International Practices* (CUP 2011). Adler and Pouliot, in turn, were drawing upon a rich literature on practices in sociology, anthropology, and other disciplines. Eg, Theodore Schatzki et al (eds), *The Practice Turn in Contemporary Theory* (Routledge 2001); Pierre Bourdieu, *Outline of a Theory of Practice* (CUP 1977).

[4] Adler and Pouliot, 'International Practices' (n 3) 6. [5] ibid 6. [6] ibid 6–7.

[7] Emanuel Adler and Vincent Pouliot, 'International Practices: Introduction and Framework' in Adler and Pouliot (eds), *International Practices* (n 3) 7–8.

[8] Jutta Brunnée and Stephen Toope, 'Interactional International Law and the Practice of Legality' in Adler and Pouliot (eds), *International Practices* (n 3) 108; Jutta Brunnée and Stephen Toope, *Legitimacy and Legality in International Law: An Interactional Account* (CUP 2010).

[9] Brunnée and Toope, *Legitimacy and Legality* (n 8) 63 (quoting Etienne Wenger, *Communities of Practice: Learning, Meaning, and Identity* (CUP 1998) 73).

[10] Brunnée and Toope, 'Interactional International Law' (n 8) 109.

While Brunnée and Toope do not analyse international courts, Jens Meierhenrich and his colleagues have taken this step in a comprehensive study of practices undertaken in and around the International Criminal Court (ICC).[11] The contributors to this project explore not only the practices of ICC judges, but also those of related communities of practice, including other ICC organs (the Registry and the Office of the Prosecutor), lawyers representing the defendants before the court, and other members of the broader international criminal law community.[12] These papers do much to illuminate the everyday practices associated with the investigation, prosecution, defence, and adjudication of cases at the ICC.

We seek to build on and extend this literature, in two ways. First, unlike previous scholarship, we place international *judicial* practices at the centre of the analysis, putting forth a typology of such practices and demonstrating that they vary substantially across international courts. Second, we depart from the scholars discussed above with respect to what might be called the 'level of aggregation', or level of abstraction at which we identify and analyse specific practices. As Adler and Pouliot write, '[c]onceptually, any given practice can be appraised through different levels of aggregation', with, for example, small individual practices such as work meetings and press conferences aggregating into broader practices such as summitry or diplomacy.[13] There is no single, correct level of aggregation for the study of practices; rather, the appropriate level of aggregation should be based on the specific research question at issue, informed by the experience of the performers themselves.

For Brunnée and Toope, a high level of aggregation, and the identification of a single 'practice of legality', is sensible given their desire to construct a grand theory of international legal obligation. Their omission of courts and judges is likewise understandable given the limited role of courts in the issue-areas that they foreground, such as climate change and use of force. Given our interest in mid-range theory, rather than grand theory, it is more useful to disaggregate the practice of legality into a number of discrete practices undertaken by different actors, including particularly international judges. This is especially true with respect to issue-areas—including trade law, human rights law, investment law, and international criminal law—in which international courts and tribunals hear many cases and are increasingly central actors.

Our approach to *comparative* international judicial practices also differs from the level of aggregation found in the ICC project. In one sense, our approach is narrower in that we focus on how *judges* organize and carry out their day-to-day work. By contrast, the majority of the contributions to the ICC project focus on the practices

[11] Jens Meierhenrich, 'The Practice of International Law: A Theoretical Analysis' (2013) 76 L and Contemporary Problems 1.

[12] Alex Whiting, 'Dynamic Investigative Practice at the International Criminal Court' (2013) 76 L and Contemporary Problems 163; Karim AA Kahn and Anand A Shah, 'Defensive Practices: Representing Clients Before the International Criminal Court' (2013) 76 L and Contemporary Problems 191; Noah Weisbord, 'Bargaining Practices: Negotiating the Kampala Compromise for the International Criminal Court' (2013) 76 L and Contemporary Problems 85; Frédéric Mégret, 'Practices of Stigmatization' (2013) 76 L and Contemporary Problems 287.

[13] Adler and Pouliot, 'International Practices' (n 8).

of actors *other* than judges, including the member states that negotiated the Rome Statute, the Office of the Prosecutor, the defence bar, and others. While the practices highlighted in these papers are important and interesting in their own right, they fall largely outside the scope of our inquiry. In another respect, however, our approach is substantially broader than that of Meierhenrich and his colleagues, who explicitly disavow any interest in generalizing beyond the ICC, and do not compare the ICC to other international criminal tribunals, or the broader universe of international courts.[14] Our approach, in contrast, is explicitly *comparative*, exploring practices, such as deliberation and opinion-drafting, that are common to many or all international courts, but that take different forms across different courts.[15]

We now turn our attention to this effort, and provide an initial and preliminary attempt to identify and analyse international judicial practices across different international courts.

3 International Judicial Practices

International judges undertake many activities that exhibit the five features of practice highlighted by Adler and Pouliot. Specifically, in the course of their professional activities, international judges (1) engage in multiple *performances*, both private (within the secrecy of deliberations) and public (in their conduct of judicial hearings, composition of judicial decisions, speeches, etc). These judicial practices are (2) highly *patterned*, taking place within the socially organized, even ritualized, context of international law and litigation. Moreover, judicial practices are (3) more or less *competent* as measured by a particular public or publics—be they litigants, member states, 'the invisible college of international lawyers', or larger publics—against some set of intersubjective standards. Judicial decisions, and other actions, (4) rest on *background knowledge* of treaties, custom, case-law, rules of court, as well as informal norms of 'proper' judicial behaviour. Finally, judicial practices (5) weave together and implicate both the discursive and material worlds, taking the form of legal discourse yet having material implications for the litigants in any given case.

In the pages that follow, we provide a synoptic overview of international judicial practices. We begin by distinguishing international judicial practices into two broad categories, namely those that are not directly related to the litigation process and

[14] See eg, Meierhenrich (n 11) 78 (counselling 'a *deliberate eschewing* of generalization about the practice of international law', in favour of detailed, interpretive, site-specific research).

[15] Finally, our approach differs from that found in a sophisticated body of sociological writings on courts. Eg, Yves Dezalay and Bryant G Garth, *Dealing in Virtue: International Commercial Arbitration and the Construction of a Transnational Legal Order* (U Chicago P 1996); Antoine Vauchez and Bruno de Witte (eds), *Lawyering Europe: European Law as a Transnational Social Field* (Hart 2013); Mikael Rask Madsen, 'Sociological Approaches to International Courts' in Cesare PR Romano, Karen J Alter, and Chrisanthi Avgerou (eds), *Oxford Handbook of International Adjudication* (OUP 2013) 388. While we share these literatures' epistemological instinct to treat courts as a site consisting of specific social practices, we are more interested in the courts themselves than many sociologically inclined scholars, and less focused on seeing courts as a site of contestation between different forms of expertise and competing sets of elites.

those that are. The first group of practices structure the organization of a court and the judges' relationships with other actors, both inside and outside the court. The second group of litigation-centred practices are in turn divided into categories that correspond to different stages of the litigation process, including (a) judicial practices that contribute to the 'institutional' or 'background' features of the litigation environment; (b) judicial practices concerning written pleadings; (c) judicial practices concerning oral hearings; (d) judicial practices concerning the production and receipt of evidence and fact finding; and (e) practices concerning deliberations and opinion-writing. Given the range and number of international judicial practices, our descriptions are necessarily brief, although by way of illustration we provide more detailed analyses of a few practices at a handful of the most prominent international tribunals.

To orient the reader to the discussion that follows, Table 5.1 provides a simplified typology of international judicial practices common to most, if not all, international tribunals.

This table underscores several key points regarding international judicial practices. First, it demonstrates the breadth and diversity of practices that international judges engage in, many of which are separate from or prior to litigation. Second, litigation-oriented practices exist throughout a litigation's life-cycle, from the moment a case is started to the choreographed release of a final judgment. Third, judicial practices concerning the litigation process are not 'free standing' or 'isolated' activities. Rather, they are interdependent; a court's practices regarding oral proceedings, for example, will be, in part, a function of its practices regarding written proceedings. Fourth, as emphasized below, while there is a broad overlap among international courts in the areas where practices take place, there is considerable variation across courts in the specific *content* of their practices. Fifth and finally, as we shall presently see, the statutes and formal procedural laws of different international courts inform and set constraints on judicial practices, but are underdetermining, leaving judges with choices about how to organize those practices.

3.1 Practices not directly related to the litigation process

Judicial practices most obviously occur in the litigation context. But international judges often engage in repeated and structured interactions with actors inside and outside of the courthouse. By way of illustration, we provide an extended analysis of one of these practices, concerning relations with coordinate treaty bodies, and much briefer discussions of other non-litigation practices.

3.1.1 Practices concerning relations with coordinate political bodies

Many international courts are embedded within treaty-based institutional structures. Constitutive treaties often provide little guidance regarding the relations between international courts and coordinate treaty bodies. Nonetheless, international judges interact with actors from coordinate bodies in myriad ways. Consider, for example,

Table 5.1 International judicial practices

Practices not directly related to the litigation process

- Practices concerning relations with coordinate treaty bodies
  - Practices concerning preparation and submission of annual reports
  - Practices concerning requests for material support for courts
- Practices concerning relations between judges and other court officials
  - Practices concerning relations with the Registry or Secretariat
  - Practices concerning relations with the Prosecutor
  - Practices concerning relations with Defence counsel
- Practices concerning relations with judges of other international courts
  - Practices concerning exchange of case law and other information
  - Practices concerning joint seminars, workshops, and the like
- Practices concerning relations with domestic officials
  - Practices concerning relations with domestic judges
- Practices concerning internal administrative and budgetary matters
- Practices concerning training of new judges
- Practices concerning extra-judicial activities
  - Practices concerning off-the-bench writings and speeches
  - Practices concerning academic conferences and workshops

Practices related to the litigation process

- Practices concerning the 'institutional' or 'background' features of the litigation environment
  - Linguistic practices
  - Practices concerning whether case is heard by full tribunal or chambers
  - Practices concerning access to the court, and who can represent parties
- Practices concerning the written pleadings
  - number, sequencing of, time limit for pleadings
  - submission of evidence via written pleadings
  - ability of entities other than parties to submit written pleadings
- Practices concerning the oral pleadings
  - length of oral hearings
  - structure of oral hearings (emphasis on statements of counsel, introduction of evidence, questions from the bench, etc)
  - practices concerning transparency, including whether hearings are open or available online
- Practices concerning production and receipt of evidence and fact-finding
  - adversarial, inquisitorial, managerial, other styles
  - site visits
  - treatment of facts found by other international actors
- Practices concerning experts
  - party retained experts
  - experts retained by court

Table 5.1 Continued

- Practices concerning burden of proof
- Practices concerning standard of proof
- Practices concerning deliberations and opinion-writing
  - practices concerning lead role of *juge rapporteur*, use of drafting committee, or drafting by entire court
  - practices concerning role of clerks and/or registry in drafting of opinions
  - practices concerning court's dominant mode of interpretation
  - practices concerning citation to case law of other tribunals
  - practices concerning use or non-use of separate or dissenting opinions

the International Court of Justice (ICJ)'s practice of preparing and submitting annual reports to the United Nations (UN) General Assembly, and the related practice of the ICJ President's annual speech to the General Assembly. These annual reports are conventionally understood as useful compendia of a court's recent activity and as a useful mechanism for promoting oversight by and accountability to the political bodies that receive these reports.

A practice-oriented perspective starts by noting that nothing in the ICJ's Statute or Rules requires an annual report,[16] and that the Court did not always submit annual reports. Indeed, the Permanent Court of International Justice (PCIJ) judges did not prepare annual reports, and ICJ judges did not submit annual reports to the General Assembly until 1968, begging the questions of what motivated judges to institute this practice, and what purpose it serves.

The roots of this practice are found in the highly critical reaction to the Court's 1966 decision in the *South West Africa* cases.[17] In response to the firestorm the decision triggered, the judges launched various efforts designed to repair the political damage. In particular, in April 1967 the Court created a 'Committee on Relations', consisting of three judges, responsible for the development of the Court's relations with other UN organs and international bodies.[18] Shortly thereafter, for the first time, ICJ judges visited and addressed the International Law Commission. In 1968 the judges issued their first annual report; hosted, for the first time, a visit by the UN Secretary General; and the ICJ President presented, for the first time, an oral report to the General Assembly. In 2000, the ICJ President initiated the practice of providing a private briefing to the Security Council.

[16] At some tribunals, an annual report is legally required. For example, the International Criminal Tribunal for Rwanda (ICTR) and International Criminal Tribunal for the former Yugoslavia (ICTY) submit annual reports pursuant to provisions in the Statutes creating these courts.

[17] Eg, DP Forsythe, 'The International Court of Justice at Fifty' in AS Muller et al (eds), *The International Court of Justice: Its Future Role After Fifty Years* (Springer 1997) 385, 393 ('*South West Africa* was the ICJ's Dred Scott decision').

[18] International Court of Justice, *International Court of Justice Yearbook (1967–68)* (The Hague 1968) 92–93.

The ICJ's annual report, the President's annual speech to the General Assembly, and the yearly briefing of the Security Council, are repetitive and patterned performances that occur within the highly organized context of UN politics and procedures. This context includes the rules surrounding the timing and organization of the General Assembly's annual sessions as well as informal rules regarding the diplomatic protocol associated with UN proceedings. Within these various structural constraints, ICJ judges exercise substantial agency, as they have wide discretion regarding whether and how to frame an appeal for greater material support, urge use of certain mechanisms to expand the Court's case load, or signal how political bodies can best enhance the likelihood of compliance with ICJ decisions. Moreover, these practices can be performed more or less competently, referring *not* to whether the report accurately describes the Court's activities over the past year, but rather to the report's efficacy in communicating a message that enhances the Court's stature or legitimacy with the General Assembly, Security Council, and other audiences. These practices likewise weave together discursive and material worlds. The annual report's text and President's briefings are discursive practices which, if performed competently, can impact the political and material support the UN's political bodies provide to the Court. In this sense, these practices convey 'social meanings', which have much more to do with efforts to enhance the Court's standing among relevant constituencies than it does with the ostensible informational purpose of publicizing the Court's activities over the past year.

3.1.2 Practices concerning relations with judges of other international courts

International courts operate in a highly decentralized and nonhierarchical setting, and rarely have treaty-based relations with one another. Nevertheless, international judges from different courts often engage with each other in highly patterned ways, including in face-to-face interactions at various workshops, conferences, seminars, and a variety of other fora. For example, the ICJ regularly hosts seminars on topics of mutual interest with judges from other international and regional courts; the European Court of Justice (ECJ) judges hold annual meetings with the judges of the European Court of Human Rights (ECtHR); and the judges from the Inter-American Court of Human Rights and ECtHR exchange visits to discuss issues of mutual concern. The participation of international judges from different international courts in these various fora has given rise to a set of patterned interactions with strong performative dimensions that can be analysed under the vernacular of practice theory.

3.1.3 Practices concerning relations between judges and other court officials, particularly the registry

International courts are typically comprised of various organs. For example, every international court has a registry, which is generally responsible for providing administrative support to the court in the exercise of its judicial functions. In addition to processing cases, registries are variously responsible for information technology, media and public relations, the court library, translations of judgments, and other administrative matters. Although registries are independent, they typically function under the authority of the court, and through their various activities engage in sustained and regularized interactions with the judges, both individually and collectively. These interactions can be analysed under the rubric of practice theory. In addition, and significantly, at some courts registry officials also play important roles in the drafting of opinions, a practice we analyse in detail elsewhere.

3.1.4 Practices concerning relations with domestic officials

Judges at some international courts engage in patterned interactions with domestic officials. The most prominent and developed set of relationships is that between the ECJ and national courts of EU member states. A large literature details how the ECJ skilfully 'recruited' domestic courts, using the mechanism of the preliminary ruling and the direct effect doctrine, to build domestic constituencies for EU law and help drive European integration.[19] The academic community has paid substantially less attention to other types of regularized and patterned interactions involving the ECJ and domestic legal actors, including domestic judges. In particular, over the years the ECJ has organized and run a number of seminars and training sessions for domestic judges. These sessions provide an opportunity for ECJ judges to explain the preliminary reference system, develop professional networks, and, indirectly, encourage the submission of additional cases. ECJ judges also interact with other domestic officials. For example, the ECJ prepares a dossier of 'historic case law' that is provided to states about to join the Union.[20] The selection of cases provides a highly selective, and contestable, vision of the trajectory and evolution of EU law that emphasizes a 'Court centric view of European integration'.[21] These, and other, practices involving domestic officials are thus essentially about the creation and communication of social meaning, and lend themselves to analysis under the rubric of practice theory.

3.1.5 Practices concerning extra-judicial activities

International judges undertake significant off-the-bench, law-related activities including delivering speeches, participating in academic seminars and conferences, and publishing scholarly and popular writings. These varied activities are undertaken in light of a shared body of background knowledge, such as that judges should not comment in any substantive way on pending disputes or deliberations in any

[19] See, eg, Joseph HH Weiler, 'The Transformation of Europe' (1991) 100 Yale LJ 2403; Alec Stone Sweet and Thomas Brunell, 'Constructing a Supranational Constitution: Dispute Resolution and Governance in the European Community' (1998) 92 American Political Science Rev 63.

[20] See <curia.europa.eu/jcms/jcam/Jo2_14955>.

[21] Urska Sadl and Mikael Rask Madsen, 'A "Selfie" from Luxembourg: The Court of Justice and the Fabrication of the Pre-Accession Case-Law Dossiers' (2016) 22 Columbia J of Eur L 327.

particular case. Hence, judges' off-the-bench activities are *constrained* by a substantial body of background knowledge.

Just as importantly, judges' off-the-bench activities can *create* a body of background knowledge. For example, Antoine Vauchez has perceptively argued that the regularized and frequent participation of ECJ judges in various 'Festschriften, tributes, eulogies, [and] Courts' jubilees' constitute a form of 'institutional rites' whereby the participating judges define and transmit the Court's 'institutional identity' to future judges and the relevant community of practice.[22] Judges at other courts deploy many of these commemorative strategies as well. ICJ judges, for example, often participate in Festschrifts and other events that serve to celebrate the Court as an institution and socialize participants (and readers) into the ways of the Court.[23] Likewise, a substantial number of current and former Appellate Body (AB) members have regularly, in off-the-bench writings, described the AB's birth and analysed efforts by the AB's founding members to establish the legitimacy and authority of their tribunal.[24] These extra-judicial writings can usefully be analysed as a practice, a form of patterned activity that draws on shared background knowledge, and whose social meaning involves the creation of an institutional narrative and the transmission of a set of core institutional values and principles.

3.2 Practices related to the litigation process

International judges engage in a wide variety of practices associated with the litigation process. For ease of exposition, we categorize these practices in terms of which stage of the litigation process they are relevant to. Thus, we discuss judicial practices that contribute to the 'institutional' or 'background' features of the litigation environment, as well as those concerning written pleadings, oral pleadings, evidence and fact finding, and judicial deliberation and opinion writing. These categories are necessarily porous, as many practices are relevant to more than one stage of the litigation process. The discussion that follows is intended to be illustrative, rather than exhaustive.

3.2.1 Judicial practices that contribute to the 'institutional' or 'background' features of the litigation environment

3.2.1.1 Orientation and training

New international judges bring with them a wide range of professional backgrounds, cultural understandings, and linguistic preferences. To meld a diverse group of individuals into a well-functioning bench, many courts offer incoming

[22] Antoine Vauchez, 'Keeping the Dream Alive: the European Court of Justice and the Transnational Fabric of Integrationist Jurisprudence' (2012) 4 Eur Political Science Rev 51.

[23] To take just one recent example, consider Ulrich Fastenrath et al (eds), *From Bilateralism to Community Interest: Essays in Honor of Bruno Simma* (OUP 2011) (containing contributions from numerous past, present, and future ICJ judges, as well as from judges of other international courts).

[24] Eg, nine current and former AB members contributed to Gabrielle Marceau (ed), *A History of Law and Lawyers in the GATT/WTO: The Development of the Rule of Law in the Multilateral Trading System* (CUP 2015).

judges orientation or training intended to familiarize them with how the court operates. At the same time, however, these sessions are also efforts to inculcate certain institutional values. Significantly, neither the structure nor the content of these training efforts is mandated by treaty, but rather reflects decisions made over time by the judges at each court, and vary widely across courts. At some courts, more experienced judges are expected to take newer judges under their wings and 'show them the ropes', a process colloquially known at the ECJ as the 'godfather system'.[25] At other tribunals, training and orientation is largely the responsibility of registry officials rather than sitting judges. At still others, such as the ECtHR, new judges are generally left largely to their own devices. As an academic matter, the socialization of new judges at international tribunals remains uncharted territory, and can be usefully explored using practice theory.

3.2.1.1 Linguistic practices

International tribunals have specified working or official languages.[26] The selection of official languages can help determine which individuals are qualified to serve as judges, the effectiveness of different judges, and even the way that different legal concepts are understood and used. Tribunals often distinguish between the language(s) of the proceedings, and the language of the Court's internal workings. At the ICJ and International Tribunal for the Law of the Sea (ITLOS), submissions are accepted, proceedings conducted, and judgments rendered only in the official languages of French and English. On the other hand, the ECJ and ECtHR accept applications in the language of any member states, although the ECJ judges deliberate in French, and, at the ECtHR, in French or English. At the WTO, the official languages are English, French, and Spanish, but—as a matter of practice—panel and AB proceedings are virtually always conducted in English. And, at the ICC, the official languages are Arabic, Chinese, English, French, Russian, and Spanish, although the court's working languages are English and French. A judge fluent only in a less frequently used official language is likely to be less influential than her peers given her limited ability to communicate with colleagues.

Language practices also impact a court's interactions with parties and the larger public. At the International Criminal Tribunal for the former Yugoslavia (ICTY), many witnesses and defence counsel speak Bosnian, Croatian, and/or Serbian. In such cases, many judges are wholly dependent upon interpreters, and typically not in a position to evaluate the quality of the interpretation. In addition, since the ICTY's judgments are issued in English and French, the official versions of these

[25] Daniel Terris et al, *The International Judge: An Introduction to the Men and Women who Decide the World's Cases* (OUP 2007) 66.

[26] The issue is sometimes addressed in the statutes creating courts, eg, ICJ Statute, art 39 ('official languages of the Court shall be French and English'), and sometimes in judge-created rules. Eg, IACtHR Rules of Procedure, art 21 ('official languages of the Court shall be those of the OAS [Organization of American States], which are Spanish, English, Portuguese, and French', while 'working languages shall be those agreed upon by the Court each year').

texts cannot necessarily be read by the tribunal's primary regional audience in the Balkans.

Finally, and perhaps most significantly, a court's language practices can substantially impact its jurisprudence. Language differences may lead to differences in style, emphasis, and terminology. In particular, the rise of English as the dominant language in much international adjudication is thought to bring with it an overrepresentation of native English speakers as lawyers, judges, and registry officials, an infusion and privileging of common law orientations and concepts over civil law alternatives, and an increasing 'Americanization' of international litigation practices.[27]

3.2.2 Judicial practices concerning written pleadings

Written submissions seek to persuade. To do so, they must comply with the written and unwritten norms governing these submissions. These norms speak to the structure, format, and content of the written submissions. Courts differ, however, with respect to many issues that impact the written pleadings, including the number of submissions, the sequencing and order of submissions (seriatim or simultaneous), time limits for pleadings, and whether submissions are available to the public. Courts also vary widely concerning whether third parties or *amicus curiae* are permitted to file written pleadings. Moreover, courts differ as to the relative importance of the written and oral pleadings. In some instances, the written pleading is a litigant's only opportunity to persuade the court of the merits of its case. Very few of these issues are typically addressed in court statutes; in most instances therefore these issues are governed by judge-made rules and practices. And different judicial approaches to each of these issues will substantially impact the nature and content of parties' submissions which, in turn, help frame the judges' disposition of the action.

3.2.3 Judicial practices concerning the oral proceedings

The variation across international courts respecting oral proceedings is, if anything, even larger than the variation regarding written pleadings—including whether or not oral hearings are even held. For current purposes, we limit our discussion to variations in the length, structure, and format of the oral proceedings, although variations in many other practices exist.

At the ICJ, the length of merits hearings varies considerably by case, but often takes between two and six weeks.[28] Historically, ICJ oral proceedings largely consisted of the reading by counsel of prepared texts that often replicated the content of the written submission.[29] In recent years, however, the Court has made efforts

[27] Terris et al (n 25) 78.

[28] Andreas Zimmermann et al (eds), *The Statute of the International Court of Justice: A Commentary* (OUP 2006) 1128.

[29] This practice produced hearings that were 'often tedious and forbidding exercises. Long days are spent listening to the gentle droning of counsel monotonously ploughing through the reading of their prepared texts.' Robert Kolb, *The International Court of Justice* (Hart 2013) 971.

to limit the time devoted to counsel's oral presentations, and hearings today often devote time to the examination of witnesses and other forms of receiving evidence.

Hearings at the WTO's AB, in contrast, often last a day or two. Apart from brief opening and closing statements delivered by counsel, hearings primarily consist of questions from AB members and responses. At other tribunals, oral proceedings are considerably shorter. At the ECJ, the normal speaking time of the initial oral submissions was recently reduced from twenty to fifteen minutes, and—in a considerable change from past practice—today a significant part of the hearing 'is devoted to questions that the members of the Court wish to put to the participants after their initial oral submissions and eventually also to a discussion between the parties or interested persons with respect to the questions raised'.[30]

ITLOS judges follow yet a different model. They created a practice where a 'Timetable' is established in each case which sets out time-limits for each party for the presentation of evidence and arguments. The ITLOS judges have also developed a practice whereby questions to parties are not posed by individual judges. Rather, they are either conveyed by the President to the agents during his consultations with them, or communicated to the parties by the Registrar.

3.2.4 Judicial practices concerning the production and receipt of evidence and fact-finding

Although accurate fact-finding is essential in litigation, international court statutes generally contain only vague provisions regarding evidentiary matters. In exercising their broad discretion regarding evidentiary matters, judges at different courts have developed a variety of practices.

3.2.4.1 Judicial practices regarding experts

At virtually every international court, parties can present evidence through party-selected experts. In addition, many international tribunals have the authority to appoint their own experts. But courts vary in their exercise of this authority.

WTO panellists have been quite active in appointing experts. Over a dozen WTO panels have used scientific experts, and input has been sought from other international organizations, presumably because of their expertise, in an additional nineteen disputes.[31] On the other hand, ICJ judges rarely appoint outside experts, even when the parties request that they do so. This practice has come under substantial criticism, including in the recent *Pulp Mills* case, where several judges questioned the decision not to appoint independent experts.[32] The ECJ likewise has rarely exercised its power to appoint experts. These courts may be reluctant to appoint experts due to the expense involved, which would fall on the court; a fear of delaying the

[30] Allan Rosas, 'Oral Hearings Before the European Court of Justice' (2014) 21 Maastricht J 596, 609.

[31] Gabrielle Z Marceau and Jennifer K Hawkins, 'Experts in WTO Dispute Settlement' (2012) 3 J International Dispute Settlement 493, 494–95.

[32] *Pulp Mills on the River Uruguay (Argentina v Uruguay)* (Merits) [2010] ICJ Rep 14, 110.

proceedings; or to avoid a perception that they are delegating part of the judicial function to an outside party. Whatever the reason, courts' divergent practices with respect to experts has implications for the quality of the court's fact-finding and judgment,[33] as well as for the parties' litigation strategies.

3.2.4.2 The standard of proof

To prevail, a party must satisfy the appropriate 'standard of proof'; a prosecutor, for example, must prove guilt 'beyond a reasonable doubt'. Yet, with the exception of the international criminal courts, international tribunal statutes and rules of procedure typically do not address the standard of proof. Thus, it falls to the judges themselves to decide upon and apply a standard. Once again, we see wide variation in judicial practice, both across courts and, sometimes, among judges on the same court.

ICJ judges have articulated a variety of standards, sometimes in the same case. In *Corfu Channel*, its first contentious case, the judgment refers variously to evidence that is 'free from any doubt'; 'not sufficient ... to constitute decisive legal proof'; and 'fall[s] short of conclusive evidence'. Judicial pronouncements in subsequent cases have done little to clarify the applicable standard of proof. At various times, ICJ judges have invoked the 'preponderance of the evidence' standard widely used in common law systems,[34] or have spoken of proof 'beyond a reasonable doubt',[35] or that is 'convincing' or 'conclusive'.[36] In yet other cases, ICJ judges have reached conclusions 'on the basis of a balance of evidence', 'on a balance of probabilities', 'in all probability', and 'consistent with the probabilities'.[37]

The standard of proof at other tribunals is similarly unclear. The WTO Dispute Settlement Understanding (DSU) does not expressly address the standard of proof, and AB members have repeatedly declined to articulate a standard of proof, emphasizing instead that the nature and scope of evidence required to prevail 'will necessarily vary from measure to measure, provision to provision, and case to case'.[38] Judges at the ECtHR frequently state that, to prevail, a complainant must establish 'proof beyond a reasonable doubt'.[39] This sounds like the familiar criminal law standard of proof. But the judges have expressly stated that this standard 'should not be interpreted as requiring such a high degree of probability as in criminal trials'[40]—without

[33] Jeffrey L Dunoff and Mark A Pollack, 'International Judicial Performances and the Performance of International Courts' in Theresa Squatrito et al (eds), *The Performance of International Courts* (CUP 2017).

[34] *Kasikili/Sedudu Island (Botswana/Namibia)* (Merits) [1999] ICJ Rep 1045, 1233.

[35] *Land and Maritime Boundary (Cameroon v Nigeria)* (Merits) [2002] ICJ Rep 303.

[36] *Armed Activities on the Territory of the Congo (Democratic Republic of the Congo v Uganda)* (Merits) [2005] ICJ Rep 168, para 303.

[37] Katherine Del Mar, 'The International Court of Justice and Standards of Proof' in Karine Bannelier et al (eds), *The ICJ and the Evolution of International Law: The Enduring Impact of the Corfu Channel Case* (Routledge 2012).

[38] Eg, WTO, *Chile—Price Band System and Safeguard Measures Relating to Certain Agricultural Products* (23 September 2002) WT/DS207/AB/RW.

[39] *Veznedaroglu v Turkey*, App no. 32357/96, Eur Ct HR 35 (2000); *Kilic v Turkey*, App no. 22492/93, 2000-II Eur Ct HR (2000).

[40] *Nachova v Bulgaria*, App nos 43577/98 and 43579/98, Chamber Judgment, 26 February 2004, Grand Chamber Judgment, 6 July 2005, para 166.

being entirely clear on what specific degree of probability is required. Similarly, at the Inter-American Court of Human Rights, judges have stated that the standard of proof 'is less formal in an international legal proceeding than in a domestic one',[41] and self-consciously avoided 'making a rigid determination of the amount of evidence required to support a judgment'.[42]

To be sure, many evidentiary practices can be analysed in conventional doctrinal terms. Practice theory is a useful supplement insofar as it highlights that these practices are contingent judicial decisions that occupy the liminal space between structure and agency. These evidentiary practices are performative. For example, a judicial pronouncement that evidence has or has not met the relevant standard of proof is performative in that it reframes and reorganizes the evidence that it purports to describe, in ways that bring the facts into line with legal categorizations. Moreover, these performances are highly patterned, taking place within the genre of the judicial opinion. Evidentiary pronouncements weave together the discursive and material worlds. The pronouncements of the relevant standard of proof are made in written judicial decisions. At the same time, the finding that a party has or has not met the standard of proof on various issues has material implications for the litigants. And, as a growing body of literature demonstrates, these evidentiary practices can be undertaken more or less competently.[43]

3.2.5 Judicial practices regarding deliberations and opinion-writing

International judicial deliberations and opinion-writing are characterized by a wide range of judicial practices, ranging from interpretative strategies to citation practices to the use or non-use of dissenting and separate opinions. Given space constraints, we highlight just two practices involving deliberation and opinion-writing. In each case, we foreground judicial practices at the ICJ, and compare and contrast practices across different courts.

3.2.5.1 Which judges participate?

The ICJ typically hears cases in plenary. After the oral hearings, each judge prepares a written 'note' outlining her tentative views of how each of the issues in the case should be resolved. After these notes are anonymized and distributed, the judges meet in private to deliberate. At this meeting, each judge speaks, beginning with any judges ad hoc and proceeding in inverse order of seniority, from most junior to most senior. At the conclusion of this process, which might span several meetings, the main areas of agreement have emerged, and a three-person drafting committee is elected.

41 *Velasquez Rodriguez v Honduras*, Inter-Am Ct HR (ser C) No 4 (1988).

42 *Cesti Hurtado v Peru* (Reparations and Costs), Inter-Am Ct HR (ser C), No 78 (31 May 2001).

43 See, eg, Anna Riddell and Brendan Plant, *Evidence Before the International Court of Justice* (BIICL 2009); Nancy A Combs, *Fact-Finding Without Facts: The Uncertain Evidentiary Foundations of International Criminal Convictions* (CUP 2010); Michelle Grando, *Evidence, Proof, and Fact-Finding in WTO Dispute Settlement* (CUP 2009).

The drafting committee prepares and circulates a draft judgment. After other judges offer suggestions, a revised draft judgment is circulated. The full court then meets to discuss this text on a paragraph-by-paragraph basis. After this 'first reading', an amended draft is distributed and subject to a second reading. At the end of the second reading, a final vote is taken on the operative part of the judgment. On each point, each judge orally votes 'yes' or 'no', in order of inverse seniority, with the decision on each issue taken by a majority of the judges present.

This labour-intensive and highly inclusive process is *not* required by the Court's Statute. Rather it reflects a set of practices developed and refined over the years by the judges themselves, which has changed little from the PCIJ era.[44] Moreover, it has been purposefully designed and refined to ensure 'that every judge is involved at every phase of the drafting process—a practice that appears to be unique among international courts'.[45]

The modalities of deliberation at other tribunals are very different, and they are likewise the product of judicial practice rather than treaty rule. For example, the DSU provides that the WTO AB 'shall be composed of seven persons, three of whom shall serve on any one case'. Notwithstanding this seemingly clear treaty text, AB members themselves developed a system whereby all seven AB members participate in the consideration of a case. As memorialized in the AB's Working Procedures, the members hearing a case 'shall exchange views with the other [AB] members' before finalizing a report. To implement this provision, 'it has been the practice for all [AB] members to come to Geneva for a few days ... to consult with the three members of the Division hearing the appeal' in what has come to be known as the 'exchange of views'.[46] The practice of involving members of a tribunal *not* responsible for hearing a case in the deliberations is unique in international dispute settlement.

By contrast, at many other courts, particularly those with larger case loads such as the ECJ and the ECtHR, the vast majority of cases are considered and decided by a 'chamber' consisting of fewer than all members of the court. In these instances, deliberation practices are *not* designed to ensure that judicial opinions reflect the views of the entire bench. For example, at both the ECJ and the ECtHR, draft opinions are prepared by a single *juge rapporteur*, and although there are deliberations among the members of the chamber, the final opinion often bears the strong influence of the *juge rapporteur*. Moreover, in stark contrast to the AB, the members of the Court who are outside the chamber are not included in the process of deliberation or drafting.[47]

In short, international judges have, within the parameters set by their governing statutes and rules, developed their own diverse set of practices regarding the number and identity of judges that participate in deliberation and opinion drafting, and these vary dramatically across courts.

[44] Gleider I Hernández, *The International Court of Justice and the Judicial Function* (CUP 2014) 104.

[45] Philippa Webb, *International Judicial Integration and Fragmentation* (OUP 2013) 191.

[46] DP Steger, 'Improvements and Reforms of the WTO Appellate Body' in Federico Ortino and Ernst-Ulrich Petersmann (eds), *The WTO Dispute Settlement System* (Kluwer 2004) 41, 44.

[47] Nina-Louisa Arold, *The Legal Culture of the European Court of Human Rights* (Brill 2007) 75.

3.2.5.2 The use of separate and dissenting opinions

A similar level of variation is seen when we shift from judicial input (ie, who deliberates, who drafts) to judicial output (ie, the content and form of judicial opinions). Thus, international courts display great variation in interpretative methods, in citation practices, and in the nature and quality of legal reasoning. For now, we limit our discussion to one dimension of judicial output, the use or non-use of separate or dissenting opinions.

Judicial statutes frequently permit, but do not require, separate opinions. The ICJ Statute, for example, provides that 'if the judgment does not represent . . . the unanimous opinion of the judges, any judge shall be entitled to deliver a separate opinion', and virtually identical language is found in the treaties creating ITLOS and the ECtHR. The Rome Statute of the ICC provides that members of the Appeals Chamber 'may deliver a separate or dissenting opinion on a question of law'. The WTO DSU implicitly contemplates dissents, providing that 'opinions expressed in the Appellate Body report by individuals serving on the Appellate Body shall be anonymous'. One important potential exception is the ECJ Statute, which does not explicitly mention dissent, but does provide that 'the deliberations of the Court shall be and remain secret'. ECJ judges have interpreted this clause to preclude the issuance of separate opinions. Given that the statutes of other tribunals require deliberations to remain secret, yet judgments from these courts frequently contain separate opinions, we believe the ECJ judges' interpretation is not compelled by the treaty language.

Notwithstanding the broad similarities in treaty text, international courts have adopted very different practices with respect to separate opinions. At some international courts, the use of separate concurring and dissenting opinions is highly common. ICJ judgments are virtually always accompanied by multiple dissents. By way of example, the ICJ's five most recent merits judgments have been accompanied by ten,[48] twelve,[49] eleven,[50] ten,[51] and seven[52] separate dissenting and concurring opinions, respectively. At ITLOS, every single contentious case to proceed to judgment, and every single provisional measures order, has been accompanied by one or more concurring or dissenting opinions. The last five ITLOS decisions have been accompanied by ten,[53] six,[54] five,[55] four,[56] and thirteen[57] concurring or dissenting

[48] *Certain Activities Carried out by Nicaragua in the Border Area (Costa Rica v Nicaragua)*, 16 December 2015.

[49] *Application of the Convention on the Prevention and Punishment of the Crime of Genocide (Croatia v Serbia)*, 3 February 2015.

[50] *Whaling in the Antarctic (Australia v Japan, New Zealand intervening)* (Merits) [2014] ICJ Rep 226.

[51] *Maritime Dispute (Peru v Chile)* (Merits) [2014] ICJ Rep 3.

[52] *Territorial and Maritime Dispute (Nicaragua v Colombia)* (Merits) [2012] ICJ Rep 624.

[53] *The 'Enrica Lexie' Incident (Italy v India)* (Provisional Measures, Order of 24 August 2015).

[54] *The 'Arctic Sunrise' Case (Kingdom of the Netherlands v Russian Federation)* (Provisional Measures, Order of 22 November 2013).

[55] *Request for an Advisory Opinion Submitted by the Sub-Regional Fisheries Commission* (Advisory Opinion, Order of 2 April 2015).

[56] *The 'ARA Libertad' Case (Argentina v Ghana)* (Provisional Measures, Order of 15 December 2012).

[57] *The M/V 'Virginia G' Case (Panama/Guinea-Bissau)* (Judgment of 14 April 2014).

opinions, respectively. Separate opinions are likewise quite common at the ICC and the ECtHR.

At other international tribunals, in contrast, separate opinions are never, or rarely, issued. In over sixty years of operations, the ECJ has *never* issued a judgment with separate or dissenting opinions. The DSU and the AB's Working Procedures expressly contemplate separate opinions. Notwithstanding this language, the initial members of the AB entered into a secret agreement among themselves not to issue dissents. This agreement held for several years; the first AB report with a concurring statement was issued in 2001, and the first AB report with a dissent was issued in 2005. Separate opinions are still extremely rare; over the first two decades of WTO dispute settlement, roughly 8 per cent of panel reports and less than 5 per cent of AB reports contained separate or dissenting opinions.

In short, the use or non-use of separate opinions is less a function of the design choices made by states than of decisions made by judges on international courts. Elsewhere, we have explored the consequences of these decisions on, inter alia, judicial collegiality, independence, legitimacy, and the quality and development of the law.[58] For current purposes, it is sufficient to note that the diverse patterns regarding use of separate opinions can be understood as judicial practices, not driven by statutes, but rather as patterned performances that can be performed more or less competently. Moreover, these practices convey social meaning. As we have explained elsewhere, at courts that do not issue separate opinions, judges claim that speaking with one voice enhances the legitimacy and the coherence of judicial doctrine and the independence of the judges. Judges at courts with frequent separate opinions, by contrast, claim that this practice enhances the transparency, and hence the legitimacy, of the judicial process, and that separate opinions sharpen judicial doctrine by clarifying the strength of any precedent.

This incomplete and partial overview provides a sense of the range and number of international judicial practices. For current purposes, two points are particularly salient. First, these activities exhibit all of the characteristics of practices identified by Adler and Pouliot. In particular, they have a marked performative dimension, whether in the order of speaking in the privacy of deliberations, in the making of extrajudicial pronouncements, and in the rhetorical style and argumentative techniques of the judicial opinion. These practices are strongly patterned, as they regularly and repeatedly occur within the litigation context, and yet permit judges to exercise considerable agency. They can be, and are, performed more or less competently, as ascertained by the relevant communities of practice. Thus, over time, international judges become known for their skill in crafting arguments, drafting opinions, or in managing a trial courtroom. Judicial practices rest upon, and instantiate, background knowledge of substantive law as well as unwritten norms of appropriate judicial conduct. And, finally, these practices involve both discursive and material elements. Judicial dialogue and opinions are discursive practices that have substantial material ramifications for litigants and, potentially, many other actors.

[58] Jeffrey L Dunoff and Mark A Pollack, 'International Judicial Dissent: Causes and Consequences' (unpublished manuscript).

Second, these important practices vary substantially, and in some cases dramatically, across international tribunals. Although international courts engage in similar tasks—namely, the authoritative interpretation and application of international legal texts to determine if one actor breached another's legal rights—courts perform these tasks in substantially different ways. This variation motivates our commitment to a study of *comparative* international judicial practice.

4 Towards a Practice-Oriented Research Agenda

A primary goal of this chapter is to provide a conceptual framework and analytic tools to understand the day-to-day activities of international judges. The typology we develop raises questions regarding the empirical determinants and normative implications of the diverse judicial practices we survey. Although analysis of these issues is well beyond the scope of this short chapter, it is nonetheless useful to identify several topics that future scholars might address. Both individually and together, the lines of inquiry described below outline a robust research agenda intended to advance our understanding of international judicial practices.

First, it is possible for future studies to expand on the typology set forth above by going *wider* and *deeper*. Going wider means expanding beyond the handful of prominent tribunals discussed in section 3. Since there are at least twenty-four operational international tribunals, it is evident that the discussion in this chapter does no more than scratch the surface of the large universe of international courts. Beyond courts, practice theory can be usefully applied to international arbitral tribunals and other law-applying bodies, such as human rights committees. The empirical terrain of international judicial (and quasi-judicial) practices is vast.

The list of practices identified above, moreover, is illustrative, rather than exhaustive. Future scholars can *go deeper* by studying a fuller body of practices than those we identify. Going deeper will require in-depth knowledge of the on-the-ground realities at various courts. As it would be difficult for any one scholar to possess this level of knowledge regarding multiple tribunals, 'going deeper' in the study of judicial practices will likely take the form of research by teams of scholars expert in the study of specific international courts.

Second, future scholars can introduce temporality to the analysis, studying how, and why, practices change over time. Many of the practices surveyed above display great continuity over time. For example, dissent practices at international courts have not changed over decades. Some deliberation practices, on the other hand, do change over time, as the ICJ's recent decision to eliminate the preparation of 'notes' by each judge following hearings on jurisdictional matters illustrates. These examples underscore the importance of inquiry into patterns of inheritance and adaptation, habit, and innovation. Thus a second frontier of research would explore issues of *continuity and change over time* in international judicial practices.

Third, future scholars should devote substantial attention to the *consequences of judicial practices*. While the practice turn has thus far been used for primarily interpretivist purposes, our preliminary research suggests that variations in international judicial practices can have systematic impacts on judicial outputs, and future scholars can pursue a positivist research agenda for the study of the causes and consequences of judicial practices. Indeed, while the everyday practices of international judges are worth studying in their own right, drawing connections between specific practices and specific outcomes may produce the most important payoff for scholars seeking to understand the role of courts and judges in the international legal order.

5 Conclusion

As the other contributions to this volume demonstrate, the rise in number and importance of international courts has sparked a sophisticated literature on the judicialization of international relations. The day-to-day internal workings of international courts, in contrast, have remained almost entirely opaque. This chapter argues that it is time to open the black box of international courts, and introduces a practice-oriented approach that is well-suited for this purpose. This approach links the normative and legal concerns of traditional IL writings with the empirical concerns of IR scholars, while correcting both disciplines' neglect of the inner workings of courts. Focusing on judicial practices promises to reveal a wide range of otherwise concealed patterns and activities that, together, constitute international tribunals' inner workings and decision-making processes. It should therefore be attractive to interpretivist scholars, as it explains a wider range of judicial activities and provides a richer account of the judicial experience. It should also be attractive to positivist scholars more focused on explaining and predicting judicial outcomes.

Drawing links between different practices and different outcomes promises to enhance understanding of international courts. Just as importantly, as judicial practices can be designed and modified to better achieve specific goals, the study of judicial practices can provide concrete tools to those who seek to ensure that the advantages of the increased use of international courts outweigh their disadvantages, rendering these bodies less of a mixed blessing, and more a powerful tool for the achievement of international law's goals.

PART III

BACKLASH/CRITICISM

6

NGOs for International Justice

Criminal or Victims' Justice?

Kjersti Lohne

1 Introduction

Academics and legal practitioners have pointed out that doctrines and practices of international criminal law violate the fundamental principle of legality and fair trial rights, such as the presumption of innocence and the equality of arms.[1] Others have noted the dearth of penal theory and fuzzy penological objectives with international punishment,[2] with some even suggesting that international criminal justice inevitably ends up producing 'show trials' wherein the defendant merely serves an instrumental role for ulterior purposes, such as establishing 'truth', 'memory', and 'justice for victims'.[3] Meanwhile, the figure of the victim has taken central stage in international criminal justice.[4] Victims are now invoked as the *raison d'être* and telos of the work of the International Criminal Court (ICC) by academics, practitioners, and promoters of international criminal justice alike, often—as demonstrated by the Rome Statute's Preamble—in association with the need to 'end impunity' as a foundational value of the ICC.[5] According to Bassiouni, '[o]ne of the most important recognitions of the victim as a subject of international criminal law is contained

[1] George P Fletcher and Jens David Ohlin, 'Reclaiming Fundamental Principles of Criminal Law in the Darfur Case' (2005) 3 Journal of International Criminal Justice 539; Darryl Robinson, 'The Identity Crisis of International Criminal Law' (2008) 21 Leiden Journal of International Law 925; Dov Jacobs, 'A Tale of Four Illusions: The Rights of the Defence before International Criminal Tribunals' in C Rohan and G Zyberi (eds), *Defence Perspectives on International Criminal Justice* (CUP 2017).

[2] Immi Tallgren, 'The Sensibility and Sense of International Criminal Law' (2002) 13 European Journal of International Law 561; Mark A Drumbl, *Atrocity, Punishment and International Law* (CUP 2007); Barbora Holá and Joris van Wijk, 'Life after Conviction at International Criminal Tribunals: An Empirical Overview' (2014) 12 Journal of International Criminal Justice 109.

[3] Martti Koskenniemi, 'Between Impunity and Show Trials' (2002) 6 Max Planck Yearbook of United Nations Law Online 1.

[4] Sofia Stolk, 'The Victim, the International Criminal Court and the Search for Truth: On the Interdependence and Incompatibility of Truths About Mass Atrocity' (2015) 13 Journal of International Criminal Justice 973.

[5] Sara Kendall and Sarah Nouwen, 'Representational Practices at the International Criminal Court: The Gap between Juridified and Abstract Victimhood' (2014) 76 Law and Contemporary Problems 235.

NGOs for International Justice: Criminal or Victims' Justice? Kjersti Lohne.

in the ICC Statute'.[6] The provisions regarding rights for victims of international crimes *as victims* in the ICC's Rome Statute and Rules of Procedure and Evidence are therefore celebrated as '[o]ne of the major innovations of the International Criminal Court',[7] with the ICC recognizing and outlining principles of victim participation in court proceedings, protection of victims and witnesses during proceedings, rights to compensation or reparations, and the creation of a Trust Fund for Victims from which reparations may be made.

Thus here we are at a critical juncture for international criminal justice. As already observed by others, 'going too far in the direction of victims will, aside from creating well-known liberal fears for the defendant, transform international criminal justice so as to deny it its very character as a criminal law enterprise'.[8] Aside from constituting 'justice' as a zero-sum game between these two different constituencies, the victim–perpetrator issue speaks to broader and deeper notions about the 'identity' of the international criminal justice project, and specifically to Robinson's and Mégret's respective diagnosis of international criminal justice as in a state of 'identity crisis'[9] and as 'riddled by anxieties'.[10] As an amalgam of different legal fields—criminal law, human rights law, and humanitarian law—international criminal law's norms and practitioners 'draw a deep intellectual inheritance from human rights and humanitarian law', pointing in particular to the interpretative, substantive, and ideological assumptions travelling with a 'victim-focused teleological reasoning'.[11] In a similar vein, Dixon and Tenove suggest that international criminal justice is constituted at the intersection of three global fields—interstate diplomacy, criminal justice, and human rights advocacy—with the latter especially influencing its approach to victims.[12]

While the associations between international criminal courts and human rights non-governmental organizations (NGOs) are well-observed,[13] there is far less empirical analysis of the underlying arrangements and assumptions of those working to influence the field. This matters because in as much as a question of 'being' is a question of 'being as', the identity of international criminal justice is at the mercy

[6] M Cherif Bassiouni, 'International Recognition of Victims' Rights' (2006) 6 Human Rights Law Review 203, 230.

[7] Jo-Anne Wemmers, 'Victims and the International Criminal Court (ICC): Evaluating the Success of the ICC with Respect to Victims' (2009) 16 International Review of Victimology 211, 211.

[8] Frédéric Mégret, 'The Anxieties of International Criminal Justice' (2016) 29 Leiden Journal of International Law 197, 211.

[9] Robinson (n 1). [10] Mégret (n 8).

[11] Robinson (n 1) 961. See also other important contributions on international criminal justice as an amalgam of legal regimes and traditions (domestic criminal law, human rights law, humanitarian law, and transitional justice): Allison Marston Danner and Jenny S Martinez, 'Guilty Associations: Joint Criminal Enterprise, Command Responsibility, and the Development of International Criminal Law' (2005) California Law Review 75; Peter Dixon and Chris Tenove, 'International Criminal Justice as a Transnational Field: Rules, Authority and Victims' (2013) 7 International Journal of Transitional Justice 393.

[12] Dixon and Tenove (n 11).

[13] Margaret E Keck and Kathryn Sikkink, *Activists Beyond Borders: Advocacy Networks in International Politics* (Cornell University Press 1998); Marlies Glasius, *The International Criminal Court: A Global Civil Society Achievement* (Routledge 2006); Kathryn Sikkink, *The Justice Cascade: How Human Rights Prosecutions Are Changing World Politics* (WW Norton & Company 2011).

of interpretations narrated through the stories told about it, and 'to what' international criminal justice is compared to and associated with.[14] To this end, the chapter specifically approaches the victim–perpetrator tension in international criminal justice through a legal sociology approach to NGO advocacy at the ICC, adopting a view 'from the outside' in order to explore how international criminal law and justice are embedded in and by wider social processes. Based on fieldwork observations and interviews, the chapter analyzes the imbalance in victim–perpetrator focus in NGO advocacy in international criminal justice through an exploration of NGO advocacy at the ICC. It argues that the significant imbalance in attention towards victims and defendants in NGO advocacy at the Court can shed additional light on the 'identity' of international criminal justice as victims' rather than criminal justice.

Following a contextualization of NGOs in international (criminal) law and a method section, the analysis proceeds in five sections where the victim–perpetrator dichotomy in NGO advocacy is incrementally explored. The first section describes and 'unpacks' core non-governmental *organization* for the ICC, revealing that there is only one major NGO advocating the rights of defendants—the International Bar Association (IBA). Their organization is further explored in section 2, where it is suggested that there is a separation between 'rule of law' advocacy and 'human rights' advocacy in international criminal justice. Section 3 probes deeper into the associations between human rights advocacy as victims' advocacy, and argues that the 'fight against impunity' demonstrates interesting 'pro-prosecution' sensibilities at the international level that to some extent contradicts NGO engagement with domestic systems of criminal justice in western democracies. This apparent contradiction is further explored in section 4, which focuses on NGOs' approach to legal aid. What is explored here are the social conditions of NGO advocacy as centred on victims' justice through analysing part of what can be referred to as the field's moral economy, that is, to the norms and sensibilities lending legitimacy to market rationalities:[15] materially, victims are a more fundable constituency for human rights NGOs to advocate on behalf of; imaginatively, as explored in the chapter's final section, the presumption that defendants might indeed be innocent seems to be, at best, weak. Having thus enquired into what type of justice international criminal justice is imagined to provide—and for whom—the chapter concludes that for those advocating international criminal justice, the justice imagined is that for victims.

[14] For a narrative concept of the state, see Erik Ringmar, 'On the Ontological Status of the State' (1996) 2 European Journal of International Relations 439.

[15] Susanne Karstedt and Stephen Farrall, 'The Moral Economy of Everyday Crime: Markets, Consumers and Citizens' (2006) 46 British Journal of Criminology 1011; Kristin Bergtora Sandvik, 'The Political and Moral Economies of Dual Technology Transfers: Arming Police Drones' in *Drones and Unmanned Aerial Systems* (Springer 2016).

2 Approaching NGOs in International Criminal Justice

As aptly put by Philippe Sands in his keynote speech at the European Society of International Law's annual conference in Oslo, '[o]ur legal world is no longer just about states'.[16] The presence and participation of NGOs in international law and policy development are familiar by now. They have advanced the creation of treaties and international organizations, and lobbied for implementation and enforcement of international rules at the domestic level.[17] Their activities 'encompass virtually every area of international concern',[18] and the growth in numbers of international NGOs alone makes it eminently reasonable to enquire into not only if they matter, but how and when they matter.[19]

Writing about the United Nations, Donini declared more than two decades ago that 'the Temple of States would be a rather dull place without nongovernmental organizations'.[20] It reflects a more general claim about NGOs' contribution to the humanization of international law and policy,[21] that is, to the normative shift in the international legal order towards a focus on human security—the security of peoples and persons—rather than an exclusive focus on state security.[22] In particular, the work of human rights NGOs has pushed the evolution of human rights norms and its legal institutionalization and dispersion around the world.[23] As seen by Glasius,[24] '[t]hese two features are, of course, interrelated: the development of a more people-empowering international rule of law, and the emergence of a global civil society capable of contributing to such a rule of law, feed and drive one another'.

The development of international criminal justice is considered part of the advance towards a more 'people-empowering' international rule of law. Indeed, the creation of the ICC is referred to as a 'global civil society achievement',[25] or even, an

[16] Philippe Sands, 'Reflections on International Judicialization' (2017) 27 European Journal of International Law 885, 889.

[17] Steve Charnovitz, 'Nongovernmental Organizations and International Law' (2006) 100 The American Journal of International Law 348.

[18] Karsten Nowrot, 'Legal Consequences of Globalization: The Status of Non-Governmental Organizations under International Law' (1999) 6 Indiana Journal of Global Legal Studies 579, 589.

[19] Eg, in 1990 there were approximately 20,300 organizations listed as international NGOs in the Yearbook of International Organizations. Two decades later there were 56,000 international NGOs. By 2013, this number had risen to just over 58,500. See UIA, *Yearbook of International Organizations* (Brill 2014).

[20] Antonio Donini, 'The Bureaucracy and the Free Spirits: Stagnation and Innovation in the Relationship between the UN and NGOs' (1995) 16 Third World Quarterly 421, 421.

[21] Charnovitz (n 17); see generally Keck and Sikkink (n 13); Ruti G Teitel, *Humanity's Law* (OUP 2011).

[22] Teitel (n 21).

[23] Keck and Sikkink (n 13); Risse Thomas, Stephen C Ropp, and Kathryn Sikkink, *The Power of Human Rights: International Norms and Domestic Change* (CUP 1999).

[24] Marlies Glasius, 'Expertise in the Cause of Justice: Global Civil Society Influence on the Statute for an International Criminal Court' in Marlies Glasius, Mary Kaldor, and Helmut K Anheier (eds), *Global Civil Society* (OUP 2002).

[25] Glasius (n 13).

'achievement of the masses organized'.[26] According to scholars and advocates, the emergence of the NGO *Coalition for the International Criminal Court* (CICC) as 'the most advanced and sophisticated organization thus far created collectively by civil society to influence and shape multilateral treaty-making is an irresistibly compelling feature of the story of the Rome Statute'.[27] Therefore, alongside the legacy of Nuremberg,[28] the crafting of the ICC can also be seen as emerging from the globalization of human rights and the proliferation of NGOs in the late 1980s, and specifically, to the emergence of an international campaign against impunity.

By the time of the Rome Conference—the United Nations Diplomatic Conference on Plenipotentiaries on the Establishment of an International Criminal Court—in 1998, the CICC comprised a transnational advocacy network of approximately 800 organizations. Out of these, 236 NGOs were accredited to the conference, and were represented by about 500 individuals. The CICC was thus the biggest 'delegation' in Rome, in numbers and expertise far surpassing state delegations. They provided a number of functions, such as lobbying state and intergovernmental representatives; writing expert documents, reports, and journal articles; convening seminars and conferences; disseminating the Court ideal to a wider audience; seeking and giving financial support for Southern NGOs and expert participation in the debates; providing experts and interns to smaller and poorer government delegations; and street action.[29] Through process tracing, Glasius examines the specific contribution of NGOs to three specific provisions to the Statute, finding that NGOs played a significant role in influencing the drafting and adoption of an independent prosecutor and gender-specific crimes in the Rome Statute, while being less successful regarding their attempts to include prohibitions on the use of indiscriminate weapons in the Rome Statute.[30]

While there is a substantial amount of literature on the role of NGOs in the ICC treaty negotiations, as it has become somewhat of an emblem for the 'new diplomacy' of the 1990s,[31] much less has been written on the continued significance of these actors for the Court and for the development and identity of international criminal justice generally. Since 'Rome' however, the role of NGOs has developed in tandem with the ICC's institutionalization,[32] fulfilling a number of functions at the international level that, arguably, would be inconceivable within western systems

[26] Cenap Cakmak, 'Transnational Activism in World Politics and Effectiveness of a Loosely Organised Principled Global Network: The Case of the NGO Coalition for an International Criminal Court' (2008) 12 The International Journal of Human Rights 373, 373.

[27] Fanny Benedetti, Karine Bonneau, and John L Washburn, *Negotiating the International Criminal Court: New York to Rome, 1994–1998* (Nijhoff 2014).

[28] Geoffrey Best, *War and Law since 1945* (Clarendon 1994); Antonio Cassese, *International Criminal Law* (2nd edn, OUP 2008).

[29] Glasius (n 24).

[30] ibid; Comparing the efforts of NGOs in these three areas, she suggests that core features such as strength in numbers, experience as 'conference-goers', and internal support largely affected the success of the campaigns.

[31] David Davenport, 'The New Diplomacy' (2002) 116 Policy Review 17.

[32] Heidi Nichols Haddad, 'After the Norm Cascade: NGO Mission Expansion and the Coalition for the International Criminal Court' (2013) 19 Global Governance: A Review of Multilateralism and International Organizations 187.

of criminal justice.[33] In addition to their 'traditional' roles of advocacy and agenda-setting, they identify and represent victims to the Court; they provide evidence and *amicus curia* briefs, draft penal codes, and lobby for their implementation in domestic systems of criminal justice, to give but a few examples.[34]

As Pearson observes however, '[i]n any situation where the subtleties and complexities of human dynamics are crucial to the outcome, as they are in the case of the ICC negotiations, such evidence is neither available nor quantifiable'.[35] The intention of this chapter is thus not to identify a direct effect of NGOs to specific developments in international criminal law. Rather, the importance of analysis of NGOs' interaction with international criminal law is in observing the dynamics of their involvement, and in the complexities of processes shaping the field of international law. In this manner, the role of human rights NGOs in providing moral authority, visibility, and legitimacy to international criminal justice is as important[36]—if not more—than states adopting NGOs' positions on specific wordings or interpretation of statutory provisions, namely because it recognizes the normative orderings within which legal norms operate. The empirical analysis is therefore concerned with norms, values, and material relations, as these are constitutive of social conditions for the practice and development of international criminal law. In lieu of democratic accountability, transparency in international law-making processes as well as the social conditions on which law—broadly understood—is administered, interpreted, and enforced, is fundamental to its legitimacy.[37] A legal sociology approach that sees international criminal law from 'the outside'—as constitutive of and by society—enables an empirically founded critique of the power that international criminal law embodies.

Therefore, mindful to the way in which human rights NGOs are assumed as 'particularly important for mobilizing moral authority'[38] to the field of international criminal justice, the aim of this chapter is to probe into the material and ideational aspects of this role. Who are they and how are they organized; what issues matter to them, and why? In focusing on the materialities and imaginations of non-governmental *organization* for the ICC, the empirical analysis below reveals significant imbalances in attention towards the rights of victims and defendants in international criminal justice, which, on a broader level, reveal important dimensions of the social conditions informing the identity of international criminal justice as embodied by the ICC.

[33] At the domestic level however, NGOs are engaged to a much greater extent on behalf of the defendant. See section 4.

[34] Kjersti Lohne, *Advocates of Humanity: Human Rights NGOs in International Criminal Justice* (OUP forthcoming 2018).

[35] Zoe Pearson, 'Non-Governmental Organizations and the International Criminal Court: Changing Landscapes of International Law' (2006) 39 Cornell International Law Journal 243, 254.

[36] Cakmak (n 26); Dixon and Tenove (n 11); Kjersti Lohne, 'Global Civil Society, the ICC, and Legitimacy in International Criminal Justice' in N Hayashi and C Bailliet (eds), *The Legitimacy of International Criminal Tribunals* (CUP 2017).

[37] Jürgen Habermas, 'The Constitutionalization of International Law and the Legitimation Problems of a Constitution for World Society' (2008) 15 Constellations 444.

[38] Dixon and Tenove (n 11).

3 Methods

The data for this chapter is based on parts of the author's doctoral research, which is a transnational, multi-sited ethnography of human rights NGOs in international criminal justice.[39] As the hub of global justice-making, The Hague has been the primary perspective in research and analysis.[40] This chapter specifically draws on data from observations in The Hague and interviews conducted in 2013 with all staff members of the CICC's secretariat office in The Hague (seven informants), except from the administration and finance officer, in addition to the CICC's convenor, one regional staff member, and two representatives from their national coalitions. Moreover, the analysis builds on interviews conducted with NGO informants working on international justice issues from the IBA, Human Rights Watch, Open Society Justice Initiative, Parliamentarians for Global Action, and REDRESS. Two people who formerly had been central NGO actors were interviewed in their capacities as independent victims' rights experts, now acting as consultants and experts on the ICC and victims' rights in particular. The analysis of the organizational make-up of NGO advocacy has been further informed by the NGOs' online representations of issue agendas and activities. The triangulation of interviews, observations, and (online) representations provide a holistic analysis of non-governmental *organization* for the ICC, in comparison to methodological approaches that, for instance, base analysis upon online representations.[41]

The analysis was done through a series of coding in NVivo, a qualitative analysis software, where the data was assigned to thematic, conceptual, and analytic codes.[42] Narrative analysis was used to analyse interviews, which is an approach that underlines informants' self-presentations of identities and values. In other words, what has been important in analysis has been the search for informants' meaning-making, and how agency is conditioned by culture and context.[43] The research process can therefore be described as a swirl of interpretation, moving in and out of theory, method, and data. Hence, in employing this methodological approach to the role of NGOs in order to say something about the 'identity' of international criminal justice, '[o]bjectivity is not measured by procedures that assure an accurate mapping of the world but by the growth of knowledge; that is, the imaginative and parsimonious reconstruction of theory to accommodate anomalies'.[44]

39 Lohne (n 34).

40 The CICC also has a secretariat in New York, the 'UN office', and many of the international human rights NGOs that are the focus in this analysis likewise have representatives in New York or Washington. While there is reason to believe that data from New York would have provided different insights, in studying law in its cultural, social, and political contexts I considered proximity to the actual workings of the Court more important than a New York-based analysis on global justice lobbyism.

41 R Charli Carpenter and Betcy Jose, 'Transnational Issue Networks in Real and Virtual Space: The Case of Women, Peace and Security' (2012) 12 Global Networks 525.

42 See eg Johnny Saldaña, *The Coding Manual for Qualitative Researchers* (Sage 2009) 32.

43 Lois Presser, 'The Narratives of Offenders' (2009) 13 Theoretical Criminology 177; Sveinung Sandberg, 'Are Self-Narratives Strategic or Determined, Unified or Fragmented? Reading Breivik's Manifesto in Light of Narrative Criminology' (2013) 56 Acta Sociologica 69.

44 Michael Burawoy, 'The Extended Case Method' (1998) 16 Sociological Theory 4, 5.

Importantly though, international criminal justice is a field in constant flux, driven by events that have the potential to significantly change the landscape in which international criminal justice operates. Since the empirical research was conducted, there has been an articulation of a legitimacy crisis for the ICC, and several African countries have already sent, or are voicing their intention to, send notice of withdrawal from the ICC and the Rome Statute. To a certain extent then, empirical analysis is contextual—informed by the specificities of space and time. Yet the analytical aim is nonetheless to tease out elements and qualities in international criminal justice-making that are more stable, by way of identifying trends, characteristics, and dynamics of the field. Such an approach can in turn deepen the understanding of the pushback and legitimacy 'crisis' that international criminal justice-making is currently experiencing. In what follows, the chapter demonstrates the skewed nature of the international criminal justice project through an analysis of the significant imbalance in attention towards victims and defendants in NGO advocacy at the Court.

4 The Victim–Perpetrator Dichotomy in NGO Advocacy

4.1 Non-governmental *organization* for the ICC

Today, the CICC has developed into an institution of international criminal justice. According to its own website and description,

> The Coalition for the International Criminal Court includes 2,500 civil society organizations in 150 different countries working in partnership to strengthen international cooperation with the ICC; ensure that the Court is fair, effective and independent; make justice both visible and universal; and advance stronger national laws that deliver justice to victims of war crimes, crimes against humanity and genocide. [45]

Cooperation between the ICC and NGOs is endorsed by the ICC Rules of Procedure and Evidence. While having formal roles, such as dealing with accreditation of civil society to the annual Assembly of States Parties (ASP) meetings,[46] the NGOs also serve a range of informal roles in the functioning of the ICC. For example, the CICC facilitates access between the Court and civil society in situation countries, they do outreach to explain the Court's mandate to affected communities, lobby states parties for political and financial support to the Court, and organize a host of events and awareness-building activities such as lectures, seminars, and side events at the ASP meetings as well as in the everyday life of international criminal justice in The Hague. Such engagement has led to characterizations of the relationship between the ICC and the CICC as one of 'synergy', to the extent that for those unacquainted

[45] 'About the Coalition' (*Coalition for the International Criminal Court)* <www.iccnow.org/?mod=coalition> (accessed 8 February 2014).

[46] Assembly of States Parties to the Rome Statute of the International Criminal Court, 'Handbook for Participants' (20 October 2015) <www.asp.icc-cpi.int/iccdocs/asp_docs/ASP14/ASP14-Handbook-ENG.pdf> (accessed 27 June 2016).

with the internal dynamics of international criminal justice, the latter has been confused with being an organ of the former.[47] Moreover, the role of the CICC can be seen as both mobilizers and monitors of international criminal justice, both of which play into their lobbyism and legal assistance, campaigns, capacity-building, and outreach. Their activities thus span both sides of a common division characterizing NGOs: advocacy and service provision.[48] However, service provision, such as building capacity and giving assistance to local civil society organizations in ICC situation countries, or offering legal and technical assistance to governments, are still services imbued with norms, values, and imaginations of justice. Hence, advocacy and service provision are not mutually exclusive aims, but rather different strategies used by NGOs in their promotion of international criminal justice.

The CICC's structure can be understood as having three different parts: a secretariat, a transnational advocacy network of supporting NGOs, and a group of steering committee members. The steering committee provides policy and programme coherence for the CICC's activities, and includes many of the founding members of the Coalition. Given their central roles in NGO advocacy for the ICC, Amnesty International, the International Federation for Human Rights, Human Rights Watch, No Peace Without Justice, Parliamentarians for Global Action, REDRESS, Women's Initiatives for Gender Justice, and the World Federalist Movement-Institute for Global Policy can be identified as core steering committee members.[49] Next to these eight organizations, Open Society Justice Initiative and the IBA can also be identified as belonging to the group of NGOs that are particularly active in ICC advocacy.

Known as the 'drafters' or the 'usual suspects' by people in the field, these organizations are all international, western-based organizations with a human rights profile: They have campaigns or programmes to do with international criminal justice, and most have staff members working specifically on ICC-related issues, which reflects both their resource capabilities and their perception of international criminal justice as a critical human rights issue. Most of them have offices and permanent representation in The Hague. There they monitor the progress of international criminal law coming out of the ICC, they draft proposals and recommendations, and lobby states parties at The Hague Working Group meetings, which are diplomatic working group meetings between state members of the Court—a type of mini-ASPs on particular issues. This core group of NGOs have become conspicuous participants in the field of international criminal justice and at the ASP meetings in particular; here, they give plenary statements to the General Debate, host shadow meetings and side events where, for instance, they bring together their own expertise

[47] Lohne (n 36).

[48] Amanda Murdie and David R Davis, 'Looking in the Mirror: Comparing INGO Networks across Issue Areas' (2012) 7 The Review of International Organizations 177.

[49] In addition, the following organizations were steering committee members at the time of research: Adaleh Center for Human Rights Studies, Andean Commission of Jurists, Asian Forum for Human Rights and Development, Asociación Pro Derechos Humanos, Civil Resource Development and Documentation Centre, Georgian Young Lawyers Association, Human Rights Network-Uganda, and Justice Without Frontiers.

with states' representatives, ICC officials, and other international criminal law professionals. In the everyday life of international criminal justice in The Hague, they drink coffee with, and lobby state representatives, they organize and participate as expert voices in conferences and seminars, and attend and hold receptions for international criminal justice professionals in the city.

In order not to duplicate each other's work and to maximize their combined efforts, the CICC's advocacy issues are organized in NGO issue-specific teams and 'thematic caucuses'. However, there is a significant organizational imbalance between attention to victims and defendants in international criminal justice advocacy. While the Victims' Rights Working Group (VRWG) is by far the largest thematic caucus—according to their website, they are a 'network of over 300 national and international civil society groups and experts'[50]—there is no thematic caucus or issue-team that focuses on the rights and interests of the defence in international criminal justice. Moreover, out of the ten organizations identified as the most central advocates of international criminal justice in The Hague, this leaves only one, namely the IBA, dealing with the latter.

4.2 The IBA, the rule of law, and the lack of imagination

Out of the core group of international NGOs in The Hague, the only organization that specifically focuses on defence rights is the IBA, which is a federation of national bar associations supporting the human rights and independence of lawyers and the judiciary. The IBA's ICC programme is twofold. The first part of their mandate is to monitor the ICC as a legal institution and workplace, representing the 'global voice of the legal profession'. The second part of their mandate is geared towards advocacy and especially monitoring the ICC, as is also the case for the other NGOs. However, the IBA does not consider itself an NGO, but is nonetheless listed as such in the Yearbook of International Organizations. Their representatives explain that they are often associated with being an NGO 'because of the type of work we do'—the ICC programme is a branch of the IBA's Human Rights Institute based in London. They thus identify as a 'hybrid' organization, a 'not-for-profit association', and their focus on human rights are those that concern the legal profession, and especially the independence of the judiciary and the upholding of the rule of law.

In their work on the ICC, a major part of their monitoring work is focused on fair trial rights as, according to one of their representatives, 'without fair trial rights you don't have rule of law, and secondly, there was an enormous gap in this area. We're the only organisation in The Hague—well, others touch on it, but nobody is focusing on these issues.' In part then, their motivation for focusing on fair trial rights can be explained by carving out an issue for themselves as part of a 'division of labour' among international justice advocacy at the ICC. A more articulated motivation however, and that can also help explain the variation of issue emergence and adoption among the 'usual suspects' of NGOs at the ICC, is the IBA's principled and

[50] 'Who we are' (*VRWG*) <www.vrwg.org/about-vrwg/who-we-are> (accessed 27 June 2016).

pre-existing moral standards regarding the rule of law.[51] As an association of legal practitioners and bar associations, it is the rule of law as interpreted by international legal professionals, rather than human rights as interpreted and advocated by transnational networks of human rights NGOs, that inform their work. What emerges into view is thus a separation of organizations in NGO advocacy for international criminal justice: whereas human rights organizations primarily focus on victims, defence issues are dealt with by lawyers' associations.

A question may thus be asked about how this imbalance in victim and defendant advocacy plays into the perception of fairness in international criminal justice[52]—and the bent to identify grievances. An IBA representative explains that 'The fairness aspect is there—it is in the statutes, the rules and frameworks—but the means and the will are not there!' This lack of 'means and will' is seen to cause a lack of thinking and imagination in international criminal justice, especially as concerns defendants' rights. For example, after the ICC's first acquittal in its second case, Congolese Mathieu Ngudjolo Chui filed for asylum on the grounds of being unable to return to the Democratic Republic of the Congo (DRC) for personal security reasons after having implicated the Congolese government. After having spent months following his acquittal at Schiphol's immigration detention centre, he was transferred to the ICC's 'protection ... in a hotel in The Hague' while awaiting a decision by a Dutch district court regarding his appeal for asylum in the Netherlands.[53] While his claim for asylum (and compensation) were in turn denied, and Ngudjolo expelled back to the DRC in May 2015,[54] his situation stirred up frustration as indicative of legal and moral 'loopholes' in the field.[55] As the IBA representative asserted: 'The Court didn't imagine what would happen after someone have been acquitted. They only imagined what would happen if someone was found guilty.'

While the articulation of the acquitted accused as a 'forgotten party' in international criminal justice is not new,[56] it is however interesting to note that such sensibilities are still strong among observers in the field. In their understanding, it is simply not what 'people in the field want to focus on'. I ask why not.

> Atrocity crimes bring a lot of emotion, and obviously, the first thing on people's minds are the victims, which is very understandable. Most NGOs in the field are looking at human rights and victims, making sure states are signing up, that arrests are happening. The train is always moving in that direction, and yes, fair trial rights do get lost in the shuffle.

[51] R Charli Carpenter, 'Setting the Advocacy Agenda: Theorizing Issue Emergence and Nonemergence in Transnational Advocacy Networks' (2007) 51 International Studies Quarterly 99.

[52] Mégret (n 8).

[53] Tjitske Lingsma, 'Acquitted by the ICC, but Still Not Free', *International Justice Tribune* (The Hague, 4 April 2014) 4.

[54] Joris Van Wijk and Barbora Hola, 'Acquittals in International Criminal Justice: Pyrrhic Victories?' (2016) Leiden Journal of International Law 1.

[55] Joris van Wijk, 'When International Criminal Justice Collides with Principles of International Protection: Assessing the Consequences of ICC Witnesses Seeking Asylum, Defendants Being Acquitted, and Convicted Being Released' (2013) 26 Leiden Journal of International Law 173.

[56] Benoit Henry, 'The Acquitted Accused, a Forgotten Party of the ICTR' (2005) 12 New England Journal of International and Comparative Law 81.

What is pointed to here resonates with Bass' observation that in international criminal justice, legalism is not enough: one also needs moral outrage.[57] International criminal justice taps into and is propelled by the humanitarian impetus to 'do something' about the suffering of others. This is also the *raison d'être* of human rights NGOs, as mobilizers of moral outrage on behalf of distant others, predicated on a theory of change that knowledge about suffering produces action.[58] As part of this, victims—more so than perpetrators—are in the hearts and minds of international justice advocates.

4.3 Victims' advocates and the 'punitive turn'

As recognized by Wemmers, the 'major innovation and shift in the status of victims before the court is due, in part, to pressure from non-governmental organizations'.[59] In the ICC negotiations in Rome, victims' rights were at the top of many of the NGOs' agendas, uniting under the VRWG. The working group was facilitated by REDRESS, a London-based human rights organization that, in spite of its relatively small size compared to the other NGOs, holds a particularly central position in victims' advocacy. According to their website, the VRWG work to promote the rights and interests of victims before the Court, and focus particularly on participation and legal representation, protection and support, reparations, ensuring victims' voices are heard in considering the interest of victims, and a gender-sensitive approach.[60]

In considering victim participation, a central argument for including victims in the criminal justice process is their potential to contribute 'facts', 'truth', and 'memory'. For example, NGO informants pointed to how victims participating in the *Lubanga* case have helped clarify social conventions, such as the use of names in DRC, which benefited criminal proceedings. Another such example is the way in which sexual- and gender-based violence were brought to 'public' attention through victims participating in the ad hoc tribunals as witnesses.[61] As part of this, a central issue has been to advocate for ICC charges brought against alleged perpetrators being 'reflective' of the conflict, as expressed here: 'As a victims' advocate I think one of the main reasons why you want to have victim participation is to have some sort of control on the type of charges that are brought being representative of what actually happened.'

This is seen as an important element in considering trials as 'memory', or, rather, as writing history. As such, this rationale is closely associated with a preference for the ICC's prosecutorial strategy to be reflective of the underlying patterns of the conflict in question. Although most of the human rights NGOs were involved,

[57] Gary Jonathan Bass, *Stay the Hand of Vengeance: The Politics of War Crimes Tribunals* (Princeton University Press 2000).

[58] Richard Ashby Wilson and Richard D Brown, *Humanitarianism and Suffering: The Mobilization of Empathy* (CUP 2009).

[59] Wemmers (n 7) 211.

[60] 'Strategy' *(VRWG)* <www.vrwg.org/about-vrwg/strategy> (accessed 27 June 2016).

[61] See also Mariana Pena and Gaelle Carayon, 'Is the ICC Making the Most of Victim Participation?' (2013) International Journal of Transitional Justice.

the International Federation for Human Rights (FIDH), consisting of 178 human rights organizations, has been particularly active in pushing for and implementing victim participation. Through their Legal Action Group, comprising a network of pro-bono lawyers, FIDH has provided legal support for victims of international crimes, and have inter alia represented victims in proceedings at the ICC. Part of FIDH's strategy of facilitating victim participation was to challenge the Prosecutor's policy in relation to cases and charges, strategically using victim participation as a means to make advocacy for prosecutions of international crimes.[62]

Before going any further, however, it is important to note that the turn to criminal law has required a significant adjustment of thinking for human rights NGOs. In the early days of the human rights movement, the criminal justice system was associated with repression—a system inherently repressive due to its potential for violence. 'While some criminal justice systems might have been more suspect than others, all were considered as capable of abusing power.'[63] The human rights focus was originally aimed at the rights of the defendant and of the political prisoner of authoritarian regimes. While there are nuances within organizations, amnesty and the release of political prisoners were at the very core of Amnesty International's foundation in 1961, an organization that since spearheaded the movement and became an 'iconic global symbol of moral authority'.[64]As the organization grew, they started to work more broadly on prisoners' and defence rights: on issues such as unlawful detention and the right to fair trial. Yet in 1972, Amnesty International suggested the creation of an international tribunal to investigate torture around the world in their *Campaign for the Abolition of Torture*, based on a mistrust in the ability of any national system to deal with the matter systematically.[65] From a former position of scepticism then, human rights NGOs gradually came to embrace the criminal justice system as a tool for the work of liberation and emancipation *from* repression.

This shift is especially apparent as concerns human rights NGOs' approach to amnesties for international crimes, as 'impunity' is now widely framed as a human rights violation 'in and of itself'.[66] In general, human rights organizations oppose amnesties for international crimes on the grounds that they are impermissible according to international law. Amnesty International's position is especially interesting, both as being representative of the human rights movement generally and also because of the aforementioned shift in approach to the criminal justice system. For example, in their press release immediately following the opening of

[62] FIDH, *Supporting the Participation of Victims from DRC before the International Criminal Court* (Report of the FIDH Legal Action Group, 2006).

[63] Karen Engle, 'Self-Critique, (Anti)Politics and Criminalization: Reflections on the History and Trajectory of the Human Rights Movement' in José María Beneyto and David Kennedy (eds), *New Approaches to International Law* (TMC Asser Press 2012) 58.

[64] Stephen Hopgood, *Keepers of the Flame: Understanding Amnesty International* (Cornell University Press 2006) 2.

[65] Sikkink (n 13).

[66] William A Schabas, 'Sentencing by International Tribunals: A Human Rights Approach' (1996) 7 Duke Journal of Comparative & International Law 461, 515.

ICC investigations in Uganda, they write that '[u]nder no circumstances should amnesty laws include crimes under international law', and further that 'Amnesty International opposes amnesties, pardons and similar measures of impunity for crimes under international law in all circumstances where they would prevent a judicial determination of guilt or innocence, the discovery of the truth or full reparations'.[67] Four years later they reiterate their position in a report commenting on an agreement between the Lord's Resistance Army (LRA) and the Ugandan government on Accountability and Reconciliation, resulting from peace negotiations, saying that the

> Amnesty Act of 2000 is a serious barrier to accountability and justice to tens of thousands of victims of Uganda's conflict ... Amnesty International has repeatedly called on Uganda to repeal the Act and revoke all amnesties granted to ensure justice, truth and reparations for all crimes under international law committed during the conflict.[68]

It is interesting to note that, not only is the organization opposing the use of amnesties, but it is also advocating that Uganda should 'revoke' the amnesties already granted to LRA rebels who have defected, as the agreement between the LRA and the Ugandan government 'severely undermines the commitment to accountability by exempting the more than 20,000 persons who have been granted amnesty'.[69] Human Rights Watch has adopted a similarly punitive position, both in specific cases such as the situation in Uganda, and also generally, saying 'No Amnesty for Atrocities'.[70]

As there is no direct prohibition of amnesty in international law, the legal argumentation and reasoning of human rights NGOs is worth particular attention.[71] According to Scharf, 'there are several articles of the Rome Statute that might be read as permitting the Court under certain circumstances to recognize an amnesty exception to its jurisdiction', and '[t]he Rome Statute is purposely ambiguous on the question of whether the International Criminal Court should defer to such an amnesty-for-peace arrangement in deciding whether to exercise its jurisdiction'.[72] Importantly then, it is the NGOs' interpretation of international law that is put forth in their advocacy.

Indicative of what can be called this 'punitive turn' in human rights advocacy, in the run up to the treaty negotiations in Rome, Amnesty International also argued that substantive defences such as the statutes of limitation, superior orders, duress,

[67] Amnesty International, 'Uganda: First Steps to Investigate Crimes Must Be Part of Comprehensive Plan to End Impunity' (30 January 2004) AFR 59/001/2004 2.

[68] Amnesty International, 'Agreement and Annex on Accountability and Reconciliation falls short of a comprehensive plan to end impunity' (March 2008) AFR 59/001/2008 21–22.

[69] ibid 21.

[70] Human Rights Watch, 'Letter to Obama on Targeted Killings and Drones' (7 December 2010) <www.hrw.org/news/2010/12/07/letter-obama-targeted-killings-and-drones> (accessed 27 June 2016).

[71] Kieran McEvoy and Louise Mallinder, 'Amnesties in Transition: Punishment, Restoration, and the Governance of Mercy' (2012) 39 Journal of Law and Society 410.

[72] Michael P Scharf, 'The Amnesty Exception to the Jurisdiction of the International Criminal Court' (1999) 32 Cornell International Law Journal 507, 522, 526.

coercion, and other 'negation of responsibility' were 'impermissible' and 'inappropriate' as defences for the ICC statute.[73] In fact, as observed by Wilson, 'the AI "blacklist", if adopted, would have left available to international criminal defendants and their lawyers only a narrow range of defences such as insanity or other mental impairment, alibi, and failure of proof'.[74] Albeit human rights NGOs are stronger on procedural defences, the analysis provided here reveals that this is not what human rights NGOs in international criminal justice prioritize. It thus appears that in international criminal justice,

> [m]any traditionally liberal actors (such as non-governmental organizations or academics), who in a national system would vigilantly protect defendants and potential defendants, are among the most strident pro-prosecution voices, arguing for broad definitions and modes of liability and for narrow defences, in order to secure convictions and thereby fulfil the victim's right to justice.[75]

4.4 Legal aid and the domestic paradox

Even though victims have gained a more prominent status in western systems of criminal justice in the past decades,[76] what emerges into view is an interesting paradox in relation to domestic systems of criminal justice in established democracies. It may look like as if human rights NGOs tend to speak on behalf of, and represent, directly or by proxy, different constituencies depending on whether their concern is criminal justice at the international level or at the domestic level in western democracies: Internationally, human rights NGOs are, largely, victims' advocates; at the domestic level, they advocate for the rights of defendants and prisoners. For example, many of the central human rights NGOs advocating victims' rights to justice at the ICC (Amnesty International, Human Rights Watch, REDRESS) are at the same time among the most vocal and active advocates for defendants' rights vis-à-vis military commissions at Guantanamo Bay (albeit the latter operates beyond the US civil and criminal justice system).[77] As observed by Robinson, domestically, 'liberal sensitivities focus on constraining the use of the state's coercive power against individuals. In ICL, however, prosecution and conviction are often conceptualized as the fulfilment of the victims' human right to remedy.'[78]

This distinction is particularly apparent when considering how human rights NGOs approach legal aid at the ICC. Whereas legal aid is mainly provided to defendants in western domestic criminal justice systems, in international criminal justice, NGOs' judicial assistance and legal aid is primarily provided to victims of international crimes. To understand better the underlying social conditions for this

[73] Amnesty International, 'The Quest for International Justice: Defining the Crimes and Defences for the International Criminal Court' (February 1997) IOR 40/06/97.

[74] Richard J Wilson, 'Defenses in Contemporary International Criminal Law. By Geert-Jan Gj Knoops' (2002) 96 AJIL 517, 518.

[75] Robinson (n 1) 930.

[76] See generally Sandra Walklate, *Handbook of Victims and Victimology* (Willan Publishing 2007).

[77] Kjersti Lohne, 'Prisoners' Advocates at Gitmo: The Role of NGOs in (De)Legitimising Punishment in Response to Cosmopolitan Dilemmas' (International Studies Association Annual Convention).

[78] Robinson (n 1) 930.

difference, one needs to acknowledge the central role of 'the victim' to the human rights industry, and the way that it connects to the role of NGOs in international criminal justice. Consider the following excerpt from one informant, as we discuss the role of NGOs as particularly significant in international criminal justice.

> Why is it that international criminal justice has developed this [strong] role for NGOs? Is it because NGOs put their foot in the door to start with? Maybe. Is it because they almost started the whole thing anyway? [. . .] I think it is because justice is ultimately about and for victims.

Rather than a direct remedy for victims' suffering, criminal law has traditionally been conceptualized as the state's reaction to an offence and the offender.[79] The claim reproduced above, then, which was widespread among my informants, differs from the dominant justifications for criminal law and state punishment. Yet the perception that justice is 'ultimately about and for victims' says something important about what kind of justice international criminal courts are expected to deliver among those working within the field.[80] Albeit 'natural' given the atrociousness of the crimes in question, and the large numbers of victims accordingly perceived as 'beneficiaries' of this type of humanitarianism/justice, the expectation of international criminal justice to serve 'victims' justice' by human rights NGOs inescapably influences the direction of their efforts. In this manner, legal aid has predominantly become a 'victims' issue' in international criminal justice.

As regards the legal aid programme, critical concern among NGOs has been to ensure its adequate funding. As an NGO representative put it: 'One of the main worries at the moment is that they are not trying to make the system better; they are trying to make it cheaper!' Another NGO representative elaborated on the matter:

> How to represent victims is being viewed from a purely budgetary perspective, like 'what's the way we can represent a thousand victims?' Our point of view is that it should be the other way around: What do victims need? And then look at how much it will cost and the most efficient way of doing that.

Importantly, unlike most domestic systems of justice, the ICC has to negotiate its budget annually at the ASP meetings, and the legal aid programme has to demonstrate to the States Parties how it contributes to the Court's objectives. It is therefore interesting to observe how over the years the ICC budget has become one of the major advocacy issues for the Coalition, with Amnesty International heading the Coalition's working group on budget. On the face of it, budget issues seem a long way away from what is generally considered human rights advocacy. As a universal membership organization financed by private donations, members' dues, and fund-raising campaigns, it seems even further from Amnesty International's trademark letter writing campaigns. Budget issues are far from 'sexy' enough to attract popular support, which a member-based campaign organization such as Amnesty International relies upon. For these reasons, budget was initially a controversial issue

[79] Nicola Lacey, *State Punishment: Political Principles and Community Values* (Routledge 1988).

[80] Carolyn Hoyle and Leila Ullrich, 'New Court, New Justice?: The Evolution of "Justice for Victims" at Domestic Courts and at the International Criminal Court' (2014) 12 Journal of International Criminal Justice 681.

within the CICC, and sparked resistance from its members. A CICC representative explains that there has been a significant change of opinion as regards budget advocacy: 'No matter what (former Chief Prosecutor) Moreno Ocampo or (former) President Kirsch said, or the Registrar, if it wasn't in the budget, then it wasn't there. So now Amnesty and Human Rights Watch are the primary monitors of the budget.'

As the legal aid programme finances legal counsels and representatives for both victims and perpetrators, the budgetary discussion adds another dimension to the inclusion of victims in criminal justice proceedings—namely the extent to which victims' rights come at the expense of defendants'.[81] While international criminal judges and defence counsel alike have voiced considerable concern for the principle of equality of arms, particularly as regards material resources made available to the defence,[82] human rights NGOs have primarily focused on the cost implications for victims.[83] During an interview with a Coalition representative, I asked about the major organizations working on legal aid and victim representation:

INFORMANT: Redress, Amnesty International, and FIDH are very big on it, as well as a number of organizations in situation countries who work with victims on a daily basis, such as Advocats Sans Frontiers. So yes, a lot of them! Defence legal aid is another one but that is more the bar organizations that are interested in that, the International Criminal Bar.

AUTHOR: So these are more rule of law oriented organizations?

INFORMANT: Well, they are legal profession organization whereas others are more human rights, so obviously they focus more on victims' issues—not to say they're not interested in defence rights, but they focus more on victims. It is also a matter of resources ...

Commenting on the imbalance between victim and defendant advocacy among Coalition members, another informant explains that victims are much more interesting for NGOs, also because they are directly related to funding flows. In the moral economy of international criminal justice, victims are the driving engine, just as they are for human rights NGOs. Defence rights are simply 'not as sexy', she said:

> Victims' issues are of course at the heart of many human rights institutions and organizations, and this is what our Coalition is made up of, so there is a much greater focus on victims' issues, to ensure that the best interests of victims are met ... At the end of the day, it's the victimhood, the victimized—that's what we're here for and working on.

While the 'imperative to represent or stand in for the figure of the absent victim permeates the discourse of those who "practice" international criminal law—whether as lawyers, diplomats or activists',[84] claims to 'speak for', 'give voice to', and 'represent'

[81] Salvatore Zappalà, 'The Rights of Victims v. The Rights of the Accused' (2010) 8 Journal of International Criminal Justice 137.

[82] Christine Van den Wyngaert, 'Victims before International Criminal Courts: Some Views and Concerns of an ICC Trial Judge' (2011) 44 Case Western Reserve Journal of International Law 475; Masha Fedorova, 'The Principle of Equality of Arms in International Criminal Proceedings' in C Rohan and G Zyberi (eds), *Defence Perspectives in International Criminal Justice* (CUP 2017).

[83] FIDH and Montserrat Carboni, *Cutting the Weakest Link: Budget Discussions and Their Impact on Victims Rights to Participate in the Proceedings* (Position Paper, 11th Session of the Assembly of States Parties to the Rome Statute, 2012).

[84] Kendall and Nouwen (n 5) 240.

the interests of victims are significantly embedded in the practice of human rights NGOs. According to Mutua, the representation of the victim is the 'giant engine' of human rights organizations, asserting that '[w]ithout the victim there is no savage or savior, and the entire human rights enterprise collapses'.[85] In a similar manner, it is the figure of the victim that drives international criminal justice advocacy.

4.5 Smeared by association

However, the focus on victims rather than defendants is not just a question of resources and interests. In this final section, it is considered how defence rights are also viewed as a difficult topic to focus on vis-à-vis a general public opinion, and therefore far from ideal for human rights NGOs to mobilize and advocate on behalf of. An NGO representative articulates it in the following manner, explaining that in the working field of international criminal justice, 'It's more difficult to come home and say "I'm going to represent Gbagbo" than to say "Hi, I found a job at ICC in Chambers".'[86] Using 'home' as a symbol of 'general public opinion', she says that 'That's just how it is'. There is neither sympathy nor moral outrage to be gained from working on the defence side, namely because criminal defendants in international criminal justice are hardly perceived innocent until proven guilty. There is a sense of defending the defendant in international criminal justice as being morally problematic, indicating antipathy towards the criminal defendant in international criminal justice. As argued by Jacobs:

> One explanation for this can be found in a very basic psychological trope: guilt by association. Defence lawyers are seen to be defending the 'scum of the world', as one Prosecutor was heard saying to a Defense Counsel at the ICC ... Who would ever expect Muammar Ghadaffi, Saddam Hussein or tomorrow, Assad or Bashir to be acquitted? For such political figures, international trials are purely symbolic; a formal validation of what everybody thinks they already know about what they did.[87]

Indeed, this perception of the trial being a 'formal validation', or a show trial really, seem to be lurking underneath the surface in the mentalities of some of the NGO representatives most central in ICC advocacy too. Before meeting with one of my NGO informants, I had been observing trial proceedings against Laurent Gbagbo at the ICC the same day. During our interview, my informant refers to the sensibilities emerging when sitting up close, observing and monitoring trial proceedings at the Court:

> What were you feeling when you watch him, and you sit there, with Gbagbo's supporters (next to you)? Maybe a bit apprehension. But at the end of the day, if you really believe in the rule of law, you know. But that's a very narrow lawyer's perspective, and I do understand that, but innocent until proven guilty ... That's very narrow (whispers).

[85] Makau Mutua, 'Savages, Victims, and Saviors: The Metaphor of Human Rights' (2001) 42 Harvard International Law Journal 201, 227.

[86] Former President of Côte d'Ivoire Laurent Gbagbo is currently on trial at the ICC, charged with four counts of crimes against humanity as indirect co-perpetrator allegedly committed in post-election violence in Côte d'Ivoire in 2010–2011.

[87] Jacobs (n 1) 582.

What is expressed here is an appreciation of the presumption of innocence as a legal principle according to the rule of law. That is a principled stance. Yet, it should give pause for thought when central NGO representatives in international criminal justice advocacy suggest that this is a 'narrow' view, precisely because these are the people and organizations that act as intermediaries between the courts, member states, affected communities, and a generalized (mostly online) globalized public.

5 Discussion and Conclusion

This chapter has approached international criminal justice from a legal sociology perspective with the aim to shed light on the anxiety and hybridity in international criminal justice as 'being' criminal justice or victims' justice. Continuing the story of NGO influence upon the Rome Statute system of justice, the chapter has provided an analysis of their organizational structures and advocacy issues, and the rationalities and sensibilities therein. It has revealed a fundamental discrepancy between advocacy on behalf of victims and defendants in international criminal justice. Out of the central NGOs promoting international criminal justice, the IBA is the only organization that has a primary focus on defence rights at the ICC. In contrast to the fight against impunity focus of human rights organizations, the IBA promotes a 'rule of law' focus, indicating different perceptions on what type of 'justice' international criminal justice is imagined to provide among its different stakeholders. While legal professionals' associations emphasize parallels with domestic systems of criminal justice in terms of due process and the objectives of criminal law procedures, human rights NGOs appear to put a greater emphasis on international criminal justice as part of transitional justice, seeking to help the criminal justice process establish 'truth' and 'memory' and public recognition of victims' suffering. For human rights NGOs, international criminal justice is primarily a means to enforce human rights; indeed, the 'punitive turn' in the human rights movement indicates that the fight against impunity has become a central human rights issue. In consequence, it is victims—not defendants—that are the focus of human rights advocacy in international criminal justice. And yet while victims' advocacy can be both unproblematic and morally defensible when seen in isolation, when taken together, the dominance of victims' advocates can in part explain how imbalances and tensions between 'victims' or 'criminal' justice emerge in the field of international criminal justice.

The comparison of advocacy on behalf of victims and defendants in international criminal justice thus offers insight into the skewed nature of the international criminal justice project—into where it has developed from, and perhaps where it is going. In lieu of democratic legitimacy, international criminal law and justice has sought legitimacy in global universals; to not leave unpunished those atrocities that shock the 'conscience of humanity'. Yet, in alleging *hostis humani generis*, a part of humanity is abstracted from the rest, called to answer for the part that suffers. Riddled with anxiety at this paradoxical state, torn between two parts of an inseparable whole, it appears the justice imagined is one of victims' justice—rather than fairness in a substantive, international, criminal justice sense.

7

The Revolving Door in International Investment Arbitration[a]

Malcolm Langford,[*] Daniel Behn,[**] and Runar Lie[***]

1 Introduction

It is regularly but anecdotally observed that international investment arbitration is marked by a 'revolving door'. Single individual actors play multiple roles as arbitrators, counsel, expert witnesses, and tribunal secretaries within this fragmented and ad hoc adjudicative system of investment arbitration. The movement between roles may be *sequential*[1] or even *simultaneous.* The latter practice is often referred to as 'double hatting' and has attracted significant criticism on the grounds of conflict of interests.[2] However, the nature and extent of the revolving door in international investment arbitration has never been empirically determined and its sociological and normative implications remain largely unexplored.

This chapter presents the first-ever analysis of the entire international investment arbitration community since its inception. It draws on our PITAD[3] database of

[a] This chapter was first published in the Journal of International Economic Law, 20(2) (2017). The piece was partly inspired by the closing speech by Philippe Sands at the European Society International Law annual conference in 2015, and which forms the final chapter in this volume. We would like to thank the peer reviewers and Wolfgang Alschner, Joost Pauwelyn, and Sergio Puig for their comments on the original version. We note that double hatting index data in Section 5 has been slightly updated and is the same as reported in Langford, Behn, and Lie, 'Ethics and Empirics of Double Hatting' (2017) 6(7) ESIL Reflections 1.

* Professor, Faculty of Law, University of Oslo and Co-Director, Centre on Law and Social Transformation, University of Bergen and CMI. Email: malcolm.langford@jus.uio.no.

** Senior Research Fellow, PluriCourts Centre of Excellence, Faculty of Law, University of Oslo and Lecturer in Law, The Liverpool Law School, University of Liverpool. Email: d.f.behn@jus.uio.no.

*** Researcher, PluriCourts Centre of Excellence and Forum for Law and Social Science, Faculty of Law, University of Oslo.

[1] Eg, an arbitrator may act as legal counsel in a case, then as an arbitrator in another case, an expert witness in a third, and then back to legal counsel work in a fourth case.

[2] See Phillipe Sands, 'Conflict and Conflicts in Investment Treaty Arbitration: Ethical Standards for Counsel' in Arthur Rovine (ed), *Contemporary Issues in International Arbitration and Mediation: The Fordham Papers* (Brill 2012), at 28–49; Phillipe Sands, 'Judicialization and its Challenges', this volume.

[3] PluriCourts Investment Treaty Arbitration Database (PITAD) as of 1 January 2017.

1,039 international investment arbitration cases and ICSID[4] annulment proceedings in order to first map the identity and relationships of 3,910 individuals in their different roles, using social network analysis and various indexes. In addition, we examine sociologically whether the revolving door phenomenon challenges our understanding of who has power within the international investment arbitration community; and we empirically assess normative concerns over double hatting by determining the extent to which it occurs and whether the practice has eased or worsened over time.

In doing so, we seek to advance the existing literature on international investment arbitration in *three* discrete ways. Our first contribution is *descriptive*. By focusing on a broad group of actors, we partly return to Dezalay and Garth's vision of the 'field' as the analytical unit. The focus is less on specific institutional roles (particularly those of the arbitrator), but instead the 'networks and relationships organized' around arbitration and the 'space for positions and struggles'.[5] To be sure, Dezalay and Garth were significantly concerned with arbitrators. After extensive empirical work they observed that a coterie of 'grand old men' dominated the field of international commercial arbitration.[6] Small in number, linked closely, and mostly European, they even referred to themselves as a 'club' or a 'mafia'.[7] After a period of 'generational warfare', these figures were joined and complemented by Anglo-American arbitration technocrats and law firms.[8] Since then scholars have continued to map the field with a focus on gender, nationality, education, and employment background.[9] Recent medium-N surveys confirm elite educational backgrounds and male and Western identities of arbitrators,[10] but also the possible rise of a third and more pluralistic generation of managerial arbitrators within commercial, but not investment treaty, arbitration.[11]

However, Dezalay and Garth's work also showed the peculiar symbolic (and legal) capital of those actors that crossed institutional lines. They devoted significant space to the role of legal counsel, law firms, and witnesses and noted implicitly the potential role and power of a revolving door. One vignette is telling: an Anglo-American litigator, with his first case in international commercial arbitration, learnt the importance of appointing distinguished arbitrators as counsel. With the 'combination of Lalive and Goldman' he commented, 'I was a conductor of virtuosos and prima donnas'.[12] Thus, we map the roles of all types of actors in investment arbitration

[4] International Centre for Settlement of Investment Disputes.

[5] Yves Dezalay and Bryant Garth, *Dealing in Virtue: International Commercial Arbitration and the Construction of a Transnational Legal Order* (Chicago: Chicago University Press 1996) 20.

[6] ibid. [7] ibid, 10. [8] ibid.

[9] See eg Susan Franck, 'Empirically Evaluating Claims about Investment Treaty Arbitration', (2007) 86 North Carolina Law Review 1; Michael Waibel and Yanhui Wu, 'Are Arbitrators Political?' Working Paper (December 2011); Paul Friedland and Stavros Brekoulakis, '2012 International Arbitration Survey: Current and Preferred Practices in the Arbitral Process' (2013) 8 Constitutional Law International 39; Sergio Puig, 'Social Capital in the Arbitration Market' (2014) 25 European Journal of International Law 387; Susan Franck et al, 'International Arbitration: Demographics, Precision and Justice' (2015) ICCA Congress Series No 18: Legitimacy: Myths, Realities, Challenges 33; Thomas Schultz and Robert Kovacs, 'The Rise of a Third Generation of Arbitrators? Fifteen Years after Dezalay and Garth' (2012) 28(2) Arbitration International 161.

[10] Franck et al (n 9). [11] Schultz and Kovacs (n 9). [12] ibid, 109.

and provide the first quantitative perspective of the field and empirical estimation of the revolving door. In doing so, we also identify key attributes of all actors such as gender and nationality.[13]

Our second contribution is to build on *sociological* work that seeks to identify who has the power in the investment arbitration community and the extent of that power. In Dezalay and Garth's account, power was measured in largely qualitative terms—an actor's symbolic capital. This power was determined by the combination of 'social class, education, career and expertise', which aspiring arbitrators needed to optimally combine in order to project neutrality, competence, and authority.[14] Puig, however, provides an essentially quantitative perspective of power in his recent social network analysis of investment arbitrators. By counting the number of roles and different types of ties between arbitrators, power is measured by an individual's exposure in the system.[15] Tracking all arbitral appointments at ICSID between 1972 and 2014 he identifies a core of approximately twenty-five arbitrators whom he calls 'power brokers'.[16] Notably, with the exception of a few 'formidable women', Puig found that grand old men from Europe and North America continue to 'dominate the arbitration profession'.[17] He argues that the maintenance of a core over a long period may support Ginsburg's theory that the imbalance in appointments is a result of *strategic* action: that the rapid global spread of arbitration incentivizes insider arbitrators to raise the barriers to keep out new entrants.

Using social network analysis, our study builds on Puig in order to better understand the biographic dynamics of this core group. However, it differs in three important ways. First, we analyze a much larger dataset, which includes non-ICSID cases—roughly doubling the sample size. Second, we expand the actors to include all known legal counsel, expert witnesses, and tribunal secretaries.[18] In our view, Puig undercounts the importance of legal counsel and expert witnesses in the system. Not only are legal counsel tasked with directing much of the cases, they are also deeply involved in arbitrator appointments—they are the key gatekeepers in the system. This methodological innovation also means we are able to reflect anew on existing explanatory theories of monopolistic behaviour in the arbitration market. We can highlight and quantify the role of legal counsel in strategic and (often undervalued) structural explanations.[19]

[13] In a companion article, we have analyzed the gender roles and causes of gender segregation in international investment arbitration: see Taylor St John et al, 'Glass Ceilings and Arbitral Dealings: Explaining the Gender Gap in Investment Arbitration', *Gender on the International Bench, PluriCourts-iCourts Workshop*, Oslo, 23–24 March 2017.

[14] Dezalay and Garth (n 5), 20. [15] Puig (n 9). [16] ibid.

[17] ibid, 387. Recent medium-N surveys find similar patterns.

[18] The data collected in PITAD is limited by instances where awards and documents listing arbitrators, legal counsel, expert witnesses, and tribunal secretaries are not publicly available. Furthermore, as ICSID provides the most complete and comprehensive publicly available registry on arbitral appointments, legal counsel, and tribunal secretaries, that data on ICSID arbitrations will be more complete than that of all non-ICSID arbitration. In this respect, the study illustrates the benefits of datasets as they grow in size: see discussion by Wolfgang Alschner, Joost Pauwelyn, and Sergio Puig, 'The Data-Driven Future of International Economic Law' (2017) 20(2) Journal of International Economic Law 1.

[19] See discussion of the results on power brokers in Section 4.

Third, we weight the different roles of arbitrators. As far as we have determined, Puig has equally weighted presiding arbitrators and claimant/respondent-appointed wing arbitrators. Yet, the president of an arbitration represents the most prestigious role in arbitration, possesses the most responsibility in case management, and exercises the most influence in the final decision as they are usually not appointed solely by one party. In light of this, we weight arbitrators differently and thus introduce a more qualitative measurement of power—recognizing that the symbolic capital of a presiding arbitrator is higher than a wing arbitrator. In doing so, we avoid an anomaly produced by Puig's method, in which some wing arbitrators have a rank that does not intuitively cohere with their actual power in the system.

Our final contribution is to ground *normative* debates on double hatting in an empirical reality. Various scholars have raised concerns with conflicts of interests about arbitrators simultaneously acting as legal counsel and arbitrator in different cases.[20] However, the extent of double hatting has never been measured. It remains the subject of anecdote and casual observation. Furthermore, it is not uncommon to hear claims that the practice is decreasing over time with the implication that the ethical concerns are less sharp today—but no evidence is offered for such assertions.

Determining the nature and extent of double hatting is particularly important in the current political climate. Concern with this practice has strengthened the many contemporary critiques of the investment arbitration system; and will become even more relevant as investment arbitration continues on a growth trajectory (in terms of the annual number of cases filed). Many of these critiques focus on the arbitral system. It has been slated for its 'pale, male, and stale' character (that arbitrators are overwhelmingly older white men),[21] lack of transparency in the selection of arbitrators,[22] third-party funders,[23] law firm-driven litigation,[24] excessive collegiality,[25] and high levels of fees and costs.[26] These critiques all share with double hatting a

[20] See Sands, 'Conflict and Conflicts' (n 2); Sands, 'Geopolitics' (n 2); Judith Levine, 'Dealing with Arbitrator "Issue Conflicts" in International Arbitration' (2006) 61 Dispute Resolution Journal 60; Ruth Mackenzie and Phillipe Sands, 'International Courts and Tribunals and the Independence of the International Judge' (2003) 44 Harvard International Law Journal 271; Joseph Brubaker, 'The Judge Who Knew Too Much: Issue Conflicts in International Adjudication' (2008) 26(1) Berkeley Journal of International Law 111. Double hatting as an expert witness while at the same time acting as arbitrator or legal counsel in another case may also be problematic, but that requires a more nuanced ethical discussion.

[21] See eg Lucy Greenwood and C Mark Baker, 'Getting a Better Balance on International Arbitration Tribunals' (2012) 28 Arbitration International 653; Susan Franck et al, 'The Diversity Challenge: Exploring the "Invisible College" of International Arbitration' (2015) 53 Columbia Journal of Transnational Law 429; Gus Van Harten, 'The (Lack of) Women Arbitrators in Investment Treaty Arbitration', Columbia FDI Perspectives No 59 (6 February 2012).

[22] See eg Chiara Giorgetti, 'Who Decides Who in International Investment Arbitration' (2014) 35(2) University of Pennsylvania Journal of International Law 431; Sergio Puig, 'Blinding International Justice' (2016) 56(3) *Virginia Journal of International Law* 648.

[23] Catherine Rogers, 'Gamblers, Loan Sharks and Third-Party Funders' in Catherine Rogers (ed), *Ethics in International Arbitration* (OUP 2014).

[24] See eg Pia Eberhardt and Cecilia Olivet, 'Profiting from Injustice: How Law Firms, Arbitrators, and Financiers are Fueling an Investment Arbitration Boom', Corporate Europe Observatory (November 2012).

[25] Puig (n 9), 400.

[26] Focusing at least on transparency of costs awards, see Susan Franck, 'Rationalizing Costs in Investment Treaty Arbitration' (2011) 88 Washington University Law Review 769.

similar concern: the closed nature of the community and its ability to engage in self-dealing.

Moreover, these critiques have all contributed to the so-called legitimacy crisis in investment arbitration. With over 831 known investment treaty arbitrations initiated to date (almost all coming in the past fifteen years),[27] and a significant number of instances in which the threat of treaty arbitration has been used, states hosting foreign investors are increasingly finding themselves having to defend their laws and policies before and in the shadow of international arbitral tribunals. In addition to the process of legitimacy concerns above, states and other stakeholders have been raising concerns over *outcomes*. Arbitration awards have been perceived as excessively pro-investor,[28] pro-investment,[29] and anti-developing state.[30] Thus, a failure to clarify or address a *process* legitimacy concern such as double hatting only compounds the sense of crisis.

This chapter proceeds as follows. In Section 2 we describe the international investment arbitration regime and present our dataset. In Section 3 we set out data separately for each of the four types of roles and analyze their relative importance through social network analysis and/or case ranks. In Section 4, we bring the roles together to analyze the entire field and examine who are the power brokers in the community. In Section 5, we analyze the extent to which double hatting is occurring and whether there is real cause for normative concern.

2 The International Investment Arbitration Regime

The modern international investment regime can be described in multiple ways, but generally includes the international institutions and rules governing the regulation of trans-border investments. Built on a network of more than 3,500 signed bilateral investment treaties (BITs), regional free trade agreements (FTAs),[31] and a handful of plurilateral investment treaties,[32] the regime gives a foreign investor a number

[27] PITAD (n 3).

[28] For instance, tribunals exhibit a bias that disproportionately favours the interests and rights of individual foreign investors when pitted against the duty of a state to regulate and legislate in the broader public interest. See eg Gus Van Harten, 'Arbitrator Behaviour in Asymmetrical Adjudication: An Empirical Study of Investment Treaty Arbitration' (2012) 50 Osgoode Hall Law Journal 211, 251.

[29] For instance, tribunals exhibit a bias that disproportionately favours liberal economic rights and values over other equally important public welfare objectives such as public health, environmental protection, or fundamental human rights. See eg Jorge Viñuales, *Foreign Investment and the Environment in International Law* (CUP 2012).

[30] For instance, tribunals are disproportionately more likely to rule against less developed respondent states. See eg Thomas Schultz and Cedric Dupont, 'Investment Arbitration: Promoting the Rule of Law or Over-Empowering Investors? A Quantitative Empirical Study' (2014) 25 European Journal of International Law 1147; Daniel Behn, Tarald Berge, and Malcolm Langford, 'Poor States or Poor Governance: Explaining Outcomes in Investment Treaty Arbitration', *PluriCourts Research Paper No 16-04* (2016), available at: http://ssrn.com/ abstract=2740516 (accessed 1 February 2018).

[31] UNCTAD provides an extensive database on IIAs, available at: <http://investmentpolicyhub.unctad.org/IIA> (accessed 1 February 2018).

[32] See eg Energy Charter Treaty (ECT), North American Free Trade Agreement (NAFTA), Association of South-East Asian Nations (ASEAN) Comprehensive Investment Agreement, Central American-Dominican Republic Free Trade Agreement (DR-CAFTA), as well as, recently concluded or

of substantive protections and rights,[33] including, most importantly, investor–state dispute settlement (ISDS) provisions. While this regime has its roots in the immediate post-Second World War period, it was not until the 1990s that the annual number of international investment agreements (IIAs) exploded.

For the purposes of this chapter, we are focused on the institution of, and networks arising out of, international arbitration between a foreign investor and the state hosting their investments: this prominently includes investment treaty arbitration (ITA), but can also include cases arising out of contracts or concessions and/or a host state's foreign investment laws. An ITA case commonly arises when a foreign investor alleges that the beneficiary rights they are granted under an IIA has been breached by the state hosting its investments. Investment arbitration can also occur in cases between foreign investors and host states under arbitration agreements allowing for investor–state arbitration (as embedded in various forms of investment contracts or concessions) or national foreign direct investment (FDI) laws. These particular forms of arbitration are often administered under ICSID. But they can also arise under ad hoc procedures or the rules of international commercial arbitration centres.

We have tracked and coded all these cases in our new and first-of-its-kind database (PITAD). It includes all known treaty-based arbitrations, all ICSID contract and FDI law-based arbitrations and all ICSID annulment committee proceedings; and each case is coded for up to 138 different variables. The dataset would ideally include all international commercial arbitrations and all non-ICSID contract-based investment arbitrations, but given the default confidentiality of such processes, the data available remains far from complete or accessible.[34] In any case, our dataset has a certain coherence. It covers all known cases whose legal claim is procedurally or substantively based on an international treaty: whether through the ICSID Convention and/or various IIAs. This consequent 'public law' nature of the arbitration arguably heightens concerns around transparency and conflicts of interests raised by the revolving door phenomenon.[35]

However, the number of international investment arbitrations arising out of contracts or FDI laws pales in comparison with the exponential increase in investment treaty-based arbitrations over the past two decades (see Figure 7.1 which is dawn

late-round negotiated treaties: Trans-Pacific Partnership (TPP) Agreement, Canada-EU Comprehensive Economic and Trade Agreement (CETA), Singapore-EU Free Trade Agreement, Transatlantic Trade and Investment Partnership (TTIP) Agreement, and the Pan-Asian Regional Comprehensive Economic Partnership (RCEP) Agreement.

[33] IIAs typically include: prohibitions against expropriation without adequate compensation, full protection and security, fair and equitable treatment (FET), most-favoured nation (MFN) treatment, and national treatment.

[34] Indeed, there is a significant overlap between individuals within the international commercial arbitration community and the international investment arbitration community. See discussion of data limitations in Alschner, Pauwelyn, and Puig (n 18).

[35] Stephan Schill, 'Enhancing International Investment Law's Legitimacy: Conceptual and Methodological Foundations of a New Public Law Approach' (2012) 52 Virginia Journal of International Law 57. We have discovered though that our field-based approach to international investment arbitration picks up a number of key actors in international commercial arbitration. Quite a number that play roles as legal counsel, arbitrators, and secretaries in international investment arbitration are also regularly involved in international commercial arbitrations.

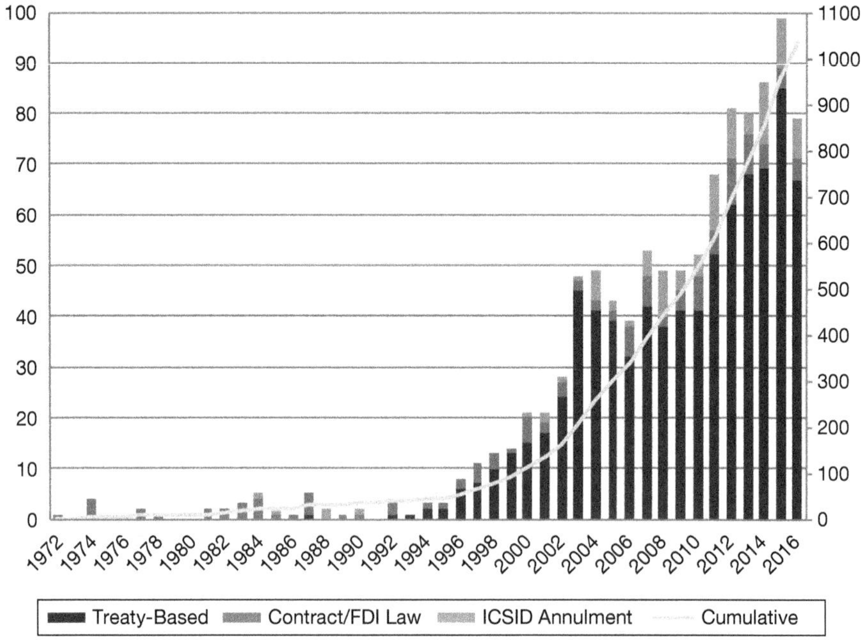

Figure 7.1 International investment arbitration cases registered by year (1987–2016)

from PITAD). In fact, the most distinct feature of this treaty-based regime is the explosion of litigation. It is this meteoric rise in the instances of ITA over the past two decades that has led some to claim there is 'no other category of private individuals' that are 'given such expansive rights in international law as are private actors investing across borders'.[36]

Prior to the year 2000, there were only a small number of ITA cases registered.[37] These cases raised seemingly few concerns and went largely unnoticed by the international legal community. This changed at the beginning of the millennium as the annual number of ITA cases surged, with an average of forty cases per year in the 2000s, and fifty cases per year in the 2010s. Of the 831 treaty-based cases registered to date, 111 different states have acted as respondents, compared with claimants from sixty-seven different home states;[38] and by the end of the first decade of the 2000s, the use of ITA had become a global, prominent, and lucrative area of

[36] Beth Simmons, 'Bargaining over BITS, Arbitrating Awards: The Regime for Protection and Promotion of International Investment' (2014) 66 World Politics 12, 42.

[37] The first treaty-based arbitration to be registered was in 1987: *Asian Agricultural Products Ltd (AAPL) v Republic of Sri Lanka*, ICSID Case No ARB/87/3, Award (27 June 1990).

[38] PITAD (n 3).

international adjudication, while at the same time coming under increasing scrutiny from a growing number of states, scholars, and civil society actors.

By comparison, the number of ICSID-based contract or FDI law arbitrations have totalled 118 to date with an average of about five cases registered per year since the first case in 1972.[39] While the initiation of non-treaty based ICSID cases still occurs, these cases only comprise less than 10 per cent of the ICSID caseload today. In addition, there have been ninety ICSID annulment committee cases registered over the past two decades (see also Figure 7.1). Under Article 53(1) of the ICSID Convention, a party may seek an annulment of their award on one of five narrow grounds: the arbitral tribunal was not properly constituted, it exceeded its powers, it failed to give reasons, it was tainted by corruption, or there had been a serious departure from a rule or procedure. While these annulments concern existing litigation, they are staffed with new arbitration panels and are thus included as separate cases.

Not all of the cases have been concluded and claimant-investor success rates vary. Of the 949 international investment arbitration cases that have been registered (treaty-based, ICSID contract-based, or FDI law-based) as of 1 January 2017, the outcomes are as follows:[40] 419 have been concluded,[41] 301 remain pending, and an additional 229 were settled or discontinued. Of the concluded cases, claimant-investors have won on the merits in 47 per cent of cases and lost on jurisdiction or the merits in 53 per cent. The remaining 'cases' are the annulments. Of these, forty-one have been concluded, fourteen remain pending and an additional twenty-five have either been settled or discontinued. Of the concluded annulments, 32 per cent resulted in a full or partial annulment of the underlying case and 68 per cent in rejection of the annulment request.[42]

3 Mapping the Actors

In this section, we identify and map the individuals in each actor role in international investment arbitration: arbitrators, legal counsel, expert witness, and tribunal secretary. This mapping is partly done by a simple count of number of cases and an identification of attributes such as nationality, gender, legal role, and/or institutional role. In addition, we provide a separate social network analysis for arbitrators. A full social network analysis of the entire community is undertaken in the next section.

Social network analysis constitutes both a theory and a method.[43] Theoretically, social network analysis emphasizes the importance that ties between individuals

[39] The first ICSID arbitration to be registered: *Holiday Inns SA and others v Kingdom of Morocco*, ICSID Case No ARB/72/1, Settled.

[40] PITAD (n 3).

[41] A concluded case is one where the claimant-investor has either won on the merits or lost on jurisdiction or the merits. It does not include discontinued or settled cases.

[42] Thus, all combined, 1,039 investment arbitrations are analyzed.

[43] Stanley Wasserman and Katherine Faust, *Social Network Analysis: Methods and Applications* (CUP 1994); Brian Carolan, *Social Network Analysis and Education: Theory, Methods and Applications* (SAGE Publications 2014) 3–22.

may have for their behaviour and transmission of 'resources'. This pattern of relations may also provide either opportunities for, or constraints on, individual action, which is especially relevant in the case of a market such as international investment arbitration. Methodologically, social network analysis provides tools and measurements for visualizing and understanding the relationships between individuals and similar individuals. At the core of such methods, is the identification of *nodes* (in our case individual actors) and *edges* (relationships between individual actors participating in the same arbitral dispute). Social network methods also provide the opportunities to measure different aspects of network *centrality*. In this respect, social network analysis theory is an ideal method to analyze the arbitration community: almost all observers note the important role of networks in securing appointments.

To be sure, network analysis is not only relevant to social relations between legal actors—it can also be applied to law itself. However, the underlying theoretical perspectives and methodological approaches remain the same for both types of network analysis.[44]

3.1 Arbitrators

In international investment arbitration, each party to the dispute will customarily appoint one of three arbitrators; and in many cases the parties (or the co-arbitrators) will jointly appoint the presiding arbitrator. However, there is a large degree of variation in the manner of appointment. While the default is that the parties will appoint the two wing arbitrators, the presiding arbitrator can be appointed by the parties, the two wing arbitrators or by the institution hosting the arbitration. For ICSID annulment committee cases, all three annulment committee members are appointed by the Secretary-General of ICSID.

Of all the possible configurations for the appointment of arbitrators in international investment arbitration cases, however, there is an underlying constant: all arbitrators are selected for a particular dispute on an ad hoc basis. This structure means that for every arbitration, there are individuals (either the parties, legal counsel representing the parties, arbitral institutions, or co-arbitrators) that are making selection decisions for each of the 1,039 cases in our dataset.

The top twenty-five arbitrators by numbers of appointments are listed in Table 7.1. There is a familiar pattern of well-known grand old men and two 'formidable women' (Stern and Kaufmann-Kohler), as Puig christened them. With the exception of four arbitrators, all those listed are nationals of Western states. Yet, even these four are not particularly representative of the rest of the world. The single arbitrator from Eastern Europe, Alexandrov, has been a resident in the USA for almost three decades—with education and employment experience from US institutions.[45] The other three are

[44] See eg Damien Charlotin, 'The Place of Investment Awards and WTO Decisions in International Law: A Citation Analysis' (2017) 20(2) Journal of International Economic Law 1; Mattias Derlén and Johan Lindholm, 'Is it Good Law? Network Analysis and the CJEU's Internal Market Jurisprudence' (2017) 20(2) Journal of International Economic Law 1.

[45] On the importance of converging institutional practices, see Paul DiMaggio and Walter Powell, 'The Iron Cage Revisited: Collective Rationality and Institutional Isomorphism in Organizational Fields' (1983) 48(2) American Sociological Review 147.

Table 7.1 International investment arbitrators—top twenty-five by appointments

Rank	Arbitrator	Nationality	Presiding	Claimant-appointed	Respondent-appointed	Annulment committee	Total cases
1	Brigitte Stern	France	4	1	82	1	**88**
2	Gabrielle Kaufmann-Kohler	Switzerland	38	15	2	1	**56**
3	L Yves Fortier	Canada	24	25	2	2	**53**
4	Charles Brower	US	1	50	0	1	**52**
5	Francisco Orrego Vicuña	Chile	18	27	3	1	**49**
6	Albert Jan van den Berg	Netherlands	15	16	12	1	**44**
7	J Christopher Thomas	Canada	0	1	42	0	**43**
8	Bernard Hanotiau	Belgium	12	18	5	5	**40**
8	Karl-Heinz Böckstiegel	Germany	26	8	2	4	**40**
10	VV Veeder	UK	25	6	6	0	**37**
10	Bernardo Cremades	Spain	14	10	10	3	**37**
12	Piero Bernardini	Italy	11	13	3	9	**36**
13	Marc Lalonde	Canada	8	20	7	0	**35**
14	Rodrigo Oreamuno	Costa Rica	15	0	14	5	**34**
15	Stanimir Alexandrov	Bulgaria	3	25	1	3	**32**
16	Phillipe Sands	UK	1	4	25	0	**30**
15	Juan Fernández-Armesto	Spain	21	1	3	4	**29**
17	Jan Paulsson	France	13	12	2	1	**28**
18	Horacio Grigera Naón	Argentina	2	24	2	0	**28**
18	David Williams	New Zealand	10	17	0	1	**28**
21	James Crawford	Australia	12	2	10	3	**27**
22	Pierre Tercier	Switzerland	22	0	3	0	**25**
23	Toby Landau	UK	3	1	20	0	**24**
23	Vaughan Lowe	UK	13	2	9	0	**24**
23	Franklin Berman	UK	10	5	4	5	**24**

from high income Latin American states, and either live or have their professional practice based in the US or Western Europe. Most of these top twenty-five arbitrators also have a sizeable number of influential and prestigious presiding chair appointments. Only three are consistently appointed by the claimant (Brower, Alexandrov, and Naón) and three consistently appointed by the respondent (Stern, Thomas, and Sands). The number of total appointments of this group is also formidable. The top twenty-five arbitrators account for 4 per cent of all investment arbitrators (629 in total) but are represented in just over a third of all arbitral appointments (991 of 2,676) in our dataset.

We now conduct a social network analysis of this community of investment arbitrators. In Figure 7.2, we provide a visual representation of this network. This diagram charts the centrality of the arbitrators according to the number, place, and

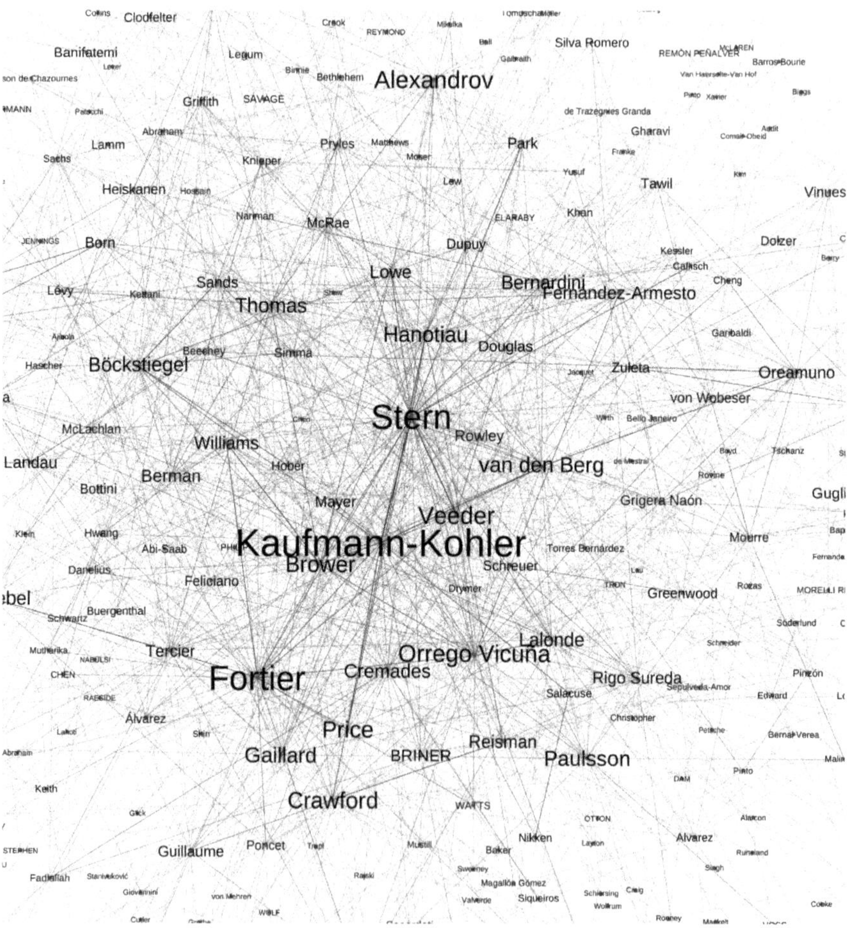

Figure 7.2 Mapping the international investment arbitrator network

weight of their edges. As foreshadowed, we have weighted arbitrators slightly differently from Puig. The relationships are weighed according to a relationship matrix where a discount is given depending on the perceived importance of the role in relation to the other nodes, role, and allegiance.

For arbitrators, this weighting is directed so that a single working relationship between two arbitrators will have two unique scores. In the case of a presiding arbitrator and a wing arbitrator, the president's relationship will be given a score of 1 while the wing arbitrators' relationship will be given a score of 0.75, reflecting the perceived discrepancy of power between the roles. These weighted and directed relationships form the basis for the two subsequent scores—Page Rank and HITS Hub.[46] While describing these scoring systems in detail is beyond the scope of this chapter, both are cumulative ranking systems that use every possible path in the graph to determine the relative importance of the node. The HITS Hub score expands on page rank including a measure of consensus between the nodes and ranks it according to the total accumulative value of the relationships that the node owns. The figure maps the community according to the HITS Hub score. This is because it measures the importance of the relationships, and hence the power that any given arbitrator can likely assert.

Eyeballing the map suggests an inner core of influential arbitrators followed by a second ring of arbitrators. We therefore test the presence of a strong core-periphery by presenting an alternative visualization in Figure 7.3. As with Figure 7.2, names are scaled according to their HITS Hub score. Each arbitrator is ranked counterclockwise according to the same ranking. The inner circle comprises the top twenty-five arbitrators found in Table 7.2. The diagram illustrates the substantial weight of relationships between the top twenty-five arbitrators as well as their consistent dominance of roles in comparison to the rest of the network.

A closer inspection of the figures shows why some international investment arbitrators feature prominently in the network analysis. In Table 7.2, we rank the top twenty-five arbitrators according to their spatial influence in the network. The table presents four factors for evaluating an arbitrator's importance: degrees—weighted and unweighted, Page Rank, and HITS Hub score. The table is ranked by the HITS Hub score.

Examining the results, the order changes in comparison to the number of appointments (compare columns 1 and 2 in Table 7.2). Some regularly-appointed arbitrators drop out of the top twenty-five appointment list completely (see Table 7.1) while others such as Stern, Brower, Thomas, Paulsson, and Cremades drop down on the rankings. The reason is clear on closer inspection. Arbitrators which predominantly represent one party in arbitration (ie they are primarily appointed by either the claimant or respondent) slide down the ranking. Notably, this is only partly a function of the different weightings. It also occurs because wing arbitrators tend to be

[46] Pooja Devil, Ashlesha Gupta, and Ashutosh Dixit, 'Comparative Study of HITS and PageRank Link based Ranking Algorithms' (2014) 3(2) International Journal of Advanced Research in Computer and Communication Engineering 5749. We note that Derlén and Lindholm (n 44) also favour PageRank and Hub scores.

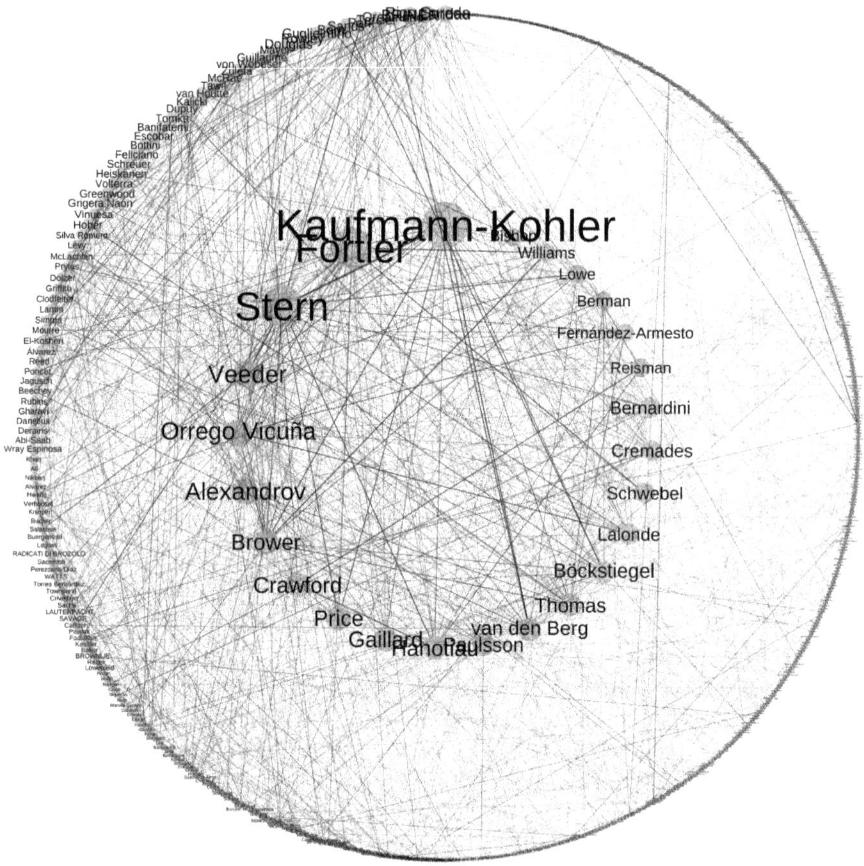

Figure 7.3 Mapping the international investment arbitrator network

further out in the network compared to those who have a more even representation in terms of appointments (ie those that are appointed as either presiding arbitrator, claimant-appointed arbitrator, *or* respondent-appointed arbitrator). Thus, the pattern of their connections and subsequent connections revealed that predominantly party-appointed arbitrators were not as close to the core.

For the sake of comparison, we also provide the arbitrator's rankings from Puig's analysis (based on the degrees score).[47] This shows the difference gained in adding non-ICSID cases and in weighing presiding and wing arbitrators differently. While our general rankings are not totally dissimilar from Puig's unweighted network analysis of ICSID cases,[48] we have uncovered some new and important arbitrators in the top twenty-five, including Price, Park, Riga Sureda, and Gaillard. These arbitrators frequently are chosen to arbitrate in non-ICSID cases. Another

[47] Puig (n 9), 415. [48] ibid.

Table 7.2 Arbitrator network rankings—centrality and influence (top 25)

Rank	Rank (Table 7.1)	Rank (Puig)	Arbitrator	Nationality	HITS hub	Page rank	Degrees out (Weighted)
1	2	5	Gabrielle Kaufmann-Kohler	Switzerland	1.00000	0.01300	123 (110)
2	1	1	Brigitte Stern	France	0.90342	0.02097	185 (125)
3	9	11	VV Veeder	UK	0.71088	0.00994	85 (76)
4	3	8	L Yves Fortier	Canada	0.63079	0.01531	128 (108)
5	4	6	Charles Brower	USA	0.61830	0.01229	114 (78)
6	NI*	2	Francisco Orrego Vicuña	Chile	0.57162	0.01281	104 (83)
7	6	9	Albert Jan van den Berg	Netherlands	0.51763	0.01225	97 (76)
8	8	13	Bernard Hanotiau	Belgium	0.48508	0.01025	85 (68)
9	8	16	Karl-Heinz Böckstiegel	Germany	0.44687	0.01135	84 (75)
10	19	22	Vaughan Lowe	UK	0.43337	0.00750	57 (49)
11	16	15	David Williams	New Zealand	0.43253	0.00695	61 (47)
12	11	4	Marc Lalonde	Canada	0.42718	0.01011	77 (57)
13	7	17	J Christopher Thomas	Canada	0.40380	0.01153	96 (65)
14	10	10	Piero Bernardini	Italy	0.39353	0.01027	76 (62)
15	15	18	Juan Fernández-Armesto	Spain	0.36776	0.00827	63 (60)
16	18	7	Pierre Tercier	Switzerland	0.34175	0.00725	55 (53)
17	NI	NI**	Daniel Price	USA	0.33412	0.00307	46 (33)
18	NI	NI	William Park	USA	0.32939	0.00618	47 (39)
19	19	NI	Franklin Berman	UK	0.31241	0.00605	49 (42)
20	9	3	Bernardo Cremades	Spain	0.30521	0.00982	76 (62)
21	12	14	Rodrigo Oreamuno	Costa Rica	0.30327	0.00994	74 (63)
22	NI	NI	Andrés Rigo Sureda	Spain	0.29313	0.00681	51 (50)
23	13	25	Stanimir Alexandrov	Bulgaria	0.28874	0.00826	69 (50)
24	NI	NI	Emmanuel Gaillard	France	0.28640	0.00681	56 (42)
25	16	12	Jan Paulsson	France	0.28262	0.00708	57 (47)

*NI: Not included in the list of top 25 arbitrators by number of appointments (Table 7.1 above)

** NI: Not included in the list of top 25 arbitrators in Puig's analysis.

Source: Sergio Puig, 'Social Capital in the Arbitration Market', (2014) 25 European Journal of International Law 387, at 415.

interesting distinction is that some arbitrators that rank highly on Puig's scoring, drop down the rankings considerably in our index (compare columns 1 with 3 in Table 7.2). For example, Cremades, Paulsson, and Tercier are significantly lower in Puig's ranking when compared with ours (largely a function of taking few arbitral appointments in the past two to three years). Contrariwise, Lowe and Veeder jump up nearly a dozen places. These shifts are attributable to differentiated scoring (Lowe and Veeder primarily act as presiding arbitrators) but it is also a function of the increased number of appointments that these arbitrators have received in the past two to three years.[49]

3.2 Legal counsel

We now turn to the role of legal counsel in the international investment arbitration network. They represent a paradox. On one hand, they are numerous. We have identified 2,699 distinct lawyers that have represented claimants and respondents: see Figure 7.4. On the other hand, there is a core of lawyers who dominate the caseload. Only 14 per cent (382 lawyers) have litigated more than two cases, while only 1 per cent (the top twenty-five) have litigated more than thirteen cases: see Table 7.3. A member of this top 1 per cent of litigators has thus appeared on average in every second case in international investment arbitration (530 of 1,039).

3.2.1 ICSID annulments counted additionally

Examining this group more closely, Western nationals and law firms clearly dominate. Moreover, almost without exception, the non-Western contingent only represent their home state as in-house counsel (ie Argentina)[50] or only act as respondent state counsel within their home states' region (ie Mexico and Czech Republic).[51] Tellingly, the only two non-Western legal counsel that have represented claimant-investors in international investment arbitration cases are long-term residents of the US (Alexandrov) and France (Gharavi), with elite education from these states. Moreover, a number of top arbitrators also feature on this legal counsel list;[52] and we will return to this important revolving door phenomenon in the next section. The one (slightly) positive sign of diversity in this group concerns women. Compared to the arbitrator cluster, they are better represented with five of the top twenty-five being women (20%).[53] The final feature worth noting is the role of the law firms of legal counsel. Anglo-American and French law firms dwarf the list—even for counsel that represent predominantly respondent states. Only four of the top twenty-eight have spent some time as government-employed counsel and only one exclusively so—the last legal counsel on the list.[54]

[49] Indeed, one challenge of network analysis is that it is often cross-sectional and poorly integrates change over time. See discussion in Charlotin (n 44).

[50] Guglielmino and Abbona.

[51] Pekař and Álvarez-Avila.

[52] Crawford, Alexandrov, Paulsson, Gaillard, Gharavi, Volterra, Price, and Kalicki.

[53] Abbona, Álvarez-Avila, Kalicki, Carlson, and Gill.

[54] Pedroza.

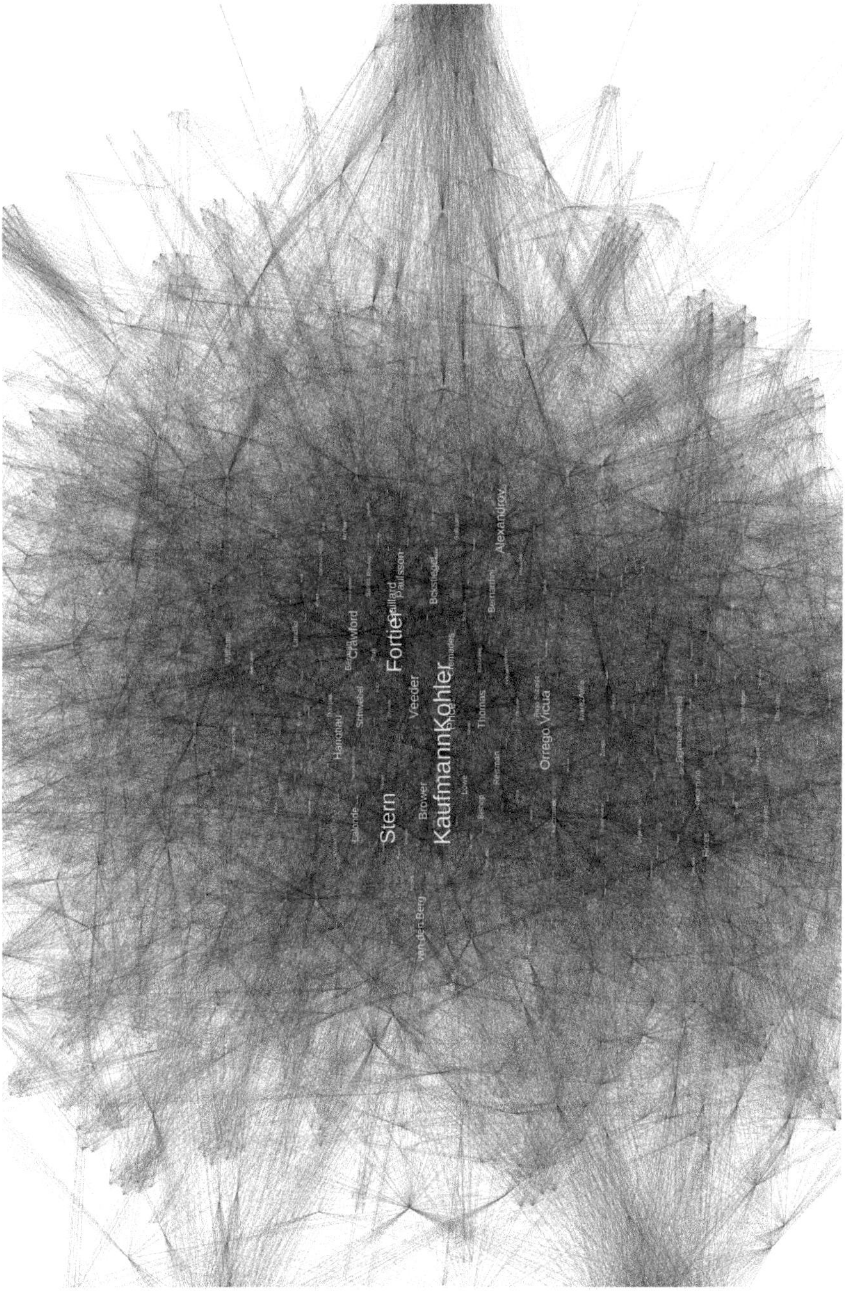

Figure 7.4 Mapping the full network

Table 7.3 Legal counsel—cases, nationality, and law firm (top 25)

Rank	Counsel	Nationality	Law firm(s)	For claimant	For resp.	Total cases*
1	Stanimir Alexandrov	Bulgaria	Sidley Austin | Powell Goldstein	13	18	**31**
2	Nigel Blackaby	UK	Freshfields	26	4	30
3	Osvaldo Guglielmino	Argentina	Argentina Ministry	0	25	25
4	Emmanuel Gaillard	France	Shearman & Sterling	14	7	**21**
5	Todd Weiler	Canada	Todd Weiler	20	0	**20**
6	Angelina Abbona	Argentina	Argentina Ministry	0	19	**19**
6	Ronald Goodman	US	Foley Hoag | White & Case	3	16	**19**
8	Stephen Jagusch	New Zealand	Quinn Emanuel | Allen & Overy	12	6	**18**
8	Gabriela Álvarez-Avila	Mexico	Curtis Mallet	0	18	**18**
8	Jan Paulsson	France	Freshfields | Three Crowns | Coudert	7	11	**18**
8	Hamid Gharavi	France	Derains & Gharavi	11	7	**18**
12	Stephen Anway	US	Squire Patton Boggs | Squire Sanders	1	16	**17**
13	Rostislav Pekař	Czech	Squire Patton Boggs | Squire Sanders	2	14	**16**
13	George Kahale	US	Curtis Mallet	0	16	**16**
13	R Doak Bishop	US	King & Spalding	16	0	**16**
13	Paolo Di Rosa	US	Arnold & Porter | Winston & Strawn	3	13	**16**
13	Robert Volterra	Canada	Latham & Watkins | Volterra Fietta	9	7	**16**
13	Jean Kalicki	US	Arnold & Porter	5	11	**16**
19	Mark Clodfelter	US	US Ministry | Foley Hoag	1	14	**15**
19	Marinn Carlson	US	Sidley Austin	5	10	**15**
21	Barry Appleton	Canada	Appleton & Associates	14	0	**14**
21	Judith Gill	UK	Allen & Overy	10	4	**14**
21	James Crawford	Australia	Matrix Chambers	8	6	**14**
21	Craig Miles	US	King & Spalding	14	0	**14**
25	Daniel Price	US	Sidley Austin | Powell Goldstein	8	5	**13**

* ICSID Annulments counted additionally

3.3 Expert witnesses

Expert witnesses have not been a focus in previous studies of the international investment arbitration community.[55] However, in constructing the PITAD database, we were continually surprised by the regular appearance of familiar names amongst the expert witnesses. Moreover, some of this expert advice addressed rather pedestrian points in international investment law. On its face, it was not clear why such calibre of expert testimony was required. Our suspicion was that parties were also using leading figures (often other arbitrators) as part of a symbolic strategy, something that Dezalay and Garth also found in their interviews. To be sure, expert witnesses possess more than symbolic power, particularly if they are the only expert witness on a particular point or they are providing valuations for the damages/quantum phase of the arbitration. The material and legal power of these expert witnesses in the system should not be undervalued.

Table 7.4 ranks the top twenty-five expert witnesses according to their number of appearances in international investment arbitration cases. It is notable that only

Table 7.4 Expert witnesses—cases, nationality, and roles (top 25)

Rank	Expert	Nationality	Role	For claimant	For resp.	Total cases
1	Brent Kaczmarek	US	Quantum/ Industry Expert	17	11	28
2	Rudolf Dolzer	Germany	International Law Expert	13	4	17
3	W Michael Reisman	US	International Law Expert	9	7	16
4	Christoph Schreuer	Austria	International Law Expert	11	2	13
5	Manuel Abdala	US	Quantum/ Industry Expert	5	1	6
6	Anne-Marie Slaughter	US	International Law Expert	0	5	5
6	Ismael Mata	Argentina	National Law Expert	0	5	5
6	James Crawford	Australia	International Law Expert	1	4	5
6	James Dow	US	Quantum/ Industry Expert	0	5	5
6	Joseph Kalt	US	Quantum/ Industry Expert	4	1	5
6	Nico Schrijver	Netherlands	International Law Expert	2	3	5

(*continued*)

[55] Christopher Drahozal makes a similar observation in 'Empirical Findings on International Arbitration: An Overview' in Thomas Schultz and Federico Ortino (eds), *Oxford Handbook on International Arbitration* (OUP 2017).

Table 7.4 Continued

Rank	Expert	Nationality	Role	For claimant	For resp.	Total cases
6	Pablo Spiller	US	Quantum/ Industry Expert	4	1	5
13	Alberto Bianchi	Argentina	Domestic Law Expert	4	0	4
13	Jan Paulsson	France	International Law Expert	3	1	4
13	Juan Andrade	Ecuador	National Law Expert	0	4	4
13	Lucian Mihai	Romania	National Law Expert	1	3	4
13	William Burke-White	US	International Law Expert	0	4	4
18	Adnan Amkhan	UK	International Law Expert	2	1	3
18	Benedict Kingsbury	Australia	International Law Expert	0	3	3
18	David Caron	US	International Law Expert	3	0	3
18	Hernán Pérez Loose	Chile	National Law Expert	3	0	3
18	José Alvarez	US	International Law Expert	3	0	3
18	Kenneth Vandevelde	US	International Law Expert	2	1	3
18	Robert Howse	Canada	International Law Expert	3	0	3
18	Thomas Waelde	Germany	International Law Expert	2	1	3

five expert witnesses have appeared more than five times and together account for eighty-two cases (11% of all known expert witness appearances and more than half of the top twenty-five). They appear to play an almost orator-like role in the system. Two of these experts are quantum/industry experts (Kaczmarek and Abdala); and three are international law academics (but also arbitrators: Reisman, Dolzer, and Schreuer). Of these, three have appeared for both claimants and respondents on a relatively regular basis.

Moving to the top twenty-five, we see a pattern of almost exclusively Western expert witnesses and only one woman (Slaughter). Given the number of female professors in international economic law and public international law, this low usage of female international law expert witnesses is quite striking. Although, it may not be surprising given numerous psychological studies concerning gender cognitive bias in assessing the reliability of witnesses.[56] The same could be said of the absence

[56] See eg Blake McKimmie et al, 'Jurors Responses to Expert Witness Testimony: The Effects of Gender Stereotypes' (2004) 7(2) Group Processes and Intergroup Relations 131.

of non-Western international law professors. Indeed, the regular selection by legal counsel and law firms of Western male expert witnesses implicitly suggests what international investment arbitrators view as credible. It may also give credence to the hypothesis (and indirect evidence) of a possible cognitive arbitral bias against less developed states in international investment arbitration.[57]

3.4 Tribunal secretaries

Finally, we include tribunal secretaries. While often invisible to the outside world, the role of tribunal secretaries in shaping and influencing international litigation has gained increased scholarly and political attention. While earlier studies indicated that their role was largely confined to the non-substantive parts of award drafting,[58] recent accounts suggest that tribunal secretaries may be more influential.[59]

Table 7.5 ranks the number of tribunal secretaries—in the 568 cases in which we have information. Notably, the top twenty-five are responsible for administering 68 per cent of these cases. Interestingly, it is only at this point that we see any signs of gender or regional diversity—a majority are women and slightly more than half come from non-Western states.[60]

4 Who are the Power Brokers?

The previous section mapped the different actors in the system. We now draw this mapping analysis together to analyze the investment arbitration community as a whole, and focus on the issue of power. As discussed in the introduction, we seek to measure power in both quantitative and qualitative terms. *Quantitatively*, we count the number of cases and connections as a measure of institutional power. Thus, individuals who are regularly engaged in international investment arbitration have the opportunity to exercise significant material influence in the system. Moreover, high numbers of appointments in any role usually increasing the chances of future appointment—a sign of symbolic power.[61]

[57] See Behn, Berge, and Langford (n 30).

[58] Joint Report of the International Commercial Disputes Committee and the Committee on Arbitration of the New York City Bar Association, 'Secretaries to International Arbitral Tribunals' (2006) 17 American Review of International Arbitration 575, 585.

[59] Taylor St John, 'Tribunal Secretaries', *PluriCourts Investment Arbitrator Behavior Workshop*, Oslo, 25 May 2016. See also in relation to the WTO: Cossette Creamer, 'Between the Letter of the Law and the Demands of Politics: The Judicial Balancing of Trade Authority within the WTO', Working Paper (2015), available at: <http://scholar.harvard.edu/cosettecreamer/publications/between-letter-law-and-demands-politics-balancing-authority-wto-dispute> (accessed 1 February 2018).

[60] It may be that there is a selection bias. Most of the publicly available information about tribunal secretaries comes from ICSID cases, which are hosted by the World Bank. This institution has a partial commitment to regional diversity as an intergovernmental organization. However, we note that women appeared to be well-represented in many arbitration centres along with increasingly a greater number of non-Western nationals. But this is a subject for further investigation.

[61] See extended discussion in St John et al (n 12).

Table 7.5 Tribunal secretaries—cases, nationality, and institution (top 25)

Rank	Secretary name	Nationality	Institution	Total cases
1	Gonzalo Flores	Chile	ICSID	38
2	Martina Polasek	Czech Republic	ICSID	30
3	Eloïse Obadia	France	ICSID	28
4	Aurélia Antonietti	France	ICSID	25
5	Ucheora Onwuamaegbu	Nigeria	ICSID	24
6	Natalí Sequeira	Costa Rica	ICSID	21
7	Claudia Frutos-Peterson	Mexico	ICSID	20
8	Gabriela Alvarez-Avila	Mexico	ICSID	19
9	Mercedes Cordido-Freytes de Kurowski	Venezuela	ICSID	16
10	Aïssatou Diop	Senegal	ICSID	15
10	Anneliese Fleckenstein	Venezuela	ICSID	15
12	Marco Monañés-Rumayor	Mexico	ICSID	13
12	Milanka Kostadinova	Bulgaria	ICSID	13
14	Paul-Jean Le Cannu	France	ICSID/PCA	12
15	Alicia Martín Blanco	Spain	ICSID	11
16	Frauke Nitschke	Germany	ICSID	10
16	Janet Whittaker	UK	ICSID	10
18	Tomás Solís	El Salvador	ICSID	9
18	Alejandro Escobar	Chile	ICSID	9
18	Ann Catherine Kettlewell	Mexico	ICSID	9
21	Margrete Stevens	Denmark	ICSID	8
22	Martin Doe	Canada	PCA	7
22	Mairée Uran-Bidegain	Colombia	ICSID	7
24	Geraldine Fischer	US	ICSID	6
24	Katia Yannaca-Small	Greece	ICSID	6

Qualitatively, we are concerned with shading the degree of material and symbolic power that comes with a particular position in arbitration. Thus we further expand our relationship matrix to facilitate the perceived variances of influence between the different roles and the parties they represent. This weighting attempts to normalize and avoid overemphasis of lesser roles in the system. Therefore, we rank arbitrators higher than counsel and counsel higher than tribunal secretaries and witnesses. In addition, we assign further weights for distance between actors, according to the structure of arbitration.

These weightings are of course somewhat arbitrary but we describe and justify them as follows. First, as discussed above, presiding arbitrators are given a weighting of 1 and wing arbitrators (0.75). Second, we weight counsel at (0.5) but introduce also a *distance* weighting. We weight the relationship between a claimant counsel and claimant-appointed wing arbitrator at (1.25); yet for the same claimant counsel and the respondent arbitrator we weight the relationship at (0.75). The former is done because the relationship is close (and one is involved in nominating the other), while the latter is done because the two actors are much further apart. The same logic is applied in reverse to a respondent counsel. Third, we weight tribunal secretaries at (0.375) and witnesses at (0.25). We also apply distance weightings to the expert witnesses. Thus, the relationship between a claimant witness and claimant counsel is weighted at (1.25), but (0.75) for a claimant witness and respondent counsel.

Based on this methodology, we can identify the power brokers in the system. In Table 7.6, we provide a new and alternative picture of the most powerful actors.

Table 7.6 All actors—network rankings (top 25)

Rank	Name	Nationality	Arb.	Counsel	Exp.	Sec.	HITS hub	Page rank	Degrees out (weighted)
1	Gabrielle Kaufmann-Kohler	Switzerland	56	0	0	0	1.00000	0.00373	753 (641)
2	L Yves Fortier	Canada	53	0	0	0	0.87664	0.00423	761 (655)
3	Brigitte Stern	France	88	0	0	0	0.87278	0.00622	1067 (727)
4	VV Veeder	UK	37	2	0	0	0.55004	0.00298	493 (419)
5	Francisco Orrego Vicuña	Chile	49	0	0	0	0.54280	0.00322	542 (428)
6	Stanimir Alexandrov	Bulgaria	32	31	0	0	0.52113	0.00411	781 (424)
7	Charles Brower	US	52	0	0	0	0.48111	0.00314	582 (386)
8	James Crawford	Australia	27	14	5	0	0.48067	0.00394	697 (408)
9	Daniel Price	US	18	13	0	0	0.48031	0.00190	470 (260)
10	Emmanuel Gaillard	France	23	21	0	0	0.47015	0.00344	676 (370)
11	Bernard Hanotiau	Belgium	40	3	0	0	0.44905	0.00304	497 (394)
12	Jan Paulsson	France	28	18	4	0	0.4454	0.00378	662 (363)
13	Albert Jan van den Berg	Netherlands	44	0	0	0	0.44069	0.00324	533 (405)
14	J Christopher Thomas	Canada	43	3	0	0	0.42114	0.00299	520 (340)
15	Karl-Heinz Böckstiegel	Germany	40	0	0	0	0.41590	0.00273	400 (359)
16	Marc Lalonde	Canada	35	0	0	0	0.39232	0.00258	452 (330)
17	Stephen Schwebel	US	18	9	0	0	0.38389	0.00202	396 (232)
18	Bernardo Cremades	Spain	37	2	0	0	0.37650	0.00249	400 (303)
19	Piero Bernardini	Italy	36	1	0	0	0.37495	0.00234	357 (304)
20	Gonzalo Flores	Chile	0	0	0	38	0.34236	0.00334	662 (251)

(continued)

Table 7.6 Continued

Rank	Name	Nationality	Arb.	Counsel	Exp.	Sec.	HITS hub	Page rank	Degrees out (weighted)
21	W. Michael Reisman	US	19	1	16	0	0.33781	0.00298	607 (253)
22	Juan Fernández-Armesto	Spain	29	0	0	0	0.32955	0.00220	325 (308)
23	Franklin Berman	UK	24	0	0	0	0.32912	0.00164	290 (250)
24	Vaughan Lowe	UK	24	1	1	0	0.32573	0.00206	339 (271)
25	Gabriela Álvarez-Avila	Mexico	0	18	0	19	0.32565	0.00330	610 (252)

For certain actors, there is a clear jump up the ladder. Arbitrators that have worn multiple hats or individuals with other hats constitute this surging group. They have served as both legal counsel and arbitrator (eg Alexandrov, Crawford, Price, Paulsson, Gilliard, and Schwebel); both expert witness and arbitrator (eg Reisman); or frequently as tribunal secretaries (eg Alvarez-Avila and Flores).

The existence of a differently configured group of arbitrators allows us also to revisit existing explanatory theories on arbitrator selection. Importantly, our findings highlight the often implicit but under-emphasized role of counsel and others in those explanations. As noted earlier, Ginsburg's theory emphasized *strategic* action and the use of barriers to keep out new entrants. However, it was Rogers who noted the role of information asymmetries as a key strategic entry barrier. Information asymmetries are typical of ad hoc systems and benefit insiders, and she noted specifically the role of counsel and tribunal secretaries.[62] Indeed, one arbitration lawyer recently boasted that their competitive advantage lies in what is 'not written down'.[63] Thus, the existence of a core group of counsel, which includes a significant number that also act as arbitrators, may enhance the maintenance of those information asymmetries.

Moreover, Rogers highlighted two structural factors that shape the imperfect competitive nature of the arbitration market. These are the (i) role of insiders in making arbitration appointments[64] and (ii) lack of regulation (with an absence of legal/judicial oversight and little room for reputational sanction).[65] The existence of a strong core group beyond pure arbitrators accentuates potentially both aspects. First, legal counsel and tribunal secretaries are pivotal in making or influencing appointments. They are the clear power brokers in the first phase of an arbitration. Indeed, we might speculate that a revolving door increases incentives for a special

[62] Catherine Rogers, 'The Vocation of the International Arbitrator' (2004) 20 American University International Law Review 957, 968–69.

[63] GAR, *Global Arbitration Review 100: The Guide to Specialist Arbitration Firms 2012* (Geneva: GAR 2012), 3, cited in Eberhardt and Olivet (n 24).

[64] 'Arbitrator selection is often in the hands of members of the same "club," who are either operating in the institutions or already appointed as party-appointed arbitrators.' Rogers (n 23), 12.

[65] ibid, 970–75.

form of oligopolistic behaviour: making appointments in expectation of a return favour. In future research, we will test the likelihood that counsel nominate arbitrators that may be more likely to appoint them when these arbitrators act as counsel: a reciprocal revolving door. Second, the closeness and ties in the community may not incentivize public reputational sanctions. The power that insider legal counsel hold in appointments may strongly disincentivize critique. In other words, those who are too critical can be quickly subject to exclusion or relegation to a wing arbitrator role.

Thus, by foregrounding the role of the broader arbitration community we can enrich existing theories about the arbitration market. It especially allows us to identify the deeply embedded power brokers who may determine the ability of outsiders to enter and insiders to remain.

5 Double Hatting

We now turn to the question of whether there is double hatting—the simultaneous fulfilment of two roles, especially arbitrator and counsel. The issue of whether it is acceptable for an individual to sit simultaneously as an arbitrator in one case and act as legal counsel in another case has been the subject of a long-running and heated debate within the international commercial arbitration community;[66] and it moved to centre stage with the rise of treaty-based arbitration in the 2000s. Critics of the international investment arbitration regime have continually pointed to the legitimacy concerns that arise when a system of adjudication permits adjudicators to act as arbitrator in one case and as legal counsel in another. One of the interesting points about the legitimacy of this double hatting issue in international investment arbitration is that it is not only subject to criticism from the outside, but is a practice where insiders in the community have remained actively split over the past decade.

Leading the charge against the practice of double hatting from the inside is Sands, who over the past decade has repeatedly written and lectured about the legitimacy concerns tied to double hatting in international arbitration.[67] For Sands, the conflict issues that can arise are relatively clear:

> [It] is possible to recognise the difficulty that may arise if a lawyer spends a morning drafting an arbitral award that addresses a contentious legal issue, and then in the afternoon as counsel in a different case drafts a pleading making arguments on the same legal issue. Can that lawyer, while acting as arbitrator, cut herself off entirely from her simultaneous role as counsel? The issue is not whether she thinks it can be done, but whether a reasonable observer would so conclude. Speaking for myself, I find it difficult to imagine that I could do so without, in some way, potentially being seen to run the risk of allowing myself to be influenced, however subconsciously.[68]

While acknowledging that many of his colleagues believe that they can effectively separate the different roles that they may play in different arbitrations, Sands

[66] For a summary of the discourse on this issue, see Sebastian Perry, 'Arbitrator and Counsel: the Double-Hat Syndrome', Global Arbitration Review (15 March 2012).
[67] See eg Luke Eric Peterson, 'Arbitrator Decries "Revolving Door" Roles of Lawyers in Investment Treaty Arbitration', Investment Arbitration Reporter (25 February 2010).
[68] Sands (n 20), 31–32.

articulates that this practice nonetheless is problematic in international arbitration. It can never fully shield itself against questions of perceived bias. In terms of legitimacy for the system, it is a practice that should be avoided.[69] Likewise, Judge Thomas Buergenthal of the International Court of Justice, in a 2006 lecture, summarized the issues that can arise when arbitrators act simultaneously or sequentially as counsel:

> I have long believed that the practice of allowing arbitrators to serve as counsel, and counsel to serve as arbitrators, raises due process of law issues. In my view, arbitrators and counsel should be required to decide to be one or the other, and be held to the choice they have made, at least for a specific period of time. That is necessary, in my opinion, in order to ensure that an arbitrator will not be tempted, consciously or unconsciously, to seek to obtain a result in an arbitral decision that might advance the interests of a client in a case he or she is handling as counsel. ICSID is particularly vulnerable to this problem because the interpretation and application of the same or similar legal instruments—the Bilateral Investment Treaties, for example—are regularly at issue in different cases before it […]. These revolving-door problems—counsel selecting an arbitrator who, the next time around when the arbitrator is counsel, selects the previous counsel as arbitrator—should be avoided. *Manus manum lavat*, in other words—you scratch my back and I'll scratch yours, does not advance the rule of law.[70]

While Sands, Buergenthal, and others have highlighted why the practice of double hatting is ethically undesirable for arbitrators and legal counsel to practice, it is not uncommon to hear arguments that support the practice, and these arguments draw principally upon structural and economic claims. Firstly, they hold that there is a relatively small pool of arbitrators that can sit in these types of arbitrations and that limiting qualified individuals from sitting as arbitrator due to work as legal counsel would undermine the quality and rigour of the adjudicators acting in the current system.[71] Secondly, they claim that there is an economic argument for not restricting the practice of double hatting: many legal counsel seeking to become full-time arbitrators cannot justify giving up their counsel practice when there is no guarantee that arbitral appointments will come in the future.[72] Therefore, under this scenario, it is inevitable that some double hatting will occur during the transitionary period between the time an individual acts primarily as counsel to the time that they become a full-time arbitrator.

[69] Some arbitrators have clarified their role in similar terms although on a more individual basis: 'I don't feel the need to stand on the rooftops and preach about my own practice. I have not appeared as counsel in investor-state arbitration or indeed inter-state arbitration… I find it more comfortable to confine my arbitration role to being an arbitrator or member of an ICSID annulment committee.' See Interview with Sir Frank Berman in Sebastian Perry, 'To Be Frank', Global Arbitration Review (21 February 2013).

[70] Thomas Buergenthal, 'The Proliferation of Disputes, Dispute Settlement Procedures and Respect for the Rule of Law' (2006) 3(5) Transnational Dispute Management.

[71] On this point, Barton Legum, a prominent counsel and arbitrator based in Paris, has noted that: 'the pool of qualified arbitrators is already "vanishingly small" and that it would be problematic for the users of the arbitration system if efforts were made to exclude all practicing BIT counsel from this pool.' Peterson (n 65).

[72] 'I have a lot of sympathy for those who say you need arbitrators with skill and experience. How on earth does somebody get established as an arbitrator if he or she never gets a chance to start? So I think inevitably there has to be some overlap. But there may be a stage in one's career when it becomes sensible to do one thing or the other.' ibid, 2.

Empirically speaking, the first of these arguments would only hold for the 1990s. Since then, the potential pool of investment arbitrators has expanded significantly. And while there may be a shortage of qualified arbitrators in other fields such as international commercial arbitration,[73] investment arbitration appointments are viewed as highly prestigious.[74] Investment arbitration is a buyer's market not a seller's market. It is also not clear how far the second argument extends temporally. Once counsel has obtained their first or even second arbitrator appointment, they could desist from accepting future counsel appointments as they ease into a new role.

Ethically speaking, however, both of these justifications for the practice are rather unpersuasive, given that, at a minimum, the practice of double hatting can reasonably give rise to questions of potential or perceived bias or conflict. And these appearances of bias or conflict that can arise in this context are not merely hypothetical. There are a number of examples where the double hatting problem has become the subject of formal challenges.

This classic example involves French arbitrator Gaillard and an international investment arbitration case (*Telekom Malaysia v Ghana*[75]), where he was acting as the claimant-appointed arbitrator at the same time that he was also acting as claimant's counsel in an ICSID annulment proceeding in a different case (*RFCC v Morocco*[76]). Even though Gaillard disclosed that he was acting as counsel in the ICSID annulment case, the respondent state (Ghana) in the arbitration where he was acting as arbitrator lodged multiple challenges against him in the Hague District Court[77] (Netherlands was the seat of the arbitration) alleging that his role as arbitrator was incompatible with his simultaneous role as counsel in the ICSID annulment case, especially due to the fact that both cases involved similar legal issues and that Ghana was relying on the case of *RFCC v Morocco* in its submissions. Ghana argued, inter alia, that Gaillard, 'who in his capacity of counsel opposes a specific notion or approach, cannot be unbiased in his judgment of that same notion or approach in a case in which he acts as arbitrator'.[78] The Hague District Court ordered Gaillard to choose whether to continue as arbitrator or counsel, but not both. Gaillard subsequently resigned from his position as counsel in the ICSID annulment proceedings.

Even if Gaillard was able to separate his different roles in different cases, this example highlights, at a minimum, that an appearance of bias or conflict was reasonable, even if there was no showing of actual bias. Ultimately, this challenge to Gaillard was resolved through his resignation in one of his roles; however, it is important to note that neither the various arbitration rules (ie ICSID, SCC,[79] ICC,[80] and UNCITRAL) nor the *IBA Guidelines on Conflicts of Interest in International*

[73] ibid, 2. [74] Franck (n 9).

[75] *Telekom Malaysia Berhad v The Republic of Ghana*, PCA Case No 2003-03, UNCITRAL, Settled.

[76] *Consortium R.F.C.C. v Kingdom of Morocco*, ICSID Case No ARB/00/6, Decision on Annulment (18 January 2006).

[77] *Republic of Ghana v Telekom Malaysia Berhad*, Hague District Court, Challenge No 13/2004, Petition No HA/RK 2004.667, 18 October 2004; Challenge 17/2004, Petition No HA/RK/2004/778, 5 November 2004.

[78] ibid, Challenge No 13/2004, Petition No HA/RK 2004.667, p 3.

[79] Stockholm Chamber of Commerce. [80] International Chamber of Commerce.

Arbitration explicitly prohibit this practice.[81] While the *IBA Guidelines* do not provide bright line rules preventing arbitrators to act simultaneously as counsel, the *IBA Guidelines* are clear on the arbitrator's role in cases where justifiable doubts arise in regard to the arbitrator's independence or impartiality. The *IBA Guidelines* on issues of conflict of interest states:

> (a) An arbitrator shall decline to accept an appointment or, if the arbitration has already been commenced, refuse to continue to act as an arbitrator, if he or she has any doubt as to his or her ability to be impartial or independent; (b) The same principle applies if facts or circumstances exist, or have arisen since the appointment, which, from the point of view of a reasonable third person having knowledge of the relevant facts and circumstances, would give rise to justifiable doubts as to the arbitrator's impartiality or independence [...]; (c) Doubts are justifiable if a reasonable third person, having knowledge of the relevant facts and circumstances, would reach the conclusion that there is a likelihood that the arbitrator may be influenced by factors other than the merits of the case as presented by the parties in reaching his or her decision.[82]

In cases where an arbitrator is acting simultaneously in another case as counsel, there are situations—as highlighted in the above example—where an appearance of bias or conflict arises to the degree where a reasonable third person would have justifiable doubts as to the arbitrator's impartiality or independence. Yet, the *IBA Guidelines* are just that: guidelines. They do not create clear legal obligations on arbitrators that can be sanctioned. As a result, the international arbitration community must rely to a degree on 'self-regulation' or 'self-policing' if the practice of double hatting is to be minimized in the short-term.

Nonetheless, our concern is not to resolve this debate but rather assess empirically the extent to which double hatting actually occurs in international investment arbitration; and to propose some ways in which the practice could be minimized. In determining the existence of double hatting, we have developed a customized algorithm. Through a multi-factor calculation, we determine an all-time score for each individual and an annual score.

The double hatting index is calculated as follows. If a person in a given year is involved only as either arbitrator or legal counsel (ie is wearing only 'one hat'), the individual is not assigned any points. If, however, she or he is involved with a minimum of two investment arbitration cases in a minimum of two different roles, then a 'yearly score' of (2) is assigned to that individual for a given year. The score does not attempt to describe the intensity of double hatting within a calendar year, and hence the maximum score an individual can receive for a year is (2). Cases are included in the evaluation from their constitution date and until they are either discontinued, settled, or finally resolved through a decision in the form of an award. Cases that are pending as of 1 January 2017 have a concluding date as of 1 January 2017 for the purposes of our analysis. Our double hatting index is a somewhat conservative measure. It does not take into account potentially multiple conflicts of interests (due to appointments in many cases).

[81] *IBA Guidelines on Conflicts of Interest in International Arbitration*, Adopted by resolution of the IBA Council on Thursday 23 October 2014.

[82] ibid, Part I, Article 2.

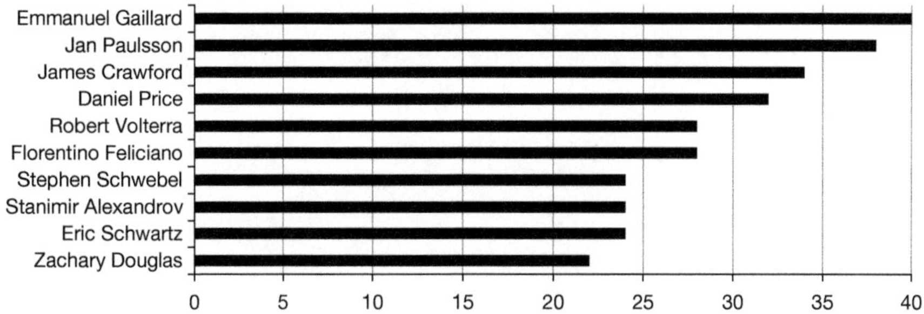

Figure 7.5 The double hatting index (top 10)

Figure 7.5 lists the top ten according to those criteria. The top four places go to actors that we have already identified as power brokers in the international investment arbitration community. These are Gaillard, Paulsson, Crawford, and Price. This group all has scores over 30, which means considerable double hatting over a long period of time. However, there is a considerable group hot on their heels with twenty arbitrators with scores over 20. Some of these are prominent arbitrators but many also represent a new generation of actors that may be transitioning to full-time arbitrator roles (ie Silva Romero, Bishop, Heiskanen, and Douglas). It is also interesting to note that those arbitrators which have made clear statements on the problem of double hatting (eg Sands and Reisman) have very low double hatting scores despite being central figures in the network.

However, it is not uncommon for the international investment arbitration community to claim that the problem of double hatting has been decreasing over time. Our index above is ahistorical and measures cross-sectionally double hatting. Thus, in Figure 7.6, we have calculated the double hatting index over time for the top twenty-five arbitrators and for all arbitrators.

The yearly results in Figure 7.6 suggest that there has not been a significant decrease (or increase) over time. Instead, the phenomenon for the top twenty-five double hatters appears to have been relatively stable since 2005—hovering between scores of 35 and 50 with only a slight decline over the past decade. It is much less stable for other individuals with a large rise up to 2014 and then a strong fall. Thus, it seems too early to conclude that there has been a dramatic change in the practice. There appears to be a select group of arbitrators that frequently double hat as legal counsel.

In order to make this continuous practice of the top ten double hatters clear on an individual basis, we have tracked each year of their double hatting (Table 7.7). What is particularly notable is that those who have ceased double hatting in the last three to four years have largely ceased taking new cases as either arbitrator or counsel as they reach retirement age (ie Schwebel). However, in some other cases, the lack of double hatting in the past few years is probably more likely the result of: having a sufficiently large caseload as arbitrator as to preclude the time or economic necessity to act as counsel simultaneously (ie Schwartz), or being appointed as judge to the International Court of Justice (ie Crawford), which restricts counsel work during the time that the individual is on the bench. Therefore, it does not appear that the individuals ceasing to

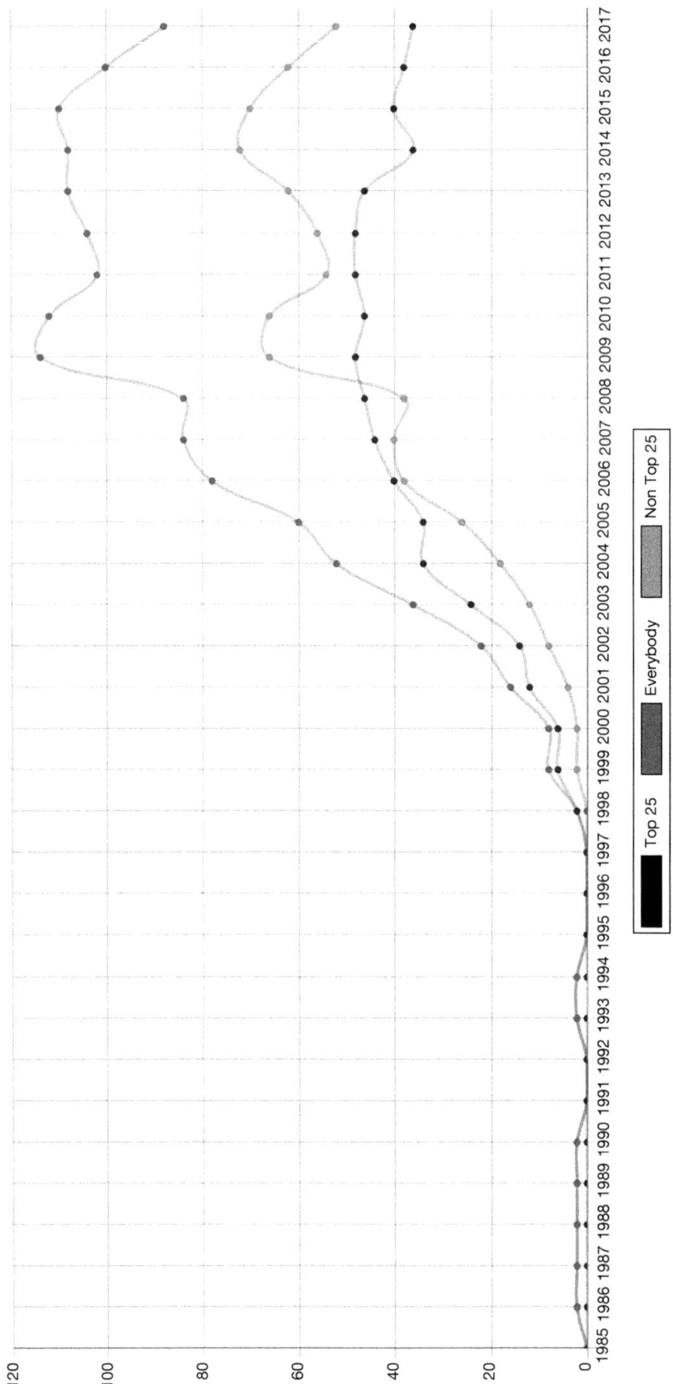

Figure 7.6 Double hatting over time

Table 7.7 Double hatting by year (top 10)

Name/Year	1998	1999	2000	2001	2002	2003	2004	2005	2006	2007	2008	2009	2010	2011	2012	2013	2014	2015	2016	2017
Emmanuel Gaillard	X	X	X	X	X	X	X	X	X	X	X	X	X	X	X	X	X	X	X	X
Jan Paulsson		X	X	X	X	X	X	X	X	X	X	X	X	X	X	X	X	X	X	X
James Crawford		X		X	X	X	X	X	X	X	X	X	X	X	X	X	X	X		
Daniel Price				X	X	X	X	X	X	X	X	X	X	X	X	X	X	X	X	
Robert Volterra						X	X	X	X	X	X	X	X	X	X	X	X	X	X	X
Florentino Feliciano						X	X	X	X	X	X	X	X	X	X	X	X	X		
Stanimir Alexandrov								X	X	X	X	X	X	X	X	X		X	X	X
Stephen Schwebel				X	X	X	X	X	X	X	X	X	X	X	X					
Eric Schwartz								X	X		X	X	X	X	X	X	X			
Zachary Douglas										X	X	X	X	X	X	X	X	X	X	X

double hat over the past few years are making this choice as a response to the ethical or conflict issues that have arisen in the discourse critiquing the practice.

6 Conclusions

The purpose of this chapter was to present a preliminary assessment of the complete network of actors in the international investment arbitration community to date. Instead of focusing on one group or type of actors within the regime, we have sought to provide a comprehensive map of all relevant actors and their roles in order to identify those actors who move between different roles and even wear multiple hats simultaneously (double hatting).

What we find is that the 1,000-plus international investment arbitration cases to date have involved almost 4,000 known individuals and that within this select group of individuals there is a prominent core that is both highly influential and powerful within the system. Our social network analysis suggests a deep set of 'power brokers' across the field, as those passing regularly through the revolving door score quite highly on our measures of power. This suggests that an analysis of power cannot be constrained to the arbitral role. As we have highlighted, the key explanatory theories of the uncompetitive nature of the arbitration markets implicitly or explicitly take into account this structural feature.

In terms of double hatting, we find that the practice continues to exist. In reality, it is a very small group but it is constituted by highly influential and well-known individuals. In other words, double hatting is not a common or widespread practice across the entire network of cases (ie breadth), it is practised so consistently by a highly visible and powerful core of some of the most influential actors in the system (ie depth). Given that critiques of double hatting focus on the *perceived* bias and lack of impartiality, independence, and legitimacy that such a practice can have on the reasonable outside observer, its prevalence amongst influential actors is questionable even if there is a debate on its actual effects on independence.

Turning to reform, if about ten to fifteen individuals agreed to stop double hatting, it is highly probable that the major critiques against its practice would evaporate. While it would be preferable for the legitimacy of the system for top double hatters to self-regulate in this manner, there are potential rule changes that could mandate the termination of this practice. One way would be to include a double hatting ban in new IIAs that have been signed (as for eg in the recent CETA[83]) or through a reform or modification of the institutional rules governing the vast majority of these arbitrations.[84]

[83] Article 8.30(1) of the *Canada-EU Comprehensive Economic and Trade Agreement* stipulates that members of the Tribunal: '. . . shall be independent . . . In addition, upon appointment, they shall refrain from acting as counsel or as party-appointed expert or witness in any pending or new investment dispute under this or any other international agreement.'

[84] For a detailed assessment of the rules governing international investment arbitration and their relation to double hatting, see Nathalie Bernasconi-Osterwalder, Lise Johnson, and Fiona Marshall, *Arbitrator Independence and Impartiality: Examining the Dual Role of Arbitrator and Counsel* (Winnipeg: IISD 2010).

8

Dissecting Backlash

The Unarticulated Causes of Backlash and its Unintended Consequences

David Caron and Esmé Shirlow

In October 2015, a newspaper in the United Kingdom ran an opinion piece in which it was asserted that:

> TTIP's [the Transatlantic Trade and Investment Partnership's] biggest threat to society is its inherent assault on democracy. One of the main aims of TTIP is the introduction of Investor-State Dispute Settlements (ISDS), which allow companies to sue governments if those governments' policies cause a loss of profits. In effect it means unelected transnational corporations can dictate the policies of democratically elected governments.[1]

In the same month, over 150,000 protestors took to the streets of Germany to protest against the same treaty.[2] Such incidents, along with others, are increasingly cited as evidence of 'a rising backlash' against the regime of investor-State arbitration.[3]

[1] Lee Williams, 'What Is TTIP? And Six Reasons Why the Answer Should Scare You' *The Independent* (6 October 2015) <http://www.independent.co.uk/voices/comment/what-is-ttip-and-six-reasons-why-the-answer-should-scare-you-9779688.html>.

[2] Janosch Delcker and Cynthia Kroet, 'More than 150,000 Protest against EU-US Trade Deal' *Politico* (10 October 2015) <http://www.politico.eu/article/germany-mobilizes-against-eu-u-s-trade-deal-merkel-ttip-ceta/>. Some reports put the number of protestors as high as 250,000: 'Hundreds of Thousands Protest in Berlin against EU-U.S. Trade Deal' *Reuters* (Berlin, 10 October 2015) <http://www.reuters.com/article/us-trade-germany-ttip-protests-idUSKCN0S40L720151010>; Chris Johnston, 'Berlin Anti-TTIP Trade Deal Protest Attracts Hundreds of Thousands' *The Guardian* (10 October 2015) <http://www.theguardian.com/world/2015/oct/10/berlin-anti-ttip-trade-deal-rally-hundreds-thousands-protesters>.

[3] See, eg: Asha Kaushal, 'Revisiting History: How the Past Matters for the Present Backlash Against the Foreign Investment Regime' (2009) 50 Harvard International Law Journal 491, 492; Charles N Brower and Stephan Schill, 'Is Arbitration a Threat or a Boon to the Legitimacy of International Investment Law?' (2008) 9 Chicago Journal of International Law 471, 473; Francesco Francioni, 'Foreign Investments, Sovereignty and the Public Good' (2014) 23(1) Italian Yearbook of International Law 1, 4–5; Vernon Cassin, '"Investment Arbitration Is Now On Broadway, And The Critics Are Not Being Kind"' <http://kluwerarbitrationblog.com/2015/01/23/investment-arbitration-is-now-on-broadway-and-the-critics-are-not-being-kind/>.

Other chapters of this book raise thoughtful cautionary notes concerning the meaning of the notion of 'backlash'. The term 'backlash' indicates the presence of something more than scrutiny, critique, or even crisis.[4] Whereas critique of a system might lead to suggestions for reform, 'backlash' implies actions taken in opposition to the system itself. Extrapolating from a definition proffered by Sunstein, 'backlash' can be defined as: *Intense and sustained public disapproval of a system accompanied by aggressive steps to resist the system and to remove its legal force.*[5] 'Backlash', therefore, manifests as 'intense', 'sustained', and 'aggressive' calls for the abandonment of a system or for the adoption of a radically alternative structure.

Taking this definition of backlash as its starting point, this chapter considers how 'backlash' against investor-State arbitration has manifested (Section 1). In particular, it considers the forms of backlash, from whom or what it comes, and what motivates it. The chapter suggests that 'backlash' is a complex phenomenon, and argues that much of the 'backlash' against investor-State arbitration materializes as a result of, and therefore reflects, broader concerns about globalization. The concerns underlying the latter cannot, however, necessarily be addressed by reforms to investor-State arbitration. With this in mind, the chapter moves to consider how the regime of investment arbitration has evolved, and what has prompted that evolution (Section 2). The chapter charts key procedural and substantive reforms to the regime, highlighting that care must be taken in characterizing such reform as evidence of backlash or a response to it. Finally, the chapter considers the unintended consequences of backlash (Section 3). Whereas, as Section 2 shows, reform founded on critique can be sweeping, it is at the same time measured and reasoned. By contrast, reform prompted by backlash is rooted in anger and is as likely to do harm as it is to do good. Where Francis Bacon observed that 'Revenge is a kind of wild justice', we suggest that 'Backlash is a kind of wild reform'.[6] By exploring these themes, the chapter illustrates how concerns about diffuse forces such as globalization add hyperbole to critiques of investment treaty arbitration, turning them into a 'backlash'. Section 2 illustrates how reform has sought to separate the rhetoric from reality. States and institutions have responded to changing circumstances—rather than backlash—to implement a raft of modifications to investment treaty arbitration. To the extent that backlash raises issues incapable of being addressed within the existing investment arbitration regime, Section 3 identifies its potentially unintended consequences.

While the chapter focusses upon investment treaty arbitration, it seeks also to illuminate the complexities of evaluating opposition to international regimes, as well as the cyclical nature of contestation and reform. These issues hold particular relevance to investor-State arbitration given current negotiations of major bi- and multi-lateral treaties with investor-State protections. These issues are also likely to gain in relevance

[4] Cf Michael Albert Waibel (ed), *The Backlash against Investment Arbitration: Perceptions and Reality* (Wolters Kluwer Law & Business 2010) xxxvii.

[5] Cass R Sunstein, 'Backlash's Travels' (2007) 42 Harvard Civil Rights—Civil Liberties Law Review 435, 435. Sunstein focusses on backlash against particular cases in domestic law, defining backlash as 'Intense and sustained public disapproval of a judicial ruling, accompanied by aggressive steps to resist that ruling and to remove its legal force'.

[6] Francis Bacon, 'On Revenge' (1625) available at <https://www.bl.uk/collection-items/bacons-essays-on-revenge-envy-and-deformity>.

in light of the many investment treaties which will in the coming period come up for renewal or termination.[7]

1 Backlash against What? The Forms, Sources, and Focal Points of Backlash

A large range of acts are cited under the banner of 'backlash'. These include decisions of States to review,[8] not renew,[9] terminate, or withdraw from existing treaties;[10] refusals by States to negotiate or sign investment treaties;[11] and changes in the approaches of States to the negotiation of new treaties.[12] In these senses, backlash is not merely a critique and request for a particular reform, but rather action away from the regime even if the alternative is not fully articulated. There are also forms of 'backlash' which are not manifested in the actions of States, but arise instead from civil society, non-governmental organizations, and academia. For these groups, 'backlash' often manifests in the form of protests, comments in public consultation processes, and increased reporting and academic discussion of the 'crisis' said to face

[7] 'International Investment Policymaking in Transition: Challenges and Opportunities of Treaty Renewal' (United Nations Conference on Trade and Development 2013) IIA Issues Note No. 4 <http://unctad.org/en/PublicationsLibrary/webdiaepcb2013d9_en.pdf>.

[8] Jan Kleinheisterkamp, 'Investment Treaty Law and the Fear for Sovereignty: Transnational Challenges and Solutions' (2015) 78 (5) Modern Law Review 798; Luke Eric Peterson, 'Norway Proposes Significant Reforms to Its Investment Treaty Practices' *IISD Investment Treaty News* (27 March 2008) <http://www.iisd.org/pdf/2008/itn_mar27_2008.pdf>; Damon Vis-Dunbar, 'Norway Shelves Its Draft Model Bilateral Investment Treaty' *IISD Investment Treaty News* (8 June 2009) <http://www.iisd.org/itn/2009/06/08/norway-shelves-its-proposed-model-bilateral-investment-treaty/>; B Bland and S Donnan, 'Indonesia to Terminate More than 60 Bilateral Investment Treaties' *Financial Times* (26 March 2014) <http://www.ft.com/cms/s/0/3755c1b2-b4e2-11e3-af92-00144feabdc0.html>; UNCTAD (ed), *Reforming International Investment Governance* (United Nations 2015); SA Spears, 'The Quest for Policy Space in a New Generation of International Investment Agreements' (2010) 13 Journal of International Economic Law 1037, 1043.

[9] Anne van Aaken, 'Perils of Success? The Case of International Investment Protection' (2008) 9 European Business Organization Law Review (EBOR) 24 <http://www.journals.cambridge.org/abstract_S1566752908000013> (accessed 12 January 2016).

[10] Emmanuel Gaillard, 'The Denunciation of the ICSID Convention' (2007) 237 New York Law Journal; van Aaken (n 9) 24; UNCTAD, *Reforming International Investment Governance* (n 8); UNCTAD (ed), *Investing in the SDGs: An Action Plan* (United Nations 2014); Damon Vis-Dunbar, Luke Eric Peterson, and Fernando Carbrera Diaz, 'Bolivia Notifies World Bank of Withdrawal from ICSID, Pursues BIT Revisions' <http://www.bilaterals.org/?bolivia-notifies-world-bank-of>; Fernando Carbrera Diaz, 'Ecuador Continues Exit from ICSID' <http://www.iisd.org/itn/2009/06/05/ecuador-continues-exit-from-icsid/>.

[11] Spears (n 8) 1043; van Aaken (n 9) 9, 22. Cf: Stephan Schill, 'The Sixth Path: Reforming Investment Law from Within', *Society of International Economic Law* (Online Proceedings, Working Paper 2014) 4; Charles N Brower and Sadie Blanchard, 'What's in a Meme? The Truth about Investor-State Arbitration: Why It Need Not, and Must Not, Be Repossessed by States' (2013) 52 Columbia Journal of Transnational Law 689, 701.

[12] Andreas Kulick, 'Narrating Narratives of International Investment Law: History and Epistemic Forces' in Rainer Hofmann, Christian Tams, and Stephan Schill (eds), *International Investment Law and History* (Edward Elgar 2016) 20; Cassin (n 3); Jürgen Kurtz, 'Australia's Rejection of Investor-State Arbitration: Causation, Omission and Implications' [2012] ICSID Review—Foreign Investment Law Journal; van Aaken (n 9) 23.

the regime.[13] Currently, non-governmental organizations, some governments, and various national publics focus critically on bi- or multi-lateral agreements such as the TTIP and TPP and specifically the foreign investment chapters of these treaties. The acts and criticisms directed at those treaties are often described as a 'backlash' against investment arbitration generally.

Backlash against investment arbitration may emanate from a variety of sources. These sources include civil society or 'the public' generally, non-governmental organizations, academics, the media, and States themselves.[14] The source of backlash matters because it may influence the form in which such backlash is expressed as well as the motivations and focal points of that backlash. Identifying the sources of backlash is furthermore important because it influences the appropriate responses to backlash, dictating to whom (or to what) such responses are being offered. Finally, identifying the sources and forms of backlash might indicate shifts in the relevant debates and their focal points over time.

Of course, any one source or form of 'backlash' necessarily interacts with and informs the other sources and forms through which 'backlash' might be expressed. Take, for example, the European Commission's 2014 'public consultation on modalities for investment protection and ISDS in TTIP'.[15] The consultation process garnered almost 150,000 responses. While not all responses were critical of TTIP, the sources of those responses are nevertheless instructive in considering from where responses criticizing the regime may actually originate.[16] While 148,830 of the responses came from 'citizens', 'approximately 145,000 of these were submitted through NGOs [non-governmental organizations] which had provided respondents with "pre-defined" answers'.[17] In this case, then, there is a mixed source of 'backlash' comprising a range of actors including individuals, academics, and NGOs. This example also illustrates that there are, furthermore, many strands to the critique where expert opinion and public opinion reinforce and shape one another in a more generalized way.[18]

[13] Francioni (n 3) 4–5; UNCTAD, *Reforming International Investment Governance* (n 8) 176; Karsten Nowrot, 'How to Include Environmental Protection, Human Rights and Sustainability in International Investment Law?' (2014) 15 The Journal of World Investment & Trade 612, 619; Malcolm Langford, 'Cosmopolitan Competition: The Case of International Investment' in Cecilia Bailliet and Katja Aas (eds), *Cosmopolitan Justice and its Discontents* (Routledge 2011) 178, 183.

[14] Cassin (n 3) (contending that 'In Germany, a public consensus appears to have formed that investor-state dispute settlement should be dropped entirely from the TTIP'). See, also, Kulick (n 12) 19 (noting that 'International investment law is in the limelight, not only in international law scholarship but in mainstream public opinion'); Chen Huiping, 'The Expansion of Jurisdiction by ICSID Tribunals: Approaches, Reasons and Damages' (2011) 12 Journal of World Investment & Trade 671, 671.

[15] The consultation process was open from 27 March–13 July 2014: European Commission, 'Online Public Consultation on Investment Protection and Investor-to-State Dispute Settlement (ISDS) in the Transatlantic Trade and Investment Partnership Agreement (TTIP)' (2015) Commission Staff Working Document—Report SWD(2015) 3 Final.

[16] ibid 9. [17] ibid 10.

[18] Anthea Roberts, 'Clash of Paradigms: Actors and Analogies Shaping the Investment Treaty System' (2013) 107 American Journal of International Law 45, 84.

The diverse range of sources and forms of 'backlash' necessarily means that that backlash may reflect a range of differing motivations and concerns. Teasing apart the types of acts said to constitute 'backlash', it is clear that they are diverse and specific to both the situation and source. Apart from the question of what it means to say there is a backlash, then, there is an important and complex question of stating what the backlash is against. Is it against a particular tribunal or investment arbitration generally, or is it against something else? The aim here is not to scrutinize each critique of the investment arbitration regime or to offer responses to, or endorsements of, the positions articulated therein. Instead, the critical point here is to highlight that some cases of 'backlash' focus upon a particular tribunal or the arbitration regime because they provide a focal point for criticism that is discrete and focused, while the force motivating that 'backlash' is actually directed at a more diffuse target other than investor-State arbitration. It is clear in our analysis that the critique is not directed solely, or even in all cases, at tribunals. Rather, tribunals form a focal point for broader concerns.

A primary concern underlying much of the 'backlash' said to be about investor-State arbitration is globalization. The concept of 'globalization' covers many phenomena and is difficult to define. Indeed, those motivated by concerns related to globalization themselves may not necessarily share a common understanding of what it comprises. It suffices for present purposes to observe that, at base, 'globalization' results in the 'denationalization of clusters of political, economic, and social activities that undermine the ability of the sovereign state to control activities on its territory'.[19] In so doing, globalization 'challenges the idea of the state as the sovereign guardian of the public interest',[20] and gives increased power to non-national actors, including multinational corporations. Concerns about the perceived negative effects of globalization are very frequently articulated through critique of investor-State arbitration.[21] The linkage of investor-State arbitration with broader concerns about globalization has resulted in a 'strong ideological and functional opposition' to investment arbitration.[22] Many see it as the embodiment of broader forces with which they are concerned, including the 'upward transfer of wealth,

[19] Karsten Nowrot, 'Legal Consequences of Globalization: The Status of Non-Governmental Organizations Under International Law' (1999) 6 Ind. Law Journal 579, 586.

[20] Barnali Choudhury, 'Recapturing Public Power: Is Investment Arbitration's Engagement of the Public Interest Contributing to the Democratic Deficit?' (2008) 41 Vanderbilt Journal of Transnational Law 775, 777.

[21] See, eg: Claire Provost and Matt Kennard, 'The Obscure Legal System That Lets Corporations Sue Countries' *The Guardian* (10 June 2015) <https://www.theguardian.com/business/2015/jun/10/obscure-legal-system-lets-corportations-sue-states-ttip-icsid> (observing that 'it seems increasingly likely that the massive financial risks associated with investor-state arbitration will effectively grant foreign investors a veto over government decisions'). George Monbiot, 'This Transatlantic Trade Deal Is a Full-Frontal Assault on Democracy' *The Guardian* (4 November 2013) <http://www.theguardian.com/commentisfree/2013/nov/04/us-trade-deal-full-frontal-assault-on-democracy> (observing that the TTIP 'would allow a secretive panel of corporate lawyers to overrule the will of parliament and destroy our legal protections').

[22] LE Trakman, 'Resolving Investor-State Disputes under a Transpacific Partnership Agreement—What Lies Ahead?' [2012] Transnational Dispute Management 9.

constraint of government, and liberalization of markets'.[23] Concern about foreign investment is thus in part directly a concern about the fairness and legitimacy of investor-State arbitration. It is also, however, a manifestation of broader concerns about globalization, about economic dislocation and other social interests, about jobs and livelihoods.[24]

Such underlying concerns are reflected, for example, in the statements of Senator Warren—a vocal opponent of investment arbitration. Senator Warren has asked:

> Who will benefit from the TPP? American workers? Consumers? Small businesses? Taxpayers? Or the biggest multinational corporations in the world? ... Agreeing to ISDS in this enormous new treaty would tilt the playing field in the United States further in favor of big multinational corporations. Worse, it would undermine U.S. sovereignty ... ISDS would allow foreign companies to challenge U.S. laws—and potentially to pick up huge payouts from taxpayers—without ever stepping foot in a U.S. court.[25]

Underlying Senator Warren's critique of investment arbitration is a broader concern about the forces of globalization and denationalization. And yet, '[t]he focus of her ire is the Investor-State Dispute Settlement (ISDS) process'.[26] For Senator Warren, investment arbitration forms a focal point for the articulation of a broader concern about a more diffuse target: globalization. Similarly, looking more closely at the placards held by protestors at the 2015 TTIP rally in Germany, it is clear that many reflect broader concerns, predominantly relating to fear of foreign takeover and a shifting of domestic decision-making power to geographically removed actors.[27] In these cases, '[t]hose who advocate withdrawal from the investment law regime' are also 'those who argue against globalization more generally'.[28] Former US President Obama has noted that he 'understand[s] the skepticism people have about trade agreements, particularly in communities where the effects of automation and globalization have hit workers and families the hardest'.[29] More than this,

[23] Gus Van Harten, 'Five Justifications for Investment Treaties: A Critical Discussion' (2010) 2 Trade, Law and Development 19, 24.

[24] See, also, Langford (n 13) 182.

[25] Elizabeth Warren, 'The Trans-Pacific Partnership Clause Everyone Should Oppose' *Washington Post* (25 February 2015) <https://www.washingtonpost.com/opinions/kill-the-dispute-settlement-language-in-the-trans-pacific-partnership/2015/02/25/ec7705a2-bd1e-11e4-b274-e5209a3bc9a9_story.html>.

[26] Kevin O'Marah, 'Elizabeth Warren On TPP: Bad For Business' *Forbes* (22 May 2015) <https://www.forbes.com/sites/kevinomarah/2015/05/22/elizabeth-warren-on-the-tpp-bad-for-business/#76a21e7d685d>.

[27] See, eg: Caroline Copley, 'Hundreds of Thousands Protest in Berlin against EU-US Trade Deal' *The Sydney Morning Herald* (11 October 2015) <http://www.smh.com.au/world/hundreds-of-thousands-protest-in-berlin-against-euus-trade-deal-20151011-gk66kx.html>.

[28] Spears (n 8) 1074. See, also, Brigitte Stern, 'The Future of International Investment Law: A Balance Between the Protection of Investors and the States' Capacity to Regulate' in Alvarez (ed), *The Evolving International Investment Regime: Expectations, Realities, Options* (2011) 175 ('I wondered whether there had not been some confusion between the difficulties raised by globalization in general and the difficulties encountered within the investment arbitration system in particular. Of course, I know that some are more or less embedded in the others, but I am still not sure that we can solve them with the same solutions, and at the same level.').

[29] Barack Obama, 'Obama Op-Ed—"The TPP Would Let America, Not China, Lead the Way on Global Trade"' *The Washington Post* (2 May 2016) <https://www.washingtonpost.com/opinions/president-obama-the-tpp-would-let-america-not-china-lead-the-way-on-global-trade/2016/05/02/680540e4-0fd0-11e6-93ae-50921721165d_story.html>.

though, we would suggest that investment arbitration has attracted such strong critique because it forms a focal point for the articulation of concerns about globalization. Globalization, as a diffuse force, does not itself form a concrete enough target.

A similar phenomenon was associated with the protests that accompanied the 1999 World Trade Organization (WTO) Ministerial Conference in Seattle. In the context of immense civil society protest against the WTO in Seattle, Professor Georges Abi Saab argued that it should not be surprising that the WTO was the object of such protests. He observed that the forces of globalization were diffuse, that there is no clear agent of globalization and that in such a situation protests often centre on particular symbols of the more general phenomenon of concern.[30] The focus placed on investment arbitration within the TTIP is similar.[31] Many parts of the TTIP will have far greater social impact than the arbitration scheme or the worst possible single arbitration one can imagine. One macroeconomic study, for example, predicts that the TTIP will result in net export and job losses, as well as a lowering of wages and growth rates, with northern European economies suffering the largest losses.[32] The particular focus upon the investor-State arbitration provisions in TTIP, however, is something that provides a relatively clear focus for the articulation of concern about these more general impacts. This is borne out in the European Commission's Report on the European Union (EU)'s TTIP Consultation Process. In that Report, the Commission notes that '[w]hile the scope of the consultation was limited to the proposed EU approach to investment protection/ISDS in TTIP, a first category of statements indicates opposition or concerns to TTIP in general'.[33] In fact, 'quite a majority of replies oppos[ed] TTIP in general'.[34] Arguably, here, responses criticize the investor-State provisions of the TTIP because that is the focus of the consultation process: although other chapters of the TTIP may arguably have a greater effect in terms of displacement, they are not as public and therefore not as apt a site for criticism and input in the same way as the investment chapter.

Let us be clear. We are not suggesting that investment arbitration is not deserving of reform, or that it should not be held to the highest standard. What we are suggesting is that there are complexities to backlash, and the investment arbitration mechanism may not in fact be the principal reason for the intensity of the backlash directed against it. The concerns are in part concerns about investment arbitration, but they also reflect and manifest concerns that are deeper and broader. This is critically important for three reasons. First, it is important because it means that reform of the investment arbitration regime may not be capable of responding to all of the concerns underlying

[30] See, also, Langford (n 13) 183.

[31] See, also, Roger Alford, 'Scholars Debate Investment Arbitration Chapter in TPP and TTIP' *Kluwer Arbitration Blog* (7 April 2015) <http://arbitrationblog.kluwerarbitration.com/2015/04/07/scholars-debate-investment-arbitration-chapter-in-tpp-and-ttip/>; Langford (n 13) 178, 182, 183–84.

[32] Jeronim Capaldo, 'The Trans-Atlantic Trade and Investment Partnership: European Disintegration, Unemployment and Instability' (2014) Working Paper No. 14-03 Global Development and Environment Institute Working Paper.

[33] European Commission (n 15) 3.

[34] ibid 14.

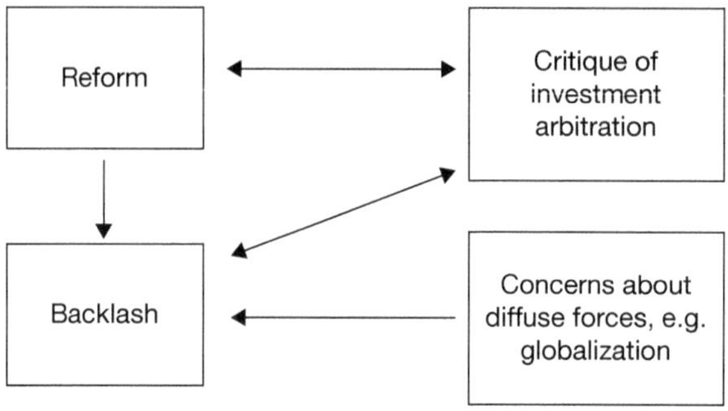

Figure 8.1 The complexities of backlash (arrows indicating direction of influence)

the criticisms directed against it. Second, there is a danger in characterizing acts manifesting these concerns as a 'backlash' directed solely against the investment arbitration regime insofar as that may over-inflate the level of public dissatisfaction with that regime itself. Brower and Blanchard have argued in this respect that 'backlash' stems from, and results in, the proliferation of a 'meme … of a broken system'.[35] They argue that 'objections that began as ideologically driven polemics have come to be widely, but inaccurately, presumed as truths'.[36] Finally, it is important because it risks missing and leaving unaddressed broader underlying concerns. As Irene Ten Cate argues:

> societal opposition to the investment law regime does not stem from hostility to the concept of foreign investment or to the objective of establishing international rules to govern foreign investment per se, but rather from concerns about the non-participatory manner in which the global economy's rules are being written and about restrictions on governments' ability to address the pernicious effects of globalization. Eliminating the global economy's rules or foreign investors' rights under [international investment agreements] all together would not be a productive way to address these two fundamental concerns.[37]

To assume that the strength of backlash is directed at investor-State arbitration rather than globalization risks misdirecting reform efforts. Whether or not one agrees with this particular conclusion, the underlying observation remains: it is necessary to dissect the motivations of backlash from its focal point(s) before it is possible to identify the responses appropriate to it. In identifying what backlash is against, one must ask whether the apparent backlash is against a particular institution or something else entirely. In identifying the possible responses to backlash, it is necessary to thus bear in mind its complexities. As Figure 8.1 illustrates, these complexities relate, in particular, to the interrelationships between motivations, focal points, and

[35] Brower and Blanchard (n 11) 699. The authors define a 'meme' as 'a unit of cultural transmission that replicates itself through individuals by inducing repetition'.

[36] ibid.

[37] Irene M Ten Cate, 'International Arbitration and the Ends of Appellate Review' (2012) 44 New York University Journal of International Law and Politics 1109, 1111. See also, Trakman (n 22) 17–18.

responses to backlash. Section 2 further expands on the relationship between these features of backlash.

2 Responding to Backlash

As noted in Section 1, a range of State initiatives and actions to reform the investor-State arbitration regime have themselves been cited as evidence of (or at least acts in response to) the perceived backlash against the regime. This Section emphasizes two points. Section 2.1 examines the history of reform over the past approximately fifteen years to illustrate how the regime has evolved and adapted.[38] It is argued that the significant range of both procedural and substantive reforms that have taken place within investment arbitration over this period reinforces Section 1's observation that backlash is not a reaction only to investment arbitration, but rather a response to something broader. Section 2.2 illustrates that the actions of States in reforming the investment arbitration regime are primarily taken in response to shifting circumstances, and would arguably have occurred even absent the backlash against investment arbitration itself. This highlights that it is important not to assume that all actions and reforms are forms of, or responses to, backlash. As a whole, the Section illustrates how investment arbitration has been reformed to respond to concrete critiques and concerns, but has nevertheless been unable to reform in a way capable of dissipating the backlash directed against it. The Section thus seeks to illustrate that there are elements to backlash which reform to the investment arbitration regime may be incapable of addressing.

2.1 A story of reform

The last fifteen years have seen the investment arbitration regime evolve significantly. In fact, one would be hard pressed to identify an international dispute settlement mechanism that has reformed more over the same period, or indeed any equivalent length of time.[39] Since at least 2000, States have been engaged in an active process of reform. Reform has taken place both at the level of individual State treaty practice as well as institutionally, and has encompassed procedural, substantive, and systemic changes. Given the extent of the regime's evolution, this is not the place to consider each reform in detail. Instead, this subsection briefly traces the major components of that reform to support the following subsection's consideration of what has motivated that reform.

[38] Note that the investment arbitration 'regime' is comprised of 'large networks of components with no central control'. In this sense, not all reforms impact upon all elements of the 'regime'. The Section thus illustrates some of the more major reforms having a significant impact upon important components of the regime. Melanie Mitchell, *Complexity: A Guided Tour* (OUP 2009) x.

[39] Nowrot (n 13) 620.

2.1.1 Procedural reforms

The first generation of investment treaties only incidentally addressed issues of arbitral procedure, instead relying upon institutional rules to fill the gaps.[40] The last fifteen years have seen a shift in treaty drafting practice towards more detailed procedural provisions, as well as reforms to treaty and institutional rules.

Changes to the procedural rules governing transparency are a good example of this evolution. Very few, if any, early investment treaties expressly regulated the issue of transparency. Instead, these treaties opted to leave the matter to the discretion of each arbitral tribunal for decision in accordance with the applicable procedural rules. Until the mid-2000s, the majority of such procedural rules contained only minimal transparency provisions, which usually provided for transparency to operate on an opt-in basis (ie, with the consent of both parties).[41] This minimal regulation of transparency did not, however, persist for long.

At the level of treaty practice, States made a raft of changes from the early 2000s onwards to increase the transparency of investor-State proceedings. As Table 8.1 highlights, these included joint interpretations on the transparency regime governing arbitrations under existing treaties as well as a commitment to negotiating for increased transparency in future treaties.[42] This resulted in the negotiation of a 'new generation' of investment treaties providing for greater transparency of arbitral proceedings.[43] This included provision for public hearings, the publication of arbitral documents, and *amicus curiae* intervention.[44] This trend has been solidified in

[40] David Gaukrodger and Kathryn Gordon, 'Investor-State Dispute Settlement: A Scoping Paper for the Investment Policy Community' [2012] OECD Working Papers on International Investment 64.

[41] Andrew P Tuck, 'Investor-State Arbitration Revised: A Critical Analysis of the Revisions and Proposed Reforms to the ICSID and UNCITRAL Arbitration Rules' (2007) 13 Law & Business Review of the Americas 885, 897. The ICSID Convention and Rules, eg, provided that awards could not be published without party consent: Rules of Arbitration of the International Centre for Settlement of Investment Disputes. Similarly, the 1976 UNCITRAL Arbitration Rules provided for closed hearings and the non-publication of awards absent party agreement to the contrary: Arbitration Rules of the United Nations Commission on International Trade Law 1976.

[42] See, eg: Trade Act of 2002 s 2102 (providing that future US treaties should adopt 'the fullest measure of transparency in the dispute settlement mechanism'); Canada, 'Model Investment Treaty' art 38; Norway Model Investment Treaty art 19; NAFTA Free Trade Commission, 'Notes of Interpretation of Certain Chapter 11 Provisions' ('[n]othing in the NAFTA imposes a general duty of confidentiality on the disputing parties [or] … precludes the Parties from providing public access to documents submitted to, or issued by, a Chapter Eleven Tribunal'). See, further: David Gantz, 'The Evolution of FTA Investment Provisions: From NAFTA to the United States-Chile Free Trade Agreement' (2003) 19 American University of International Law Review 679, 704; Mary Footer, 'BITs and Pieces: Social and Environmental Protection in the Regulation of Foreign Investment' (2009) 18 Michigan State University College of Law Journal of International Law 33, 47.

[43] Gantz (n 42) 707.

[44] See, eg: Korea-Australia Free Trade Agreement 2014; Athina Fouchard Papaefstratiou, 'The EU Proposal Regarding Investment Protection: The End of Investment Arbitration as we Know It?' <http://kluwerarbitrationblog.com/2015/12/29/the-eu-proposal-regarding-investment-protection-the-end-of-investment-arbitration-as-we-know-it/>; Sonja Heppneron, 'A Right of Public Access to Investor-State Arbitral Proceedings?' <http://kluwerarbitrationblog.com/2015/12/09/a-right-of-public-access-to-investor-state-arbitral-proceedings/>; European Parliament Directorate-General for External Policies, 'The Investment Chapters of the EU's International Trade and Investment Agreements in a Comparative Perspective' (2015) EP/EXPO/B/INTA/2015/01 74.

Table 8.1 15 Years of Procedural Change

	2000–2001	2002–2003	2004–2005	2006–2007	2008–2009	2010–2011	2012–2013	2014–2015
Treaty-based Developments	NAFTA FTC interpretation, including on transparency (2001)	US TPA: pro-transparency position in future negotiations (2002)	CAFTA-DR: increased transparency for ISDS proceedings (2004)	Norway Model BIT: increased transparency for ISDS proceedings (2007)				EU-Singapore Free Trade Agreement, detailed disclosure requirements for arbitrators (2014)
			US Model BIT: increased transparency for ISDS proceedings (2004)					EU-Canada Comprehensive Economic and Trade Agreement, guidance on arbitrator regulation (2014)
								Norway Model BIT: increased transparency for ISDS proceedings (2015)
								India draft Model BIT: provisions regulating arbitrator conflicts of interest (2015)
								TPP: provisions for mandatory public disclosure of certain documents, open hearings, *amicus curiae* participation (2015)
								German Model BIT: standing appellate body (2015)
Institutional Developments			IBA Guidelines on Conflicts of Interest (2004)	Amendment of ICSID Rules (2006)		Amendment of UNCITRAL Rules (2010)	UNCITRAL Transparency Rules (2012)	UN Convention on Transparency (2014)

(*continued*)

Table 8.1 Continued

	2000–2001	2002–2003	2004–2005	2006–2007	2008–2009	2010–2011	2012–2013	2014–2015
			ICSID Secretariat working papers on possible reforms (2004–2005)			ICC Statement of Independence for Arbitrators (2010)	ICSID report on annulment mechanism (2012)	Revised IBA Guidelines on Conflicts of Interest (2014)
						LCIA starts publishing abstracts on arbitrator challenges (2011)	ICC revised practice notes on duties and remuneration of administrative secretaries (2012)	
							IBA Guidelines on Party Representation (2013)	

recent treaty practice. Broadly speaking, the past fifteen years have seen a shift from silence on the issue of transparency, to an opt-in transparency regime, to a regime which increasingly imposes a 'duty of transparency'.[45] In fact, as the European Parliament's Directorate-General for External Policies has noted, some provisions on transparency currently being negotiated 'go beyond the level of transparency and public access that can be found in developed domestic legal orders'.[46] At the very least, these reforms have meant that '[i]nvestor-State treaty arbitration ceased to be hidden from public view long ago'.[47]

These changes in State treaty drafting practice have been accompanied by a range of amendments to applicable procedural rules. In 2004, the ICSID (International Centre for Settlement of Investment Disputes) Secretariat published a working paper focusing, inter alia, upon possible responses to the lack or delayed publication of information from ICSID proceedings as well as the scope for third party access to such proceedings.[48] In 2005, the Secretariat published a follow-up paper which contained text to implement the reforms flagged in the 2004 paper.[49] In 2006, both the ICSID and ICSID Additional Facility Rules were amended to include detailed provisions on the filing of *amicus curiae* submissions as well as provision for public hearings.[50] The UNCITRAL Rules likewise underwent a process of revision in 2010. During this process, the issue of transparency was identified as an area for particular reform. Subsequently, the UNCITRAL (United Nations Commission on International Trade Law) Rules on Transparency in Treaty-Based Investor-State Arbitration were negotiated and incorporated into the 2013 UNCITRAL Arbitration Rules. The Transparency Rules operate to 'reverse the presumptions of confidentiality and privacy in investment treaty arbitration in favour of a presumption of openness'.[51] Thereafter, a further treaty was drafted to provide additional scope for the application of the Rules on Transparency, including in non-UNCITRAL proceedings.[52]

Treaties and institutional rules have also been revised to address 'the characteristics, selection and regulation of arbitrators in ISDS'.[53] Early provisions regulating arbitrator conduct provided codes of conduct addressing disclosure requirements,

[45] Federico Ortino, 'External Transparency of Investment Awards' (2008) Working Paper No. 49/08 SIEL Online Proceedings Working Papers 1.

[46] European Parliament Directorate-General for External Policies (n 44) 74.

[47] Brower and Blanchard (n 11) 717. See, also, Roberts (n 18) 92.

[48] ICSID Secretariat, 'Possible Improvements of the Framework for ICSID Arbitration' (2004) 7–11 <https://icsid.worldbank.org/apps/ICSIDWEB/resources/Documents/Possible%20Improvements%20of%20the%20Framework%20of%20ICSID%20Arbitration.pdf>.

[49] ICSID Secretariat, 'Suggested Changes to the ICSID Rules and Regulations' (2005) 3–4 <https://icsid.worldbank.org/apps/ICSIDWEB/resources/Documents/Suggested%20Changes%20to%20the%20ICSID%20Rules%20and%20Regulations.pdf>.

[50] Rules of Arbitration of the International Centre for Settlement of Investment Disputes (n 41) Rules 32 and 37; ICSID Additional Facility Arbitration Rules arts 39 and 41.

[51] Stephan Schill, 'Transparency as a Global Norm in International Investment Law' <http://kluwerarbitrationblog.com/2014/09/15/transparency-as-a-global-norm-in-international-investment-law/>.

[52] UN Convention on Transparency in Treaty-Based Investor-State Arbitration.

[53] Gaukrodger and Gordon (n 40) 3, 44. See, also, European Parliament Directorate-General for External Policies (n 44) 59.

conflicts of interest, and confidentiality obligations.[54] A number of other treaties provided for the creation of pre-established rosters of arbitrators.[55] Once again, these treaty practices were supplemented by institutional reform. Institutional reforms to arbitrator regulation were encapsulated in ICSID's 2004–2006 reform process discussed above. That process resulted in amendments to the ICSID Rules in 2006 to impose additional disclosure requirements on arbitrators.[56] In the same year, the International Bar Association (IBA) adopted Guidelines on Conflicts of Interest in International Arbitration.[57] In 2014, the IBA Guidelines were amended, to address 'a number of issues that have received attention in international arbitration practice since 2004'.[58] A number of institutions have also sought to provide greater information about expectations around conflicts of interest and disclosure, including through publication of decisions on arbitrator challenges or the release of guidance notes.[59] These issues have also been subjected to detailed study. In 2015, for example, a Task Force of the American Society of International Law and the International Council for Commercial Arbitration released a draft report and recommendations on issue conflicts in investor-State arbitration.[60] More recently, in September 2015, the EU Commission released a proposal in the context of the TTIP negotiations which elaborates on requirements for the selection and appointment of arbitrators in investor-State disputes.[61]

The issue of the cost of investment arbitration has also been a further site for reform. Arbitrator fees, for example, were reviewed institutionally by ICSID as part of its 2004 reform process. In 2006 the ICSID Rules were amended to allow

[54] See, eg: EU-Singapore Free Trade Agreement 2014 art 9.21.

[55] See, eg: EU-Canada Comprehensive Economic and Trade Agreement 2014; EU-Singapore Free Trade Agreement (n 54). European Parliament Directorate-General for External Policies (n 44) 10. On proposals on the same for future treaties, see: Athina Fouchard Papaefstratiou, 'TTIP: The French Proposal For A Permanent European Court for Investment Arbitration' <http://kluwerarbitrationblog.com/2015/07/22/ttip-the-french-proposal-for-a-permanent-european-court-for-investment-arbitration/>.

[56] See, for further information about these reforms: Tuck (n 41) 892, 900; Choudhury (n 20) 820; International Law Association, 'Final Report of the Committee on the International Law of Foreign Investment' (2008) 73 International Law Ass'n Rep Conf 752, 783.

[57] International Bar Association Guidelines on Conflicts of Interest in International Arbitration 2004. These Guidelines are referred to in a number of treaties, see eg: EU-Canada Comprehensive Economic and Trade Agreement (n 55). The Guidelines have also been applied in a number of arbitral proceedings: European Parliament Directorate-General for External Policies (n 44).

[58] International Bar Association Guidelines on Conflicts of Interest in International Arbitration 2014 ii.

[59] The London Court of International Arbitration (LCIA) began publishing abstracts of arbitrator challenge decisions in 2011: Herbert Smith Freehills, 'LCIA Publishes Arbitrator Challenge Decisions' <http://hsfnotes.com/arbitration/2011/11/24/lcia-publishes-arbitrator-challenge-decisions/>. See, for further discussion of such amendments: Catherine Rogers, 'What If the Ghost of Christmas Present Visited the International Arbitration Community of 1995?' <http://kluwerarbitrationblog.com/2015/12/26/what-if-the-ghost-of-christmas-present-visited-the-international-arbitration-community-of-1995/>.

[60] ICCA-ASIL Joint Task Force, 'Report of ICCA-ASIL Joint Task Force (Discussion Draft)' <https://www.asil.org/sites/default/files/ASIL-ICCA%20Joint%20Task%20Force%20-%20Discussion%20Draft%2010%20March%202015.pdf>.

[61] Fouchard Papaefstratiou (n 55); Fouchard Papaefstratiou (n 44).

for the 'prompt termination of meritless claims'.[62] The 2010 amendments to the UNCITRAL Rules also sought to improve efficiency, incorporating the option for parties to request that an arbitrator indicate that they can 'devote the time necessary to conduct [the] arbitration diligently, efficiently and in accordance with the time limits in the Rules'.[63] Other institutions, too, have issued 'practice notes' on matters such as arbitrator fees or efficient case management.[64]

Of course, many further areas of procedural reform could be cited. Looking only to these reforms, as set out in Table 8.1, however, it is evident that the system has done much to evolve procedurally in the space of fifteen years.

2.1.2 *Substantive reform*

As to substance, the changes are even more substantial. At a general level, treaties in this time have moved from less to more detailed treaty provisions, that is, from 'light touch regulation' to 'more comprehensive regulation'.[65] During this period, States have amended the standards of substantive protection in both model and actual investment treaties.[66] Treaties have become both more detailed and more nuanced in their approach to the protection of investment, including by restricting the substantive protections accorded to investors under their terms.[67] In addition, treaties are increasingly also referring to non-investment related objectives that are presumably to play some role in limiting the scope of the protection of investment protection. For example, 'sustainable development-oriented clauses are on the rise', as are references to the 'right to regulate' and 'environmental protection'.[68] Equally, exceptions

[62] Rules of Arbitration of the International Centre for Settlement of Investment Disputes (n 41) Rule 41(5). See, for further background on these reforms: ICSID Secretariat (n 48); Gaukrodger and Gordon (n 40) 21.

[63] UNCITRAL Arbitration Rules 2010.

[64] See, eg: 'UNCITRAL Notes on Organizing Arbitral Proceedings'; 'ICC Techniques for Controlling Time and Costs in Arbitration'; Remy Gerbay, 'The LCIA's New Guidance Notes—An (Uneasy) Exercise in Relative Normativity' <http://kluwerarbitrationblog.com/2015/09/01/the-lcias-new-guidance-notes-an-uneasy-exercise-in-relative-normativity/>.

[65] European Parliament Directorate-General for External Policies (n 44) 8. See, also, Footer (n 42) 37; Nowrot (n 13) 624.

[66] See, eg: Canada, Foreign Investment Protection Agreement 2004; Norway Model Investment Treaty (n 42); United States Model Investment Treaty 2012; India, Model Investment Treaty. See, further: UNCTAD, *Reforming International Investment Governance* (n 8); Kaushal (n 3) 534.

[67] For further consideration of such changes, see further: UNCTAD, 'Bilateral Investment Treaties 1995–2006: Trends in Investment Rulemaking' (2007); Footer (n 42) 42; Spears (n 8) 1071; Roberts (n 18) 80.

[68] UNCTAD, 'Recent Trends in IIAs and ISDS' (2015) IIA Issues Note No 1 <http://unctad.org/en/PublicationsLibrary/webdiaepcb2015d1_en.pdf>. See, eg: EU-Canada Comprehensive Economic and Trade Agreement (n 55) Preamble; India-Singapore Free Trade Agreement 2005 Preamble. See, further: Spears (n 8) 1068; National Board of Trade (Sweden), 'The Right to Regulate' in the Trade Agreement between the EU and Canada—and Its Implications for the Agreement with the USA' 4; European Parliament Directorate-General for External Policies (n 44) 8; Alessandra Asteriti, 'Waiting for the Environmentalists: Environmental Language in Investment Treaties' id2028405 SSRN; Kathryn Gordon and Joachim Pohl, 'Environmental Concerns in International Investment Agreements: A Survey' (2011) Paper No 2011/1 OECD Working Papers on International Investment 3, 7, 10 <www.oecd.org/daf/investment>.

and carve-outs to obligations placed on the host State are both increasingly included and expanding in scope.[69] A range of measures are being placed outside the scope of liability, including public health measures, prudential regulations, or measures related to public morality, social welfare, or sustainable development.[70] A number of standards of protection have also been the subject of refinement, clarification, or exclusion. The fair and equitable treatment standard, for example, has been the subject of reform, including through express linkage to the minimum standard of treatment under customary international law or the inclusion of open or closed lists of the treatment included within its scope.[71] Expropriation, too, has been made the subject of detailed annexures setting out the treaty parties' understanding of what does (and does not) constitute expropriation, along with the tests that ought to be applied by tribunals in assessing allegedly expropriatory acts.[72] Umbrella clauses have also been the subject of reform, having been restricted, clarified, or excluded altogether.[73]

2.1.3 Implications: frequent adaptation, responsiveness to critique, backlash is not only about investor-State arbitration

This brief historical overview supports three key observations. First, the investor-State regime has adapted—a lot, and frequently. It is commonly recognized that there has been an exponential increase in both the conclusion of treaties and the incidence of arbitral proceedings.[74] The above history of adaptation shows the resilience of the regime: its ability to absorb a significant amount of change whilst maintaining a high degree of stability and function.[75] Second, this history illustrates that many

[69] European Parliament Directorate-General for External Policies (n 44) 136; Spears (n 8) 1059; M Sornarajah, 'Mutations of Neo-Liberalism in International Investment Law' (2011) 3 Trade, Law and Development 203, 229; Kenneth Vandevelde, 'Rebalancing through Exceptions' (2013) 17 Lewis & Clark Law Review 449, 451.

[70] See, eg: US–Peru Free Trade Agreement 2006 art 10.21; Comprehensive Economic Cooperation Agreement between the Republic of India and the Republic of Singapore; US-Colombia Free Trade Agreement 2006 art 10.21; United States Model Investment Treaty (n 66) Annex B. See, further: Andrew Newcombe, 'General Exceptions in International Investment Agreements', *BIICL Eighth Annual WTO Conference* (2008) 7 <http://www.biicl.org/files/3866_andrew_newcombe.pdf>; International Law Association (n 56) 771.

[71] United States Model Investment Treaty (2004) art 5; Canada, Foreign Investment Protection Agreement (n 66) art 5; EU-Canada Comprehensive Economic and Trade Agreement (n 55); EU-Singapore Free Trade Agreement (n 54). See, further: European Parliament Directorate-General for External Policies (n 44) 139.

[72] See, eg: United States Model Investment Treaty (2004) (n 71); Canada, Foreign Investment Protection Agreement (n 66); India-Singapore Free Trade Agreement (n 68); 2007 COMESA Common Investment Area Agreement; EU-Singapore Free Trade Agreement (n 54); United States Model Investment Treaty (n 66); Treaty Between the United States of America and the Oriental Republic of Uruguay Concerning the Encouragement and Reciprocal Protection of Investment 2005.

[73] See, eg: EU-Canada Comprehensive Economic and Trade Agreement (n 55) (omitting the clause altogether); EU-Singapore Free Trade Agreement (n 54) (restricting the clause). See, further: UNCTAD, *Reforming International Investment Governance* (n 8) 144; European Parliament Directorate-General for External Policies (n 44) 162.

[74] Daniel S Meyers, 'In Defense of the International Treaty Arbitration System' (2008) 31 Houston Journal of International Law 47, 80.

[75] Langford (n 13) 185; Roberts (n 18) 91; Meyers (n 74) 80; Ten Cate (n 37) 1114.

features of the regime forming the subject of current 'backlash' have not gone unaddressed.[76] This throws into question the widespread assumption that the regime is facing some kind of pressing 'crisis'.[77] In this context, it must be asked whether continued criticism of the regime fails to take historic reforms into account;[78] exhibits some kind of inadvertent or even strategic blindness to those reforms;[79] or merely illustrates that the reforms have failed, have not had widespread impact, or are yet to influence arbitral approaches in any appreciable way.[80] Third, the history and success of these reforms reinforces the earlier point that backlash is not only about arbitration. If backlash were only about the arbitration mechanism, it would be reasonable to expect that that backlash would decrease as the regime adapted in a manner apt to respond to the backlash. Instead, the opposite has been witnessed: backlash has increased alongside reform.[81] This is not to suggest that the agenda of reform is complete. Investment arbitration, like any other regime, can always do better.[82] Rather, it is to highlight the necessity of asking how responsive any reform agenda *can* be to the concerns underlying the current backlash.

2.2 Responding to what?

There is an equally crucial issue of *to what* exactly the above reforms responded. As with the forms and sources of backlash, the motivations underlying the regime's history of reform are also diverse.[83] The suggestion in this subsection is that the actions of States to substantively limit the protections afforded to foreign investors, and to modify the procedures attaching to investor-State proceedings, are not responses to (or indications of) 'backlash' per se but are instead primarily an action taken in response to shifting circumstances. In particular, States are engaged in an iterative process of modification in response to arbitral jurisprudence as well as their own changing risk profiles.[84] The particular circumstances to which States

[76] Paul Michael Blyschak, 'State Consent, Investor Interests and the Future of Investment Arbitration: Reanalyzing the Jurisdiction of Investor-State Tribunals in Hard Cases' (2009) 9 Asper Rev International Business and Trade Law 99, 99; European Parliament Directorate-General for External Policies (n 44) 20; Kleinheisterkamp (n 8) 797.

[77] Sergio Puig, 'Recasting ICSID's Legitimacy Debate: Towards a Goal-Based Empirical Agenda' (2013) 36 Fordham International Law Journal 465, 468.

[78] National Board of Trade (Sweden) (n 68) 4.

[79] Douglas Johnston, 'Functionalism in the Theory of International Law' (1988) 26 Canadian Yearbook of International Law 3, 3; Eric Ip, 'Globalization and the Future of the Law of the Sovereign State' (2010) 8 International Journal Const Law 636, 649 (suggesting that '[t]he public belief that sovereignty is under stress provides officials and lawyers with fuel to shift the blame to transnational forces').

[80] Brower and Schill (n 3) 473; European Parliament Directorate-General for External Policies (n 44) 139, 142; Spears (n 8) 1045; Nowrot (n 13) 644; Asteriti (n 68) 154.

[81] Meyers (n 74) 80.

[82] Leon Trakman, 'The ICSID Under Siege' (2013) 45 Cornell International Law Journal 603, 656; David Caron, 'Investor State Arbitration: Strategic and Tactical Perspectives on Legitimacy' (2008) 32 Suffolk Transnational Law Review 513, 515; Kaushal (n 3) 534.

[83] Nowrot (n 13) 618.

[84] Jurgen Kurtz, 'Building Legitimacy Through Interpretation: Investor-State Arbitration: On Consistency, Coherence and the Identification of Applicable Law' in Zachary Douglas, Joost Pauwelyn, and Jorge Vinuales (eds), *The Foundations of International Investment Law: Bridging Theory Into Practice* (OUP 2014).

are responding can be broken into four key groups, which are each canvassed in the following paragraphs. Of course, critiques of investment arbitration may themselves also be prompted by these factors. What the following subsection illustrates, however, is: first, in responding to these factors, State actions may be mistakenly taken as themselves evidence of 'backlash' and, in turn, generate further unwarranted critique; and second, 'backlash' itself typically does not prompt reform, which is instead motivated by other factors.

2.2.1 Responding to case law

Many amendments in investment treaty practice have occurred in response to the application of treaties in investment treaty cases. The 'first generation' treaties of the 1990s were negotiated at a time before the first arbitral claims, and thus were uninformed by interpretations or procedures adopted by arbitral tribunals.[85] For some time, 'the system of resolving investment treaty claims remained relatively untested' and as such 'there was little need to re-evaluate the status quo'.[86] Arbitral claims, however, subsequently 'surged' and there was a concomitant increase in arbitral jurisprudence and practice.[87] As tribunals interpreted and applied investment treaties, States acted to ' "correct" developments in the jurisprudence that [they] did not foresee or with which [they do] not agree'.[88] This prompted amendments to both treaties and institutional rules. The 2004–2006 reform process at ICSID, for example, was prompted by increased use of ICSID as a dispute settlement institution.[89] Similarly, arbitral interpretations of vague 'first generation' treaty standards prompted States to include greater detail in subsequent treaties.[90] Whereas expropriation and fair and equitable treatment provisions in first generation treaties were only a few sentences long, for example, later treaties were revised to include greater detail to guide arbitral tribunals in assessing compliance with these provisions.[91] Similarly, carve-outs or exceptions were incorporated into treaties in response to arbitral proceedings applying earlier generation treaties that had been silent, or otherwise circumspect, on the circumstances to which such exceptions might apply. The TPP tobacco carve-out is a good example of this latter type of reform.[92]

[85] Blyschak (n 76) 166.

[86] Susan Franck, 'Challenges Facing Investment Disputes: Reconsidering Dispute Resolution in International Investment Agreements' 1427590 Washington & Lee Public Legal Studies Research Paper Series 155.

[87] Meyers (n 74) 48; European Parliament Directorate-General for External Policies (n 44) 161; van Aaken (n 9) 9.

[88] Brower and Schill (n 3) 496. See, also, Kleinheisterkamp (n 8) 799; Chen Huiping, 'The Investor-State Dispute Settlement Mechanism: Where to Go in the 21st Century?' (2008) 9 Journal of World Investment & Trade 467, 483; Blyschak (n 76) 166; Spears (n 8) 1048; Langford (n 13) 182; Kaushal (n 3) 534; van Aaken (n 9) 22, 24.

[89] Tuck (n 41) 892.

[90] Blyschak (n 76) 166.

[91] Sornarajah (n 69) 229; European Parliament Directorate-General for External Policies (n 44) 136, 139; Brower and Schill (n 3) 495.

[92] Trans-Pacific Partnership art 29.5.

The increase in proceedings also indicated that claimants were impugning different State acts than had perhaps been expected. As South Africa, in reviewing its approach to investment treaty arbitration in 2009, stated '[e]xisting dispute settlement institutions were not designed to address complex issues of public policy that now routinely come into play in investor-state disputes'.[93] Whilst early expropriations were mostly 'formal expropriations where the title of ownership was transferred',[94] for example, '[t]his pattern has changed and indirect action, often in the form of regulations' became a more commonly impugned measure.[95] As such, new investment treaties increasingly had to accommodate more detailed guidance on the scope of indirect expropriation provisions.[96] A similar phenomenon occurred with respect to the fair and equitable treatment clause, which—in contrast to early expectations—nowadays is widely credited as the 'most important standard in investment disputes'.[97]

States also responded to arbitral jurisprudence to make explicit the assumptions underpinning their treaties.[98] The introduction of the first umbrella clauses into treaties occurred, for example, at a time when those clauses had yet to be applied by arbitral tribunals.[99] Thomas Wälde has argued that the development of the umbrella clause 'envisaged not a commercial law breach, but rather governmental action abrogating a long-term-mostly concession-like-agreement'.[100] Blyschak contends that this underlying assumption meant that 'nobody expected that the umbrella clause, when coupled with investment arbitration and freed from the supervision of the host state, would suddenly make private commercial contract claims arguably actionable under international law'.[101] Yet, in many cases, this is precisely what happened.[102] It is perhaps to be expected, then, that those States which negotiated umbrella clauses with the above expectations in mind would, in light of this jurisprudence, seek to restrict or exclude those clauses altogether in newer treaties. Some argue that the regime itself was originally designed to support this iterative cycle of interpretation and recalibration.[103] At the least, it is clear that this iterative process of refinement

[93] Republic of South Africa, 'Bilateral Investment Treaty Policy Framework Review: Government Position Paper' (Department of Trade and Industry 2009) 45.

[94] Ursula Kriebaum, 'Regulatory Takings: Balancing the Interests of the Investor and the State' (2007) 8 Journal of World Investment & Trade 717, 717.

[95] ibid. [96] ibid.

[97] Gus Van Harten, *International Treaty Arbitration and Public Law* (OUP 2007) 87; European Parliament Directorate-General for External Policies (n 44) 136; Christoph Schreuer, 'Fair and Equitable Treatment in Arbitral Practice' [2005] J w I T 357, 357.

[98] Blyschak (n 76) 166.

[99] Axel Weissenfels, 'Independent BIT Standard or Mere Affirmative Commitment? The Umbrella Clause Interpreted' (2005) 10 Austrian Review of International and European Law 95, 95.

[100] Thomas W Wälde, 'The "Umbrella" (or Sanctity of Contract/Pacta Sunt Servanda) Clause in Investment Arbitration: A Comment on Original Intentions and Recent' Presentation at British Institute of Comparative and International Law 6.

[101] Blyschak (n 76) 146.

[102] European Parliament Directorate-General for External Policies (n 44) 161; van Aaken (n 9) 7.

[103] Santiago Montt Oyarzún, *State Liability in Investment Treaty Arbitration: Global Constitutional and Administrative Law in the BIT Generation* (Hart 2009) 157.

is likely to continue into the future. As newer treaties are applied and interpreted, States are likely to have ongoing cause to engage in further recalibration.[104]

2.2.2 *Responding to changing risk profiles*

In amending the substantive and procedural rules applicable to investor-State arbitration, States have also responded to their changing risk profiles. The majority of early investment treaties resulted from asymmetric negotiations between an essentially capital-exporting and an essentially capital-importing State. In these negotiations, capital-exporting States placed an 'almost exclusive emphasis on the protection of foreign investment'.[105] They sought only the protection of their own investors in the capital-importing State, and were largely unconcerned with the implications of those treaties for their own liability. Nowadays, the picture is more nuanced. It is increasingly difficult to classify States as solely 'capital-exporting' or 'capital-importing'. Treaties, too, are no longer concluded on a solely asymmetric basis.[106] Instead, States which were traditionally capital-exporters are becoming also capital-importers, and vice-versa.[107] Simultaneously, 'the number of states counting themselves as respondents has also increased dramatically'.[108] The 'increased likelihood that both Contracting Parties may find themselves in the respondent seat in an investor-state arbitration' changes their 'perceptions of the risks and rewards inherent in their treaty programs'.[109] The United States, for example, initiated reforms to its model treaty and negotiating practice 'just after it was challenged by the first NAFTA claim'.[110] Changes in State risk profiles means that an increasing number of States are seeking to balance their regulatory space with the protection of their overseas investors.[111] This necessarily results in modifications to treaty practice.[112]

2.2.3 *Responding to changing expectations about investment*

The expectations of States in entering into investment treaties are also changing. Whereas the conclusion of treaties in the 1990s was 'based on the widely shared

[104] Luke Nottage and Kate Miles, '"Back to the Future" for Investor-State Arbitrations: Revising Rules in Australia and Japan to Meet Public Interests' Paper No. 08/62 Sydney Law School Legal Studies Research Paper 5; Tuck (n 41) 902.
[105] Footer (n 42) 37; Christopher M Ryan, 'Meeting Expectations: Assessing the Long-Term Legitimacy and Stability of International Investment Law' (2007) 29 University of Pennsylvania Journal of International Law 725, 726; Spears (n 8) 1042.
[106] UNCTAD (ed), *World Investment Report 2010: Investing in a Low-Carbon Economy* (United Nations 2010) 18–20, 82.
[107] Kulick (n 12) 21.
[108] Roberts (n 18) 90. See, also, European Parliament Directorate-General for External Policies (n 44) 13; van Aaken (n 9) 25; Kulick (n 12) 19.
[109] Roberts (n 18) 90; Kulick (n 12) 22.
[110] Huiping (n 88) 482. See, also, G Gagné and JF Morin, 'The Evolving American Policy on Investment Protection: Evidence from Recent FTAs and the 2004 Model BIT' (2006) 9 Journal of International Economic Law 357.
[111] Spears (n 8) 1042. [112] van Aaken (n 9) 25; Ryan (n 105) 756.

belief that this would increase foreign investment',[113] empirical evidence as to the expected benefits of entering into investment treaties is increasingly becoming more nuanced.[114] So, too, are State attitudes towards foreign investment. As Brower and Blanchard note, '[t]he increase in criticism of the investment law regime has occurred in tandem with a cyclical cooling of certain states' attitudes toward foreign direct investment generally'.[115] Changing expectations as to the benefits of investment treaties, or of foreign investment more generally, have resulted in shifts in State treaty practice. As van Aaken explains 'the point of optimality between commitment costs and benefits of FDI still needs to be found'.[116]

2.2.4 Responding to changing expectations about dispute settlement

Finally, States have implemented reforms as their expectations of investment arbitration have changed. Investment treaty arbitration was initially modelled from international commercial arbitration, and as such commercial 'philosophies about the role of law, the state, and the function of dispute resolution' informed its early design.[117] Over time, investor-State arbitration came also to be conceptualized as a regime of public international law, or even 'international public law'.[118] As a result, States showed 'a greater willingness to draw inspiration from litigation-based models of dispute resolution' as well as international and public law paradigms.[119] As Catherine Rogers notes, these changing paradigms led to the development of 'an entirely new set of expectations' about how investor-State arbitration should function.[120] Focusing on procedural rules, for example, Rogers argues that:

> [w]ords like 'transparency' and 'accountability' today seem like obvious requirements for a process and important and delicate as arbitrator selection. In 1995, these terms were anathemas.[121]

As different paradigms are used to conceptualize investor-State arbitration, and as new practitioners with particular professional backgrounds enter the field, it is only natural to see a different set of expectations and operating assumptions gain prominence.[122] These new expectations also result in modifications to treaty drafting practice and arbitral procedures.

[113] Roberts (n 18) 90; European Parliament Directorate-General for External Policies (n 44) 20; Spears (n 8) 1040–41.

[114] See, eg: Jason Webb Yackee, 'Are BITs Such a Bright Idea? Exploring the Ideational Basis of Investment Treaty Enthusiasm' (2005) 12 U C Davis Journal of International Law and Policy 195.

[115] Brower and Blanchard (n 11) 764–65.

[116] van Aaken (n 9) 26. See, also, Nowrot (n 13) 644.

[117] Franck (n 86) 155; Roberts (n 18) 54.

[118] Roberts (n 18) 54.

[119] Tuck (n 41) 887; Roberts (n 18) 78.

[120] Rogers (n 59).

[121] ibid.

[122] Roberts (n 18) 55, 84.

2.2.5 Conclusions

This subsection has sought to highlight the range of circumstances to which State reforms of the investment treaty arbitration system have responded. It also bears a cautionary note: it is possible that, in responding to these changing circumstances (or, indeed, backlash generated by reference to these circumstances), State actions are mistakenly being taken as themselves evidence of 'backlash'. In taking care to identify the motivations underlying these reforms, the danger of detecting an exponential increase in 'backlash' as a result of system adaptation and refinement is avoided.

3 Unintended Consequences of Backlash

This Section considers briefly the possible unintended consequences of backlash.

The most extreme consequence of backlash is for the mechanism of treaty arbitration to be replaced with something else entirely.[123] Given that there is evidently a flow of investment disputes, the question is where they would go without treaty arbitration. What are the alternatives?

For many, the assumption is that investment disputes, absent an arbitration mechanism, will go to the national courts of host States. This has been proposed in the statements of various non-governmental organizations as well as some States.[124] At base, it is undeniable that all States 'should strengthen their domestic justice systems for the benefit of all citizens and communities, including investors'.[125] While such a result may be desirable, however, there are nevertheless a number of hurdles to be overcome before it is possible. In particular, there is the issue of how to test whether national courts at present are an appropriate or feasible alternative to treaty arbitration. One option is the development of a ratings or indexing system to assess the adequacy of the treaty arbitration system as compared to national courts.[126] The World Justice Project, for example, issues a Rule of Law Index reporting on ninety-nine countries. Using the Index's methodology, might it be possible to assess the adequacy of the international commercial arbitration system and the treaty arbitration system? For some States, the arbitration system would probably in many respects rank rather high in a list of national judiciaries. Some national courts, for example, are 'not perceived to be sufficiently neutral in resolving disputes between foreign

[123] Chris Campbell, Sophie Nappert, and Luke Nottage, 'Assessing Treaty-Based Investor-State Dispute Settlement: Abandon, Retain or Reform?' (2013) Paper No. 13/40 Sydney Law School Legal Studies Research Paper 1.

[124] See, eg: 'Gillard Government Trade Policy Statement: Trading Our Way to More Jobs and Prosperity' (Australian Department of Foreign Affairs and Trade 2011).

[125] Gus Van Harten and others, 'Public Statement on the International Investment Regime' (2010) <http://www.osgoode.yorku.ca/public-statement-international-investment-regime-31-august-2010/>.

[126] See, further: Caron (n 82). See, also, John Gaffney, 'When Is Investor-State Dispute Settlement Appropriate to Resolve Investment Disputes? An Idea for a Rule-of-Law Ratings Mechanism' (2015) 149 Columbia FDI Perspectives, Perspectives on Topical Foreign Direct Investment Issues (suggesting the use of the EU Justice Scoreboard).

investors and host states'[127] or otherwise inefficient as compared to arbitration in doing so.[128] One can also imagine pairings of countries with national judiciaries both ranked higher than treaty arbitration, and in that instance it could be argued that mutual recourse to national courts for investment disputes is appropriate.

The issues associated with assessing the appropriateness or feasibility of national courts aside, however, a further hurdle arises: investors would retain the ability to negotiate agreements directly with host States providing for dispute settlement through other means.[129] There is some indication, for example, that in the absence of investment treaties investors will seek concessions from States to better protect their investments.[130] These concessions very frequently channel disputes to commercial arbitration proceedings. Such a situation could lead to significant unintended consequences.[131] It would, for example, benefit the most powerful investors and would also privilege those types of investment capable of protection through contractual arrangements.[132] It also pushes disputes underground, subjecting them to less transparent and largely unregulated procedures as compared to those which would apply in the case of an investment treaty arbitration.

Less extreme consequences are, however, also conceivable. Indeed, there is significant scope for States to continue to build upon, rather than discard, the present regime.[133] Doing so allows them to derive the benefits of the rich history of experimentation and reform sketched above.[134] Whilst critiques manifesting as 'backlash' can thus direct attention to possibilities for improvement of the regime, care must be taken to ensure that such critiques do not cause us to 'overlook the value of that system and the concerns in response to which the system emerged'.[135] In particular, in considering responses to backlash, care must be taken to avoid the trap of assuming that alternatives offer greener pastures.[136] A different system may simply lead to new problems,[137] or may result in current issues manifesting in different ways.[138]

4 Conclusions

This chapter has sought to tease apart the forms and focus of 'backlash' against the investment treaty regime, whilst also considering responses and consequences. It has highlighted the complex and multifaceted nature of these issues, and raised a number of points for further consideration. In particular, it has questioned the claim that State acts to reform the investment treaty regime are a response to, or even a form of, backlash against that regime. Rather, States have worked to refine the regime in light of changing circumstances, and in order to avoid the unintended consequences that

[127] Brower and Schill (n 3) 479. [128] ibid. [129] Roberts (n 18) 90.
[130] H Inadomi, *Independent Power Projects in Developing Countries* (Wolters Kluwer 2010).
[131] Langford (n 13) 187–88.
[132] Brower and Schill (n 3) 481, 482; European Parliament Directorate-General for External Policies (n 44) 163.
[133] Brower and Schill (n 3) 475. [134] Meyers (n 74) 50. [135] ibid 48.
[136] European Parliament Directorate-General for External Policies (n 44) 106.
[137] ibid. [138] Franck (n 86) 157.

might be associated with its complete abandonment. To borrow words from a different context, the chapter has illustrated how 'backlash' against the investor-State regime is not necessarily 'a swelling tide of history but i[s] more like a series of waves that lap on an international beach, retreating repeatedly into domestic seas but leaving incremental changes on the shore'.[139]

[139] S Tarrow, *The New Transnational Activism* (CUP 2005) 219.

9

Non-Participation in Compulsory Procedures of Dispute Settlement

The People's Republic of China's Position Paper in the *South China Sea Arbitration* and Beyond

Erik Franckx and Marco Benatar***

In recent times, a sharp increase can be noticed on the official webpage of the Permanent Court of Arbitration (PCA) of its inter-state cases, mainly as a result of disputes brought under Annex VII of the United Nations Convention on the Law of the Sea (1982 Convention) that make use of the registry of the PCA.[1] This heightened activity would be cause for unbridled optimism among supporters of international dispute settlement, were it not for a parallel development of considerable concern: the re-emergence of non-participation after nearly three decades.[2] The

* Research professor, President of the Department of International and European Law, and Vice-dean for Internationalization, Faculty of Law and Criminology, Vrije Universiteit Brussel (VUB). He holds teaching assignments at Vesalius College (VUB); Université Libre de Bruxelles; Brussels School of International Studies (University of Kent); Institute of European Studies (VUB); Université Paris-Sorbonne Abu Dhabi, United Arab Emirates; and the University of Akureyri, Iceland. He is appointed by Belgium as: expert in maritime boundary delimitation to the IHO (2005–); member of the Permanent Court of Arbitration (2006–); arbitrator under the United Nations Convention on the Law of the Sea (2014–); expert on marine scientific research for use in Special Arbitration under Annex VIII of the United Nations Convention on the Law of the Sea (2015–); and member of the National Commission for the Reform of Private and Public Maritime Law (2012–). Publication list is available at <http://www.vub.ac.be/people/erik-franckx>.

** Research Fellow, Max Planck Institute Luxembourg for Procedural Law. Researcher, Department of International and European Law, Faculty of Law and Criminology, Vrije Universiteit Brussel (VUB).

[1] PCA, 'United Nations Convention on the Law of the Sea' <http://pca-cpa.org/en/services/arbitration-services/unclos/> (accessed 1 September 2016); Dapo Akande, 'The Peace Palace Heats Up Again: But Is Inter-State Arbitration Overtaking the ICJ?' (EJIL: *Talk!*, 17 February 2014) <www.ejiltalk.org/the-peace-palace-heats-up-again-but-is-inter-state-arbitration-overtaking-the-icj/> (accessed 1 September 2016).

[2] The last instance of non-participation being that of the United States in the merits phase of *Military and Paramilitary Activities in and against Nicaragua (Nicaragua v United States)* before the International Court of Justice (ICJ). The prevalence of defaulting respondent states in previous decades garnered considerable scholarly attention, not in the least from the Institut de droit international. See Institut de droit international, 'Resolution on Non-Appearance Before the International Court of Justice' (1991) <www.justitiaetpace.org/idiE/resolutionsE/1991_bal_01_en.PDF> (accessed 1 September 2016).

Non-Participation in Compulsory Procedures of Dispute Settlement: The People's Republic of China's Position Paper in the South China Sea Arbitration *and Beyond.* Erik Franckx and Marco Benatar.

lull was broken in 2013, when the Philippines brought a case, the *South China Sea Arbitration*, against the People's Republic of China (PRC).[3] Shortly after the institution of proceedings, the PRC made its intentions known that it would not participate in the case. That very same year, the Russian Federation stated that it would not take part in the *Arctic Sunrise Arbitration*, which was initiated by the Netherlands to resolve a dispute over a Greenpeace vessel flying the Dutch flag. A noteworthy feature in both PCA-administered cases is the respondent states' use of so-called 'position papers', aimed at influencing the adjudicators on matters of fact and law, while formally adhering to their policy of non-participation.

The present contribution intends to demonstrate that, as a general trend, courts and tribunals will try to be as flexible as possible in order to take cognizance of the arguments developed by the non-participating state, as expressed in a number of different ways. Position papers, whether on jurisdiction or on the merits of the case, have clearly been a preferred method of non-participating states, as indicated by recent practice. At the same time, however, this contribution will argue that this flexibility has its limits.

In order to test these assertions, the PRC's reliance on position papers in its dealings with its South China Sea (SCS) neighbours will serve as a starting point. After providing some background to the dispute in the SCS, the chapter will turn to official declarations presented by the Chinese government (section 1). We will take a closer look at a number of statements formulated by the PRC in a non-adjudicatory context, namely the Haiyang Shiyou 981 incident between the PRC and Vietnam during the spring of 2014 (section 2). The next section will examine the PRC's position paper in the *South China Sea Arbitration* and how it was received by the Arbitral Tribunal (section 3). In this section comparisons will also be drawn with the *Arctic Sunrise Arbitration*. The next section will assess the value attached to these position papers by the tribunals involved (section 4). In the conclusions (section 5) the potential ramifications of the PRC's 'position paper' strategy will be addressed as well as recent developments in this respect.

1 Background of the Dispute

The claim reflected in the nine-dashed line was for the first time endorsed by the Chinese government at the international level in connection with state-to-state disputes in 2009. It came in response to submissions made by Malaysia and Vietnam regarding their continental shelf claims beyond 200 nautical miles in the SCS.[4] After Malaysia and Vietnam sent their joint submission to the Commission on the

[3] *South China Sea Arbitration (Philippines v China)* <https://pcacases.com/web/view/7> (accessed 1 September 2016).

[4] The use of the denomination 'South China Sea' has no legal implications as to the entitlements to these waters or the insular features they contain. See Erik Franckx, Marco Benatar, Nkeiru Joe, and Koen Van den Bossche, 'The Naming of Maritime Features Viewed from an International Law Perspective' (2011) 11 China Oceans L R 1. The present chapter simply uses this term because it is the nomenclature commonly used in the English language. See for instance International Hydrographic Organization, *Limits of Oceans and Seas* (3rd edn, Imp Monégasque 1953) 30–31. This publication states in its preface: 'These limits have no political significance whatsoever' (2).

Limits of the Continental Shelf on 6 May 2009[5] and Vietnam filed its individual submission for another part of its continental shelf beyond 200 nautical miles the following day,[6] the PRC reacted by submitting two identical letters to the Secretary-General of the United Nations (UN) outlining its legal claims in the SCS.[7] These Chinese letters of 7 May 2009 contained the following paragraph:

> China has indisputable sovereignty over the islands in the South China Sea and the *adjacent waters*, and enjoys sovereign rights and jurisdiction over the *relevant waters* as well as the seabed and subsoil thereof (see attached map). The above position is consistently held by the Chinese Government, and is widely known by the international community.[8]

As neither the terms 'adjacent waters' nor 'relevant waters' are to be found in the so-called Constitution for the Oceans,[9] the first ever codification of the whole law of the sea in a single document,[10] one expects to find clarifications in the 'attached map' to which these Chinese letters of 7 May 2009 refer.[11] But instead of clarifying these terms, the attached map simply depicts nine dashes. And even though the only legend accompanying the map is a scale indicating distances, it should be noted that the typographical signs used to represent the dashes, namely '· –·', are exactly the same as those used to depict the land boundary between the PRC and Vietnam in the upper left corner of that map. Instead of furthering one's understanding of the notions of 'adjacent waters' and 'relevant waters', the 2009 Map creates a new enigma because, as of present, the PRC has not officially specified what these dashes represent on the map. This situation creates a 'flou artistique', a touch of deliberate

[5] Malaysia-Vietnam, 'Joint Submission to the Commission on the Limits of the Continental Shelf Pursuant to Article 76, paragraph 8 of the United Nations Convention on the Law of the Sea 1982 in Respect of the Southern Part of the South China Sea, Executive Summary' (UN, May 2009) <www.un.org/Depts/los/clcs_new/submissions_files/mysvnm33_09/mys_vnm2009excutivesummary.pdf> (accessed 1 September 2016). As indicated by the letter of the Secretary-General of the UN, acknowledging receipt, this join submission was made on 6 May 2009 <www.un.org/depts/los/clcs_new/submissions_files/mysvnm33_09/mysvnm_clcs33_2009e.pdf> (accessed 1 September 2016).

[6] Vietnam, 'Submission to the Commission on the Limits of the Continental Shelf Pursuant to Article 76, paragraph 8 of the United Nations Convention on the Law of the Sea 1982, Partial Submission in Respect of Vietnam's Extended Continental Shelf: North Area (VNM-N), Executive Summary' (UN, April 2009) <www.un.org/Depts/los/clcs_new/submissions_files/vnm37_09/vnm2009n_executivesummary.pdf> (accessed 1 September 2016). As indicated by the letter of the UN Secretary-General, acknowledging receipt, this submission was made on 7 May 2009 <www.un.org/depts/los/clcs_new/submissions_files/vnm37_09/vnm_clcs37_2009e.pdf> (accessed 1 September 2016).

[7] China, 'Letter to the Secretary-General of the United Nations—CML/17/2009' (UN, 7 May 2009) <www.un.org/Depts/los/clcs_new/submissions_files/mysvnm33_09/chn_2009re_mys_vnm_e.pdf> (accessed 1 September 2016); China, 'Letter to the Secretary-General of the United Nations—CML/18/2009' (UN, 7 May 2009) <www.un.org/Depts/los/clcs_new/submissions_files/vnm37_09/chn_2009re_vnm.pdf> (accessed 1 September 2016) (Chinese letters of 7 May 2009).

[8] ibid. Our emphasis.

[9] United Nations Convention on the Law of the Sea (adopted 10 December 1982, entered into force 16 November 1994) 1833 UNTS 397 (1982 Convention).

[10] Contrary to the four separate conventions adopted in 1958, namely the Convention on the Territorial Sea and the Contiguous Zone (adopted 29 April 1958, entered into force 10 September 1964) 516 UNTS 205; Convention on the Continental Shelf (adopted 29 April 1958, entered into force 10 June 1964) 499 UNTS 311; Convention on the High Seas (adopted 29 April 1958, entered into force 30 September 1962) 450 UNTS 11; Convention on Fishing and Conservation of the Living Resources of the High Seas (adopted 29 April 1958, entered into force 20 March 1966) 559 UNTS 285.

[11] This map has been reproduced in Annex 1 to this chapter (2009 Map).

soft focus causing a blurred image, since no one can tell with certainty what China means by these notions or the 2009 Map for that matter.[12]

The inclusion of the 2009 Map in an official document addressed to the UN Secretary-General, and thus intended for wide dissemination in the international community, was a significant event. This can be inferred not only from the strong diplomatic interest this map triggered in the form of governmental protests,[13] but also from the flurry of scholarly attention it received. Journals specialized in the law of the sea dedicated issues to this matter[14] whereas a leading general international law review found the 2009 Map important enough to devote an agora to the questions it raised.[15]

The conclusion can therefore be reached that although the territorial claims of the PRC over features in the SCS may have been clearly expressed in the past, the same cannot be said of its maritime claims in the region. As far as the 2009 Map is concerned, moreover, an additional question can be raised as to the legal value of such cartographic evidence.[16]

The PRC has so far been steadfast in its opinion that all issues in the SCS, be they related to sovereignty claims over features or the rights derived therefrom (eg fisheries, maritime delimitation), should be settled on a bilateral basis with its maritime neighbours.[17]

The publication of the 2009 Map, *urbi et orbi*, was therefore quite a noteworthy event, for it took this map out of the bilateral sphere and made it subject to international scrutiny. Lately, the PRC has also started to engage with its maritime

[12] Erik Franckx, 'Chinese Claims in the East China Sea and South China Sea: A Legal Assessment of Cartographic Evidence' in Françoise Nicolas, Céline Pajon, and John Seaman (eds), *The Asian Century: What International Norms and Practices?* (IFRI 2014) 25.

[13] See for instance the communications by Indonesia specifically addressing the issue of the 'nine-dotted-lines map' (UN, 8 July 2010) <www.un.org/depts/los/clcs_new/submissions_files/mysvnm33_09/idn_2010re_mys_vnm_e.pdf> (accessed 1 September 2016); US Dept of State, Office of Ocean and Polar Affairs, Bureau of Oceans and International Environmental and Scientific Affairs, 'China: Maritime Claims in the South China Sea' (2014) <www.state.gov/documents/organization/234936.pdf> (accessed 1 September 2016).

[14] Such as the journal *Ocean Development and International Law* in its first issue of 2012. In the order of appearance in the journal: Miyoshi Masahiro, 'China's "U-Shaped Line" Claim in the South China Sea: Any Validity Under International Law?' (2012) 43 Ocean Development and Intl L 1; Keyuan Zou, 'China's U-Shaped Line in the South China Sea Revisited' (2012) 43 Ocean Development and Intl L 18; Thang Nguyen-Dang and Thao Nguyen Hong, 'China's Nine Dotted Lines in the South China Sea: The 2011 Exchange of Diplomatic Notes Between the Philippines and China' (2012) 43 Ocean Development and Intl L 35; Gau Michael Sheng-Ti, 'The U-Shaped Line and a Categorization of the Ocean Disputes in the South China Sea' (2012) 43 Ocean Development and Intl L 57.

[15] Namely the *American Journal of International Law* in 2013. In the order of appearance in the journal: Lori Fisler Damrosch and Bernard H Oxman, 'Agora: The South China Sea. Editors' Introduction' (2013) 107 AJIL 95; Zhiguo Gao and Bing Bing Jia, 'The Nine-Dash Line in the South China Sea: History, Status, and Implications' (2013) 107 AJIL 98; Florian Dupuy and Pierre-Marie Dupuy, 'A Legal Analysis of China's Historic Rights Claim in the South China Sea' (2013) 107 AJIL 124; Robert Beckman, 'The UN Convention on the Law of the Sea and the Maritime Disputes in the South China Sea' (2013) 107 AJIL 142.

[16] Erik Franckx and Marco Benatar, 'Dots and Lines in the South China Sea: Insights from the Law of Map Evidence' (2012) 2 Asian J Intl L 89.

[17] 'Why is the South China Sea Contentious?' *BBC News* (12 July 2016) <www.bbc.com/news/world-asia-pacific-13748349> (accessed 1 September 2016).

neighbours through the exchange of legal arguments in the public sphere. Two examples relating to the SCS will be further developed. The first concerns the incident surrounding the Haiyang Shiyou 981 oil platform during the summer of 2014, the second is the *South China Sea Arbitration*.

2 Haiyang Shiyou 981 Oil Platform

No better illustration of this shift from the private bilateral to the public multilateral level can be found than the incident that arose between the PRC and Vietnam when the Chinese state-owned China National Offshore Oil Corporation decided to move its deep-water oil platform Haiyang Shiyou 981 in disputed waters in the region of the Paracels, claimed by both countries. When drilling commenced on 2 May 2014, this quickly escalated into a major bilateral crisis until the platform was removed from the area on 15 July 2014, that is one month ahead of the planned withdrawal date.[18]

Soon after the start of the incident, Vietnam addressed an official letter to the UN Secretary-General explaining its legal position and requesting the PRC to immediately withdraw the oil platform from the area.[19] The PRC responded later the same month by submitting in a similar manner its own legal arguments in a document entitled 'position paper'.[20] Like the preceding Vietnamese letter, the Chinese document requested the UN Secretary-General to circulate the letter and annex amongst the UN member states. Vietnam responded with two letters, one dealing with the sovereignty aspect[21] and the other concerning the maritime claims.[22] China replied with another 'position paper' containing a more elaborate argumentation,[23] which was also posted on the website of its Ministry of Foreign Affairs.[24] This in turn

[18] For a good recent overview article of this incident, see for instance Ankit Panda, '1 Year Later: Reflections on China's Oil Rig "Sovereignty-Making" in the South China Sea' (*The Diplomat*, 12 May 2015) <thediplomat.com/2015/05/1-year-later-reflections-on-chinas-oil-rig-sovereignty-making-in-the-south-china-sea/> (accessed 1 September 2016).

[19] Vietnam, 'Letter dated 7 May 2014 from the Permanent Representative of Viet Nam to the United Nations Addressed to the Secretary-General' (9 May 2014) UN Doc A/68/870. The letter itself containing the position of the Ministry of Foreign Affairs was included as annex and dated 4 May 2014.

[20] China, 'Letter dated 22 May 2014 from the Chargé d'affaires a.i. of the Permanent Mission of China to the United Nations addressed to the Secretary-General' (27 May 2014) UN Doc A/68/887. The Chinese Position Paper was included as annex (PRC Oil Platform Position Paper 1).

[21] Vietnam, 'Letter dated 28 May 2014 from the Chargé d'affaires a.i. of the Permanent Mission of Viet Nam to the United Nations addressed to the Secretary-General' (30 May 2014) UN Doc A/68/897. The letter itself containing the position of the Ministry of Foreign Affairs was included as annex.

[22] Vietnam, 'Letter dated 6 June 2014 from the Permanent Representative of Viet Nam to the United Nations addressed to the Secretary-General' (9 June 2014) UN Doc A/68/906. The letter itself containing the position of the Ministry of Foreign Affairs was included as annex and dated 4 June 2014.

[23] China, 'Letter dated 9 June 2014 from the Chargé d'affaires a.i. of the Permanent Mission of China to the United Nations addressed to the Secretary-General' (9 June 2014) UN Doc A/68/907. The Chinese position paper, entitled 'The operation of the HYSY 981 drilling rig: Viet Nam's provocation and China's position', was included as annex, containing itself three enclosures (PRC Oil Platform Position Paper 2).

[24] China, 'The Operation of the HYSY 981 Drilling Rig: Vietnam's Provocation and China's Position' (Chinese Ministry of Foreign Affairs, 2014) <www.fmprc.gov.cn/mfa_eng/zxxx_662805/t1163264.

triggered another reaction from Vietnam on the sovereignty issue[25] as well as on the maritime claims in the area,[26] to which China reacted by issuing yet another 'position paper'.[27] This series of exchanges ended that year with a last reply of Vietnam more than a month after the withdrawal of the oil platform[28] and an additional 'position paper' by China in December 2014.[29]

These four rounds of diplomatic notes following the Haiyang Shiyou 981 oil platform incident are interesting in that they lift part of the veil to the world at large of the PRC's maritime claims in the SCS. These diplomatic notes are significant in that they emanate from the PRC government and thus represent state practice under international law. Even though none of them shed light on the exact meaning of the dashes depicted on the 2009 Map, a number of relevant arguments are developed.[30]

2.1 The non-existence of a dispute concerning the Paracels

A first salient aspect of the diplomatic correspondence is that the PRC is of the firm opinion that no legal dispute exists with Vietnam as far as the Paracels are concerned.[31] It is however well-established that the determination of whether a dispute exists 'is a matter for objective determination. The mere denial of the existence of

shtml> (accessed 1 September 2016). This version contained two more enclosures than the PRC Oil Platform Position Paper 2 (n 23).

[25] Vietnam, 'Letter dated 3 July 2014 from the Permanent Representative of Viet Nam to the United Nations addressed to the Secretary-General' (9 July 2014) UN Doc A/68/942. The letter itself containing the position of Vietnam, entitled 'The sovereignty of Viet Nam over the Hoang Sa Archipelago' was included as annex.

[26] Vietnam, 'Letter dated 3 July 2014 from the Permanent Representative of Viet Nam to the United Nations addressed to the Secretary-General' (9 July 2014) UN Doc A/68/943. The letter itself containing the position of Vietnam, entitled 'China's illegal placement of the Haiyang Shiyou 981 oil rig in the exclusive economic zone and continental shelf of Viet Nam' was included as annex.

[27] China, 'Letter Dated 24 July 2014 from the Permanent Representative of China to the United Nations addressed to the Secretary-General' (28 July 2014) UN Doc A/68/956. The Chinese Position Paper was included as annex (PRC Oil Platform Position Paper 3).

[28] Again two separate letters were sent. A first one relating to the maritime claims: Vietnam, 'Letter dated 22 August 2014 from the Permanent Representative of Viet Nam to the United Nations addressed to the Secretary-General' (27 August 2014) UN Doc A/68/980. The letter itself containing the position of Vietnam, entitled 'China's illegal placement of the *Haiyang Shiyou 981* oil rig in the exclusive economic zone and continental shelf of Viet Nam', was included as annex. A second letter concerned the sovereignty claims: Vietnam, 'Letter dated 3 July 2014 from the Permanent Representative of Viet Nam to the United Nations addressed to the Secretary-General' (9 July 2014) UN Doc A/68/981. The letter itself containing the position of Vietnam, entitled 'The sovereignty of Viet Nam over the Hoang Sa Archipelago', was included as annex.

[29] China, 'Letter Dated 8 December 2014 from the Permanent Representative of China to the United Nations addressed to the Secretary-General' (10 December 2014) UN Doc A/69/645. The Chinese Position Paper was included as annex (PRC Oil Platform Position Paper 4).

[30] The following three sections (2.1, 2 and 3) are based on an initial assessment made by one of the present authors elsewhere, as further elaborated in Franckx (n 12) 29–32.

[31] This is stressed in all four position papers of the PRC. See PRC Oil Platform Position Paper 1 (n 20) para 2; PRC Oil Platform Position Paper 2 (n 23) point IV, para 1; PRC Oil Platform Position Paper 3 (n 27) para 1 ('China stands firmly against and by no means accepts the so-called "Xisha disputes" that Viet Nam attempts to fabricate'); PRC Oil Platform Position Paper 4 (n 29) para 1 ('there is not the slightest dispute').

a dispute does not prove its non-existence.'[32] And even though it must be admitted that '[a] mere assertion is not sufficient to prove the existence of a dispute any more than a mere denial of the existence of the dispute proves its non-existence', what is required is that 'the claim of one party is positively opposed by the other',[33] which seems clearly to be implied from the above-mentioned exchange of diplomatic notes.[34]

2.2 Continuation of business as usual

For China, the drilling in the continental shelf was merely business as usual. After having conducted exploration activities for more than ten years in the area, including two- and three-dimensional seismic operations, the present drilling activities are claimed to be a simple continuation of these previous routine activities.[35] Even if, *arguendo*, it is assumed that the Paracels belong to the PRC and that there is no dispute on this point with Vietnam,[36] the PRC admits that there are 'overlapping claims' which both countries are trying to settle.[37] Given the highly unpredictable influence of maritime features like islands, rocks, reefs, and low-tide elevations on maritime delimitation,[38] even under this hypothesis the better approach might well be that states should try to enter into provisional arrangements of a practical nature.[39] This of course applies *a fortiori* to the disputed sovereignty over the Paracels claimed by the two countries. The statement that the 2014 activities are a continuation of business as usual should be contrasted with the following passage taken from the *Guyana v Suriname Arbitration* concerning oil and gas activities in undelimited, disputed areas:

In the context of activities surrounding hydrocarbon exploration and exploitation, two classes of activities in disputed waters are therefore permissible. The first comprises activities

[32] *Interpretation of Peace Treaties with Bulgaria, Hungary and Romania* (Advisory Opinion) (First Phase) [1950] ICJ Rep 65, 74.

[33] *South West Africa Cases (Ethiopia v South Africa, Liberia v South Africa)* (Preliminary Objections) [1962] ICJ Rep 319, 328.

[34] See Malcolm N Shaw, *International Law* (7th edn, CUP 2014) 774 referring to a 'relatively low threshold' in this respect.

[35] PRC Oil Platform Position Paper 1 (n 20) para 2; PRC Oil Platform Position Paper 2 (n 23) point I, para 2.

[36] See however section 2.1 of this chapter.

[37] PRC Oil Platform Position Paper 4 (n 29) para 1.

[38] Derek Bowett, 'Islands, Rocks, Reefs, and Low-tide Elevations in Maritime Boundary Delimitations' in Jonathan I Charney and Lewis M Alexander (eds), *International Maritime Boundaries*, vol 1 (Martinus Nijhoff 1993) 150: 'It is clear that the presence of islands, rocks, reefs, and low-tide elevations is a frequent, complicating factor in delimitation. The situations are so diverse that generalizations are hazardous, and to attempt to postulate "rules" would be to fall into the error which the courts have persistently, and rightly, avoided. The most that can be done is to identify certain tendencies in state practice.' The categorical affirmation that the area of operation of the Haiyang Shiyou 981 oil platform during the summer of 2014 'will never fall within the scope of Vietnam's EEZ and continental shelf, no matter which principle is applied in the delimitation' (PRC Oil Platform Position Paper 4 (n 29) para 1) seems therefore to be somewhat overstretched, even in the hypothesis, evoked above for the sake of argumentation, that the Paracels would fall under the sovereignty of the PRC.

[39] In accordance with the 1982 Convention (n 9) arts 74(3) and 83(3).

undertaken by the parties pursuant to provisional arrangements of a practical nature. The second class is composed of acts which, although unilateral, would not have the effect of jeopardizing or hampering the reaching of a final agreement on the delimitation of the maritime boundary.

The Tribunal is of the view that unilateral acts which do not cause a physical change to the marine environment would generally fall into the second class. However, acts that do cause physical change would have to be undertaken pursuant to an agreement between the parties to be permissible, as they may hamper or jeopardise the reaching of a final agreement on delimitation. A distinction is therefore to be made between activities of the kind that lead to a permanent physical change, such as exploitation of oil and gas reserves, and those that do not, such as seismic exploration.[40]

Instead of being business as usual, the drilling operations undertaken by the Haiyang Shiyou 981 oil platform form the next step in the exploration and exploitation activities of the PRC in that area, which under contemporary international law fall into a totally different category than the seismic testing undertaken previously in that area by the Chinese state-owned oil company.

2.3 The applicable legal framework is the 1982 Convention

The PRC acknowledges that the 1982 Convention forms part of the applicable international legal framework with respect to the maritime claims in the SCS.[41] But as with the Chinese letters of 7 May 2009, the use of some terms in these diplomatic notes is puzzling, not because they do not appear in the 1982 Convention, but rather because they seem to be totally unrelated to the activities undertaken. The emphasis placed on the drilling activities having taken place in the contiguous zone of the PRC,[42] a zone in which the coastal state has certain competences limited to customs, fiscal, immigration, and sanitary matters,[43] for instance, does not seem to bear much relevance from a legal point of view. Its specific mention in the PRC Oil Platform Position Paper 2 therefore remains perplexing.

These diplomatic notes also rely on the Chinese baselines around the Paracels to determine the exact location of the drilling.[44] Explicit reference is made to the Declaration of the Government of the PRC on the Baselines of the Territorial Sea of the PRC, dated 15 May 1996,[45] duly deposited with the UN Secretary-General.[46] This Declaration is said to have been enacted 'in complete compliance

[40] *Guyana v Suriname* (Award of 17 September 2007) 30 RIAA 1 paras 466–467.

[41] PRC Oil Platform Position Paper 2 (n 23) point II, para 2 and point III, para 1; PRC Oil Platform Position Paper 4 (n 29) point 2.

[42] PRC Oil Platform Position Paper 2 (n 23) point I, para 1.

[43] 1982 Convention (n 9) art 33.

[44] PRC Oil Platform Position Paper 2 (n 23) point I, para 1.

[45] China, 'Declaration of the Government of the People's Republic of China on the Baselines of the Territorial Sea, 15 May 1996' (1996) 32 L Sea Bull 37 (PRC Territorial Sea Declaration).

[46] PRC Oil Platform Position Paper 4 (n 29) point 2. The originals of the deposited baselines are available at UN Division for Ocean Affairs and the Law of the Sea, 'Maritime Space: Maritime Zones and Maritime Delimitation' <www.un.org/Depts/los/LEGISLATIONANDTREATIES/PDFFILES/DEPOSIT/chn_mzn7_1996.pdf> (accessed 1 September 2016).

with international law'.[47] By encircling the Paracels by means of straight baselines connecting its outermost features, the PRC gives the impression of relying on those provisions of the 1982 Convention that concern outlying archipelagos.[48] This would be problematic, as this system only applies to states constituted wholly by one or more archipelagos or islands and excludes mainland (or continental) states.[49] This restriction was clearly part of the compromise when the concept of the archipelagic state was for the first time codified in the 1982 Convention.[50] If not archipelagic baselines, the only remaining possibility is that the baselines drawn around the Paracels are straight baselines.[51] But also this line of reasoning seems difficult to reconcile with the International Court of Justice's (ICJ) *obiter dictum* in the *Qatar v Bahrain Case*:

> The Court observes that the method of straight baselines, which is an exception to the normal rules for the determination of baselines, may only be applied if a number of conditions are met. This method must be applied restrictively. Such conditions are primarily that either the coastline is deeply indented and cut into, or that there is a fringe of islands along the coast in its immediate vicinity.[52]

The application of straight baselines to offshore archipelagos was criticized in the *South China Sea Arbitration*. While acknowledging the existence of state practice to this effect, the Arbitral Tribunal held that such deviations from the 1982 Convention had not given rise to a new norm of customary international law that would permit any departures from the established rules.[53] Hence, no matter how one tries to justify the straight baselines drawn around the Paracels, they remain highly problematic from a legal point of view unless the Paracels were to become an independent state, not belonging to either China or Vietnam, because the latter two countries both have a continental landmass.[54]

A final remarkable point, at least if one agrees that the 1982 Convention is the governing legal framework, is the map attached to PRC Oil Platform Position Paper 2 depicting the two locations where the oil platform Haiyang Shiyou 981 was positioned during the summer of 2014.[55] Informative as this 2014 Map may be with

[47] PRC Oil Platform Position Paper 4 (n 29) point 2.

[48] More particularly 1982 Convention (n 9) art 47, concerning archipelagic baselines.

[49] ibid art 46(1), providing a definition of the notion 'archipelagic state', the only state able to apply archipelagic baselines under art 47. *South China Sea Arbitration* (n 3) (Merits) para 573.

[50] For a more developed argumentation by the present authors, see Erik Franckx and Marco Benatar, 'Straight Baselines Around Insular Formations Not Constituting an Archipelagic State' in CJ Jenner and Thuy Tran Truong (eds), *The South China Sea: A Crucible of Regional Cooperation or Conflict-making Sovereignty Claims?* (CUP 2016) 186–201.

[51] 1982 Convention (n 9) art 7.

[52] *Maritime Delimitation and Territorial Questions between Qatar and Bahrain (Qatar v Bahrain)* (Merits) [2001] ICJ Rep 40, 103, para 212. The Court refused to accept the construction of a system of straight baselines around Bahrain (paras 213–215), a state that could possibly have claimed archipelagic status, but had not done so.

[53] *South China Sea Arbitration* (n 3) (Merits) paras 575–576.

[54] US Dept of State, Office of Ocean Affairs, Bureau of Oceans and International Environmental and Scientific Affairs, 'Straight Baselines Claim: China' (1996) 8 <www.state.gov/documents/organization/57692.pdf> (accessed 1 September 2016).

[55] This map has been reproduced in Annex 2 to this chapter (2014 Map).

respect to the exact positions of the drilling operations, it is troubling in terms of international law: it depicts one of the nine dashes, marked as a state boundary,[56] attributing about 63 per cent of the maritime area between the Vietnamese mainland[57] and Triton Island[58] to the PRC. Leaving aside the issue of contested sovereignty, this apportionment hardly seems 'equitable' from the perspective of maritime delimitation under the 1982 Convention.[59]

3 The PRC's Position Paper in the *South China Sea Arbitration*

3.1 The *South China Sea Arbitration*

On 22 January 2013 the Philippines informed the PRC of its decision to institute legal proceedings under Annex VII of the 1982 Convention in an effort to challenge certain of the Chinese maritime claims and actions in the SCS. The PRC reacted by means of a diplomatic note dated 19 February 2013, stating that the PRC rejected and returned the Philippines' *note verbale* and notification.[60] In that diplomatic note, the PRC described 'the Position of China on the South China Sea issues'.[61] After having been invited by the Arbitral Tribunal to comment on the draft Rules of Procedure, the PRC responded by means of a *note verbale* of 1 August 2013 addressed to the PCA maintaining its position that it did not accept the arbitration and consequently would not be participating in the procedure.[62]

The Philippines submitted its memorial on 30 March 2014,[63] following which the Arbitral Tribunal set 15 December 2014 as the deadline for the PRC to submit its counter-memorial.[64] After the parties had once more been given the opportunity to comment on the scheduling, the PRC sent another *note verbale* in which it reiterated its position that it did not accept the arbitration while emphasizing that the present *note verbale* 'shall not be regarded as China's acceptance of or participation in the proceedings'.[65] In the PRC's absence, the Arbitral Tribunal rendered two decisions, that is a first Award on Jurisdiction and Admissibility on 29 October 2015 (2015 Award)[66] and a second Award on 12 July 2016 (2016

[56] See supra (n 12) and accompanying text.

[57] This does not take into account the Vietnamese system of straight baselines or the islands in front of the Vietnamese coasts that serve as basepoints for these straight baselines.

[58] Constituting the most western point of the baseline system proclaimed by the PRC around the Paracels in 1996. See supra (n 45) and accompanying text.

[59] 1982 Convention (n 9) arts 74(1) and 83(1).

[60] China, 'Chinese Spokesperson Hong Lei's remarks on China returned the Philippines' Notification on the submission of South China Sea issue to international Arbitration' (Chinese Ministry of Foreign Affairs, 2013) <http://ph.china-embassy.org/eng/xwfb/t1014903.htm> (accessed 1 September 2016).

[61] *South China Sea Arbitration* (n 3) 'First Press Release' (PCA, 27 August 2013). See also ibid (Merits) para 29.

[62] ibid 'First Press Release' (PCA, 27 August 2013). The Arbitral Tribunal, after having received the comments of the Philippines the day before, subsequently adopted the Rules of Procedure in its first Procedural Order.

[63] This date had been fixed by the Arbitral Tribunal in its first Procedural Order. ibid.

[64] *South China Sea Arbitration* (n 3) 'Second Press Release' (PCA, 3 June 2014).

[65] ibid.

[66] *South China Sea Arbitration* (n 3) (Jurisdiction and Admissibility).

Award).[67] The latter decision inter alia invalidated a number of China's maritime claims and declared its conduct to be contrary to the 1982 Convention and general international law.

Despite what one might surmise from this chain of events, the PRC's legal position, both on jurisdiction as well as the merits, was conveyed. Many Chinese scholars published scientific papers on the subject in authoritative journals.[68] A whole book was devoted to the Chinese perspective on this arbitration.[69] But irrespective of the position held by some of these authors, the arguments developed in those publications cannot, as a rule, be attributed to the PRC.[70]

That is why the position paper of 7 December 2014, which was posted on the website of the PRC's Ministry of Foreign Affairs, carries special weight as it represents the official governmental position.[71] Although the PRC refused to participate in the proceedings of the *South China Sea Arbitration* until the very end, the 2014 Position Paper was clearly written with this case in mind. It contains a number of legal arguments setting out why the PRC believes that the Arbitral Tribunal has no jurisdiction. The timing of the release of the position paper is also salient, as it was made public about a week before the deadline for the PRC to deposit its counter-memorial.[72]

This 2014 Position Paper has only one purpose and that is to prove that the Arbitral Tribunal lacks jurisdiction to entertain the case. It does not address the substantive issues raised by the Philippine memorial.[73] While it develops an argumentation that is basically addressed to the Arbitral Tribunal, much like a counter-memorial on jurisdiction, the 2014 Position Paper explicitly states that it cannot 'be regarded as China's acceptance of or participation in this arbitration'.[74] It subsequently puts forward mainly three lines of argumentation: (1) this case concerns in essence a dispute over territorial sovereignty and thus falls outside of the purview of the 1982 Convention;[75] (2) the Philippines and China have agreed to settle their

[67] ibid (Merits). The Award addresses matters of jurisdiction that were not settled in the 2015 Award and the merits of the case.

[68] The *Chinese Journal of International Law*, for instance, has published a number of articles relating to the jurisdiction as well as merits of the arbitration. See eg Sienho Yee, 'The South China Sea Arbitration (The Philippines v. China): Potential Jurisdictional Obstacles or Objections' (2014) 13 Chinese J Intl Law 663; Keyuan Zou and Xinchang Liu, 'The Legal Status of the U-shaped Line in the South China Sea and Its Legal Implications for Sovereignty, Sovereign Rights and Maritime Jurisdiction' (2015) 14 Chinese J Intl L 57. A 'Special Issue on Jurisdiction and Admissibility in the South China Sea Arbitration' of the same journal is forthcoming. See also the authoritative article by Gao and Jia (n 15). Judge Gao was at the time of writing, and still is, the Chinese judge on the ITLOS bench.

[69] Stefan Talmon and Bing Bing Jia (eds), *The South China Sea Arbitration: A Chinese Perspective* (Hart Publishing 2014).

[70] Nonetheless, following the Philippines suggestion, the Arbitral Tribunal did consult 'academic literature by individuals closely associated with Chinese authorities' in an effort to discern China's position (*South China Sea Arbitration* (n 3) (Merits) para 126).

[71] China, 'Position Paper of the Government of the PRC on the Matter of Jurisdiction in the South China Sea Arbitration Initiated by the Republic of the Philippines' (7 December 2014) <www.fmprc.gov.cn/mfa_eng/zxxx_662805/t1217147.shtml> (accessed 1 September 2016) (2014 Position Paper).

[72] See supra (n 64) accompanying text. The PRC did not submit a counter-memorial.

[73] 2014 Position Paper (n 71) para 2. [74] ibid. [75] ibid paras 4–29.

relevant disputes through negotiations, not by legal means;[76] and (3) even if the dispute were to come within the ambit of the 1982 Convention, it pertains to questions of delimitation that China has excluded from compulsory dispute settlement.[77]

The substance of the 2014 Position Paper is of less relevance for present purposes. What is of crucial importance, however, is that the PRC sent a copy of the document to the members of the Arbitral Tribunal while at the same time informing the Registry that 'the forwarding of the aforementioned Position Paper shall not be regarded as China's acceptance of or its participation in the arbitration'.[78]

These developments placed the Arbitral Tribunal in a rather uncomfortable position. On the one hand the PRC clearly wanted the Arbitral Tribunal to take its argumentation on jurisdiction into account, while at the same time maintaining its position that it did not want to accept or participate in the arbitration. In a first phase the Arbitral Tribunal made use of its powers under article 25 of its Rules of Procedure, entitled 'Failure to Appear or to Make Submissions', and requested a supplemental written submission from the appearing party, the Philippines.[79] The latter was invited 'to address, as it considers appropriate, any public statements made by the Chinese government in relation to the dispute'.[80] In a second phase, the Arbitral Tribunal, after having sought the views of the parties, decided in its fourth Procedural Order 'that it will treat China's communications (including the Position Paper) as constituting a plea concerning the Arbitral Tribunal's jurisdiction for purposes of article 20 of the Rules of Procedure'.[81] The latter provides as follows:

Preliminary Objections
Article 20

1. The Arbitral Tribunal shall have the power to rule on objections to its jurisdiction or to the admissibility of any claim made in the proceedings.
2. A plea that the Arbitral Tribunal does not have jurisdiction shall be raised no later than in the Counter-Memorial. A Party is not precluded from raising such a plea by the fact that it has appointed, or participated in the appointment of, an arbitrator. A plea that the Arbitral Tribunal is exceeding the scope of its authority shall be raised as soon as the matter alleged to be beyond the scope of its authority is raised during the arbitral proceedings. The Arbitral Tribunal may, in either case, admit a later plea if it considers the delay justified.
3. The Arbitral Tribunal shall rule on any plea concerning its jurisdiction as a preliminary question, unless the Arbitral Tribunal determines, after seeking the views of the Parties, that the objection to its jurisdiction does not possess an exclusively preliminary character, in which case it shall rule on such a plea in conjunction with the merits.
4. Prior to a ruling on any matters relating to jurisdiction or admissibility, a hearing shall be held if the Arbitral Tribunal determines that such a hearing is necessary or useful, after seeking the views of the Parties.[82]

[76] ibid paras 30–56. [77] ibid paras 57–75.

[78] *South China Sea Arbitration* (n 3) 'Third Press Release' (PCA, 17 December 2014).

[79] ibid 'Rules of Procedure' art 25(2). These rules were adopted by means of the first Procedural Order. See 'First Press Release' (n 61).

[80] 'Third Press Release' (n 78).

[81] *South China Sea Arbitration* (n 3) 'Fourth Press Release' (PCA, 22 April 2015).

[82] 'Rules of Procedure' (n 79) art 20.

It transpires from the 2015 and 2016 Awards that the Arbitral Tribunal undertook a balancing act with the goal of ensuring procedural fairness to both parties. This explains the importance given by the Arbitral Tribunal to the 2014 Position Paper. The Arbitrators held that the publication of this document to some level assuaged the Philippines' concerns that it would be forced into the 'position of having to guess' what the non-participating respondent's arguments could be.[83] Yet, the assessment of jurisdiction was not confined to tackling the objections raised by China in the aforementioned document. True to its obligation to 'satisfy itself' that it has jurisdiction,[84] the Tribunal examined, and invited the parties to address, other potential jurisdictional hurdles.[85]

3.2 Comparison with the *Arctic Sunrise Arbitration*

The present part will focus on the *Arctic Sunrise Arbitration* and more particularly on the manner in which the issue of the defaulting party played out in this litigation. For even though the legal nature of both disputes is quite different, namely maritime claims and activities in the SCS (*South China Sea Arbitration*) versus the legality of boarding and detaining a foreign-flagged vessel in the exclusive economic zone (*Arctic Sunrise Arbitration*),[86] there are some noteworthy similarities. In both cases the respondents, major powers, refused to participate in claims brought against them by smaller countries. Moreover, in each case the defaulting party, after having decided not to participate in the arbitration, deemed it useful to bring its legal argumentation to the attention of the Arbitral Tribunal: the PRC did so in the jurisdiction phase, whereas the Russian Federation acted in kind in the phase on the merits. By comparing the behaviour of the defaulting respondents striking differences can be observed.

Much like the PRC, the Russian Federation reacted swiftly. Russia responded to a Dutch note of 4 October 2013 instituting legal proceedings under Annex VII of the 1982 Convention,[87] an additional note of the Netherlands dated 21 October 2013 requesting the prescription of provisional measures by the International Tribunal for the Law of the Sea (ITLOS),[88] and a communication from ITLOS regarding said request, by means of two notes dated 22 October 2013, one addressed to the Embassy of the Netherlands in Moscow and one to the ITLOS. Both documents

[83] *South China Sea Arbitration* (n 3) (Merits) paras 126–127.

[84] 1982 Convention (n 9) annex vii, art 9.

[85] *South China Sea Arbitration* (n 3) (Merits) para 130.

[86] It should be specified that the dispute over the *Arctic Sunrise*, a Greenpeace ship flying the flag of the Netherlands that was located in the Russian exclusive economic zone at the moment of boarding by Russian authorities, gave rise to two distinct proceedings: the *Arctic Sunrise Arbitration* before an ad hoc Tribunal pursuant to Annex VII of the 1982 Convention and the *Arctic Sunrise Case*, an application to obtain provisional relief from the ITLOS (pending the constitution of the Arbitral Tribunal).

[87] *Arctic Sunrise Arbitration (Netherlands v Russia)*, 'Notification and Statement of Claims' (PCA, 4 October 2013) <www.pcacases.com/web/view/21> (accessed 1 September 2016).

[88] *Arctic Sunrise Case (Netherlands v Russia)*, 'Request for Provisional Measures Submitted by the Netherlands' (ITLOS, 21 October 2013) <www.itlos.org/cases/list-of-cases/case-no-22/> (accessed 1 September 2016).

contain similar wording, namely that the Russian Federation 'does not accept the arbitration procedure under Annex VII to the Convention [. . .] and does not intend to participate in the proceedings of the International Tribunal for the Law of the Sea in respect of the request of the Kingdom of the Netherlands for the prescription of provisional measures'.[89]

The Russian Federation did however react on one occasion, namely when the ITLOS sought Russia's comments on a request from Greenpeace International to submit an *amicus curiae*. The respondent state answered this question in the negative, but only after the deadline set by the Tribunal had passed. Indeed, it is apparent from the procedural history of the case that the ITLOS had already rejected Greenpeace International's request a day earlier.[90] In its answer, the Russian Federation specified that 'this transmission of the Russian position to the tribunal can in no way be interpreted as a form of participation of the Russian Side' in the case.[91] This was the only form of participation of the Russian Federation in the *Arctic Sunrise Case* as it was not represented at the public hearing,[92] did not reply to further questions it received,[93] and did not take up the Tribunal's invitation to present its observations before the closing of the hearing.[94] The ITLOS held that it had prima facie jurisdiction[95] and prescribed provisional measures on 22 November 2013 ordering the release of the vessel and the people on board upon the posting of a bond by the Netherlands.[96]

Turning to the arbitral proceedings, the Russian Federation made its intentions clear *ab initio* even before the tribunal held its first meeting on 17 March 2014.[97] The respondent stated that it maintained its position already expressed on 22 October 2013,[98] namely that it did not accept the arbitration and that it consequently refused 'to take part in this arbitration and abstains from providing comments both on the substance of the case and procedural matters'.[99] Russia upheld this policy throughout the proceedings. It did not send any representatives to this first meeting.[100] Adopting a different approach than in the ITLOS proceedings,[101] the Russian Federation refrained from responding to the Arbitrators' query to

[89] *Arctic Sunrise Case* (n 88) 'Note verbale of the Embassy of the Russian Federation in Berlin' (ITLOS, 22 October 2013). This note was addressed to the ITLOS, but contained in annex the note sent to the Netherlands Embassy in Moscow.

[90] The ITLOS declined the request on 5 November 2013 whereas the Russian answer was received on 6 November. *Arctic Sunrise Case* (n 88) (Provisional Measures) paras 18–19.

[91] ibid para 19. [92] ibid para 30. [93] ibid para 32. [94] ibid para 50.

[95] ibid para 45.

[96] ibid para 105. By that time the ITLOS President had also appointed Dr Alberto Szekely as arbitrator because the Russian Federation had failed to appoint the second arbitrator within the timeframe. *Arctic Sunrise Arbitration* (n 87) 'Procedural Order No 1' (PCA, 17 March 2014). The appointment was made on 15 November 2013.

[97] By then the three remaining arbitrators had been appointed by the ITLOS President. This happened on 10 January 2014. *Arctic Sunrise Arbitration* (n 87) 'Procedural Order No 1' (PCA, 17 March 2014).

[98] See supra (n 89) and accompanying text.

[99] *Arctic Sunrise Arbitration* (n 87) 'Note verbale from the Russian Federation to the PCA' (PCA, 27 February 2014).

[100] ibid 'Procedural Order No 2' (PCA, 17 March 2014); ibid 'Press Release' (PCA, 21 March 2014).

[101] See supra (n 90) and accompanying text.

comment on the request by Greenpeace International to submit an *amicus curiae* to the Arbitral Tribunal.[102] Furthermore, Russia did not inform the Arbitral Tribunal whether it would submit a counter-memorial[103] nor did it express its views on the issue of bifurcation of the proceedings.[104]

Contrary to the PRC, which by means of its 2014 Position Paper had sent the Arbitral Tribunal a clear signal that it was raising preliminary objections, the Russian Federation did not provide detailed argumentation and refused to take a position. Faced with this non-participation, the Netherlands stated on several occasions that the terse Russian *notes verbales* of 22 October 2013[105] and 27 February 2014[106] should be equated with a plea concerning the jurisdiction of the Arbitral Tribunal.[107] The Arbitral Tribunal ruled on 21 November 2014 that the Russian *note verbale* of 22 October 2013 constituted such a plea to which article 20(3) of its Rules of Procedure applied[108] and decided to rule on this plea without a hearing.[109] On 26 November 2014 the Arbitral Tribunal unanimously ruled that it had jurisdiction to hear the merits.[110]

During the phase leading up to the hearings on the merits, scheduled for 10 and 11 February 2015, the Russian Federation 'maintained its position not to participate in the proceedings'[111] and did not indicate an intention to submit comments as requested by the Arbitral Tribunal.[112] At the oral proceedings on the merits the Russian Federation was not represented and 'did not ... otherwise participate'.[113]

But then, rather unexpectedly, the Russian Federation posted on the website of its Ministry of Foreign Affairs on 5 August 2015 a document titled 'Ministry of Foreign Relations of the Russian Federation on Certain Legal Issues Highlighted by the Action of the *Arctic Sunrise* against *Prirazlomnaya* platform'.[114] This document of forty pages reads like a counter-memorial on the merits. After having repeated that the Russian Federation does not participate in the arbitration, this document nevertheless 'finds

[102] *Arctic Sunrise Arbitration* (n 87) 'Procedural Order No 3' (PCA, 8 October 2014). The Arbitral Tribunal denied this request as had the ITLOS.

[103] See supra (n 90) and accompanying text. See also ibid 'Press Release' (PCA, 7 November 2014).

[104] It abstained from doing so as well with respect to the Netherlands' request concerning a draft procedural order of the Arbitral Award. ibid 'Procedural Order No 4' (PCA, 21 November 2014).

[105] See supra (n 89) and accompanying text.

[106] See supra (n 99) and accompanying text.

[107] 'Procedural Order No 4' (n 103). As stated in the preamble of this procedural order, the Netherlands had already expressed this view in a letter to the Arbitral Tribunal of 27 February 2014, at the occasion of the first procedural meeting of 17 March 2014, as well as in its Memorial of 31 August 2014.

[108] *Arctic Sunrise Arbitration* (n 87) 'Rules of Procedure' art 20(3). These rules were adopted by means of 'Procedural Order No 2' (PCA, 17 March 2014). This provision is identical to art. 20 of the Rules of Procedure adopted in the *South China Sea Arbitration*. See supra (n 82) and accompanying text.

[109] 'Procedural Order No 4' (n 103).

[110] Arctic Sunrise Arbitration (n 8) (Jurisdiction) para 79.

[111] ibid (Merits) para 18.

[112] ibid 'Press Release' (PCA, 18 February 2015).

[113] ibid.

[114] Russia, 'The Ministry of Foreign Affairs of the Russian Federation on certain legal issues highlighted by the action of the *Arctic Sunrise* against *Prirazlomnaya* platform' (Russian Ministry of Foreign Affairs, 2015) <www.mid.ru/en/web/guest/foreign_policy/news/-/asset_publisher/cKNonkJE02Bw/content/id/1639745> (accessed 1 September 2016).

it important', given the fact that the case concerns the balance of coastal and flag state powers in the exclusive economic zone and on the continental shelf, 'to address some of those issues'.[115] For present purposes, once again,[116] the content is less important. What is worth stressing here, however, is that the Russian Federation sent this document two days later to the PCA. The Arbitral Tribunal refers to this document as 'Position Paper' in its 2015 Award on the Merits.[117] In an accompanying letter the Russian Federation stated that 'this shall in no way be interpreted as the Russian Federation's acceptance of or participation in the arbitration'.[118] After having notified the Netherlands of this development and observing that the latter country made no application in this respect, the Arbitral Tribunal decided to take no formal action on Russia's Position Paper given that: (i) it was brought to the Tribunal's attention at a very late stage of this phase of the proceedings following Russia's consistent failure to participate in this arbitration; and (ii) according to Russia, the Position Paper does not constitute a formal submission in this proceeding.[119]

In the unanimous Award on the Merits, the Arbitral Tribunal found that the Russian Federation had illegally boarded the *Arctic Sunrise* and that the Netherlands was entitled to compensation.[120]

4 The Rise of Non-participation and Position Papers?

This chapter has demonstrated that the PRC has resorted to so-called position papers in interactions with its SCS neighbours. Particularly in the *South China Sea Arbitration* this has resulted in a coherent legal argumentation defending the PRC's position at least with respect to a well-specified part of the arbitration (ie the jurisdiction of the Arbitral Tribunal). The Arbitrators each received a copy of the 2014 Position Paper. At the same time, however, the PRC addressed a communication to the Registry stressing that this did not imply that the PRC had decided to accept or participate in the arbitration.

The Arbitral Tribunal, after having consulted the parties, relied on a provision of its Rules of Procedure that deals with preliminary objections so that it could take the arguments of the 2014 Position Paper into account. This approach appears to be compatible with the provision that governs situations whereby one of the parties fails to defend its case[121] as well as with the practice of international courts and tribunals in such instances.[122]

[115] ibid para 2.2.

[116] A similar remark was made with respect to the 2014 Position Paper of China. See supra (n 78) and accompanying text.

[117] *Arctic Sunrise Arbitration* (n 87) (Merits) para 68. [118] ibid. [119] ibid.

[120] ibid para 401. At the time of writing, the compensation phase (calculation of the quantum) is still pending.

[121] 'Rules of Procedure' (n 79) art 25(2), which reads in part: 'The Arbitral Tribunal may take whatever other steps it may consider necessary, within the scope of its powers under the Convention, its Annex VII, and these Rules, to afford to each of the Parties a full opportunity to present its case'.

[122] Mincai Yu, 'China's Informal Participation in the Annex Philippines v. China Arbitral Tribunal's Proceedings' (2015) 30 Intl J Marine and Coastal L 54.

The *Arctic Sunrise Arbitration* seems to confirm this practice. There are however clear distinctions to be noted. The Russian Federation, first of all, did not find it essential to write a 'position paper' on jurisdiction. Maybe it was the precedent set by China half a year earlier in the *South China Sea Arbitration* by producing its 2014 Position Paper and the manner in which it was received by the Arbitral Tribunal that prompted the Russian Federation to act in a very similar manner with respect to the merits of its own case. But unlike the 2014 Position Paper, which the PRC submitted eight days before the deadline set by the Arbitral Tribunal to hand in its counter-memorial, the Russian action proved ill-timed, as the 2015 Russian Ministry of Foreign Affairs Document was sent to the Arbitral Tribunal only seven days before it delivered its Award on the Merits. Not only did the Tribunal decide to take no formal action on this document because of its timing and nature, as indicated above,[123] but even worse, it was able to sweep aside the whole legal argumentation presented by the Russian authorities with one concise sentence in which it remarked that 'the Tribunal is satisfied that the relevant issues are fully addressed in this Award'.[124]

5 Conclusions

Can states refuse to participate in international legal proceedings and yet have their legal arguments, developed outside of that framework, be heard by the court or tribunal involved? The answer appears to be 'yes', as the Arbitral Tribunal did everything in its power to provide the PRC with the opportunity to present its case and take on board the arguments raised in its position paper.[125] It is further submitted that the result would have been similar in the *Arctic Sunrise Arbitration*, had the Russian Federation acted in a timelier manner.

While the Arbitral Tribunal's treatment of China's position paper is consonant with its procedural rules and shows due regard for procedural fairness, it might very well prompt other states to reap the benefits of not participating in proceedings and all the while mount a legal defence through the use of position papers. Recent years had seen a greater involvement of China with international courts and tribunals as borne out by its engagement in World Trade Organization litigation and participation in advisory proceedings before the ICJ and ITLOS (both the Seabed Disputes Chamber and the full Tribunal).[126] In recent memory, Russia has actively

[123] See supra (n 119) and accompanying text.

[124] *Arctic Sunrise Arbitration* (n 87) para 68 *in fine*.

[125] 'Rules of Procedure' (n 79) art 25(2) as reprinted above (n 121).

[126] Dapo Akande, 'China's View of International Litigation: Is the WTO Special?' (EJIL: *Talk!*, 13 November 2015) <www.ejiltalk.org/chinas-view-of-international-litigation-is-the-wto-special/> (accessed 1 September 2016) (referring inter alia to *Accordance with International Law of the Unilateral Declaration of Independence in Respect of Kosovo* (Advisory Opinion) [2010] ICJ Rep 403; *Responsibilities and Obligations of States Sponsoring Persons and Entities with Respect to Activities in the Area* (Seabed Disputes Chamber) (Advisory Opinion) <www.itlos.org/en/cases/list-of-cases/case-no-17/> (accessed 1 September 2016); *Request for an Advisory Opinion Submitted by the Sub-Regional Fisheries Commission (SRFC)* (Advisory Opinion) <www.itlos.org/en/cases/list-of-cases/case-no-21/> (accessed 1 September 2016)). On historic and contemporary Chinese attitudes vis-à-vis international adjudication and arbitration, see Julian Ku, 'China and the Future of International Adjudication' (2012) 25 Maryland

participated in international proceedings, including as defendant.[127] Now it appears that both powers are promoting a policy that would encourage non-participation in international proceedings brought by unilateral application. This approach, which would substantially narrow the scope of international adjudication and arbitration, is aptly illustrated in a recent joint declaration:

> The Russian Federation and the People's Republic of China reaffirm the principle of peaceful settlement of disputes and express their firm conviction that States shall resolve their disputes through dispute settlement means and mechanisms that they have agreed upon […].
>
> This applies equally to all types and stages of dispute settlement, including political and diplomatic means when they serve a pre-requisite to the use of other mechanisms of dispute settlement. It is crucial for the maintenance of international legal order that all dispute settlement means and mechanisms are based on consent and used in good faith and in the spirit of cooperation, and their purposes shall not be undermined by abusive practices.[128]

Are these developments, namely the flexibility displayed by courts and tribunals on the one hand and the recent practice of China and Russia on the other hand, to be expected to open the floodgates for non-participation in compulsory procedures of dispute settlement? This might well be the case if the interests of the parties were secured in exactly the same manner in both instances. One can, however, seriously doubt whether the use of position papers by a non-participating state will ever be able to equal the submission of a counter-memorial and the subsequent oral pleadings in this respect. It is believed that the absence of the possibility, first to orally defend and further develop one's own written arguments contained in the counter-memorial, and second to critically assess those developed orally by the claimant, tends to weaken the position of the defendant as it will always grant the court or tribunal ample discretion in the way it weighs and makes use of the different arguments developed in the position paper.

A host of pending arbitrations have the potential to either incentivize or deter the resort to position papers. In 2009, Croatia and Slovenia concluded a *compromis*

J Intl L 154; Zhu Dan, 'China, the International Criminal Court, and International Adjudication' (2014) 61 Netherlands Intl L R 43, 46–56; Qingjiang Kong and Xiaojuan Ping, 'International Law and International Institutions: Implications for a Rising China' (2015) 1 Chinese J Global Governance 157, 164–71. See also Tommy Koh and Hao Duy Phan, 'The Asian Way to Settle Disputes' (2016) 1 Asian-Pacific J Ocean L and Policy 5.

[127] Eg *Application of the International Convention on the Elimination of All Forms of Racial Discrimination (Georgia v Russia)* (Merits) [2011] ICJ Rep 70; *The 'Hoshinmaru' Case (Japan v Russia)* (Prompt Release) <www.itlos.org/en/cases/list-of-cases/case-no-14/> (accessed 1 September 2016); *The 'Tomimaru' Case (Japan v Russia)* (Prompt Release) <www.itlos.org/en/cases/list-of-cases/case-no-15/> (accessed 1 September 2016); *Hulley Enterprises Limited (Cyprus) v Russia* <https://pcacases.com/web/view/60> (accessed 1 September 2016); *Yukos Universal Limited (Isle of Man) v Russia* <https://pcacases.com/web/view/61> (accessed 1 September 2016); *Veteran Petroleum Limited (Cyprus) v Russia* <https://pcacases.com/web/view/62> (accessed 1 September 2016). On Russian attitudes to international litigation, see Lauri Mälksoo, *Russian Approaches to International Law* (OUP 2015) 154–56.

[128] 'The Declaration of the Russian Federation and the People's Republic of China on the Promotion of International Law' (Russian Ministry of Foreign Affairs, 2016) <www.mid.ru/en/foreign_policy/news/-/asset_publisher/cKNonkJE02Bw/content/id/2331698> (accessed 1 September 2016).

submitting their territorial and maritime dispute to arbitration with the PCA acting as registry. The smooth running of the case came to a sudden halt when it was discovered that the agent for Slovenia and the arbitrator appointed by Slovenia had engaged in unlawful *ex parte* contacts. The revelations led to the departure of the original party-appointed arbitrators and the Slovenian agent. New appointments were made to replace said arbitrators. Croatia sought the discontinuance of the case,[129] whereas Slovenia requested that the Arbitral Tribunal complete its mandate. A hearing was held to address the legal implications of the incident. Croatia, which was fully engaged in the arbitral proceedings prior to the fateful event, did not participate in the hearing nor did it file formal written submissions. It had however formulated its position in diplomatic notes and letters.[130] The Croatian Ministry of Foreign and European Affairs even created an English-language website titled 'Termination of the Arbitration Process between Croatia and Slovenia: Causes and Consequences' with hyperlinks to documents providing analysis.[131] The Arbitral Tribunal made ample use of the abovementioned documentation and correspondence to assess the legal arguments expressed by Croatia. While acknowledging the breaches of the Arbitration Agreement by Slovenia, the Arbitral Tribunal decided in a Partial Award that the proceedings could and would continue.[132] Responding to the Partial Award, Croatia issued a press release commenting that it is no longer a party to the arbitration and does not consider itself bound by the decisions of the Arbitral Tribunal.[133]

In the wake of the Russian annexation of Crimea, several Ukrainian private investors and Ukrainian state-owned enterprises with investments in Crimea filed claims against Russia under UNCITRAL (United Nations Commission on International Trade Law) Arbitration Rules (1976) pursuant to the Russia-Ukraine Bilateral Investment Treaty (BIT).[134] It has been reported in most of these cases, of which all

[129] Croatia relieved its legal team of its duties and commenced a procedure under its domestic law to terminate the Arbitration Agreement. See Croatia, 'Termination of the Arbitration Process between Croatia and Slovenia: Causes and Consequences' (Croatian Ministry of Foreign and European Affairs, 2016) <www.mvep.hr/en/other/termination-of-the-arbitration-process> (accessed 1 September 2016).

[130] *Croatia v Slovenia*, 'Press Release' (PCA, 30 June 2016) <https://pcacases.com/web/view/3> (accessed 1 September 2016).

[131] ibid (Partial Award) para 61. [132] ibid para 231.

[133] Croatia, 'Press Release on Arbitral Tribunal's Decision' (Croatian Ministry of Foreign and European Affairs, 2016) <www.mvep.hr/en/info-servis/press-releases/press-release-on-arbitral-tribunal's-decision-,25852.html> (accessed 1 September 2016).

[134] *Aeroport Belbek LLC and Mr Igor Valerievich Kolomoisky v Russia* <https://pcacases.com/web/view/123> (accessed 1 September 2016); *PJSC CB PrivatBank and Finance Company Finilon LLC v Russia* <https://pcacases.com/web/view/130> (accessed 1 September 2016); *(1) Limited Liability Company Lugzor, (2) Limited Liability Company Libset, (3) Limited Liability Company Ukrinterinvest, (4) Public Joint Stock Company DniproAzot, (5) Limited Liability Company Aberon Ltd v Russia* <https://pcacases.com/web/view/124> (accessed 1 September 2016); *PJSC Ukrnafta v Russia* <https://pcacases.com/web/view/121> (accessed 1 September 2016); *(i) Stabil LLC, (ii) Rubenor LLC, (iii) Rustel LLC, (iv) Novel-Estate LLC, (v) PII Kirovograd-Nafta LLC, (vi) Crimea-Petrol LLC, (vii) Pirsan LLC, (viii) Trade-Trust LLC, (ix) Elefteria LLC, (x) VKF Satek LLC, (xi) Stemv Group LLC v Russia* <https://pcacases.com/web/view/122> (accessed 1 September 2016); *Everest Estate LLC et al v Russia* <https://pcacases.com/web/view/133> (accessed 1 September 2016). See also Sebastian Perry, 'Another Crimea Panel in Place at the PCA' *Global Arbitration Review* (19 August 2016) <http://globalarbitrationreview.com/article/1067638/another-crimea-panel-in-place-at-the-pca> (accessed 1 September 2016) (reporting on two claims filed by state-owned companies, ie *Oschadbank v Russia* and *Naftogaz v Russia*). For a detailed

but one are currently administered by the PCA,[135] that Russia did not appoint representatives and sent letters to the PCA indicating that (1) the '[Ukraine-Russia BIT] cannot serve as a basis for composing an arbitral tribunal to settle [the Claimants' claims]', (2) it 'does not recognize the jurisdiction of an international arbitral tribunal at the [PCA] in settlement of the [Claimants' claims]', and (3) nothing in its correspondence 'should be considered as consent of the Russian Federation to constitution of an arbitral tribunal, participation in arbitral proceedings, or as procedural actions taken in the framework of the proceedings'.[136] In the vast majority (if not all) of the Crimea investment cases the Russian Federation has neither responded to requests from the Arbitral Tribunals nor has it submitted statements of defence or attended hearings. A number of these Arbitral Tribunals have dealt with Russia's non-participation in the same manner: (1) continuation of the proceedings despite the respondent's failure to communicate its claim; (2) qualification of Russia's correspondence as a plea concerning jurisdiction and admissibility; and (3) bifurcation of the proceedings.[137]

The latest development that deserves to be flagged is Ukraine's decision in September 2016 to commence arbitral proceedings against Russia under Annex VII of the 1982 Convention. The application, which also originates from the situation

assessment of these investment claims, see Odysseas G Repousis, 'Why Russian Investment Treaties Could Apply to Crimea and What Would This Mean for the Ongoing Russo–Ukrainian Territorial Conflict' (2016) 32 Arbitration Intl 459.

[135] At the time of writing, it was unknown to the authors whether the notice of arbitration in *Naftogaz v Russia* had already been filed. Perry (n 134).

[136] *Aeroport Belbek LLC and Mr Igor Valerievich Kolomoisky v Russia* (n 134) 'Press Release' (PCA, 6 January 2016); *PJSC CB PrivatBank and Finance Company Finilon LLC v Russia* (n 134) 'Press Release' (PCA, 30 March 2016); *(1) Limited Liability Company Lugzor, (2) Limited Liability Company Libset, (3) Limited Liability Company Ukrinterinvest, (4) Public Joint Stock Company DniproAzot, (5) Limited Liability Company Aberon Ltd v Russia* (n 134); *PJSC Ukrnafta v Russia* (n 134) 'Press Release' (PCA, 2 May 2016); *(i) Stabil LLC, (ii) Rubenor LLC, (iii) Rustel LLC, (iv) Novel-Estate LLC, (v) PII Kirovograd-Nafta LLC, (vi) Crimea-Petrol LLC, (vii) Pirsan LLC, (viii) Trade-Trust LLC, (ix) Elefteria LLC, (x) VKF Satek LLC,(xi) Stemv Group LLC v Russia* (n 134) 'Press Release' (PCA, 2 May 2016); *Everest Estate LLC et al v Russia* (n 134) 'Press Release' (PCA, 9 August 2016).

[137] *Aeroport Belbek LLC and Mr Igor Valerievich Kolomoisky v Russia* (n 134) 'Press Release' (PCA, 6 January 2016), 'Press Release' (PCA, 30 March 2016), 'Press Release' (PCA, 15 August 2016); *PJSC CB PrivatBank and Finance Company Finilon LLC v Russia* (n 134) 'Press Release' (PCA, 30 March 2016), 'Press Release' (PCA, 15 August 2016); *Everest Estate LLC et al v Russia* (n 134) 'Press Release' (PCA, 9 August 2016). The press releases concerning *PJSC Ukrnafta v Russia* and *Stabil LLC et al v Russia* do not provide information on whether the Arbitral Tribunal, which is made of the same members in both cases, decided to treat Russia's correspondence as a plea concerning jurisdiction and admissibility. A hearing on jurisdiction common to both cases was held (*PJSC Ukrnafta v Russia* (n 134) 'Press Release' (PCA, 2 May 2016), 'Press Release' (PCA, 4 August 2016); *(i) Stabil LLC, (ii) Rubenor LLC, (iii) Rustel LLC, (iv) Novel-Estate LLC, (v) PII Kirovograd-Nafta LLC, (vi) Crimea-Petrol LLC, (vii) Pirsan LLC, (viii) Trade-Trust LLC, (ix) Elefteria LLC, (x) VKF Satek LLC,(xi) Stemv Group LLC v Russia* (n 134) 'Press Release' (PCA, 2 May 2016), 'Press Release' (PCA, 4 August 2016)). Another noteworthy development in most of these cases is that Ukraine successfully sought permission to make submissions as a non-disputing party, whereas its requests to attend and present oral arguments at hearings were denied.

in Crimea, seeks to vindicate maritime rights asserted by Ukraine in the Black Sea, Sea of Azov, and Kerch Strait and challenge Russian activities in those areas.[138] At the time of writing, the Russian Federation had at least appointed its own member on the tribunal.[139] Will the respondent defend its case head-on or stay on the sidelines?

[138] Ukraine, 'Statement of the Ministry of Foreign Affairs of Ukraine on the Initiation of Arbitration against the Russian Federation under the United Nations Convention on the Law of the Sea' (Ukrainian Ministry of Foreign Affairs, 2016) <http://mfa.gov.ua/en/press-center/news/50813-zajava-mzs-ukrajini-shhodo-porushennya-arbitrazhnogo-provadzhennya-proti-rosijsykoji-federaciji-vidpovidno-do-konvenciji-oon-z-morsykogo-prava> (accessed 20 September 2016). See also Gaiane Nuridzhanyan, 'Ukraine vs. Russia in International Courts and Tribunals' (EJIL: *Talk!*, 9 March 2016) <www.ejiltalk.org/ukraine-versus-russia-in-international-courts-and-tribunals/> (accessed 1 September 2016) (on on-going and prospective litigation before international courts and tribunals arising out of the conflict opposing Ukraine and Russia).

[139] Ukraine, 'The hearing of the case Ukraine v. Russian Federation under UNCLOS will start at the beginning of 2017' (Ukrainian Ministry of Foreign Affairs, 2016) <http://mfa.gov.ua/en/press-center/news/53422-na-pochatku-2017-roku-rozpochnetysya-rozglyad-spravi-ukrajina-proti-rosijsykoji-federaciji-zgidno-z-konvencijeju-oon-z-morsykogo-prava> accessed on 28 December 2016.

Annex 1

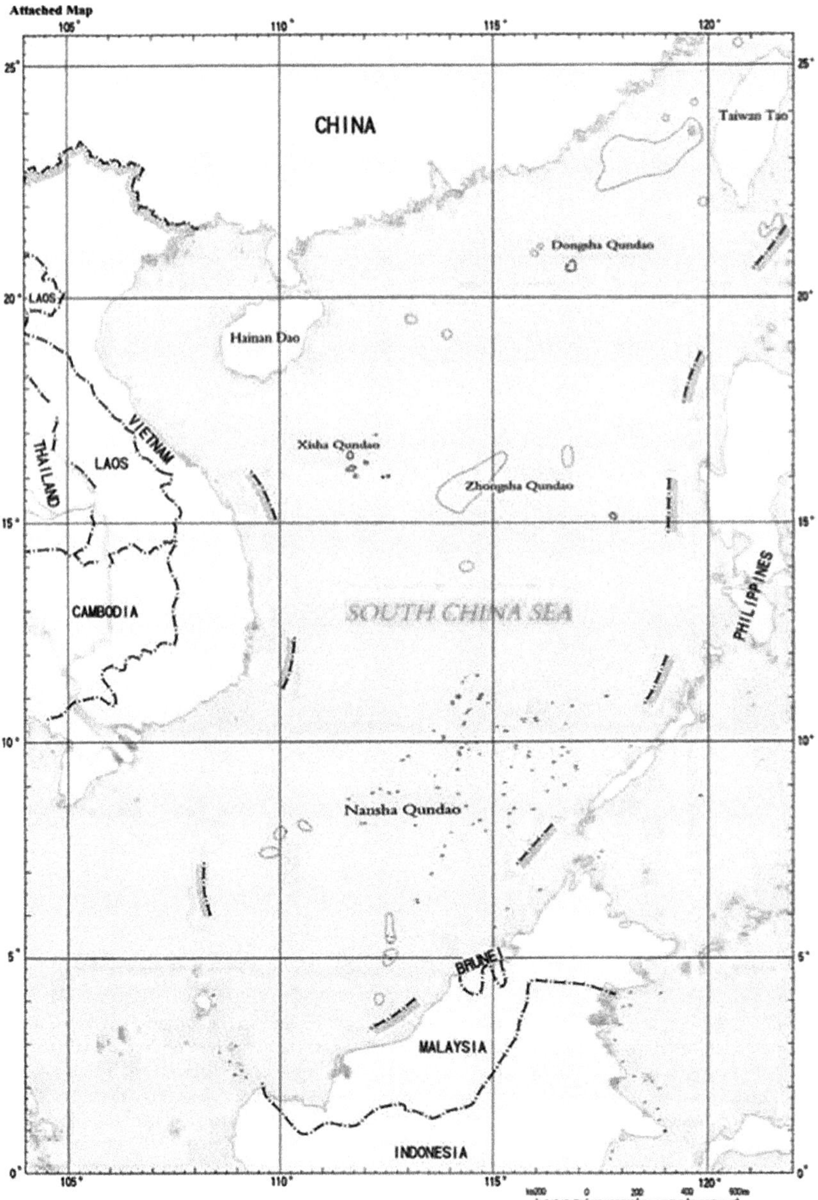

Source: China, 'Letter to the Secretary-General of the United Nations—CML/17/2009' (7 May 2009) and People's Republic of China, 'Letter to the Secretary-General of the United Nations—CML/18/2009' (7 May 2009).

Annex 2

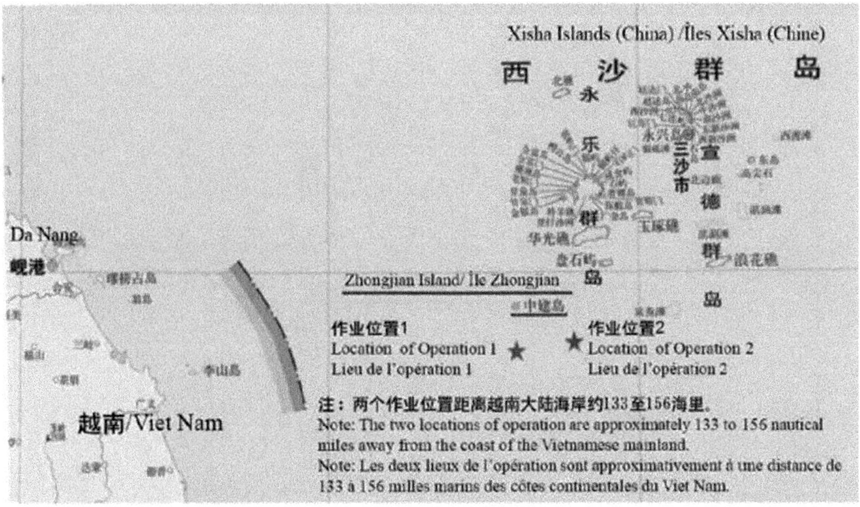

Source: China, 'Letter Dated 9 June 2014 from the Chargé d'affaires a.i. of the Permanent Mission of China to the United Nations addressed to the Secretary-General' (9 June 2014) UN Doc A/68/907, Enclosure 1.

PART IV

RESPONDING TO FRAGMENTATION

10

The Contribution of the International Court of Justice to the Promotion and Protection of Human Rights

Dominika Švarc Pipan

1 Introduction

The role of the International Court of Justice (ICJ) in the field of human rights is fairly limited, both due to the Court's specific institutional role and characteristics and due to the particular design of the global institutional framework for protection of human rights. Nevertheless, human rights have gradually become a steady and distinguishable element of both contentious and advisory proceedings before the Court, resulting in a considerable body of case-law which has significantly contributed to the overall framework for protection and promotion of human rights, both substantially and institutionally.

Conceived at the time when international protection of human rights was still at an embryonic stage, the Court's judicial function was limited to the traditional settlement of inter-State disputes on the basis of the consent of the parties and to the provision of non-binding legal advice to the organs and institutions of the United Nations system.[1] Consequently, the Court is open only to States for contentious proceedings, and to certain international organizations for advisory proceedings, while individuals consequently lack standing before the Court and cannot provide any direct procedural input to the Court's proceedings.

At the same time, international instruments aimed at protection of human rights envisage specific means of enforcement and supervision before specialized international courts and other treaty-monitoring mechanisms, which largely bypass traditional dispute-settlement procedures such as those employed by the ICJ. Only a limited number of human rights treaties (and no instrument of international humanitarian law) include jurisdictional clauses providing for the Court's jurisdiction, and many of

[1] See Charter of the United Nations (adopted 26 June 1945, entered into force 24 October 1945) art 96; Statute of the International Court of Justice (adopted 26 June 1945, entered into force 24 October 1945) arts 34 and 65.

these further restrict recourse to the Court through reservations or procedural preconditions, such as prior recourse to negotiation or other dispute-settlement procedures.[2]

Clearly, these inherent limitations considerably restrict the Court's function and role within the larger scheme of global protection of human rights. However, this does not signify that the Court could not or does not play an important role in this field. As the principal judicial organ of the United Nations, the Court has an inherent responsibility for upholding and implementing the fundamental principles of the Organization, including the promotion and protection of human rights. Moreover, as a court of general subject-matter jurisdiction, the ICJ has the competence to address *any* question of international law brought to it by States and, in certain circumstances, international organizations, including questions relating to or touching upon the rights of individuals. As the Court itself affirmed, '[t]he mere fact that it is not the rights of States which are in issue in the proceedings cannot suffice to deprive the Court of a competence expressly conferred on it by its Statute'.[3]

Indeed, human rights have featured in the Court's jurisprudence since its creation in 1946, and the subsequent evolution and increasing prominence of human rights within the overall context of international relations have been reflected in an upsurge of contentious cases and requests for advisory opinion that directly or indirectly require the Court to handle a wide range of important issues intrinsically relating to human rights. Today, its decisions routinely address such issues and, despite the lack of standing of individuals before the Court and the apparent hesitation of States to bring human rights-related disputes to the Court, the recent case-law of the Court includes a number of decisions that include findings of violations of international human rights law (IHRL) and international humanitarian law (IHL) and bear direct consequences for the fate of individuals. Along the Court's decisions, separate or dissenting opinions of individual judges, some of whom have a strong background in human rights, frequently discuss various issues relating to IHRL and IHL, additionally contributing to the academic and practical human rights discourse at the highest level of international judicial mechanisms. Unsurprisingly, the Court's increased attention to the rights of individuals and engagement in the wider human rights discourse mirrors the rise in the number of judges on the bench who had previously served on at least one international human rights tribunal or mechanism.[4]

[2] For instance, in 2011, such procedural precondition, contained in the Convention on the Elimination of All Forms of Racial Discrimination, precluded the case brought by Georgia against Russia from proceeding to the merits because, in the Court's view, the precondition of prior resort to negotiation had not been fulfilled at the date of Georgia's application. See *Application of the International Convention on the Elimination of All Forms of Racial Discrimination (Georgia v Russian Federation)* (Preliminary Objections) [2011] ICJ Rep 70 (hereafter *Georgia v Russia* (Preliminary Objections)), paras 122–184.

[3] *Application for Review of Judgment No 158 of the United Nations Administrative Tribunal* (Advisory Opinion) [1973] ICJ Rep 16, para 14.

[4] Amongst them the former Judges Rosalyn Higgins, Peter Kooijmans, Thomas Buergenthal, Bruno Simma, and Awn Shawkat Al-Khasawneh, and current Judges Antonio Cançado Trindade, Julia Sebutinde, and Patrick Robinson.

This chapter considers several aspects of the Court's contribution. The first part examines how the Court's jurisprudence contributed to the development of IHRL and IHL, including to the recognition of the relevance and normative status of these two legal regimes within the larger context of international legal order, and to the clarification of their content and scope of application, including by adopting a value-oriented approach to the interpretation of IHRL and IHL instruments, and by recognizing the extra-territorial applicability of human rights treaties and continued applicability of human rights obligations in situations of armed conflict and occupation. Nonetheless, despite its recognition of the special status of fundamental human rights norms, the Court has retained the view that certain prerogatives of State sovereignty, such as the principle of consent to the Court's jurisdiction, and jurisdictional immunities, cannot be displaced even by the most fundamental principles of IHRL and IHL.

The second part considers the Court's direct contribution to the enforcement of IHRL and IHL, both within the traditional framework of State responsibility, as well as through indication of provisional measures for protection of human rights at immediate risk of irreparable damage.

2 The Court's Contribution to the Development of International Human Rights Law and International Humanitarian Law

2.1 The relevance and normative status of human rights principles within the general international legal order

2.1.1 The 'humanization' of international relations

In two of the Court's first advisory opinions, the Court supported the ideas of internationalization of human rights and the civilizing purpose of human rights treaties. Although the issues were incidental to the main questions of treaty interpretation, the mere fact that they were dealt with by the Court helped place them on centre stage.

Thus, in the advisory opinion on the *Interpretation of Peace Treaties*, the Court indicated, albeit implicitly, that human rights were not solely a domestic affair shielded from the eyes and the interest of the outside world.[5] Further, in its advisory opinion concerning *Reservations to the Genocide Convention*, the Court also noted the civilizing purpose of human rights treaties such as the Genocide Convention, emphasizing that States have no interest of their own in such treaties, but adopt the international obligations provided therein in the interest of humanity itself.

[5] *Interpretation of Peace Treaties with Bulgaria, Hungary and Romania* (Advisory Opinion, First Phase) [1950] ICJ Rep 65, 70–71.

2.1.2 *The binding nature of human rights principles under UN Charter and Universal Declaration of Human Rights*

The Court has made valuable pronouncements on the binding nature of human rights clauses of the UN Charter and the Universal Declaration of Human Rights (UDHR).

In the *Namibia* advisory opinion, the Court confirmed the legally binding nature of human rights principles enshrined in the UN Charter, finding that the policy of apartheid as practised by South Africa in Namibia constituted a 'denial of fundamental human rights' and as such 'a flagrant violation of the purposes and principles of the [UN] Charter'.[6]

Furthermore, in the *Tehran Hostages* case, in the context of establishing the responsibility of Iran towards the United States (US) for continued detention of the US diplomatic and consular staff in Tehran, the Court noted that wrongful deprivation of a person's freedom and subjecting to physical constraint in conditions of hardship 'is in itself manifestly incompatible with the principles of the [UN Charter], as well as with the fundamental principles enunciated in the [UDHR]'.[7] While the Court refrained from making an explicit pronouncement of the legal status of the UDHR, the fact that it invoked (*proprio motu*) this instrument in its discussions of State's obligations under general international law implies its understanding that it contains binding international norms.

2.1.3 *The 'special status' of certain fundamental human rights norms*

2.1.3.1 'Elementary considerations of humanity'

In its very first contentious case, the *Corfu Channel* case between the United Kingdom (UK) and Albania, decided in 1949, the Court coined and recognized the relevance and special normative power of a concept that lies at the heart of international human rights law and international humanitarian law. In examining Albania's obligation to notify the existence of a minefield in Albanian territorial waters and warn the approaching British warships of the imminent danger to which the minefield exposed them, the Court emphasized that such an obligation derived from 'certain general and well-recognized principles, namely: *elementary considerations of humanity, even more exacting in peace than in war*' (emphasis added).[8]

Having thus elevated the notion of 'elementary considerations of humanity' to the level of a legal principle, imposing certain obligations upon a State, the Court subsequently invoked it in several other proceedings, specifically, to confirm the applicability of certain basic principles of international humanitarian law to States

[6] *Legal Consequences for States of the Continued Presence of South Africa in Namibia (South West Africa) notwithstanding Security Council Resolution 276* (Advisory Opinion) [1970] ICJ Rep 16 (hereafter *Namibia*), para 131.

[7] *United States Diplomatic and Consular Staff in Tehran (United States of America v Iran)* (Merits) [1980] ICJ Rep 3, para 91.

[8] *Corfu Channel Case (United Kingdom of Great Britain and Northern Ireland v Albania)* (Merits) [1949] ICJ Rep 4 (hereafter *UK v Albania*), 22.

as a matter of customary international law.[9] In other cases, the Court has repeatedly explicitly affirmed that certain fundamental human rights principles form part of customary international law and are thus binding on States even in the absence of an explicit conventional commitment, amongst them the prohibition of genocide[10] and the prohibition of inhuman or degrading treatment.[11]

2.1.3.2 Peremptory norms of general international law (*jus cogens*)

Eventually, the Court has recognized that certain fundamental norms of IHRL and IHL possess the character of peremptory norms of general international law—*jus cogens*. However, the Court was long reluctant to pronounce on the concept of *jus cogens* despite having had several opportunities to do so[12] and has long avoided making any reference thereto even when the concept has been expressly invoked during the proceedings.[13] While the concept has been discussed and supported by several judges in their individual opinions since the times of the Permanent Court of International Justice,[14] the Court itself explicitly recognized its existence in

[9] *Military and Paramilitary Activities in and against Nicaragua* (*Nicaragua v United States of America*) (Merits) [1986] ICJ Rep 14 (hereafter *Nicaragua v USA* (Merits)), para 218; *Legality of the Threat or Use of Nuclear Weapons* (Advisory Opinion) [1996] ICJ Rep 226 (hereafter *Nuclear Weapons*), paras 79, 82; and *Legal Consequences of the Construction of a Wall in the Occupied Palestinian Territory* (Advisory Opinion) [2004] ICJ Rep 136 (hereafter *The Wall*), para 157.

[10] *Reservations to the Convention on the Prevention and Punishment of the Crime of Genocide* (Advisory Opinion) [1951] ICJ Rep 15 (hereafter *Reservations to the Genocide Convention*), 23; see also *Application of the Convention on the Prevention and Punishment of the Crime of Genocide (Bosnia and Herzegovina v Yugoslavia)* (Preliminary Objections) [1996] ICJ Rep 595 (hereafter *Bosnia and Herzegovina v Yugoslavia* (Preliminary Objections)), para 31; *Armed Activities on the Territory of the Congo (New Application: 2002) (Democratic Republic of the Congo v Rwanda)* (Jurisdiction and Admissibility) [2002] ICJ Rep 6 (hereafter *Congo v Rwanda* (Jurisdiction and Admissibility)), para 64; *Application of the Convention on the Prevention and Punishment of the Crime of Genocide (Bosnia and Herzegovina v Serbia and Montenegro)* (Merits) [2007] ICJ Rep 43 (hereafter *Bosnia and Herzegovina v Serbia and Montenegro* (Merits)), para 161.

[11] The Court stated this in an *obiter dictum* in *Ahmadou Sadio Diallo (Republic of Guinea v Democratic Republic of the Congo)* (Merits) [2010] ICJ Reports 639 (hereafter *Guinea v Congo* (Merits)), para 87.

[12] Eg *North Sea Continental Shelf (Federal Republic of Germany/Denmark; Federal Republic of Germany/Netherlands)* (Judgment) [1969] ICJ Rep 3, para 72; *Nuclear Weapons* (n 9), paras 79–83; *Arrest Warrant of 11 April 2000 (Democratic Republic of the Congo v Belgium)* (Judgment) [2002] ICJ Rep 3 (hereafter *Congo v Belgium*), 23–26.

[13] In the advisory opinion on *Nuclear Weapons*, the Court noted that 'it has been maintained in these proceedings that [the fundamental] principles and rules of humanitarian law [were] part of *jus cogens* as defined in Article 53 of the Vienna Convention on the Law of Treaties'; however, as the Court viewed the question before as limited to the *applicability* of these norms as a matter of customary international law, rather than to their *legal character*, it considered it unnecessary to pronounce on this proposition (*Nuclear Weapons* (n 9), para 83; by contrast, Judge Weeramantry in his dissenting opinion, stated categorically that the rules of IHL have acquired a *jus cogens* status (ibid, Dissenting Opinion of Judge Weeramantry, 496)). Nevertheless, an evolving acceptance by the Court of the notion of peremptory norms might be reflected in the Court's reference to the fundamental rules of international humanitarian law as 'intransgressible principles of international customary law' (ibid, para 79).

[14] One of the earliest uses of the term *jus cogens* was made by Judge Schücking in his Separate Opinion in the Oscar Chinn case decided by the PCIJ in 1934 (*Oscar Chinn (Britain v Belgium)* (Judgment) [1934] PCIJ Rep Series A/B No 17, 149). In the jurisprudence of the ICJ, see the individual opinions of, inter alia, Judge Tanaka (*South West Africa* cases *(Ethiopia v South Africa; Liberia v South Africa)* (Second Phase) [1966] ICJ Rep 6 (hereafter *South West Africa*), Dissenting Opinion of Judge Tanaka, 298), Judge Ammoun (*Barcelona Traction, Light and Power Company, Limited (Belgium v Spain)* (Second Phase) [1970] ICJ Rep 3 (hereafter *Belgium v Spain*), Separate Opinion of Judge Ammoun, 304 and

positive international law only in 2006, in its judgment on the preliminary objections in the *Armed Activities* case between Congo and Rwanda, where it confirmed that the prohibition of genocide is 'assuredly' a *jus cogens* norm.[15] Six years later, in the *Jurisdictional Immunities* case, the Court considered that this category of norms, 'from which no derogation is permitted'[16] includes the rules of international humanitarian law 'which prohibit the murder of civilians in occupied territory, the deportation of civilian inhabitants to slave labour and the deportation of prisoners of war to slave labour'.[17] The Court also confirmed in more general terms that the rules relating to the violations of international human rights and humanitarian law amounting to crimes against humanity and war crimes, 'undoubtedly possess the character of *jus cogens*'.[18] Finally, in the case concerning the *Obligation to Prosecute or Extradite*, the Court specifically stated in an *obiter dictum* that the prohibition of torture 'has become a peremptory norm (*jus cogens*)'.[19] Along these pronouncements of the Court, a number of Judges in their individual opinions ascribed the status of *jus cogens* norms to, inter alia: (i) norms concerning human rights protection in general;[20] (ii) the right to self-determination;[21] (iii) the prohibition of torture;[22] (iv) the prohibition of ethnic cleansing, summary or extra-legal executions, and forced disappearance of persons;[23] (v) the principle of equality and non-discrimination;[24] and (vi) the 'principles of humanity' and 'dictates of the public conscience' invoked by the Martens clause.[25]

311–312), Judge Al-Khasawneh (*Congo v Belgium* (n 12), Dissenting opinion of Judge Al-Khasawneh, para 7), Judge Cançado Trindade (eg, *Questions relating to the Obligation to Prosecute or Extradite (Belgium v Senegal)* (Provisional Measures) [2009] ICJ Rep 139 (hereafter *Belgium v Senegal* (Provisional Measures)), Dissenting Opinion of Judge Cançado Trindade, para 66; *Accordance with International Law of the Unilateral Declaration of Independence in Respect of Kosovo* (Advisory Opinion) [2010] ICJ Rep 403 (hereafter *Kosovo*), Separate Opinion of Judge Cançado Trindade, para 215; *Guinea v Congo* (Merits) (n 11), Separate Opinion of Judge Cançado Trindade, para 163; *Jurisdictional Immunities of the State (Germany v Italy)* (Merits) [2012] ICJ Rep 99 (hereafter *Germany v Italy* (Merits)), Dissenting Opinion of Judge Cançado Trindade).

[15] *Congo v Rwanda* (Jurisdiction and Admissibility) (n 10), para 64. Subsequently, the Court has reaffirmed the *jus cogens* status of the prohibition of genocide in the two *Genocide* cases (*Bosnia and Herzegovina v Serbia and Montenegro* (Merits) (n 10), para 161; *Application of the Convention on the Prevention and Punishment of the Crime of Genocide (Croatia v Serbia)* (Judgment of 3 February 2015) (hereafter *Croatia v Serbia*), paras 87, 161).

[16] *Germany v Italy* (Merits) (n 14), para 95.

[17] ibid, para 93.

[18] ibid, para 95.

[19] *Congo v Belgium* (n 12), para 99.

[20] *South West Africa* (n 14), Dissenting Opinion of Judge Tanaka, 298.

[21] *Namibia* (n 6), Separate Opinion of Vice-President Ammoun, 89–90.

[22] *Belgium v Senegal* (Provisional Measures) (n 14), Dissenting Opinion of Judge Cançado Trindade, para 66; *Kosovo* (n 14), Separate Opinion of Judge Cançado Trindade, para 215.

[23] *Kosovo* (n 14), Separate Opinion of Judge Cançado Trindade, para 215.

[24] *Guinea v Congo* (Merits) (n 11), Separate Opinion of Judge Cançado Trindade, para 163; *Jurisdictional Immunities of the State (Germany v Italy)* (Counter-Claim) [2010] ICJ Rep 310 (hereafter *Germany v Italy* (Counter-Claim)), Dissenting Opinion of Judge Cançado Trindade, para 135.

[25] *Germany v Italy* (Counter-Claim) (n 24), Dissenting Opinion of Judge Cançado Trindade, para 139.

2.1.3.3 Obligations *erga omnes*

While the Court has been slow in recognizing the existence of *jus cogens* norms in positive international law, it has, by contrast, coined and developed another fundamental concept that has had a significant fortifying effect on the normative status of international human rights in the overall international legal order.[26]

In a celebrated *obiter dictum* in its 1970 judgment in the *Barcelona Traction* case, the Court identified a special category of international obligations *erga omnes*, which are, in contrast to the purely reciprocal contractual obligations, owed 'to the international community as a whole' and are '[b]y the very nature ... the concern of all States'.[27] In this and subsequent cases, the Court has gradually confirmed that this category of norms includes obligations deriving from, inter alia: (i) the outlawing of acts of aggression;[28] (ii) the outlawing of genocide;[29] (iii) the prohibition of torture;[30] (iv) the principles and rules concerning the basic rights of the human person, including protection from slavery and racial discrimination;[31] (v) the right to self-determination;[32] and (vi) certain fundamental principles of international humanitarian law.[33] The Court added that '[s]ome of the corresponding rights of protection have entered into the body of general international law' while 'others are conferred by international instruments of a universal or quasi-universal character'.[34] By recognizing that certain fundamental norms of IHRL and IHL engender obligations *erga omnes*, the Court reiterated that these norms must be respected by all States, thereby dispelling any remaining doubts that the protection of basic human rights is a matter of common concern of the international community as a whole, rather than just a matter of the domestic affairs of States.

The Court's dictum in *Barcelona Traction*, which has been acquiring increasing influence ever since, also enhanced the enforceability of these fundamental principles of IHRL and IHL, by recognizing the special consequences flowing from violations of *erga omnes* obligations in terms of the invocation of State responsibility. Since these obligations are 'the concern of all States', they may be, '[i]n view of the importance of the rights involved', invoked within the framework of State responsibility by any State.[35] This pronouncement was directly incorporated into the 2001 International Law Commission Draft Articles of State responsibility, containing a

[26] For a further discussion of the effect of the *Barcelona Traction* case on the evolution of the *erga omnes* concept, see, eg, Christian J Tams and Antonios Tzanakopoulos, 'Barcelona Traction at 40: the ICJ as an Agent of Legal Development' (2010) 23 LJIL 781, 791–94; Maurizio Ragazzi, *The Concept of International Obligations Erga Omnes* (Oxford University Press 2000).

[27] *Belgium v Spain* (n 14), para 33.

[28] ibid, para 34.

[29] ibid, para 34; *Bosnia and Herzegovina v Yugoslavia* (Preliminary Objections) (n 10), para 31; *Congo v Rwanda* (Jurisdiction and Admissibility) (n 10), para 64; *Croatia v Serbia* (n 15), para 87.

[30] *Questions relating to the Obligation to Prosecute or Extradite (Belgium v Senegal)* (Merits) [2012] ICJ Rep 422 (hereafter *Belgium v Senegal* (Merits)), paras 68–69, 103.

[31] *Belgium v Spain* (n 14), para 34.

[32] East Timor *(Portugal v Australia)* (Judgment) [1995] ICJ Rep 90 (hereafter *Portugal v Australia*), para 29; *The Wall* (n 9), paras 155–156.

[33] *The Wall* (n 9), paras 155–157.

[34] *Belgium v Spain* (n 14), para 34.

[35] ibid. The Court's pronouncement found expression in Article 48 of the International Law Commission's Draft Articles on the Responsibility of States for Internationally Wrongful Acts (2001) which allows for the invocation of responsibility by a State other than an injured State.

special set of rules for invocation of responsibility by State other than an injured State.[36] In 2012, the Court for the first time utilized this principle in the case concerning the *Obligation to Prosecute or Extradite* between Belgium and Senegal. The Court allowed Belgium (as a non-injured party) to proceed with its claims under the Torture Convention, noting that any State party to the Convention would have the right to invoke responsibility of another State party in view of the *erga omnes partes* character of the relevant rules under the Convention.[37] This development is particularly important for increasing enforceability of international human rights law, as States frequently violate human rights of their own nationals, leaving no 'injured' State to bring a claim under the traditional rules.

2.1.3.4 Limitations of the effect of the 'special status' norms on the principle of State sovereignty

Despite the growing recognition of the value of human rights and the limitations they place upon the principle of State sovereignty, the Court has retained the position that certain prerogatives of State sovereignty cannot be displaced even by the most fundamental principles of IHRL and IHL.

In particular, the Court has consistently reiterated that the substantive rules of *erga omnes* and the rules of *jus cogens* have no effect on the procedural rules determining the scope and the extent of the Court's jurisdiction and the conditions for the exercise of that jurisdiction. In the *East Timor* case, the Court, considering that 'the erga omnes character of a norm and the rule of consent to jurisdiction are two different things', held that 'when its judgment would imply an evaluation of the lawfulness of the conduct of another State which is not a party to the case' it could not act 'even if the right in question [was] a right *erga omnes*'.[38] In more general terms, the Court affirmed that 'the mere fact that rights and obligations *erga omnes* or peremptory norms of general international law (*jus cogens*) are at issue in a dispute cannot in itself constitute an exception to the principle that its jurisdiction always depends on the consent of the parties'.[39] According to the Court, no peremptory norm requires States to consent to jurisdiction where the compliance with a peremptory norm is at stake.[40]

A similar line of reasoning based on the dichotomy between the substantive rules and the procedural rules was adopted in a series of cases dealing with the question of State immunity. In the *Arrest Warrant* case, the Court held that incumbent Foreign Ministers (and by implication other high-level State officials) enjoy absolute immunity from criminal jurisdiction in a foreign State, even when charged with

[36] Art 48 of the Draft Articles on the Responsibility of States for Internationally Wrongful Acts, *Yearbook of the International Law Commission* [2001], vol II, Part Two.

[37] *Belgium v Senegal* (Merits) (n 30), paras 67–70.

[38] *Portugal v Australia* (n 32), para 29.

[39] *Congo v Rwanda* (Jurisdiction and Admissibility) (n 10), para 125; *Armed Activities on the Territory of the Congo (New Application: 2002) (Democratic Republic of the Congo v Rwanda)* (Provisional Measures) [2002] ICJ Rep 219 (hereafter *Congo v Rwanda* (Provisional Measures)), para 71. See also *Croatia v Serbia* (n 15), paras 147–148.

[40] *Congo v Rwanda* (Jurisdiction and Admissibility) (n 10), para 69; see also para 78.

a war crime or a crime against humanity,[41] which, as the Court affirmed in the *Jurisdictional Immunities*, undoubtedly possessed the character of *jus cogens*.[42] In a much-criticized[43] *obiter dictum*, the Court affirmed that this immunity continues to apply to Foreign Ministers even after they have left the office, in respect of those acts committed in an 'official capacity' as opposed to those committed 'in a private capacity'.[44] Several judges have disagreed with the Court's passing comment that 'immunity does not mean impunity' and advocated for the denial of immunity for core international crimes in pursuit of greater personal accountability and the fight against impunity.[45]

Similarly, in the *Jurisdictional Immunities* case, the Court concluded that the *jus cogens* status of the substantive rule which the State is alleged to have violated does not deprive it of its customary law entitlement to immunity from the jurisdiction of the courts of other States.[46] In other words, even though the application of a particular jurisdictional rule might operate so as to render unavailable certain procedural means by which a *jus cogens* rule could be enforced, this does not alter the applicability of the rules pertaining to the international responsibility of the State or its officials for any violation.[47] In supporting this conclusion, the Court referred to the relevant domestic and international law and practice, inter alia, to the decisions of the European Court of Human Rights (ECtHR) in *Al-Adsani v United Kingdom* and *Kalogeropoulou and others v Greece and Germany*, which likewise considered that the *jus cogens* status of a norm does not displace the State's jurisdictional immunity in foreign courts.[48]

[41] *Congo v Belgium* (n 12), para 58.

[42] *Germany v Italy* (Merits) (n 14), para 95, referring to *Congo v Belgium* (n 12), para 58.

[43] See, eg, Antonio Cassese, 'When May Senior State Officials Be Tried for International Crimes? Some Comments on the *Congo* v. *Belgium* Case' (2002) 13 EJIL 853.

[44] *Congo v Belgium* (n 12), para 61.

[45] ibid, Dissenting Opinion of Judge Al-Khasawneh, para 7; see also Dissenting Opinion of Judge ad hoc van den Wyngaert, paras 24–28. See further, Alexander Orakhelashvili, 'State Immunity and International Public Order Revisited' (2006) 49 GYIL 327, particularly 353–63; Lee M Caplan, 'State Immunity, Human Rights, and *Jus Cogens*: A Critique of the Normative Hierarchy Theory' (2003) 97 AJIL 741.

[46] Although the Court explained that its pronouncement in *Germany v Italy* relates only to the immunity of the State itself and not to the separate issue of the immunity of State officials in criminal proceedings in foreign courts (*Germany v Italy* (Merits) (n 14), para 91), its decision in *Congo v Belgium* reveals nonetheless that the Court holds the same position at least in respect of the individual criminal responsibility of high-level State officials.

[47] *Germany v Italy* (Merits) (n 14), paras 93–95 and 100; see also, in the context of the immunity of State officials from criminal jurisdiction foreign courts, *Congo v Belgium* (n 12), para 60; *Certain Questions of Mutual Assistance in Criminal Matters (Djibouti v France)* (Judgment) [2008] ICJ Rep 177, para 196.

[48] *Germany v Italy* (Merits) (n 14), para 90, citing *Al-Adsani v United Kingdom*, App no 35763/97, 21 November 2001, and *Kalogeropoulou and others v Greece and Germany*, App no 59021/00, 12 December 2002.

2.2 The special approach to the interpretation of human rights treaties

As only States have standing before the ICJ, the Court's approach to interpretation of international human rights treaties has significant implications for the level of protection accruing to individuals under these treaties. Three aspects of the Court's handling of interpretation of human rights treaties are of particular significance, namely its emphasis of their distinctive 'object and purpose', the evolutionary interpretation, and the necessity of coherent interpretation of human rights treaties across the network of judicial and quasi-judicial bodies dealing with human rights.

2.2.1 The value-oriented interpretation of human rights treaties

In its advisory opinion concerning the *Reservations to the Genocide Convention*, the Court considered that the object and purpose of the Convention, which was 'manifestly adopted for a purely humanitarian and civilizing purpose', would be the crucial criterion limiting both the freedom of States to make reservations to the Convention as well as their freedom to object to them.[49] This specific test for validity of treaty reservations was subsequently included in article 19, paragraph 3, of the Vienna Convention on the Law of Treaties (VCLT),[50] and is today widely considered as reflecting customary international law. In addition, the emphasis of the 'object and purpose' has found expression in the general rules and methods of interpretation articulated in the VCLT, which provides, in article 31, paragraph 1, that '[a] treaty shall be interpreted in good faith in accordance with the ordinary meaning to be given to the terms of the treaty in their context and in the light of its object and purpose'.

The Court further elaborated the rationale a value-oriented approach to the interpretation of human rights treaties such as the Genocide Convention, by stating that 'in this type of treaty, the contracting States do not have their own interests; they only have an overall common interest: to attain the purposes that are the *raison d'etre* of the Convention'.[51] Regional human rights courts have likewise endorsed this approach and have repeatedly affirmed that the reference to the object and purpose of a treaty assumes a particular importance in the interpretation of human rights treaties establishing obligations aimed at protection of human rights, and not subjective and reciprocal rights for States parties.[52]

[49] *Reservations to the Genocide Convention* (n 1), 23–24.

[50] Vienna Convention on the Law of Treaties (opened for signature 23 May 1969, entered into force 27 January 1980) 1155 UNTS 331.

[51] *Reservations to the Genocide Convention* (n 10), 23. See also *Croatia v Serbia*, where the Court again emphasized the relevance of 'the purely humanitarian and civilizing purpose of the Convention' in interpreting the obligations of States under the Convention (*Croatia v Serbia* (n 15), para 162), and reaffirmed that, in light of that purpose, the obligation on States to prevent genocide, expressed in Article 1 of the Convention, 'necessarily implies' a prohibition to *commit* genocide (ibid, para 166).

[52] *Restrictions to the Death Penalty (Arts 4(2) and 4(4) of the American Convention on Human Rights)*, IACtHR, Ser A No 3, OC-3/83 (1983) (Advisory Opinion), para 50; *Soering v United Kingdom*, App no 14038/88, 7 July 1989, para 87; *Baena Ricardo et al (270 workers) v Panama*, IACtHR, Ser C No 104 (2003) (Competence), para 97; *Caesar v Trinidad and Tobago*, IACtHR, Ser C No. 123 (2005) (Merits, Reparations, and Costs), Separate Opinion of Judge Cançado Trindade, paras 4–14.

2.2.2 *The dynamic interpretation of human rights treaties*

While the Court's approach to interpretation of treaties generally emphasizes the meaning that existed at the time of the adoption of a treaty (the common intention of the drafters),[53] it has normally adopted the opposite—evolutionary (dynamic) approach—to interpretation in respect of treaties directly or indirectly concerning human rights.[54]

As the Court confirmed in the *Namibia* advisory opinion, a treaty should be interpreted 'within the framework of the entire legal system prevailing at the time of the interpretation',[55] thus taking into account the developments in IHRL and IHL subsequent to the adoption of the treaties in question. This approach is followed also by the ECtHR and the Inter-American Court of Human Rights (IACtHR), both of which have expressly relied upon the Court's finding in *Namibia* in observing that evolutionary interpretation is particularly relevant in respect of human rights treaties.[56]

2.2.3 *Promoting coherent interpretation of human rights treaties*

The Court has been increasingly expressly referring to the legal and factual pronouncements of regional human rights courts, international criminal tribunals, and treaty-monitoring mechanisms, operating in the fields of international human rights law and international humanitarian law.

Of particular relevance for the question of interpretation of human rights treaties is the Court's explicit acknowledgement, in the *Diallo* case, of the considerable weight of the interpretative jurisprudence of other jurisdictions and its emphasis of the need for coherent interpretation of human rights treaties with the aim of securing 'the necessary clarity and the essential consistency of international law, as well as legal security' in this field. Relying on the jurisprudence of the Human Rights Committee (HRC) for its own interpretation of the provision of the International Covenant on Civil and Political Rights (ICCPR) concerning the prohibition of arbitrary expulsion of aliens in the *Diallo* case, the Court explained:

Although the Court is in no way obliged, in the exercise of its judicial functions, to model its own interpretation of the Covenant on that of the Committee, it believes that it should ascribe great weight to the interpretation adopted by this independent body that was established specifically to supervise the application of that treaty. The point here is to achieve the

[53] See, eg, *South West Africa* (n 14) para 16; Rights of Nationals of the United States of America in Morocco *(France v United States of America)* (Judgment) [1952] ICJ Rep 176, p 197. For one considerable exception to the inter-temporal interpretation of non-human rights treaties by the ICJ, see *Dispute Regarding Navigational and Related Rights (Costa Rica v Nicaragua)* (Judgment) [2008] ICJ Rep 213, paras 63–64, 66–68, and 70–71.

[54] Reflected to a considerable extent in Article 31(3)(c) of the VCLT.

[55] *Namibia* (n 6), para 53.

[56] *Interpretation of the American Declaration of the Rights and Duties of Man Within the Framework of Article 64 of the American Convention on Human Rights* (Advisory Opinion), IACtHR, OC-10/89, para 37; *Tyrer v the United Kingdom*, App no 5856/72, April 1978, para 31; *Loizidou v Turkey* (Preliminary Objections), App no 15318/89, March 1995, para 71.

necessary clarity and the essential consistency of international law, as well as legal security, to which both the individuals with guaranteed rights and the States obliged to comply with treaty obligations are entitled.[57]

The Court further observed that

> when [it] is called upon . . . to apply a regional instrument for the protection of human rights, it must take due account of the interpretation of that instrument adopted by the independent bodies which have been specifically created, if such has been the case, to monitor the sound application of the treaty in question.[58]

In addition, the Court cited the jurisprudence of the African Commission on Human and Peoples' Rights (AComHPR) as supportive of its own interpretation of article 12(4) of the African Charter on Human and Peoples' Rights (ACHPR) but did not stop there—it also found support in the jurisprudence of the ECtHR and the IACtHR interpreting similar provisions of the European Convention on Human Rights and the American Convention on Human Rights concerning the expulsion of aliens.[59]

Similarly, in the two *Genocide* cases the Court has relied on the findings of the International Criminal Tribunal for the Former Yugoslavia and the International Criminal Tribunal for Rwanda in interpreting the substantive provisions of the Genocide Convention.[60]

2.3 Clarifying the scope of application of human rights treaties

The Court's recent case law has also importantly clarified the scope of application of human rights instruments, confirming that human rights treaties may apply extra-territorially[61] and that they continue to apply in times of armed conflict and in the context of occupation. These pronouncements indicate that the Court handles its cases in full consciousness of the changing international security environment.

2.3.1 Extra-territorial application of human rights treaties

In its 2004 advisory opinion on *The Legal Consequences of the Construction of a Wall in the Occupied Palestinian Territory*, the Court confirmed that, specifically, the ICCPR, the International Covenant on Economic, Social and Cultural Rights (ICESCR), and the Convention on the Rights of the Child were applicable within the Occupied Palestinian Territory.[62] Specifically with regard to the ICCPR, the

[57] *Guinea v Congo* (Merits) (n 11), para 66; see also para 77.
[58] ibid, para 67.
[59] ibid, para 68.
[60] *Bosnia and Herzegovina v Serbia and Montenegro* (Merits) (n 10), paras 188, 190, 195, 198–201, 300, and 358; *Croatia v Serbia* (n 15), paras 142, 156–158, 161, 164, 188, 190, 195, and 197–201.
[61] For a detailed discussion of the Court's treatment of the question of extra-territorial applicability of human rights instruments see, eg, Ralph Wilde, 'Human Rights Beyond Borders at the World Court: The Significance of the International Court of Justice's Jurisprudence on the Extraterritorial Application of International Human Rights Law Treaties' (2013) 12 Chinese Journal of International Law 639.
[62] *The Wall* (n 9), paras 107–114.

Court considered it 'natural', in light of its 'object and purpose', that it was 'applicable in respect of acts done by a State in the exercise of its jurisdiction outside its own territory'.[63] The Court also noted that this position was consistent with the practice of the HRC.[64] In a similar vein, when determining the applicability of the ICESCR to the Occupied Palestinian Territory, the Court noted the views of the Committee on Economic, Social and Cultural Rights, that the obligations of States parties arising under the ICESCR apply to all territories and populations under its effective control.[65] A year later, in the *Armed Activities* case between Congo and Uganda, the Court affirmed this view in more general terms, stating that 'international human rights instruments are applicable "in respect of acts done by a State in the exercise of its jurisdiction outside its own territory"'.[66]

More recently, in its order indicating the provisional measures in the case concerning the *Elimination of all Forms of Racial Discrimination*, the Court, finding that the Convention on the Elimination of all Forms of Racial Discrimination contains 'no restriction of a general nature ... relating to its territorial application', confirmed that the provision of articles 2 and 5, which were at issue, are generally applicable, '*like other provisions of instruments of that nature*', to the actions of a State party outside its territory.[67] Similarly, in the *Croatia Genocide* case, the Court specifically clarified that '[t]he substantive obligations arising from Articles I and III' of the Genocide Convention 'are not on their face limited by territory' but rather, '[t]hey apply to a State wherever it may be acting or may be able to act in ways appropriate to meeting the obligations in question'.[68]

2.3.2 Application of human rights treaties in situations of armed conflict

Already in 1996, in its advisory opinion on *Nuclear Weapons*, the Court confirmed that 'the protection of the [ICCPR] does not cease in times of war, except by operation of Article 4 of the [ICCPR] whereby certain provisions may be derogated from in a time of national emergency'.[69] In the *Wall* advisory opinion and the *Armed Activities* case between Congo and Uganda, the Court expanded this conclusion to human rights treaties in general, stating that 'the protection offered by human rights conventions does not cease in case of armed conflict, save through the effect of the provisions for derogation of the kind to be found in Article 4 of the [ICCPR]'.[70]

Thus, the Court confirmed that in the context of armed conflict, the IHRL applies concurrently with IHL—the two regimes complement each other. Nevertheless, in case of a normative conflict between the two, the latter sets aside whatever standards

[63] ibid, paras 109 and 111. [64] ibid, para 109. [65] ibid, para 112.

[66] *Armed Activities on the Territory of the Congo (Democratic Republic of the Congo v Uganda)* (Merits) [2005] ICJ Rep 168 (hereafter *Congo v Uganda* (Merits)), para 216. These findings were extensively cited by the ECtHR in *Al-Skeini and Others v the United Kingdom*, App no 55721/07, 7 July 2011 (hereafter *Al-Skeini and Others v UK*), para 90.

[67] *Application of the International Convention on the Elimination of All Forms of Racial Discrimination (Georgia v Russia)* (Provisional Measures) [2008] ICJ Rep 353, paras 108–109 (emphasis added).

[68] *Croatia v Serbia* (n 15), para 183. [69] *Nuclear Weapons* (n 9), para 25.

[70] *The Wall* (n 9), para 106.

might have been provided under the former. In the *Nuclear Weapons* case, the Court explained this relationship in the specific context of discussion of the right of life, stating that the test in interpretation of human rights provisions in armed conflict is IHL as *lex specialis*:

> In principle, the right not arbitrarily to be deprived of one's life applies also in hostilities. The test of what is an arbitrary deprivation of life, however, then falls to be determined by the applicable *lex specialis*, namely, the law applicable in armed conflict which is designed to regulate the conduct of hostilities [and not by the terms of the Covenant itself].[71]

In more general terms, the Court later affirmed this position in the *Wall* advisory opinion and in the *Armed Activities* case, stating that:

> [S]ome rights may be exclusively matters of international humanitarian law; others may be exclusively matters of human rights law; yet others may be matters of both these branches of international law. In order to answer the question put to it, the Court will have to take into consideration both these branches of international law, namely human rights law and, as *lex specialis*, international humanitarian law.[72]

3 The Court's Contribution to the Enforcement of Human Rights

Apart from its contribution to the development of international human rights and international humanitarian law, the role of the ICJ in the global institutional framework for the enforcement of these two branches of international law is an important additional pillar for the invocation of State responsibility in this field.

As already noted, human rights instruments focus on individual complaint procedures. In the realm of State enforcement, they primarily provide for non-binding monitoring and reporting procedures; while some provide also for judicial mechanisms of State enforcement (either arbitration or ICJ), many of the jurisdictional clauses in human rights instruments contain reservations and/or procedural preconditions that considerably restrict the path to a legally binding judicial decision on the inter-State level. However, this enforcement gap can be reduced, at least doctrinally and technically, where it is possible, in the absence of conventionally envisaged inter-State judicial procedures, to fall back on the rules of general international law concerning State responsibility, in combination with the compulsory jurisdiction of the Court on the basis of article 36(2) of its Statute.[73] In addition, invocation of

[71] *Nuclear Weapons* (n 9), para 25.

[72] ibid; see also, subsequently, *Congo v Uganda* (Merits) (n 66), para 216. These findings were directly relied upon by the ECtHR in *Al-Skeini and Others v UK* (n 66), para 90.

[73] As was the case in the *Congo v Uganda* case. Notably, the ICJ has repeatedly confirmed the applicability of the general rules on State responsibility in the context of human rights violations by applying a number of these rules (including those concerning the right to invoke responsibility, attribution of conduct, circumstances precluding wrongfulness, succession to State responsibility, and remedies) in various human rights-related cases (where the relevant human rights treaty would not expressly contain regime-specific secondary rules) and by expressly discussing the relationship between general rules on State responsibility and rules of IHL/IHRL (see, particularly, *Bosnia and Herzegovina v Serbia and Montenegro* (Merits) (n 10), para 149; *Croatia v Serbia* (n 15), paras 114–115, 128–129).

State responsibility for human rights violation through advisory proceedings, and indication of provisional measures, provide innovative additional tools for enforcement of human rights.

3.1 Determining State responsibility and appropriate remedies for human rights violations

Whilst the majority of claims of human rights violations brought to the Court are framed in the traditional language of inter-State claims, applications were occasionally submitted within the framework of diplomatic protection on behalf of one or more individuals to be protected and were both formulated by the applicant State and handled by the Court in terms of the direct rights of the individual.[74] Remarkably, the Court has confirmed in this context that the fact that an individual lacks the capacity to independently seek redress for human rights violations does not mean that the rights in question are vested solely in the subject that has the capacity to enforce them. The Court has also confirmed that violations of human rights create an obligation on the part of the wrong-doing State to provide 'full reparation', including monetary compensation, to States *and/or individuals* for damage flowing from such violations,[75] and that, crucially, such reparation, whether claimed by the State for its own damage, or on behalf of an individual in the framework of diplomatic protection, ultimately accrues to the benefit of the injured individual(s).[76]

In the *LaGrand* and *Avena* cases concerning consular protection, the Court recognized that the obligations under article 36, paragraph 1, of the Vienna Convention on Consular Relations (VCCR) created individual rights for the detained person, which may be invoked in the Court by the national State of that person,[77] and that, consequently, the reference to 'rights' in article 36, paragraph 2, of the VCCR must be read as applying not only to the rights of the sending State, 'but also to the rights of the detained individual'.[78] Accordingly, in the *LaGrand* case, the Court held that by failing to inform the LaGrand brothers of their rights under article 36 of

[74] *Vienna Convention on Consular Relations (Paraguay v United States of America)* (Provisional Measures Order) [1998] ICJ Rep 248; *LaGrand* (*Germany v United States of America*) (Merits) [2001] ICJ Rep 466 (hereafter *Germany v USA* (Merits)); *Avena and Other Mexican Nationals (Mexico v United States of America)* (Merits) [2007] ICJ Rep 12 (hereafter *Mexico v USA* (Merits)); *Guinea v Congo* (Merits) (n 10). The Court has also stated that the scope of diplomatic protection in respect of natural persons included, inter alia, 'internationally guaranteed human rights' (*Ahmadou Sadio Diallo (Republic of Guinea v Democratic Republic of the Congo)* (Preliminary Objections) [2007] ICJ Rep 582 (hereafter *Guinea v Congo* (Preliminary Objections)), para 39).

[75] The principle of full reparation was first set out by the Permanent Court of International Justice in the *Factory at Chorzów* case (*Case Concerning the Factory at Chorzów (Germany v Poland)* (Merits) [1928] PCIJ Rep Series A No 17, 47) and has been consistently reaffirmed by the ICJ, most recently in the *Diallo* case (*Guinea v Congo* (Merits) (n 11), para 161). For a more detailed discussion, see, eg, Gentian Zyberi, 'The International Court of Justice and applied forms of reparation for international human rights and humanitarian law violations' (2011) 7 Utrecht Law Review 204.

[76] See, eg, *Ahmadou Sadio Diallo (Republic of Guinea v Democratic Republic of the Congo)* (Compensation owed by the Democratic Republic of the Congo to the Republic of Guinea) [2012] ICJ Rep 324 (hereafter *Guinea v Congo* (Compensation)), para 57.

[77] *Germany v USA* (Merits) (n 74), para 77; *Mexico v USA* (Merits) (n 74), paras 40 and 140.

[78] *Germany v USA* (Merits) (n 74), para 89.

the VCCR, the US had violated its obligations under this provision with regard to Germany *and* with regard to the brothers.[79]

Human rights violations have also been extensively discussed in the Court's 2004 advisory opinion on The Legal Consequences of the Construction of a Wall in the Occupied Palestinian Territory. The Court found, among other things, that Israel had violated provisions of several human rights instruments and its obligation to respect the right of the Palestinian people to self-determination, alongside the various violations of international humanitarian law.[80] According to the Court, Israel was under an obligation to compensate the injured persons directly, for the damage suffered.[81]

Similarly, the Court established human rights violations by the respondent State in the Armed Activities case between the Congo and Uganda, in 2005.[82] The Court held that reparations were due by Uganda to the Congo for all damages caused by Uganda's violations of its conventional and customary international obligations under international human rights law and international humanitarian law, including those that resulted in injury 'to persons on [the Congolese] territory'.[83]

In the *Bosnia Genocide* case two years later, the Court confirmed that genocide was committed in Srebrenica in 1995[84] and that Serbia had violated its obligation under the Genocide Convention to prevent and punish genocide.[85] While in its second *Genocide* case (*Croatia v Serbia*), decided in February 2015, the Court was unable to find, on the basis of evidence before it, that genocide was committed by either Croatia or Serbia, the focus on genocide should not lead down a path whereby crimes against humanity or war crimes come to be perceived as somewhat 'insignificant'. The Court's detailed analysis of the alleged crimes contributes to the recognition of the scale and gravity of the atrocities committed in the context of the conflict.

Some remarkable developments in the Court's handling of human rights issues were made in the case concerning *Ahmadou Sadio Diallo*, brought by Guinea against Congo in the context of diplomatic protection 'on behalf of Mr Diallo', alleging violations by Congo of both international economic law and human rights law as a result of his arrest, detention and eventual expulsion from Congo. While the focus of Guinea's application was initially on the former, the balance shifted heavily towards the human rights claims after the Court in 2007 declined jurisdiction over the key claims concerning violations in respect of Mr Diallo's companies and their shareholders. In its 2010 Judgment on the merits, the Court found that Congo had violated the prohibitions on arbitrary arrest, detention, and expulsion under the ICCPR and the ACHPR, as well as Mr Diallo's right to consular notification under the VCCR, and held that Congo was consequently under an obligation to pay to Guinea compensation for the damage caused by these violations.[86]

[79] ibid, para 128(3)–(4).

[80] *The Wall* (n 9), paras 120, 122, 132, 134.

[81] ibid, para 153.

[82] *Congo v Uganda* (Merits) (n 66), paras 219 and 345(3).

[83] ibid, para 259.

[84] *Bosnia and Herzegovina v Serbia and Montenegro* (Merits) (n 10), para 297.

[85] ibid, paras 450 and 471(5)–(6). A remarkable feature of this judgment was the Court's pronouncement that Article I of the Genocide Convention included not only the obligation of states parties to prevent and punish genocide, but also their obligation themselves not to commit an act of genocide.

[86] *Guinea v Congo* (Merits) (n 11), operative para 165.

Following a failure of the Parties to reach a settlement regarding compensation, the Court was subsequently asked to determine the amount of compensation for human rights violations for the first time in history. Lacking experience in this regard, the Court relied heavily on the practice of other international courts and treaty-monitoring mechanisms, including the ECtHR, the IACtHR, the HRC, and the AComHPR,[87] and determined that Congo must pay 85,000 USD for material and non-material injury suffered by Mr Diallo as a result of the established violations.[88] In line with the practice of these tribunals, the Court also affirmed that non-material injury is 'an inevitable consequence' of human rights violations such as those at stake in this case, and that such injury can thus be established even without specific evidence;[89] accordingly, the amount of compensation due for such injury 'necessarily rests on equitable considerations'.[90] By contrast, the Court, similarly to the practice of the regional human rights courts, took a stricter view in respect of material injury, and rejected for the most part Guinea's claims in this regard due to Guinea's failure to prove such damage and/or its causal nexus with the human rights violations in question.[91]

3.2 Protection of human rights through provisional measures

Along the findings of violations and determining appropriate remedies, indication of binding provisional measures is perhaps the most potent way in which the ICJ could contribute to the enforcement of human rights. In most cases, the Court indicated provisional measures for the protection of human rights precisely because compliance with those human rights formed the very subject-matter of the dispute, in particular in situations involving imminent risk to human life. But the Court has considered it necessary to order such provisional measures even where human rights norms were not strictly part of the subject-matter of the dispute, such as most recently in the territorial dispute between Cambodia and Thailand. This trend indicates that the Court's handling of provisional measures requests is increasingly permeated with human rights considerations.

The most specific provisional measures for protection of human rights were indicated in each of the three consular protection cases (*Breard*, *LaGrand*, and *Avena*), where the Court ordered the US as the respondent State to ensure that the individuals who were detained and waiting on death row were not executed pending the Court's final decision on the merits.[92] Unfortunately, none of the three orders prevented the US authorities from carrying out the planned executions, notwithstanding the Court's explicit confirmation in the *LaGrand* case, that its orders on provisional measures are legally binding.[93]

[87] ibid, paras 13, 18, 24, 33, 40, 49, 56.

[88] *Guinea v Congo* (Compensation) (n 76), operative para 61, subparas (1)–(2).

[89] ibid, para 21. [90] ibid, para 24. [91] ibid, paras 29–55.

[92] *Paraguay v USA* (Provisional Measures) (n 74), para 41; *LaGrand (Germany v United States of America)* (Provisional Measures) [1999] ICJ Rep 9, para 29; *Avena and Other Mexican Nationals (Mexico v United States of America)* (Provisional Measures) [2003] ICJ Rep 77, para 59.

[93] *Germany v USA* (Merits) (n 74), para 109.

In more general terms, in *Congo v Uganda*,[94] *Bosnia and Herzegovina v Serbia and Montenegro*,[95] *Georgia v Russia*,[96] and *Thailand v Cambodia*,[97] the Court ordered one or both parties to ensure protection of human rights and respect for the applicable provisions of international humanitarian law.

4 Conclusion

The developments discussed in this chapter demonstrate that the Court has a significant role and potential in the field of human rights protection. Since the very beginning of its work, when international human rights instruments were scarce and protection of the rights of individuals was considered a predominantly domestic affair of States, the Court was at the forefront of promoting the growing recognition of human rights in international relations and discourse. Through recognition (or in some cases, evolution) and clarification of the basic concepts and norms of IHRL and IHL, it has eventually firmly integrated these two special legal regimes into the fabric of general international law.

Moreover, despite the concern that the involvement of a generalist court like the ICJ might inhibit the more progressive developments built by the specialized human rights courts and treaty-monitoring mechanisms, and aggravate the much-feared risk fragmentation of international human rights law, the Court has been increasingly mindful and acting in concerts with these other bodies. Their case-law reveals more harmony than divergence of views and supports the proposition that international human rights law is not a series of fragmented regimes, but rather, an increasingly unified system of rules and mechanisms for the global protection of human beings.

Aside from its considerable imprint on the development and consolidation of IHRL and IHL, the Court has also contributed to the strengthening of the structural framework for the protection and enforcement of human rights on the international level. It has made an important—if often overlooked—contribution, by affirming the applicability of general rules of State responsibility to human rights violations, while at the same time influencing the evolution of those general rule of State responsibility to accommodate the special needs of the fundamental human rights principles engendering obligations of common concern. Furthermore, by

[94] *Armed Activities on the Territory of the Congo (Democratic Republic of the Congo v Uganda)* (Provisional Measures) [2000] ICJ Rep 111, para 47.

[95] *Application of the Convention on the Prevention and Punishment of the Crime of Genocide (Bosnia and Herzegovina v Yugoslavia)* (Provisional Measures) [1993] ICJ Rep 3, para 52(A); *Application of the Convention on the Prevention and Punishment of the Crime of Genocide (Bosnia and Herzegovina v Yugoslavia)* (Further Provisional Measures) [1993] ICJ Rep 325, para 61(1)–(2).

[96] *Georgia v Russia* (Provisional Measures) (n 67), para 149.

[97] Request for Interpretation of the Judgment of 15 June 1962 in the *Case Concerning the Temple of Preah Vihear (Cambodia v Thailand)* (Provisional Measures) [2011] ICJ Rep 537, para 55. See also *Land and Maritime Boundary between Cameroon and Nigeria (Cameroon v Nigeria)* (Provisional Measures) [1996] ICJ Rep 13, para 42; *United States Diplomatic and Consular Staff in Tehran (United States of America v Iran)* (Provisional Measures) [1979] ICJ Rep 7, para 47(A)(ii)–(iii).

increasingly handling straightforward human rights disputes—that is, disputes involving direct claims of human rights violations, by more frequently pronouncing on such violations and determining appropriate remedies, and by ordering provisional measures for protection of human rights—the Court is also steadily assuming a more prominent position as a forum for direct enforcement of human rights and displays a firm awareness of their growing centrality in modern international relations.

11

Should We (Still) Worry about Fragmentation?

Alain Pellet

The interactions between the different branches of international law, the tension between specialized and general law, and the relationships—or maybe more the absence of institutionalized relationship—between the judicial bodies interpreting and applying them are becoming more and more complex as their de facto interdependence grows. It raises questions of coordination and conflict. The 'proliferation' of international courts and tribunals (an institutional and 'quantitative' issue) is often put forward as the scapegoat of the multifaceted danger of fragmentation of international law (which is a 'normative' concept). The term proliferation itself is not neutral: it reflects a fast, excessive, and uncontrolled growth, almost overshadowing its virtues. As underlined by Georges Abi-Saab:

> Of course, proliferation is extremely dangerous when we speak of lethal weapons of mass destruction. But it is a totally different matter when we speak of tribunals or other law-determining agencies in a system that has notoriously suffered, throughout its existence, from the dearth (not to say lack) of objective determinations.[1]

It is indeed wiser to retain the much more neutral word 'multiplication' to name this phenomenon, which is neither a danger nor a threat for international law but its 'good fortune', as nicely described by President Bedjaoui.[2] Far from being restricted to settling disputes—an already considerable task—they contribute to the affirmation and, to a certain extent, the evolution of the international legal order.[3] Their multiplication echoes its expansion *ratione materiae* and *ratione personae* and is intrinsically linked with the highly satisfactory phenomenon of 'judicialization'.

[1] Georges Abi-Saab, 'Fragmentation or Unification: Some Concluding Remarks' (1999) 31 Journal of International Law and Politics 919, 925.

[2] Mohammed Bedjaoui, 'La multiplication des tribunaux internationaux ou la bonne fortune du droit des gens' in SFDI, *La juridictionnalisation du droit international* (Pedone 2002).

[3] See Alain Pellet, 'L'adaptation du droit international aux besoins changeants de la société internationale: conférence inaugurale, session de droit international public 2007' (2007) 329 Recueil des Cours de l'Académie de Droit International 9, 43–47 <http://www.alainpellet.eu/Documents/PELLET%20-%202007%20-%20L'adaptation%20de%20DI%20aux%20besoins%20changeants%20de%20la%20soci%C3%A9t%C3%A9%20internationale.pdf> (accessed 19 June 2016).

The irony 'lies in the fact that international lawyers, having long fought for the recognition of "their" law as "real" law, are now concerned that there may be an excess of international law. In other words, the achievements of international law may institute its own downfall.'[4] This paradox has led Prosper Weil to declare that international lawyers are 'masochists among the masochists'.[5]

There is indeed nothing to worry about—and there has never been, at least in relation to the potential dangers of fragmentation due to the multiplication of international judicial bodies. Therefore, to answer straightaway the question raised by the title of the present chapter, there is no reason to 'still worry' about fragmentation! The aim of the present chapter is to 'revisit[] issues such as whether the increasing number of international courts is in fact leading to interpretative fragmentation, whether there is a danger of forum shopping and competing jurisdiction between international courts, and whether regional courts undermine the global rule of law'.[6] This is a fair reflexion of the criticisms usually addressed to the multiplication of international courts and tribunals and it is appropriate to briefly revisit each of them in turn and to show why these criticisms are unfounded.

1 Interpretative Fragmentation?

Now, the first criticism is 'interpretative fragmentation'. The Report of the International Law Commission Study Group on Fragmentation speaks of '[f]ragmentation through conflicting interpretations of general law';[7] it could also be called conflicting jurisprudence.

Such a risk did not exist as long as there was only *one* international judicial body, as was the case of the Permanent Court of International Justice in the early 1920s. Yet, it soon coexisted with the League of Nations Administrative Tribunal, created in 1927, then with some other tribunals. But it is at the end of the Second World War that the 'multiplication' phenomenon truly started, most notably with the institution of the International Military Tribunals, the International Court of Justice (ICJ), the European Court of Human Rights (ECtHR), and the Court of Justice of the European Communities (CJEC). The second, larger, wave of multiplication occurred at the end of the Cold War when regional courts were grafted on a multitude of new economic communities and trade agreements. In total, more than a hundred international judicial and quasi-judicial organs have been created since the inception of

4 Mario Prost and Paul Kingsley Clark, 'Unity, Diversity and the Fragmentation of International Law: How Much Does the Multiplication of International Organizations Really Matter?' (2006) 5 Chinese Journal of International Law 341, 343.

5 [« Masochistes parmi les masochistes »] Prosper Weil, 'Le droit international en quête de son identité: Cours général de droit international public' (1992) 251 Recueil des Cours 9, 89.

6 See the short presentation of the ESIL Forum from which the present chapter is issued given in the Programme of the Conference <http://www.esil-sedi.eu/sites/default/files/esil-shortprogramme.pdf> (accessed 19 June 2016).

7 ILC, 'Report of the Study Group of the International Law Commission finalized by Martti Koskenniemi, Fragmentation of International Law: Difficulties Arising from the Diversification and Expansion of International Law' (1 May–9 June and 3 July–11 August 2006) UN Doc A/CN.4/L.682, Title *C*.1.(a).

modern international law.[8] Less than twenty-five however fall within the definition of 'international courts' and are currently functioning.[9] Still, such courts have collectively issued over 37,000 binding legal judgments—more than 90 per cent of which were issued after the fall of the Berlin Wall.[10] Beyond numbers, a substantial shift has occurred from voluntary dispute settlement bodies to compulsory jurisdiction, opposing 'conservative courts' preoccupied with state sovereignty, such as the ICJ, and 'progressive courts' open to non-state actors, such as the ECtHR. This situation certainly creates a risk of interpretative fragmentation. It is the unavoidable consequence of the decentralization of the international system and the ensuing absence of hierarchy between the international judicial organs. In this connection, Judge Buergenthal wondered 'whether fragmentation is the right word to describe this phenomenon. Might one not speak instead of the growing inclusiveness of international law or the broadening of the concept of international law?'[11] We certainly should!

The multiplication of international courts and tribunals is not more 'worrying' than is the coexistence of two (or three or even four if you consider the case of France)[12] supreme courts—a situation which, in effect, may lead to diverging interpretations; but the differences are always temporary and are ultimately overcome by using various techniques: interpretation in conformity or 'conciliatory' or 'neutralizing' interpretation;[13] 'normative interaction';[14] or, very simply: a change in case

[8] See a partial inventory in Robert Kolb, *The International Court of Justice* (OUP 2013) 68–69 (also in French, *La Cour internationale de Justice* (Pedone 2014) 83–84), who lists fifteen universal courts or tribunals (among which five criminal courts or tribunals) and fourteen regional judicial or quasi-judicial bodies (including the three regional Courts of human rights). For a complete inventory—to be updated, see Project on International Courts and Tribunals, *Synoptic Chart*, November 2004 <http://www.pict-pcti.org/publications/synoptic_chart/synop_c4.pdf> (accessed 19 June 2016).

[9] Cesare PR Romano, 'The Proliferation of International Judicial Bodies: The Pieces of the Puzzle' (1999) 31 International Law and Politics 709, 711–23. See also Christian Tomuschat, 'International Courts and Tribunals with Regionally Restricted and/or Specialized Jurisdiction' in Hermann Mosler and Rudolf Bernhardt (eds), *Judicial Settlement of International Disputes: International Court of Justice, Other Courts and Tribunals, Arbitration and Conciliation: An International Symposium* (Springer 1974) 290–312; Cesare PR Romano, Karen J Alter, and Yuval Shany, 'Mapping International Adjudicative Bodies, the Issues, and Players' in Cesare PR Romano, Karen J Alter, and Yuval Shany (eds), *The Oxford Handbook of International Adjudication* (OUP 2013) 5–9. See the inventory of international courts in Karen J Alter, 'The Multiplication of International Courts and Tribunals after the End of the Cold War' ibid, 66.

[10] Alter, ibid 64.

[11] Thomas Buergenthal, 'The Proliferation of Disputes, Dispute Settlement Procedures and Respect for the Rule of Law' (2006) 22 Arbitration International 495, 497.

[12] Ie, the *Conseil constitutionnel* (CC), the *Cour de cassation* (Cass), and the *Conseil d'État* (CE), respectively dealing with the constitutional, judiciary, and administrative orders; there also exists a particular tribunal, the *Tribunal des conflits*, whose sole task it is to decide cases of conflicting jurisdiction. To those could be added the ECtHR and Court of Justice of the European Union.

[13] See eg, CC Ass plén 16 April 2010 *Aziz Melki et Sélim Abdeli*; CE Ass 9 July 2010 *Fédération nationale de la libre pensée*; CE Ass 23 December 2011 *Kandyrine de Brito Paiva*; CE 15 December 2014 *SA Technicolor*. See also, eg, Elisabetta Lamarque, 'The Italian Courts and Interpretation in Conformity with the Constitution, EU Law and the ECHR' (2012) Rivista dell'Associazione Italiana dei Costituzionalisti <http://www.rivistaaic.it/the-italian-courts-and-interpretation-in-conformity-with-the-constitution-eu-law-and-the-echr.html> (accessed 19 June 2016); Gerrit Betlem and André Nollkaemper, 'Giving Effect to Public International Law and European Community Law before Domestic Courts: A Comparative Analysis of the Practice of Consistent Interpretation' (2003) 14(3) European Journal of International Law 569. As for the use of the same technique at the international level, see below n 36.

[14] See eg, CE Ass 11 March 1994 No 115052; CE Ass, 20 December 1985 No 31927, referring to the case law of the Constitutional Council. See eg, Laurence Burgorgue-Larsen, Edouard Dubout, Alexandre

law—which may and do occur in common law as well as in civil law systems, even if, admittedly, with more difficulty.[15]

The same can be said at the international level. Indeed, some divergences can be noted in the interpretation or application of identical principles to similar situations by various courts or tribunals; but direct oppositions are rare. The typical example remains that of the 'Nicaragua test' of 'effective control'[16] or the '*Tadić* test' of 'overall control'[17] for the attribution of state responsibility opposing the ICJ and the International Criminal Tribunal for the former Yugoslavia (ICTY). Yet, narrowly speaking, it is not a true example of fragmentation as there was no jurisdictional overlap between the two fora: they did not have to answer the same question nor apply the same rules.[18] Indeed, the issue at stake before the ICJ was whether the United States were to be held responsible for the conduct of the *contras*, while the ICTY was concerned with whether the armed conflict could be qualified as international (in order to then determine the applicable rules of international humanitarian law and the responsibility of the accused). Still, they both accepted that some degree of control is always necessary to engage a state's responsibility. Thus, to borrow Charney's general conclusion of his course at The Hague Academy, '[a]lthough differences exist, these tribunals are clearly engaged in the same dialectic. The fundamentals of general international law remain the same.'[19]

Nevertheless, the *Tadić* judgment triggered a wind of panic at the ICJ, as illustrated by the speeches of its Presidents before the United Nations (UN) General Assembly, addressing for three consecutive years the risk of proliferation of international courts for the unity of international law.[20] What is remarkable about these statements

Maitrot de la Motte, and Sébastien Touzé (eds), *Les interactions normatives—Droit de l'Union européenne et droit international* (Pedone 2012); Sophie Robin-Olivier, 'Normative Interactions and the Development of Labour Law, A European Perspective' (2009) 11 *Cambridge Yearbook of European Legal Studies* 377.

[15] See eg, *Brown et al v Board of Education of Topeka et al* 347 US 483 (1954) overruling *Plessy v Ferguson; Lawrence v Texas* 539 US 558 (2003) overruling *Bowers v Hardwick*. See eg, William N Eskridge, 'Overruling Statutory Precedents' (1988) 76 Georgetown Law Journal 1361.

[16] *Military and Paramilitary Activities in and against Nicaragua (Nicaragua v United States of America)* (Merits) [1986] ICJ Rep 14, 64–65 [115]. The test was forcefully reaffirmed in *Application of the Convention on the Prevention and Punishment of the Crime of Genocide (Bosnia and Herzegovina v Serbia and Montenegro)* [2007] ICJ Rep 43, 208 [399] (*Genocide (I)*).

[17] *Tadić Case* (Judgment) ICTY-94-1-A (15 July 1999) [120]. See also *Čelebići Case* (Decision) ICTY-96-21-A (20 February 2001) [26]; *Prosecutor v Thomas Lubanga Dyilo* (Judgment pursuant to Article 74 of the Statute) ICC-01/04-01/06, T Ch I (14 March 2012) [541]. For a very critical analysis—not shared by the present writer—see Karin Oellers-Frahm, 'Multiplication of International Courts and Tribunals and Conflicting Jurisdiction—Problems and Possible Solutions' (2001) 5 *Max Planck Yearbook of United Nations Law* 67, 80.

[18] See *Genocide (I)* (n 16) 210 [405]. This did not prevent the Court reacting violently to what it probably considered as a *lèse majesté* offence (ibid 209 [403]).

[19] Jonathan I Charney, 'Is International Law Threatened by Multiple International Tribunals?' (1998) 271 Recueil des Cours 101, 347.

[20] Stephen M Schwebel, 'Address to the Plenary Session of the General Assembly of the United Nations' (26 October 1999); Gilbert Guillaume, 'Address to the United Nations General Assembly' (26 October 2000); Gilbert Guillaume, 'Speech to the General Assembly of the United Nations' (30 October 2001) available on <www.icj-cij.org>. See also Gilbert Guillaume, 'The proliferation of international judicial bodies: The outlook for the international legal order', Speech to the Sixth Committee of the General Assembly of the United Nations (27 October 2000).

is not only their anxiety about what at first sight seems a rather theoretical, even esoteric problem (…) but also the narrow platform from which the critiques have emerged. In reading through the academic debates, the Presidents stand almost alone in expressing such anxiety (in addition to a small number of suspected war criminals waiting for trial at the Hague).[21]

In order to prevent fragmentation, they encouraged other courts to request advisory opinions from the ICJ on points of general international law. This echoes article 267 of the Treaty on the Functioning of the European Union which enables (or compels) national courts to question the Court of Justice on the interpretation or validity of European law. Yet, the integrated system of the European Union is fundamentally different to the horizontal logic of international law.

Judge Rosalyn Higgins, who later also acted as President of the ICJ, disagreed with the hegemonic stance of her predecessors as '[t]his seeks to re-establish the old order of things and ignores the very reasons that have occasioned the new decentralisation'.[22] Praising different approaches which represent a healthy 'level of experimentation to find the best rule to serve the international community as a whole', the late Professor Charney further warned that '[a]n overly strict hierarchical structure for third party dispute settlement could place undesirable constraints on the development of international law and specialized law for specialized areas'.[23]

Any form of hierarchy has also clearly been rejected by the ICTY in the *Čelebići* case which upheld the 'overall control' test:

The Appeals Chamber agrees that 'so far as international law is concerned, the operation of the desiderata of consistency, stability, and predictability does not stop at the frontiers of the Tribunal. […] The Appeals Chamber cannot behave as if the general state of the law in the international community whose interests it serves is none of its concern'. However, this Tribunal is an autonomous international judicial body, and although the ICJ is the 'principal judicial organ' within the United Nations system to which the Tribunal belongs, there is no hierarchical relationship between the two courts. Although the Appeals Chamber will necessarily take into consideration other decisions of international courts, it may, after careful consideration, come to a different conclusion.[24]

The fact remains that the ICJ has a tendency to place itself as superior to other courts. Such attitude is evident from its ruling in the *Genocide (I)* case which attempted—in vain—to put an end to the control test saga:

the Court attaches the utmost importance to the factual and legal findings made by the ICTY in ruling on the criminal liability of the accused before it (…). The situation is not the same for positions adopted by the ICTY on issues of general international law which do not lie within the specific purview of its jurisdiction.[25]

[21] Martti Koskenniemi and Päivi Leino, 'Fragmentation of International Law? Postmodern Anxieties' (2002) 15(3) Leiden Journal of International Law 553, 574.

[22] Rosalyn Higgins, 'Respecting Sovereign and Running a Tight Courtroom' (2001) 50(1) International and Comparative Law Quarterly 121, 122. See also Rosalyn Higgins, 'Speech to the General Assembly of the United Nations' (26 October 2006).

[23] Charney (n 19) 347–48 and 354.

[24] *Čelebići* Case (Decision) ICTY-96-21-A (20 February 2001) [24] quoting *Le Procureur v Laurent Semanza* (Decision, Sep Op Shahabuddeen) ICTR-97-20-A (31 May 2000) [25].

[25] *Genocide (I)* (n 16) 209 [403].

Beyond what appears to be a rather childish squabble, these rulings are actually encouraging as they prove Judge Simma's point that

> if there are international institutions that are constantly and painstakingly aware of the necessity to preserve the coherence of international law, it is the international courts and tribunals. (…) [A]s a rule, international judges or arbitrators have to experience an extreme sense of urgency before they would decide to straight-up contradict their colleagues in another international jurisdiction. And if such sense of urgency were based on genuine concerns about the state of development of an international legal matter, the ensuing divergencies in international jurisprudence might be welcome triggers of progress in the law.[26]

There is indeed no threat to the systemic integration of the international system[27]—at least the inter-state system, where the principle of *comitas gentium* has long been applied by international courts and tribunals[28] and largely impregnates the judicial policy of international courts and tribunals. All international courts and tribunals pay tribute to the leadership of the jurisprudence of the ICJ,[29] and the World Court itself seems to progressively come down from its ivory tower and condescends to refer to other tribunals' judgments or awards. Recently, in the *Diallo* case, the ICJ recognized that

> when the Court is called upon, as in these proceedings, to apply a regional instrument for the protection of human rights, it must take due account of the interpretation of that instrument adopted by the independent bodies which have been specifically created, if such has been the case, to monitor the sound application of the treaty in question. In the present case,

the ICJ added, 'the interpretation given above of Article 12, paragraph 4, of the African Charter is consonant with the case law of the African Commission on Human and Peoples' Rights established by Article 30 of the said Charter' which it cited.[30] And in the Wall Advisory Opinion of 2004, the Court went as far as to refer

[26] Bruno Simma, 'Fragmentation in a Positive Light' (2004) 25(4) Michigan Journal of International Law 845, 846.

[27] See Campbell McLachlan, 'The Principle of Systemic Integration and Article 31(3)(c) of the Vienna Convention' (2005) 54(2) ICLQ 279; Isabelle Van Damme, 'ILC Study Group Report on the Fragmentation of International Law: WTO Treaty Interpretation against the Background of Other International Law' (2006) 17 *Finnish Yearbook of International Law* 21; or Christian Tomuschat, 'International Law as a Coherent System: Unity or Fragmentation?' in Mahnoush Arsanjani et al (eds), *Looking to the Future, Essays on International Law in Honor of W. Michael Reisman* (Nijhoff 2011) 344.

[28] See eg, *MOX Plant Case (Ireland v United Kingdom)* (Suspension of Proceedings on Jurisdiction and Merits, and Request for Further Provisional Measures) (2003) 126 ILR 310 [28].

[29] See eg, *Azurix Corp v Argentine Republic* (Award) ICSID Case No ARB/01/12 (14 July 2006) [391]; *Wintershall Aktiengesellschaft v Argentine Republic* (Award) ICSID Case No ARB/04/14 (8 December 2008) [65]; *Tulip Real Estate and Development Netherlands BV v Republic of Turkey* (Decision on Bifurcation) ICSID Case No ARB/11/28 (5 March 2013) [45]; *ConocoPhillips v Venezuela* (Decision on jurisdiction) ICSID Case No ARB/07/30 (3 September 2013) [254]; or *Quiborax SA and Non Metallic Minerals SA v Plurinational State of Bolivia* (Award) ICSID Case No ARB/06/2 (16 September 2015) [582]. More generally see Alain Pellet, 'Lalive Lecture—The Case Law of the ICJ in Investment Arbitration' (2013) 28(2) ICSID Review 223.

[30] *Case concerning Ahmadou Sadio Diallo (Republic of Guinea v Democratic Republic of the Congo)* [2010] ICJ Rep 639, 664 [67]. However, in its earlier Judgment on preliminary objections, the ICJ showed questionable haughtiness vis-à-vis the investment case-law, considering that arbitrations relied on by Guinea to establish the principle of 'protection by substitution' are 'special cases, whether

to '[t]he constant practice' of the Human Rights Committee of which it quoted several reports.[31] Such cross-reference is all the more indispensable when the Court is called to establish the existence of a customary rule.[32]

Another note along the same lines: notwithstanding the fears which had been expressed in some circles, in the first delimitation case it had to deal with, the International Tribunal for the Law of the Sea (ITLOS) has faithfully endorsed the now well-settled jurisprudential principles posed by the ICJ.[33] The recent Order of a Special Chamber of the ITLOS in *Ghana v Côte d'Ivoire* denotes the same will not to distinguish itself from the World Court's jurisprudence regarding the conditions for the prescription of provisional measures.[34] As underlined by a former President of the ITLOS, the Hamburg Tribunal has shown 'an unequivocal reliance on the jurisprudence of other international courts'; this 'provides clear evidence that, at least in the Tribunal's case, the concerns about possible fragmentation of the jurisprudence of international courts and tribunals are unwarranted'.[35] It also proves the Tribunal's awareness that state sovereignty does not do well with surprises. Indeed, it is only by ensuring predictability, which implies a growing and coherent jurisprudence, that international courts and tribunals can increase their attractiveness and secure the consent of states to their jurisdiction.

Further, the grandiose 'general rule of interpretation' clarified in article 31 of the 1969 Vienna Convention on the Law of Treaties has been espoused by all international courts and tribunals and is a strong factor of unity of the international jurisprudence *lato sensu*. As aptly noted by Christian Tomuschat,

> the fact is that Article 31(3)(c) encapsulates the axiom of the unity of the international legal order. (…) The expression 'systemic integration' reflects in a felicitous way the accord sought

based on specific international agreements between two or more States, including the one responsible for the allegedly unlawful acts regarding the companies concerned […] or based on agreements concluded directly between a company and the State allegedly responsible for the prejudice to it […]' (*Ahmadou Sadio Diallo (Republic of Guinea v Democratic Republic of the Congo)* (Preliminary Objections) [2007] ICJ Rep 582, 615 [89]–[90]). It can be wondered how many precedents are necessary to establish the existence of a customary rule. As rightly noted by the ICSID Tribunal in *CMS Gas Transmission Company v Argentine Republic*: 'the fact is that *lex specialis* in this respect is so prevalent that it can now be considered the general rule, certainly in respect of foreign investments and increasingly in respect of other matters' (Decision on Jurisdiction) ICSID Case No ARB/01/8 (17 July 2003) [48].

[31] *Legal Consequences of the Construction of a Wall in the Occupied Palestinian Territory* (Advisory Opinion) [2004] ICJ Rep 136, 179 [109]. For more exhaustive examples, see Alain Pellet, 'Article 38' in Andreas Zimmermann et al (eds), *The Statute of the International Court of Justice: A Commentary* (OUP 2006) 787–88 [310]–[311].

[32] See eg, *Jurisdictional Immunities of the State (Germany v Italy: Greece Intervening)* [2012] ICJ Rep 99, 139 [90] referring to the case law of the ECtHR and [91] concluding that under customary international law a State is not deprived of immunity by reason of the fact that it is accused of serious violations of international human rights law or the international law of armed conflict.

[33] *Delimitation of the maritime boundary in the Bay of Bengal (Bangladesh/Myanmar)* (Judgment of 14 March 2012) ITLOS Reports 2012 [95].

[34] *Delimitation of the maritime boundary in the Atlantic Ocean (Ghana/Côte d'Ivoire)* (Provisional measures, Order of 25 April 2015) [42], [57], [63].

[35] Jose Luis Jesus, 'Statement to the Informal Meeting of Legal Advisers of Ministries of Foreign Affairs' (New York, 25 October 2010) <https://www.itlos.org/fileadmin/itlos/documents/statements_of_president/jesus/legal_advisors_251010_eng.pdf> (accessed 19 June 2016).

not only with regard to the interpretation of treaties, but in the application of any rule of international law.[36]

And tribute must be paid in this respect to the rightly celebrated formula in the very first Report of the World Trade Organization (WTO) Appellate Body which firmly stated that the GATT 'is not to be read in clinical isolation from public international law'.[37]

In the same vein, the very wrongfully criticized article 38 of the Statute of the ICJ plays its role in this 'de-fragmentation' of international law since it is very generally recognized as giving an acceptable wide description of what international law is, whether you think of articles 74 and 83 of the United Nations Convention on the Law of the Sea concerning the delimitation of maritime spaces[38] or the case-law of international criminal tribunals[39] or even that of regional courts of human rights.[40] Interestingly, this is also true of investment tribunals which, in conformity with the Report of the Executive Directors of the International Bank for Reconstruction and Development,[41] interpret the reference to 'international law' in article 42(1), of the International Centre for Settlement of Investment Disputes (ICSID) Convention, 'in the sense given to it by Article 38(1) of the Statute of the International Court of Justice, allowance being made for the fact that Article 38 was designed to apply to inter-State disputes'.[42]

These arguments all support the 'no worry answer'. If there is a concern, it is more within the investment 'non-system' that we would probably find it: the 'sovereignty' claimed by the investment tribunals sometimes results in an anarchical case-law. However, even in this respect, I am rather optimistic and I tend to agree with August Reinisch: 'the risk of fragmentation should not be exaggerated. The overall tendency of investment tribunals to adhere to previous decisions and attempt to contribute to the formation of a "*jurisprudence constante*" is likely to safeguard the coherence and predictability required of any mature legal system.'[43] Such tendency was acknowledged for example by the ICSID Tribunal in *ADC v Hungary*:

The Parties to the present case have also debated the relevance of international case law relating to expropriation. It is true that arbitral awards do not constitute binding precedent. It

[36] Tomuschat (n 27) 344–46. For an example of the application of systemic integration, see *Right of Passage over Indian Territory (Portugal v India)* (Preliminary Objections) [1957] ICJ Rep 125, 142: 'It is a rule of interpretation that a text emanating from a Government must, in principle, be interpreted as producing and as intended to produce effects in accordance with existing law and not in violation of it.'

[37] *United States—Standards for Reformulated and Conventional Gasoline* (1996) 35 ILM 621.

[38] Both articles provide that the delimitation of the exclusive economic zone and continental shelf, respectively, 'shall be effected by agreement on the basis of international law, as referred to in Article 38 of the Statute of the International Court of Justice, in order to achieve an equitable solution'.

[39] See eg, *Prosecutor v Mucić et al* (Judgment) ICTY-96-21-T (16 November 1998) [414].

[40] See eg, *Golder v The United Kingdom* (1979) 1 EHRR 524 [35]. For more exhaustive examples, see Pellet (n 31) 691–93 [49]–[53].

[41] See International Bank for Reconstruction and Development, 'Report of the Executive Directors on the Convention on the Settlement of Investment Disputes between States and Nationals of Other States' (18 March 1965) <https://icsid.worldbank.org/ICSID/StaticFiles/basicdoc/partB-section06.htm#03> (accessed on 19 June 2016) [40].

[42] ibid.

[43] August Reinisch, 'The Proliferation of International Dispute Settlement Mechanisms: The Threat of Fragmentation vs. the Promise of a More Effective System? Some Reflections From the

is also true that a number of cases are fact-driven and that the findings in those cases cannot be transposed in and of themselves to other cases. It is further true that a number of cases are based on treaties that differ from the present BIT in certain respects. However, cautious reliance on certain principles developed in a number of those cases, as persuasive authority, may advance the body of law, which in turn may serve predictability in the interest of both investors and host States.[44]

2 Forum Shopping and Competing Jurisdiction

Another fear expressed by the opponents to what they call the 'proliferation' of international tribunals concerns forum shopping and competing jurisdiction.

Here again, the investment system has a special place: it is in this respect that the choice of fora is the most striking and probably produces the most negative effects. The most outstanding examples of diverging case-law have been aptly recalled by Professor Reinisch:

> The SGS cases, where two ICSID tribunals came to divergent assessments of the meaning of umbrella clauses, the *Maffezini* tribunal and others that are split on the interpretation of MFN clauses, the *CME/Lauder v. Czech Republic* arbitrations, where the same dispute was arbitrated under two different bilateral investment agreements, and finally the *CMS v. Argentina and LG&E v. Argentina* cases which, together with subsequent cases, answered the question of whether a state of necessity prevailed differently in Argentina.[45]

However, there is no reason for losing hope: the consolidation of the jurisprudence dealing with the 'fork in the road' clause or the strengthening of the principle *electa una via*[46] could rather shortly constitute a *jurisprudence constante* partly solving the problem. Moreover, states seem to have now acknowledged the scope of the problem and start to adopt provisions completing and expressing the traditional principles—quite often reflected in investment treaties—aiming at avoiding conflicting decisions on the same case or situation: *electa una via* (fork in the road), *non bis in idem, lis pendens*, and, of course, *res judicata*. Thus, article 16 of the 2007 draft model Norwegian bilateral investment treaty provides that '[t]he Tribunal shall,

Perspective of Investment Arbitration' in Isabelle Buffard, James Crawford, Alain Pellet, and Stephan Wittich (eds), *International Law between Universalism and Fragmentation* (Nijhoff 2008) 125; see however, his analysis of four groups of cases illustrating the potential threats on uniform interpretation, ibid 114.

[44] *ADC Affiliate Limited and ADC & ADMC Management Limited v Republic of Hungary* (Award) ICSID Case No ARB/03/16 (2 October 2006) [293]. See also *Saipem SpA v The People's Republic of Bangladesh* (Decision on Jurisdiction) ICSID Case No ARB/05/07 (21 March 2007) [67] or *Mamidoil Jetoil Greek Petroleum Products Societe SA v Republic of Albania* (Award) ICSID Case No ARB/11/24 (30 March 2015) [565].

[45] Reinisch (n 43) 114. See also below n 59.

[46] See eg, *Woodruff Case* (1903) 9 RIAA 213, 222–23; *Pantechniki SA Contractors & Engineers v Albania* (Award) ICSID Case No ARB/07/21 (30 July 2009) [31] or [64]; *Getma International v Guinea* (Decision on jurisdiction) ICSID Case No ARB/11/29 (29 December 2012) [129], [134]; *Quiborax SA and Non Metallic Minerals SA v Plurinational State of Bolivia* (Award) ICSID Case No ARB/06/2 (16 September 2015) [158].

as appropriate, take into account the principles of *res judicata* and *lis pendens*, in accordance with international law, to hinder abuse of rights under this agreement, as well as otherwise exercising sound judicial economy'.

The issue also arises on the more general plane: the ITLOS and the ICJ, the regional Courts and the Committee of Human Rights, or the Dispute Settlement Understanding of the WTO and the ICJ or the EU Courts can be seized of the same dispute. There exist, indeed, 'techniques to deal with regime and rule conflict in adjudication under international law': James Crawford and Penelope Nevill count not less than nine and specify that the list is 'not closed'.[47] But they warn that '[i]t is a rather motley, incoherent collection' and 'that the various judicial strategies identified are essentially exercises in avoidance and temporising'. Moreover, placing themselves from the advocate's point of view, they add: 'there is every point in having [these techniques]: we can use one or another depending of the interest of the client'.[48] This is precisely why competing jurisdiction is criticized: the absence of clear rules to have one forum prevailing over the other(s)—and the issue is all the more complicated that sometimes the competition can be (as in investment law) between one or several international forum or fora and a national court (or several!). This was one of the issues very recently discussed before the ITLOS in the *Enrica Lexie* case.[49]

Several reflections have been engaged at the international level on the various effects of the coexistence and 'co-availability' of two or more judicial or arbitral fora and the means to limit the inconveniences of these *à la carte* menus:

- In particular, the International Law Association has analysed the principles of *res judicata* and *lis pendens* in international commercial arbitration. In 2006, it adopted recommendations for the benefit of arbitrators, on the one hand to promote efficiency, the finality of awards, as well as the role of party autonomy regarding arbitral proceedings, and on the other hand to facilitate uniformity and consistency in the interpretation and application of provisions concerning parallel proceedings and the conclusive and preclusive effects of prior arbitral awards.[50]
- A reflexion on these principles has also been undertaken by the American Law Institute and UNIDROIT regarding transnational civil procedure.[51]

[47] James Crawford and Penelope Nevill, 'Relations between International Courts and Tribunals: The "Regime Problem"' in Margaret A Young (ed), *Regime Interaction in International Law—Facing Fragmentation* (CUP 2012) 237.

[48] ibid 247.

[49] See *The 'Enrica Lexie' Incident (Italy v India)* (Provisional measures, Order of 24 August 2015) [61]–[73].

[50] See Committee on International Commercial Arbitration, 'Interim Report on *Res judicata* and Arbitration' in International Law Association Report of the Seventy-First Conference (Berlin 2004) (International Law Association 2004); 'Final Report on *Lis Pendens* and Arbitration', 'Final Report on *Res judicata* and Arbitration', 'Resolution 1/2006' in International Law Association Report of the Seventy-Second Conference (Toronto 2006) (International Law Association 2006) available on <http://www.ila-hq.org/en/committees/index.cfm/cid/19> (accessed 19 June 2016).

[51] American Law Institute/UNIDROIT, 'Principles of Transnational Civil Procedure' 2004 <http://www.unidroit.org/instruments/transnational-civil-procedure> (accessed 19 June 2016) [Principle 28].

UNIDROIT is now focusing on their regional implementation and adaptation to the peculiarities of specific legal systems. The project notably aims at avoiding a fragmentary and haphazard growth of European civil procedural law.[52]

– For its Part, the *Institut de Droit international* is currently working on the topic 'Precedents in International Law'. It examines the creation and application by international courts and tribunals of precedents and whether such recourse affects the unity and coherence of international law. It further studies the effect of precedents on the codification and progressive development of international law.[53]

As for international criminal law, an unprecedented debate on the risks of fragmentation has recently emerged following contradictory judgments issued by the ICTY and the Special Court for Sierra Leone regarding whether 'specific direction' is a condition for 'aiding and abetting' liability.[54] Here, predictability and 'legal security' are arguably even more important than in other fields, for they necessarily concern the fundamental human rights related to a fair trial and the legality principle. It is essential for any accused to be able to foresee his fate. Yet, contrary to human rights courts, which attempt to build upon their respective practice, international criminal tribunals appear to have engaged in a form of competition and militancy. The same competitive orientation might be feared between the Strasbourg and Luxembourg European Courts on human rights protection[55] and the risks of 'outbidding' would increase in case of adhesion of the EU to the ECtHR.

Be this as it may, forum shopping is 'the perfect legitimate search by parties and their counsel of the forum that appears most favourable to their interest'[56] and it 'encourages acceptance by states of the judicial or arbitral settlement of international disputes, thereby increasing the role of international law'.[57] In his Blaine Sloan Lecture, Professor Brownlie explained that

> the multiplicity of tribunals reflects the multiplicity of relations between states, the complexities of regional customs and ways of doing things. It gives a wide range of preferences. (…)

[52] See <http://www.unidroit.org/work-in-progress-studies/current-studies/transnational-civil-procedure> (accessed 19 June 2016).

[53] Commission created in 2011, Rapporteurs Alain Pellet and Mohamed Bennouna, see <http://justitiaetpace.org/commission.php> (accessed 19 June 2016).

[54] See *Prosecutor v Perišić* (Judgment) ICTY-04-81-A (28 February 2013) [25]–[44]; *Prosecutor v Taylor* (Judgment) SCSL-03-01-A (26 September 2013) [472]–[475]; *Prosecutor v Šainović et al* (Judgment) ICTY-05-87-A (23 January 2014) [1617]–[1651]. See the commentary of Guido Acquaviva, 'Aiding and Abetting International Crimes and the Value of Judicial Consistency: Reflections Prompted by the Perisic, Taylor and Sainovic Verdicts' (2014) 1 Questions of International Law 3, 11–16.

[55] Compare eg *Behrami v France* (2007) 45 EHRR SE10 with Cases C-402/05 P and C-415/05 P *Kadi and Al Barakaat International Foundation* [2008] ECR I-6351. See further Iris Canor, '*Primus Inter Pares*. Who Is the Ultimate Guardian Of Fundamental Rights in Europe?' (2000) 25(1) European Law Review 3.

[56] Tullio Treves, 'New Trends in the Settlement of Disputes and the Law of the Sea Convention' in Harry N Scheiber (ed), *Law of the Sea: The Common Heritage and Emerging Challenges* (Nijhoff 2000) 74.

[57] Hugo Caminos, 'The Growth of Specialized International Tribunals and the Fears of Fragmentation of International Law' in Nerina Boschiero et al (eds), *International Courts and the Development of International Law: Essays in Honour of Tullio Treves* (Asser 2013) 58.

> There is competition between the international courts and ad hoc courts of arbitration (...) But it is not an antagonistic competition, it is a set of options of procedural options and I see no great harm in it.[58]

And indeed there are very few non-investment cases[59] where, eventually, two different international judicial bodies have adopted opposed solutions; and when they did as might be seen as being the case of the ICJ and the ECtHR in *Georgia v Russia* for example,[60] this might be justified by the fact that the judicial bodies concerned, on the basis of their respective statutes, apply different rules in matters of jurisdiction as well as on the substance. Moreover, in fact, empirical solution will usually be found—as was eventually the case in the *Mox* case.[61]

Moreover, the multiplication of international courts and tribunals is not only a question of competition; it also results in complementarity. Just to give an example: in the cases of international crimes, the international criminal tribunals are responsible for judging the individuals charged with such crimes; and the ICJ has jurisdiction to pronounce itself on the 'institutional' responsibility of the state involved—and this has certainly very positive fallout in matters of reparation.[62]

I would, here again, rally the 'optimistic camp' and agree with PS Rao when he writes that the 'diversity of international tribunals' is 'a reflection of the growing strength of the unity and integrity of international law'; it 'is a sign of maturity and growing importance of the rule of law in international affairs'. 'The judicial enforcement of international rights and obligations reduces arbitrariness and power plays in international relations.'[63]

3 Regional Courts v the Global Rule of Law

With respect, the last range of criticisms directed at the so-called 'proliferation' of international tribunals according to which regional courts would undermine the global rule of law is pure nonsense and does not deserve long comments.

Regional courts can be considered the 'advanced bastions' of general international law. They are increasingly seized with issues pertaining to it, and actually much more

[58] Ian Brownlie, 'The Peaceful Settlement of International Disputes in Practice' (1995) 7(2) Pace International Law Review 257, 276.

[59] There might be more in investment cases. There is at least one example in which diverging solutions have been adopted by two UNCITRAL tribunals concerning the same factual issues, see *Lauder v Czech Republic* (Final Award) IIC 205 (2001) and *CME Czech Republic BV (The Netherlands) v Czech Republic* (Partial Award) IIC 61 (2001)—see Crawford and Nevill (n 47) 239–40.

[60] *Application of the International Convention on the Elimination of all forms of Racial Discrimination (Georgia v Russian Federation)* (Preliminary Objections) [2011] ICJ Rep 70; *Georgia v Russia* (2011) 52 EHRR SE14.

[61] *MOX Plant* (n 28) [28].

[62] See Alain Pellet, 'D'un crime à l'autre—La responsabilité de l'État pour violation de ses obligations en matière de droits humains' in *Mouvances du droit: Études en l'honneur du Professeur Rafâa Ben Achour* (Konrad-Adenauer-Stiftung 2015) Tome III, 317.

[63] Pemmaraju Sreenivasa Rao, 'Multiple International Judicial Forums: A Reflection of the Growing Strength of International Law or its Fragmentation?' (2004) 25(4) Michigan Journal of International Law 929, 960.

than universal courts. While, since its establishment by the UN Charter, the ICJ has judged about eighty cases, the ECtHR, created in 1951, has issued nearly 15,000 judgments[64] which often contain a section dedicated to 'relevant international law' and UN materials.[65] Quite a few international judges have even moved from one court to another, thus adding, more or less consciously, to the consistency of international jurisprudence[66]—for instance, Judges Buergenthal and Cançado Trindade have seated both at the Inter-American Court of Human Rights, then at the ICJ. However, one can only regret the small number of public international law specialists on the bench of regional courts.

Because of the more intensive solidarity between the states of a same region, they can make more progressive and integrated decisions, which, if the circumstances allow, will spread both in the domestic laws of the state of the region and at the international global level. In the words of Judge Simma,

> Let me remind you of the way in which the [ICJ] has for decades beaten around the bush concerning *jus cogens*, or its recent unnecessary negation of the character of the right to consular information as a human right.[[67] The Court has been rather timid when faced with the challenge of setting judicial limits to the powers of the UN Security Council. And if one compares the treatment of the issue of reparation in the 2007 *Genocide* judgment with certain decisions of the Inter-American Court of Human Rights on the matter of reparation of violations of human rights obligations, or with the 2003 Decision of the Human Rights Chamber for Bosnia and Herzegovina in the *Selimović (Srebrenica)* cases, one could not be blamed for indeed regarding the Hague Court as a stubborn defender of certain '*ancien regimes*' in international law.[68]

Further, regional courts have been very active in developing less formal techniques to engage in a constant inter-judicial dialogue—a cooperation that the ICJ struggles to develop due to a lack of resources. In particular, the ECtHR meets annually with the Court of Justice of the European Union, strengthened its ties with the Inter-American Court of Human Rights, exchanged legal staff with the Secretariat of the Human Rights Committee, and had substantive contacts in 2012 with the Special Tribunal for Lebanon.[69]

Therefore, much more than a threat of 'fragmentation' for the global rule of law, they are a powerful agent of progress. There must be however a limit in their

[64] See the table of international courts and cases reproduced in Marcelo Dias Varella, *Internationalization of Law: Globalization, International Law and Complexity* (Springer 2014) 274.

[65] See eg, *Sargsyan v Azerbaijan* App no 40167/06 (ECtHR, 16 June 2015) [94]–[96]; *Chiragov AO v Armenia* App no 13216/05 (ECtHR, 16 June 2015) [96]–[98]. For the reference to international law by other regional courts, see eg, *Vélasquez Rodríguez v Honduras* IACtHR Series C No 4 (29 July 1988) [127]; Case T-512/12 *Front Polisario v Council* (ECJ, 10 December 2015) notably [205]–[211].

[66] Bruno Simma, 'Universality of International Law from the Perspective of a Practitioner' (2009) 20(2) European Journal of International Law 265, 279.

[67] With respect, the present writer does not think that this is the meaning of the Court's decision. It did not negate that the right to consular information could be analysed as a human right; it only noted, that, in the circumstances, this could add nothing to its reasoning (see *Avena and Other Mexican Nationals (Mexico v United States of America)* [2004] ICJ Rep 12, 60–61 [124]).

[68] Simma (n 66) 288–89 (original footnotes omitted).

[69] ECtHR (2012) Annual Report 14.

autonomy: they must adhere to—or, if not adhere, preserve—the minimum basis of common values reflected in general international law—that is the famous and indispensable *jus cogens*. But they do, in spite of the trial and error practice of the EU Courts[70] or Human Rights Courts.[71] Just to give an example, in the *Loizidou* case, the ECtHR expressly distinguished itself from the ICJ and diverged from the consistent case-law of the latter according to which reservations in declarations of compulsory jurisdiction are legal and must be upheld.[72]

Recent tensions between regionalism and universalism have however crystallized in the will of the African Union to create an African Court of Justice and Human and Peoples' Rights.[73] On the one hand, it goes against the multiplication trend by merging the Court of Justice of the African Union and the African Court on Human and Peoples' Rights. On the other hand, it revives the question of fragmentation with its unique and extremely broad jurisdiction, including any question of international law, any legal instrument relating to human rights ratified by the States Parties concerned, and no less than fourteen international and transnational crimes. Its aim is to establish an alternative, if not a replacement forum to universal bodies, in particular the ICJ and the ICC. It is doubtful that such an ambitious project will ever be implemented, because of the enormous budget it would require, but if it were, one retrogressive provision of its Statute would from the outset constitute a case of fragmentation: the recognition of Head of State immunity for international crimes.

This being said, international courts are aware of their responsibilities and the issue of their integration within the international framework. Avoiding the inconveniences of fragmentation through cooperation is not their sole duty, it is also the responsibility of the states and international organizations which create them, elect their members and seize them. The risk of fragmentation boils down to the decentralized nature of the international legal order which is not—and will never be (as long as it remains essentially an inter-states law)—completely uniform, but its adaptability can put up with the existence of differences.

To conclude, I would like to quote from a French scholar, Denys de Béchillon, concerning what he calls the 'five French Supreme Courts'—including the European

[70] See eg, Case T-306/01 *Ahmed Ali Yusuf and Al Barakaat International Foundation v Council and Commission* [2005] ECR II-03533; Case T-315/01 *Kadi v Council and Commission* [2005] ECR II-3649; Cases C-402/05 P and C-415/05 P *Kadi and Al Barakaat International Foundation* [2008] ECR I-6351; see also Case T-49/04 *Faraj Hassan v Council and Commission* [2006] ECR II-00052; or Case T-253/02 *Chafiq Ayadi v Council* [2006] ECR II-02139.

[71] See eg, *Al-Adsani v United Kingdom* (2001) 34 EHRR 273 [60]–[61]; *Jorgic v Germany* (2008) 47 EHRR 6 [68]; *Demir and Baykara v Turkey* (2009) 48 EHRR 54 [73]; and *Michael Domingues v United States*, IACmHR Report No 62/02 (22 October 2002) [40]–[50]; *Juridical Condition and Rights of the Undocumented Migrants* (Advisory Opinion OC-18/03) IACtHR Series A No 18 (17 September 2003) [102]–[11]; or *Caesar v Trinidad y Tobago* (Merits, Reparations and Costs, Individual Opinion of Judge Cançado Trindade) IACtHR Series C No 123 (11 March 2005) [92]: 'The Inter-American Court has probably done for such identification of the expansion of *jus cogens* more than any other contemporary international tribunal'.

[72] *Loizidou v Turkey* (1995) 20 EHRR 136 [83]–[85].

[73] Protocol on the Statute of the African Court of Justice and Human Rights adopted on 1 July 2008 and Protocol on Amendments to the Protocol on the Statute of the African Court of Justice and Human Rights (adopted on 27 June 2014 not entered into force), available on <http://www.au.int/en/treaties>.

Courts of Strasbourg and Luxembourg:[74] '[a]t first sight such a polyphony may be considered as the source of a major disorder. Yet, upon closer examination, it can be seen as a precious source of enrichment both for the rule of law and the very functioning of society.'[75] The same holds true in relation with the multiplication of international courts and tribunals.

[74] See n 12 above.

[75] Denys de Béchillon, 'Cinq cours suprêmes? Apologie (mesurée) du désordre' (2011) 137 Pouvoirs 33.

PART V

EPILOGUE

12

Judicialization and its Challenges*

*Philippe Sands***

In the summer of 2014 I spent three weeks in The Hague, in the company of a man who was a hundred years old. Professor Vladimir Ibler, born on 25 June 1913 in Zagreb, when it was still a part of the Austro-Hungarian Empire, was one of my co-counsel during the arbitration proceedings between Croatia and Slovenia, heard in the Peace Palace.

Professor Ibler, diminutive in height but not in presence or character, was curious about the Peace Palace, built when he was a schoolboy, a place he had not previously had occasion to spend much time in. Each day we would slowly make our way up the central staircase in the morning, then down it later in the afternoon, past the statue of Lady Justice, to and from the Japanese room, where the hearing took place.

Professor Ibler enjoyed musing about the world, the state of international law, and the state of international courts. 'When I was born there were none', he said one morning of the courts, 'and now there are so many that I cannot keep up with them all'. He paused, then asked: 'What are they all for? What do they all mean?' The questions were left hanging, but from his cheery disposition I felt he retained a sense of hope. A centenarian whose life passed through the reigns of Emperor Franz Josef, Adolf Hitler, Josef Stalin, and Josip Tito, was somehow still able to seize on the possibility of courts as an alternative to war, which might be said to be the principal end of judicialization. He was hopeful too that Croatia and Slovenia might finally resolve their long-standing boundary dispute by arbitration proceedings under the auspices of the Permanent Court of Arbitration, conducted before a panel of five distinguished, experienced international arbitrators.

Yet Professor Ibler also sounded a note of caution, in the course of a more formal interview that I conducted for a profile to appear in the Financial Times Magazine. 'I learnt in my life not to come to fast conclusions', he told me. He continued:

> I was very happy in a lawyer's office in Zagreb from 1937 to 1939 working with Mr Korsky, and then the Nazis just shot him. I think that being in a lawyer's office you can make certain conclusions about people and about human relationships, and you can learn certain things. And what I learnt is not to be very quick to make conclusions, but to reflect all the time . . .

* First published in the European Journal of International Law, 27(4) (2016), 885–900.

** In preparing this chapter I have been greatly assisted by Luis Viveros, PhD candidate at UCL, and Dr Trpimir Socic, Faculty of Law, University of Zagreb.

'Was it a good idea to refer the dispute between Croatia and Slovenia to an international arbitral tribunal?', I enquired. 'Yes', he responded, 'of course I think positively of the idea, it was a good idea to establish the court'. And then he paused, before adding by way of a translator: 'What I am sceptical of is some of the judges that were appointed to the court, I am not entirely convinced that the tribunal has been totally independent.' He paused again, and said: 'It seems there are some invisible forces ... there are justices and injustices.'

That was June 2014. Subsequent events, to which I shall return, caused me to revisit the conversation with Professor Ibler. Fortunately I had recorded it.

'What I've learnt is not to be very quick to make conclusions.' Wise advice from a man who is a hundred years old.

Against that background, what are we to make of our current institutional judicial arrangements, and the manner in which they function? We know these courts are the product of political processes with very long roots. And we can now hardly imagine to have the rule of law without courts.

There are today far more international courts than Professor Ibler could ever have imagined, as a child, as a law student, as a middle-aged man, or even—remarkably—when he hit the age of retirement (in 1978). Back then there was no World Trade Organization Dispute Settlement Body, no International Tribunal for the Law of the Sea (ITLOS), no International Criminal Court (ICC), International Criminal Tribunal for the former Yugoslavia (ICTY), or International Criminal Tribunal for Rwanda, and no internationalized criminal courts. The Permanent Court of Arbitration (PCA) was moribund, if not dead. I recall my first teacher in international law, Robbie Jennings, in our 1980 lecture course, passing over the PCA as a historical footnote. Yet today it has well over a hundred cases, including a significant number of inter-State cases.[1] It might be said that the PCA offers hope for all institutions who have occasion to hope for more.

Two decades after Professor Ibler had reached retirement age, in 1997, Cesare Romano, Ruth Mackenzie, and I established the Project on International Courts and Tribunals (PICT), by which time the international judicial architecture had been transformed. Our first conference meeting apparently offered the first ever gathering of registrars and secretariats of the international courts, and it seemed we were awash with these bodies and their cases. Today it is virtually impossible for anyone to keep up with the totality of developments, and that has consequences, not least the emergence of new initiatives to keep us informed and help us understand, including the Pluricourts Project in Oslo,[2] and the iCourts project in Copenhagen.[3]

If not exactly an end of judicialization, one of the consequences has been the emergence of fertile academic communities that have sprung up, and that too has produced consequences. John Louth of Oxford University Press observes that

[1] PCA, 'Pending Cases' <http://www.pcacases.com/web/allcases/> (accessed 20 January 2016).
[2] 'PluriCourts' <http://www.jus.uio.no/pluricourts/english/> (accessed 4 February 2016).
[3] 'iCourts' <http://jura.ku.dk/icourts/> (accessed 4 February 2016).

fifty-five books were published on the ICC last year, a number that surely gives rise to the question: what is the purpose and utility of such a rush of publications?[4]

For all our work and effort, it must be said that it becomes ever more difficult to step back and identify trends and themes for the whole. Each court and tribunal is unique and, I am bound to add, I do believe they *are* courts and tribunals, some academics' misgivings notwithstanding. Each court and tribunal has its own rules, composition, working methods, cases, and of course its distinct legal community of bar and scholars. Invited to address 'the end(s) of judicialization', in such a context I hesitate to draw broad conclusions. We inhabit a galaxy of a thousand points of light, or more.

One thing is clear, however: our international courts are delicate and fragile creatures. We may take national courts as points of comparison, but often they have had centuries to mature. A former colleague, the distinguished English legal historian Professor Sir John Baker, would occasionally tell me that my world of international courts of today equated somewhat to the situation English courts found themselves in during the late fifteenth and early sixteenth century. I've never quite forgotten that point of comparison, as it allows us to reflect in a more contextualized way on some of the things we tend to get excited about. The reality is surely that we are engaged in a project that will extend over centuries, and it is at an early stage of development. We should therefore permit ourselves to have low expectations, even if that does not mean we should not have expectations at all. It does not mean that matters might not be improved, including by our own endeavours as observers and commentators, and occasionally as actors.

Over the past years I have been spending a significant amount of time researching a book that focuses largely on the Nuremberg Trial, and the lives of three men in that trial: Hersch Lauterpacht, Raphael Lemkin, and Hans Frank.[5] Because of this 1945 and 1946 have been very much on my mind. The idea that courts and law might supplant politics and power came to the fore in 1945, a point at which the notion that disputes could be settled by recourse to arbitration or judicial settlement began to gain traction. In the broader scheme of historical developments, that is a remarkably short period of time: just seventy years have passed. The idea and its moment was encapsulated by a memorable speech given by United States Supreme Court Justice Robert Jackson, Chief Prosecutor at Nuremberg on 21 November 1945, when he stood before the eight judges in Courtroom 600 in Nuremberg's Palace of Justice, still a working courtroom today:

'That four great nations, flushed with victory and stung with injury stay the hand of vengeance and voluntarily submit their captive enemies to the judgment of the law is one of the most significant tributes that Power has ever paid to reason',[6] he told the judges.

[4] John Louth's own publishing activities, now over many years and with so extensive a reach, will no doubt one day be the subject of a doctoral thesis, exploring the role of academic publishers in contributing to the articulation of our community and its output, including in the jurisprudence of the courts.

[5] Philippe Sands, *East West Street: On the Origins of Crimes against Humanity and Genocide* (Weidenfeld & Nicolson 2016).

[6] Nuremberg Military Tribunal, 2 IMT 98 (21 November 1945).

And in a sense that has been our guiding light—reason and the judgment of the law trumping brute force and power politics.

His friend and colleague Hersch Lauterpacht—the man who suggested that he put the concept of 'crimes against humanity' into the Nuremberg Statute (when they met in the garden of Lauterpacht's home on Cranmer Road in Cambridge, on 29 July 1945)[7]—was rather keen on courts: for enforcement within the State 'there must exist a judicial machinery', he wrote in 1944, 'accessible to every individual, for testing the conformity of legislative, judicial, and executive action with the provisions of [his proposed] Bill of Rights'.[8]

Lauterpacht was less keen about the idea of an international human rights court, and it is well worth going back to what he wrote in that remarkable book. He thought such an idea was not practicable, in part because of the absence in the international sphere of what he referred to as 'restraints upon the unavoidable power of judges'.[9] What was missing at the international level was an equivalent to the 'community of national tradition', one that reflected 'the overwhelming sentiment [. . .] of national solidarity and of the higher national interest, the corrective and deterrent influence of public opinion, and, in case of a clear abuse of judicial discretion, the relatively speedy operation of political checks and remedies'.[10]

The more you go back, and the more you read Hersch Lauterpacht, the more remarkable he appears, yet he was shown not to be right in this particular prediction. International courts of human rights were created, even if the issues he alluded too are surely pertinent today, across the range of international courts.

Still, a number of broad points can be made, as regards the 'end and the ends of judicialization' (I will include arbitration, although purists may object).

1 First, What are the *Ends* of Judicialization?

There seem to be at least three, although only two are usually referred to.

First, as Lauterpacht put it, the 'original and primary purpose was to decide disputes between States'.[11] That is a limited end, and one that has evolved, as other international actors have emerged, including individuals, corporate investors, and international organizations. Our legal world is no longer just about States, even if they do remain rather significant.

Second, as Lauterpacht also recognized—indeed he was a proponent of the idea—there was a broader role for international adjudication, as a means to develop the law—and the idea of the international rule of law—a way of gradually beefing up the content of the rules, and their effects.[12]

[7] Sands (n 5) 113.
[8] Hersch Lauterpacht, *An International Bill of the Rights of Man* (updated edn, OUP 2013) 185.
[9] ibid 13. [10] ibid.
[11] Ian GM Scobbie, 'The Theorist as Judge: Hersch Lauterpacht's Concept of the International Judicial Function' (1997) 8(2) EJIL 264, 270 (citing Lauterpacht's Provisional Report on the Revision of the Statute of the Court of 1 September 1955).
[12] ibid.

There is, I think, a *third* end for all these courts: they have themselves become new social actors, ones that contribute to evolutions in the state of human consciousness and actions. Their very existence, and the fact that they function, tends to support the notion that there is an alternative to the unlimited exercise of power, or even the possibility of an end to crime and other wrongs (although we know that to be somewhat illusory, as the experience with the ICC makes clear). It could also be said that the mere existence of these institutions offers the illusion of hope, an alternative that is often shown to have been dashed: the current problem of individuals trying to reach countries of the European Union shows rather clearly the limits of the law, and the idea of the rule of law. But it is also evident that changes of public consciousness may be effected by the activities of international courts.

I am sometimes asked which cases really made a difference, and it seems there are actually quite a few that you could settle on; the choice may be subjective, but I would certainly include, by way of illustration, the judgment in the case of *Smith and Grady v UK*[13] of the European Court of Human Rights issued in 1999, a decision that unanimously found that the investigation into and subsequent discharge of personnel from the Royal Navy on the basis that they were homosexual was a breach of their right to a private life under article 8 of the European Convention on Human Rights. That seems to have been a catalytic jurisprudential moment, one that has contributed to, if not caused, a transformation of public views in the European context on gay marriage and related matters. Courts can make a difference, that too is a reality.

2 Second, Can we Envisage the *End* of Judicialization?

It seems hard to envisage. Warts and all, international courts are now a settled part of international and domestic political processes, and they are here to stay. There will be ebbs and flows and the directions might change, but they are not going away. To be sure, there will be backlashes and whingeing and even departures and disappearances, we have heard much about that over the past two days. There will be questions about arbitration or courts, ad hoc or permanent, concerns about fragmentation and competition, and whether these features are a good or bad thing.

A prospective international litigant now has a range of choices, and that is a good thing. Competition has offered choice in decision-making—which of several judicial or arbitral possibilities might a claimant opt for?—is a question informed, in large part, by speculation as to possible outcomes. We have seen competition influence the development of the law and public consciousness: one suspects that the fact that ITLOS became the first international court to delimit a maritime boundary 200 miles beyond a coast had at least something to do with the desire to give itself an advantage against its Hague competitor which has, until now at least, refrained from

[13] *Smith and Grady v UK* Apps nos 33985/96 & 33986/96 (ECtHR, 27 September 1999).

so making such delimitation.[14] Competition allows ideas to flourish, and the battle of ideas is a hallmark of our emerging international judicial system.

There is nothing novel about this. I could mention the start of Slade's case in 1596 before the English courts—it arose because under medieval common law a claim for the repayment of a debt had to be pursued through a writ of debt in the Court of Common Pleas, a difficult, archaic, slow and very expensive process. By 1560 lawyers had found another method, enforced by a different court, called the Court of King's Bench, through the action of *assumpsit*, a form of action for deceit. Then along came another body, the Court of Exchequer Chamber, the appellate court to the Court of Common Pleas, which overruled decisions of the King's Bench on *assumpsit*, causing great friction between the courts. Courts going in different directions is not a new thing, it has happened for centuries.[15]

In Slade's Case the Exchequer Chamber gave judgment after five years—it seems there is nothing novel either about delay—ruling that *assumpsit* claims were valid and enforceable. They became the main course of action in English contract cases, and the episode is sometimes cited as an example of judicial legislation where Parliament failed to act. It could also be cited as an example of the reality of competition, and it applies equally in the international domain.

Against this background, summing up the current state and perspectives of international courts and tribunals is no easy feat. An assessment of the relative successes or failures of international justice enterprises requires an understanding of what we expect of them, both individually and collectively. It would need several hours to engage fully in the matter. All I can do, having surveyed the general landscape, is to settle on a few developments that might raise an eyebrow, or indicate the road that might yet be followed. I will briefly touch on a few examples, not wishing to suggest any particular sense of hierarchy or exclusivity, to suggest and indicate themes we might wish to think more about.

I shall plough on, encouraged to talk even about matters one prefers not to talk about, reminded of the words of psychoanalyst Nicolas Abraham, who observed: 'What haunts are not the dead, but the gaps left within us by the secrets of others.'[16] In this sense, that which is not said may be as interesting as what was said. In entering that forbidden domain, I shall draw from my own experiences.

[14] *Dispute Concerning Delimitation of the Maritime Boundary Between Bangladesh and Myanmar in the Bay of Bengal* (Judgment, 14 March 2012) ITLOS Rep. 2012, s. IX and para 506(2); *Cfr. Territorial and Maritime Dispute (Nicaragua v Colombia)* (Merits) 2012 ICJ Rep. 624, s IV; also see *Question of the Delimitation of the Continental Shelf between Nicaragua and Colombia beyond 200 nautical miles from the Nicaraguan Coast (Nicaragua v Colombia)* (Pending) <http://www.icj-cij.org/docket/index.php?p1=3&p2=3&code=nicolb&case=154&k=02> (accessed 5 February 2016).

[15] Sir John Baker, *The Oxford History of the Laws of England: Volume IV* (OUP 2003) Part III, s 5–7.

[16] Nicolas Abraham, 'Notes on the Phantom: A Complement to Freud's Metapsychology' (1987) 13(2) Trial(s) of Psychoanalysis 287 (Nicholas Rand tr).

2.1 The International Criminal Court

Recently the question has entered my mind: 'did we create the ICC too early?' It is plainly now something of a problem institution, in the eyes of many, and the causes of that situation seem to be manifold. Particularly in the African context, one has to confront a very real and—let us say it—legitimate concern: if you switch on a computer and go to the ICC webpage, you will see that every single person that has been indicted by the Prosecutor's Office at the ICC is African and black.[17] Yet Africans and black people do not have a monopoly on international crime. That record, fifteen years after the creation of the ICC, sends a troubling signal which we are bound to reflect on and address, not least since it is having political ramifications. We have seen the consequences of that in the Kenya case[18] and, more recently, in the situation of Sudan's President Al Bashir arriving in, and then leaving, South Africa, a party to the ICC Statute under an obligation to arrest him.[19] We must recognize the cogency of an argument which suggests the focus on certain individuals amounts to a form of legal neo-colonialism. Quite why there has been no indictment for the practice of torture or rendition adopted after the events of September 11th seems remarkable.[20] We have to confront this; we cannot just run away from it.

2.2 The European Court of Human Rights

Let us alight on the situation in my own country, where the dominant political party of the day has a large number of its parliamentarians—and even ministers—who seem to want to leave the European Court of Human Rights. This is because the Court is coming down with judgments they don't like, given by judges from faraway places. One of the judgments they like to focus on—the prisoner's voting case—strikes me as one that actually was correctly decided.[21]

[17] *Situation in Democratic Republic of Congo's indictees:* Thomas Lubanga Dyilo, Germain Katanga, Bosco Ntaganda, Callixte Mbarushimana, Sylvestre Mudacumura, Mathieu Ngudjolo Chui; *Situation in the Central African Republic:* Jean-Pierre Bamba Gombo, Aimé Kilolo Musamba, Jean-Jacques Mangenda Kabongo, Fidèle Babala Wandu, Narcisse Arido; *Situation in Uganda:* Ahmad Muhammad Harun ('Ahmad Harun'), Ali Muhamad Ali Abd-Al-Rahman ('Ali Kushayb'), Omar Hassan Al Bashir, Bahar Idriss Abu Garda, Abdallah Banda Abakaer Norain, Abdel Raheem Muhamad Hussein; *Situation in the Republic of Kenya:* William Samoei Ruto, Joshua Arap Sang, Uhuru Muigai Kenyatta, Walter Osapiri Barasa; *Situation in Libya:* Saif Al-Islam Gaddafi; *Situation in the Republic of Côte d'Ivoire:* Simone Gbagbo, Laurent Gbagbo, Charles Blé Goudé, Ahmad Al Faqi Al Mahdi. International Criminal Court, 'All Cases' <https://www.icc-cpi.int/en_menus/icc/situations%20and%20cases/cases/Pages/cases%20index.aspx> (accessed 19 February 2016).

[18] Owen Bowcott, 'ICC drops murder and rape charges against Kenyan president' *Guardian* (London, 5 December 2014) <http://www.theguardian.com/world/2014/dec/05/crimes-humanity-charges-kenya-president-dropped-uhuru-kenyatta> (accessed 13 February 2016).

[19] Norimitsu Onishi, 'Omar al-Bashir, Leaving South Africa, Eludes Arrest Again' *NYT* (New York, 15 June 2015) <http://www.nytimes.com/2015/06/16/world/africa/omar-hassan-al-bashir-sudan-south-africa.html> (accessed 13 February 2016).

[20] Philippe Sands, *Torture Team: Uncovering War Crimes in the Land of the Free* (Kindle edn., Penguin 2008) Ch. 'Responsibility'.

[21] *Hirst v UK No 2* App no 74025/01 (ECtHR, 6 October 2005); Mathew Holehouse, 'David Cameron: I will ignore Europe's top court on prisoner voting' *Telegraph* (London, 4 October 2015) <http://www.telegraph.co.uk/news/uknews/law-and-order/11911057/David-Cameron-I-will-ignore-Europes-top-court-on-prisoner-voting.html> (accessed 13 February 2016).

Here too we have to deal with a reality, and one that tends to be skirted around, namely that in the Council of Europe of forty-eight States, you have some that have properly functioning, independent judicial systems, and others that do not. When you create an international court that straddles so varied a group of countries, it is understandable that there may be an institutional desire to ensure that there are expressions of judicial action across the range of those countries. Which rather raises the question of whether it was a mistake to get rid of the European Commission of Human Rights, which functioned as a screening mechanism, allowing the European Court of Human Rights to deal with a more limited number of cases, those that raise serious, grave human rights issues that plainly touch on the wellbeing of Europe as a whole. Here too we have to deal with the realities of the situations we have put ourselves in, and if we have fallen into error we must be honest about it.

And of course the positions adopted by former Prime Minister Cameron in the United Kingdom[22] get seized of by friends in Russia: 'if the UK is going to withdraw, then we might as well do so'.[23] The parallel approaches of the present leadership in Russia and that of the United Kingdom is striking and worrisome.

It seems that the idea of sovereign equality means treating all countries equally, yet the reality as we know is that not all countries are equal in the context of international judicial systems. That is a reality we cannot run away from.

2.3 The European Court of Justice

Much has been talked about the recent Advisory opinion on EU ratification of the European Convention on Human Rights.[24] This decision seems difficult to justify in purely legal terms, in circumstances in which EU member states have agreed that they wish the Union to become a party. It is hard to escape the conclusion that the ECJ has basically acted to protect its own turf, to safeguard its own autonomy and put its own interests first. This suggests that one of the ends of judicialization—yet not one that our community has really focused on—is the instinct of institutional self-interest, of self-protection, and bigging up your own institution against the encroachment of others. Again, let us have strength to rise to the challenge of calling a spade a spade, and engage with what is actually going on in the functioning of the courts.

[22] Nicholas Watt, 'Cameron refuses to rule out leaving European Convention on Human Rights' *Guardian* (London, 2 June 2015) <http://www.theguardian.com/law/2015/jun/03/cameron-refuses-to-rule-out-leaving-european-convention-on-human-rights> (accessed 13 February 2016).

[23] 'The participation of the Russian Federation in any international treaty does not mean giving up national sovereignty. Neither the ECHR, nor the legal positions of the ECtHR based on it, can cancel the priority of the Constitution. Their practical implementation in the Russian legal system is only possible through recognition of the supremacy of the Constitution's legal force.' Maria Smirnova, 'Russian Constitutional Court Affirms Russian Constitution's Supremacy over ECtHR Decisions' (*EJIL:Talk!*, 15 July 2015) <http://www.ejiltalk.org/russian-constitutional-court-affirms-russian-constitutions-supremacy-over-ecthr-decisions/> (accessed 13 February 2016).

[24] Opinion 2/13 (Full Court) [2014] ECR I-2454.

2.4 ISDS—Investor State Dispute Settlement

A growing number of observers who believe that the Investor State Dispute Settlement (ISDS) system has been 'captured' by one particular stakeholder: the arbitrators (of which I am one) and the lawyers and law firms who benefit from the growth of the system.[25] It is hard to avoid the charge when reflecting on the information that comes before ISDS arbitrators, the kind of fees that are charged for discrete, small, and sometimes relatively insignificant cases: fees that run to the tens of millions of dollars for cases, legal opinions of a few pages for which a fee note of a hundred thousand dollars or more might be charged. This is what one sees sometimes when presented with a breakdown of costs. We need to look at those issues and address them realistically, and we need to join the clamour for greater transparency in the system.

There is too the most unfortunate practice of those who act as counsel and arbitrator in ISDS cases, a sort of revolving door in which the same person can spend a morning drafting a pleading on the meaning of 'fair and equitable treatment' (in one case) and then an afternoon drafting an award on the meaning of 'fair and equitable treatment' (in another case). This is sometimes referred to as 'issue conflict',[26] and some institutions have put an end to it (the International Court of Justice (ICJ) took a leadership role in eradicating that kind of practice nearly twenty years ago in its Practice Directions, which precluded individuals who acted as counsel from simultaneously sitting as ad hoc Judges;[27] the Court of Arbitration for Sport has now also prohibited the practice).

Speaking from experience, it can be an unfortunate situation to find yourself deliberating with fellow arbitrators knowing that one of more of them is actually litigating the very point that you are striving to write an award on. There is growing attention now being given to this, and rightly so. In the ISDS field the European Commission has now stepped in to call for an international investment court,[28] and the European Parliament has also made clear that it no longer wishes to tolerate that kind of practice.[29]

[25] Cecilia Olivet and Pia Eberhardt, 'Profiting from injustice: How law firms, arbitrators and financiers are fuelling an investment arbitration boom' (Transnational Institute, 27 November 2012) <https://www.tni.org/en/briefing/profiting-injustice> (accessed 13 February 2016).

[26] Philippe Sands, 'Conflict of Interest for Arbitrators and/or Counsel' in Meg Kinnear et al (eds), *Building International Investment Law: The First 50 Years of ICSID* (Kluwer 2015) 655–68.

[27] 'The Court considers that it is not in the interest of the sound administration of justice that a person sit as judge ad hoc in one case who is also acting or has recently acted as agent, counsel or advocate in another case before the Court [...]' *Practice Direction VII* (Basic Documents of the International Court of Justice) <http://www.icj-cij.org/documents/index.php?p1=4&p2=4&p3=0> (accessed 13 February 2016).

[28] 'Commission proposes new Investment Court System for TTIP and other EU trade and investment negotiations' *European Commission News Archive* (Brussels, 16 September 2015) <http://trade.ec.europa.eu/doclib/press/index.cfm?id=1364> (accessed 13 February 2016).

[29] European Parliament (2011) Resolution on the future European international investment policy (2010/2203(INI)) <http://www.europarl.europa.eu/sides/getDoc.do?type=TA&reference=P7-TA-2011-0141&language=EN> (accessed 13 February 2016).

What is the alternative? The alternative is to move away from arbitration to the establishment of a standing body or court. Whether that resolves all of these issues: who knows; whether it gives rise to other issues: who knows. One can have one's views, but these matters are now very much on the agenda. On this matter the ends of judicialization operate to prioritize the interests of certain stakeholders, including lawyers and law firms and perhaps also individual arbitrators. That is not a popular thing to say publicly, but we have to address the reality of what is actually going on.

2.5 The International Court of Justice

I turn to the ICJ, a court which probably has its strongest bench in years. It is now in a fine position to enhance its role. Yet it too might also want to examine some of its practices, some long-established, to see if there is not room for improvement.

For example, the standard applied by the court to the issue of independence and the circumstances in which a judge can and cannot sit in a case. This was addressed in the Wall Advisory Opinion,[30] giving rise to a standard that was relied upon in an Annex VII arbitration proceeding between Mauritius and the United Kingdom.[31] The approach raises some fundamental concerns: the principal judicial organ of the United Nations, which should operate to the very highest standards, seems to have the lowest standard of judicial independence in the world in terms of determining the circumstances in which a judge can and cannot sit.

Related to this is another matter that should be put on the table with some trepidation, given who is in the audience today, and that is the extracurricular activities of judges. Why is the International Court of Justice apparently the only permanent court in the world which allows its judges to sit and act as arbitrators? That strikes me as potentially problematic in terms of independence and perceptions as to the functioning of the Court itself. One has to step back from our community and ask ourselves: 'how do others perceive that practice? How do others perceive the idea that a judge might accept appointment by a party, a claimant, or a State?' One can understand, perhaps, sitting as president of a tribunal, not as party-appointed arbitrator, but even in those circumstances, how can it be that a judge who has a permanent and a full-time position and is paid a full-time salary, does not pass over any fees that are paid to the United Nations (as happened, I understand, on one occasion when an ICTY judge was allowed to sit on another case).[32]

It is not about actual bias but about perception, about ramping up our standards.

[30] *Legal Consequences of the Construction of a Wall* (Order of 30 January 2004) 2004 ICJ Rep 3 [6]–[8].

[31] *Chagos Maritime Protected Area (Mauritius v UK)* (Reasoned Decision on Challenge, 30 November 2011) 24–35.

[32] Even pending change in the practice, surely a first step would be to make publicly available on the Court website a list of all such appointments accepted by judges? As regards the future practice, the problem could be addressed by changing the status of judges and treating the appointment as part-time, as at ITLOS.

2.5.1 PCA/ad hoc inter-State arbitration

This is a convenient point to come back to the PCA and Professor Ibler. The PCA—as I mentioned—was moribund when I first studied international law, and has since had a remarkable transformation. In relation to inter-State disputes, it has been much assisted by the coming into force of Part XV of the UN Convention on the Law of the Sea. Developments at the PCA had been going seemingly well until rather recently. A couple of its cases have now involved permanent members of the Security Council—Russia and China—who have chosen not to participate in UNCLOS Annex VII cases brought against them, an approach that raises concerns which need to be addressed.[33]

That is not the only problem. One striking recent development has hardly been addressed. So delicate and sensitive, perhaps, or so recent, and that is the case of Croatia and Slovenia.[34] I declare an interest, as I was counsel for Croatia until it withdrew from the proceedings in August 2015. I am not independent, or neutral, or objective, and I must limit myself to the facts that are in the public domain. But it seems clear that what occurred—what was revealed—is like an Exocet missile that goes to the heart of the system that we are all involved and care about, a system that we wish to see succeed and improved but which, remarkably, we seem not to want to talk about, which has as its theme the functioning of international courts and tribunals.

The case was brought by an arbitration agreement between two countries, to resolve a long-standing dispute.[35] The written pleadings closed in spring of 2014. Hearings were held in May and June 2014. It's a big case involving land and sea boundaries, so it is entirely reasonable that it should take time to resolve that case and to write an award.

In February 2015 an incident occurred which gave rise to some concerns, and some attention in the media. The Slovenian Foreign Minister made a public statement in which he suggested that he had been privy to the confidential deliberations of the Tribunal. The Tribunal was alerted to these statements, and on 5 May 2015 wrote to the parties (the letter, which is strongly worded, is available on the PCA website).[36] The Tribunal noted that it was 'seriously concerned by the suggestion that one Party would have been privy to confidential information related to the

[33] *Arbitral Tribunal Constituted Under Annex VII UNCLOS (Philippines v China)* (PCA Case 2013-19); *Arctic Sunrise Arbitration (Netherlands v Russia)* (PCA Case 2014-02).

[34] *Arbitration between the Republic of Croatia and the Republic of Slovenia* (PCA Case 2012-04), information available at the PCA website <http://www.pca-cpa.org/showpage9e4c.html?pag_id=1443>, information starting from July 2015 available at <http://www.pcacases.com/web/view/3> (accessed 22 January 2016).

[35] *Arbitration Agreement between the Government of the Republic of Slovenia and the Government of the Republic of Croatia* <http://www.mzz.gov.si/fileadmin/pageuploads/Novinarsko_sredisce/Sporocila_za_javnost/Sporazum-angl.pdf> (accessed 13 February 2016).

[36] Letter from Dirk Pulkowski (Registrar) to the Agents in the Arbitration between Croatia and Slovenia (5 May 2015) <http://www.pca-cpa.org/PCA_Ltr_20150505%20(disclosed%20by%20Tribunal)1157.pdf?fil_id=2974> (accessed 22 January 2016).

Tribunal's deliberations',[37] and noted that it considered that 'such a meaning could be attributed to statements by the Slovenian Foreign Minister, and [. . .] that such statements are unhelpful for the resolution of the present dispute'.[38] The Tribunal then expressed the view, understandably, that 'safeguarding the confidentiality of the deliberations until the issuance of an award is a matter of highest priority',[39] premised as it is on the independence of the adjudicators from the Parties. In the letter the Tribunal took note of 'Slovenia's assurance that it has not received any information whatsoever as to any aspect of the outcome of the arbitration',[40] and stated that it had 'examined the arrangements that it has put in place to ensure that no confidential information may be disclosed'. It concluded: 'The Tribunal is therefore confident that no information about the likely outcome of any aspect of the arbitration has been disclosed.'[41]

And that, we expected, was the end of the matter.

I went on holiday on 22 July, on a morning flight to New York. By the time I got off the plane I had some 200 email and phone messages directed to what had emerged in the course of that day: the publication by a Serbian newspaper of the transcripts of what purported to be telephone conversations between the Agent of Slovenia and Slovenia's Party-appointed arbitrator, revealing extraordinary details about the deliberations. This was not just about the sharing of confidential information about what was going on inside the deliberations, it was also about the use of that arbitrator as a conduit for the presentation of further arguments by the Party that appointed him. Assuming they are accurate, the transcripts were very detailed, showing a two-way process in which the arbitrator gave a great deal of information to the Agent and also appeared to be acting as a conduit for the views of Slovenia, through its Agent. The question of how these recordings were obtained is of course an important one, which remains unresolved (I should mention that I have long proceeded on the assumption that any communication I engage in is recorded by someone, somewhere in the world, so I was surprised that others involved in this story did not proceed on the same basis).

On 23 July, the day after the news reports came out and the Serbian news republished, the Agent and arbitrator both resigned. That was addressed in a press release put out by the PCA. That press release itself—and here I speak in a purely personal capacity—contained an extremely unfortunate line: 'Once reconstituted, the Tribunal intends to resume its deliberations in the present arbitration without delay.'[42] No one who has read those transcripts can sensibly assume that the case can continue in any way before that arbitral tribunal. I say this having lived through the bitter experience of the Pinochet proceedings in 1998 and 1999 where the House of Lords for the first time in a 900-year history found itself having to set aside one of its own judgments in the case that had drawn more international attention than

[37] ibid. [38] ibid. [39] ibid.
[40] ibid. [41] ibid.
[42] PCA Press Release of 23 July 2015 <http://www.pcacases.com/web/sendAttach/1310> (accessed 22 January 2016).

any other in order to be seen as absolutely squeaky clean.[43] No doubt for the judges who sat on that case that it must have been a painful and difficult thing to do, all the more so on a case with such a high profile: to set aside the whole thing and start again in order to protect the system as a whole. Yet it was plainly the right thing to do, to protect the integrity of the judicial process. I shall not express any view as to what precisely ought now to happen in the *Croatia v Slovenia* case, but in deciding how to proceed the interests of the system as a whole—the integrity of the arbitral process—must surely be paramount.

On 24 July Croatia wrote to the Tribunal to say that it considered the entire arbitral process to have been tainted. It asked the Tribunal to suspend proceedings with immediate effect, and invited remaining members of the Tribunal to reflect on the grave damage that had been done to the integrity of the proceeding.[44] Five days later, on 28 July, Slovenia appointed a new arbitrator, the President of the ICJ. This was odd, since article 2 paragraph 2 of the Arbitration Agreement identifies the President of the ICJ as the appointing authority for the independent arbitrators, raising a question as to how it could be that the appointing authority could have been appointed.[45] Nevertheless, the error was quickly corrected and the President of the ICJ resigned from the arbitral Tribunal, as did Croatia's party appointed arbitrator, leaving three arbitrators sitting. Slovenia announced that it would not appoint a new arbitrator, leaving it to the President of the Tribunal to do so. In the absence of Croatia's appointing its party-appointed arbitrator, one assumes the President of the arbitral Tribunal would have to decide what to do.

And that, as far as I know, is where matters remain. Three arbitrators standing, Slovenia says the case can and must go on, Croatia says it is all over.[46]

It is hard to describe fully one's reaction to such developments. It felt extraordinarily painful, not only as a former counsel but as someone involved in the system of international justice, because it went to the very heart of the system in which we are involved, the centrality of the independence of the adjudicator. The concern must be not only that the episode will bring to a premature end a process that has

[43] *R v Bow Street Metropolitan Stipendiary Magistrate, Ex Parte Pinochet Ugarte (No 2)* [1999] 2 WLR 272.

[44] PCA Press Release of 5 August 2015 <http://www.pcacases.com/web/sendAttach/1389> (accessed 13 February 2016).

[45] Article 2(1) on the 'Composition of the Arbitral Tribunal' states that '[...] Both Parties shall appoint by common agreement the President of the Arbitral Tribunal and two members recognized for their competence in international law within fifteen days drawn from a list of candidates established by the President of the European Commission and the Member responsible for the enlargement of the European Commission. In case that they cannot agree within this delay, *the President and the two members of the Arbitral Tribunal shall be appointed by the President of the International Court of Justice from the list.*' (Emphasis not in original text) Arbitration Agreement between the Government of the Republic of Slovenia and the Government of the Republic of Croatia <http://www.assidmer.net/doc/Arbitration_Agreement_Croatia_Slovenia.pdf> (accessed 22 January 2016).

[46] Following the drafting of this piece, the President of the Arbitral Tribunal appointed Norwegian and Swiss arbitrators, HE Mr Rolf Fife and Professor Nicolas Michel and instituted a process to fill the vacant seats left by the resignation of the party-appointed arbitrators. PCA Press Release of 25 September 2015 <http://www.pcacases.com/web/sendAttach/1468> (accessed 13 February 2016). The future direction of the case remains an open question.

run over several years, but also that it will cause tremendous harm to the system of international arbitration both within and outside the PCA system, including in the context of investor-State arbitration. The trickle-down consequences are something to watch out for.

There is also a real concern that this might not be an isolated example. In my own experience that is not likely to be the case: many involved in international proceedings are aware that things go on that should not go on, even if not to the same extent as the matter I have just described. It is not entirely unusual for an agent in an inter-State case to share a conversation that he or she has had with a person sitting on a court or tribunal, a fact that causes (or should cause) a tremendous ethical difficulty. Under most rules of professional conduct counsel should not be privy to such information, and they should not want to hear such stuff or know what is going on. Other rules of professional conduct may have a different standard, and that raises a serious question about ethical standards for the international bar.

I even had a situation in one case of receiving an email from an agent in one case (it was several years ago) sending for my attention, review, and comment the deliberations of an international court or tribunal in a case in which I was involved. The reaction of a member of the English bar is to delete the email immediately, to refrain from reading the text, and to invite the appropriate person at the court or tribunal to remind its members of the duty of confidentiality.

The hope must be that this terrible episode in the course of summer 2015 will serve as a wake up call to everyone in the community to re-double their efforts in applying the very highest standards of propriety. Our international system is delicate, each court and tribunal a fragile creature, and those who wish to attack the system as a whole or individual courts will seize on these kinds of practices and will do very great damage indeed.

That—I think—is the positive that one could take out of this particular development.

What is to be done about it? Silence is not an option. Pushing uncomfortable truths under the carpet is not an option. The time has come to have an honest debate and discussion about party-appointed adjudicators and including the issue of nationality, and whether it now ought to be excluded altogether to engage in that particular process. And I think it has trickle-down consequences for who sits on what cases at permanent international courts and tribunals also. The moment should be used for an honest and constructive exploration of our own practices, to enhance the system, not to tear it apart.

Which brings me back to ask the question that hovers: How can it be that, despite the fact that these recent matters are now widely reported, even though they happened only a short while ago, that this is not talked about among scholars of international courts and tribunals? This raises a question about the nature of our community, one that is small and closed and inherently conservative, in which it is delicate and embarrassing to raise such matters and talk about them. It is understandable that younger members of the academic community would wish to tread carefully, which is why those of us who are of a more advanced age have a particular responsibility to raise such matters, even if sensitive and delicate, even if it causes difficulties in relation to our own prospects. The concern must be that our community is too cosy and too closed. Scrutiny is good, so is informed discussion and debate. The absence of scrutiny and transparency surely allows these kinds of things to happen, and then perpetuates them. Much is under the carpet, and it should be allowed—nay, encouraged—to come out.

Which brings me back to Professor Ibler.

'I learnt in my life not to come to fast conclusions', he said to me. That is surely right, and covers all the topics I have briefly touched on, and many others. I take heed of his warning and do not come to any fast conclusions.

Very regrettably—or perhaps fortunately—Professor Ibler did not live to become aware of what had happened in the case in which he had been involved: he passed away in the summer of 2015, before these matters emerged, leaving him perhaps in a happily optimistic state. He infused us with a sense of optimism—this man of a hundred years—and that is surely a good thing. So let us move on with a sense of optimism. Let us not run away from the hard, dirty, difficult things that happen in our world, and in our own narrow, small world. Let us confront them, but with courtesy, balance, and propriety. I think that is what Vladimir Ibler would have wanted.

Index